THE REVELATION

God gave

ROSS E. CASE

Posthumously edited by his son,
TIMOTHY CASE

ACW Press
Phoenix, Arizona 85013

The Revelation…God Gave
Copyright ©2003 Timothy Case
All rights reserved

Cover Design by Alpha Advertising
Interior design by Pine Hill Graphics

Packaged by ACW Press
5501 N. 7th Ave., #502
Phoenix, Arizona 85013
www.acwpress.com
The views expressed or implied in this work do not necessarily reflect those of ACW Press. Ultimate design, content, and editorial accuracy of this work is the responsibility of the author(s).

Library of Congress Cataloging-in-Publication Data

    Case, Ross E.
      The Revelation-- God gave / by Ross E. Case ;
    postumously edited by his son, Timothy Case. -- 1st ed.
      p. cm.
    ISBN: 1-892525-84-4

    1. Bible. N.T. Revelation--Criticism, interpretation,
  etc. I. Case, Timothy. II. Title.

BS2528.2.C37 2002   228'.06
                  QBI02-200473

Printed in the United States of America.

Acknowledgment

A correct understanding of Revelation is based on a correct understanding of the book of Daniel. This is because Daniel and Revelation deal with themes common to both books. (For a list of the themes that both books have in common, with appropriate references, see the footnote below.)

I am indebted to Philip Mauro's *The Seventy Weeks and the Great Tribulation*, (Reiner Publications, Swengel, Pennsylvania) for his exposition of Daniel, especially Daniel 11:36-45, and also to James Farquharson, whose earlier work gave support to Mauro's understanding of Daniel 11:40-43.

Both of these men saw in Daniel 11 and 12 a continuous prewritten history, extending from the time of Cyrus the Great to the destruction of Jerusalem in A.D. 70. Their work in this area made my work on Revelation easier, and for this I am thankful.

For those who do not have Mauro's work available to them, you will find an explanation of Daniel 11 and 12 in Appendix C. The section from Daniel 11:36-45 is taken from Philip Mauro, The *Seventy Weeks and the Great Tribulation*, pages 135-162.

I am also indebted to Finis Jennings Dake for his careful work on Daniel 11:1-35 (see *Dake's Annotated Bible*, pages 869-871, 876-877), and to Kenneth Taylor for his footnotes on the same passage in the *Living Bible*. All of these were helpful to me in my preparation of Appendix C.

Ross E. Case

Foreword

It has been a spiritually rewarding time for me to edit the notes from my father's lessons on the book of Revelation and turn them into a book. The most frequent responses I got from friends who heard what I was doing were questions along the lines of, "OK, according to your dad's theory, when is the rapture? Before or after the Great Tribulation? When does Christ return? Who is the Beast?" I have never been asked, "Can you help me understand what John prophesied?" or "How does it make any sense?"

It seems that many believers would rather have quick, canned answers than to understand the message God was conveying to His people at a critical time in history. Does this book name the "beast"? Yes (twice), and no. Does it pinpoint the return of Christ? Yes, and no.

If you want a book that tells the future like a newspaper, this isn't it. Sorry.

If you want a book that helps you understand the books of Revelation and Daniel so you can better look at world events through God's eyes, this should be very helpful.

God's Word is true; His holiness and mercy unwavering, His care for His children unceasing. Let's listen while He reveals Himself and His plans in His revelation.

Tim Case

Contents

Introduction

The word translated in our English Bibles, "revelation," is from the Greek word *apokalupsis*. The word means to unveil or to uncover. This book was not intended by its giver to be a mystery. It was rather intended to clear up a mystery, to reveal the righteousness of God in His dealings with Jerusalem and Rome, cities which had persecuted those who believed in Jesus. Revelation was also written to encourage a severely battered church with the knowledge that God would move soon to terribly punish those who were killing and persecuting them. To accomplish this, the writer of Revelation illuminated the prophetic passages of Daniel dealing with Jerusalem (Daniel 9:24-27; 12:1,7,11), and with the Roman Empire (Daniel 2:19-45; 7:1-28). It also picked up the prophecy where Daniel 11 and 12 left off (at the Jewish War of A.D. 66–70), and revealed the final events of the end times. Its very title indicates that it was to be clearly understood.

In point of fact, however, there is probably no book in the entire Bible that evokes such confusion and so many widely differing interpretations— none of which seems satisfactory—as the book of Revelation. Clearly, then, our minds have missed the mind of God in this matter. What went wrong? The author believes that there are four areas where our under- standing of the book of Revelation has led us away from the truth rather than toward the truth. With these obstacles to understanding removed, the book will stand forth clearly understood, and will become as it was intended to be, a *revelation*.

These four areas are:

1. We have not understood the Hebrew idioms and allusions to Old Testament passages and, as a consequence, we have taken many expressions literally which were intended to be taken figuratively. We will deal with this area in chapters one and two.

2. We have not realized that all of Revelation up to, and including, the return of Jesus in Revelation 19, was originally intended to have occurred in the first century A.D. We will deal with this matter in chapter three, and further explain the matter in chapters four and five.

9

3. We have not recognized that the *"one is"* phrase of Revelation 17:10, properly understood, gives us the approximate date of this revelation and, as a result, we have grossly misdated it. Then, looking at history, we have not found the events to which the book was intended to apply. We will deal with the matter of the date of Revelation in chapter six.

4. So far as Revelation from the sixth through the tenth chapters are concerned, we have not given sufficient weight to the fact that Jesus in heaven is *the same Jesus as* He was on earth! On earth, four times, in His most anguished tones, He appealed to Jerusalem and warned the city of her coming destruction. (See Luke 13:34-35; 19:41-44; 21:20-23; 23:27-31.) Jesus wept over Jerusalem (Luke 19:41), and He did not change His concern for Jerusalem after He ascended into Heaven! Are we to believe, then, that this Revelation, given in the early months of A.D. 70, will contain no reference to Jerusalem and to its soon coming destruction? This could not possibly be. Our blindness on this point, however, is a major cause for our misunderstanding of the book of Revelation.

May the blessing promised to those who read Revelation (Revelation 1:3) become even greater as you understand its message.

The Themes of Revelation

The principle themes of Revelation are presented again and again in a variety of ways so that we won't miss the essential messages. Thus, we see

(1) God's protection of the Jerusalem church

    a) 7:1-8

    b) 11:1-2 (contrasted with the destruction of the unbelieving Jews)

    c) 12:1-17a

    d) 14:1,3b-5

(2) The martyrdom of the Gentile church

    a) 6:9-11 (under Nero)

    b) 7:9-17 (under another Nero, Domitian)

    c) 13:1-18 (especially verse 7)

    d) 14:2-3a,13

    e) 14:14-16

    f) 15:2

    g) 16:6

    h) 17:6

    i) 18:20,24

    j) 19:2b

(3) God's judgment upon Jerusalem (from May to September, A.D. 70)

    a) 6:1-8

    b) 8:7–9:19

    c) 11:2

(4) God's judgment upon Rome

    a) 6:12-17

    b) 11:3-13

    c) 14:8

    d) 14:17-20

    e) 16:1-11,19

    f) 17:1–18:23

(5) The gospel preached, but unrepentance among the Gentiles

    a) 9:20-21 (But since Rome repented, this prophecy and those regarding God's judgment upon Rome and upon the beast were thrown into the future.)

    b) 14:6-7

    c) 16:9b

    d) 16:11

    e) 16:21

(6) The tragic result of worshiping the beast, or of taking the mark of the beast, or the number of his name, and the blessing upon those who don't.

    a) 13:4,8,12,15-18

    b) 14:9-16

    c) 15:2-4

    d) 19:20-21

    e) 20:4-5

    f) 21:1–22:5

(7) The return of Nero to become the beast

    a) Implied in the two separate persecutions of Revelation 6:9-11, and of Revelation 7:9-17, but developed further in the following passages.

    b) 11:7

    c) 13:3,12,14,18

    d) 17:7-8,11

(8) Jesus' soon return to destroy the beast

(I) Jesus' soon return

    a) 1:7 (while those still lived who "pierced" Him

    b) 2:25

    c) 3:11

    d) 22:7,12,20

(II) Jesus destroys the beast

    a) 16:12-16

    b) 19:11-21

Themes Common to Daniel and Revelation

The book of Revelation repeats themes from Daniel and other prophets so that a clearer picture of the prophesied event can be seen. Let's look at some examples of repeated themes.

1. The massacre by Herod the Great in his attempt to kill Jesus (Daniel 11:37,44; Revelation 12:3-5; see also Matthew 2:16-18).

2. The gospel preached (Daniel 12:3; Revelation 12:3-5).

3. Michael, the archangel, wars against Satan's angels, and defends the Jerusalem Jews who believe in Jesus, in their flight to Pella (Daniel 12:1; Revelation 12:7-12).

4. Jerusalem is destroyed in war (Daniel 9:26; 12:6-7; Revelation 6:1-8; 8:8).

5. The Jerusalem church returns from Pella to Jerusalem (Daniel 12:12, compare with 12:1; Revelation 14:1).

6. The *"Little Horn"* or Roman *"Beast"* makes war with the saints (Daniel 7:19-21; Revelation 13:7) and blasphemes against God (Daniel 7:25; Revelation 13:5).

7. This war against the saints lasts 3 1/2 years (Daniel 7:25; 12:7; Revelation 13:5).

8. Ten kings are allied with the *"Little Horn"* or *"Beast"* (Daniel 7:7,20,24; Revelation 17:3,12,16).

9. Rome is destroyed by fire (Daniel 7:11; Revelation 17:16; 18:8-9,18).

10. The three former world empires continue their existence until they, and the Roman Empire, are replaced on earth by the coming kingdom of God (Daniel 2:34-35,44; 7:12,17-18; Revelation 16:12,14,16).

Special Note

Revelation abounds in visions similar to those found in the Old Testament, but in which the shapes, colors, or numbers are changed.

Thus, both Ezekiel (1:5-25) and John (Revelation 4:6-8) saw visions of four living creatures or beasts. In both visions the appearance of a lion, an ox (or calf), a man, and an eagle were seen. But in Ezekiel's vision, he saw each creature with these four faces (1:10), while John saw each one with a single face (Revelation 4:7). Also, John's *"beasts"* had six wings like the seraphim in Isaiah's vision (6:2), while Ezekiel's *"living creatures"* had four wings (1:6).

Both Zechariah (6:1-8) and John (Revelation 6:1-8) had visions of four horses, or four groups of horses, of different colors. Zechariah also saw four chariots. The first chariot was pulled by red horses, the second by black horses, the third by white horses, and the fourth chariot by grisled and bay horses (Zechariah 6:2, 3).

John (Revelation 6:2,4-5,8) also saw four colors of horses, but these were white, red, black, and pale green.

Zechariah (4:14) and John (Revelation 11:3) also had visions of *"the two anointed ones, that stand by the Lord of the whole earth"* or *"the two witnesses."* In both visions olive trees and candlesticks were seen as representing these two, but Zechariah (4:2-3) saw one candlestick and two olive trees, while John (Revelation 11:4) saw *"two olive trees, and the two candlesticks."*

Both Daniel (12:5-7) and John (Revelation 10:2,5-6) saw similar visions of an angel or angels. Daniel (12:5) saw two angels, one on each bank of a river, and a third angel upon the river. John saw one angel who had his *"right foot upon the sea, and his left foot on the earth"* (Revelation 10:2). In both visions angels lifted hands to *"swear by him that liveth for ever,"* but Daniel's angel lifts *"his right hand and his left hand unto heaven"* (Daniel 12:7), while John's angel (Revelation 10:5) lifted one hand to heaven.

Both Ezekiel (2:9–3:3) and John (Revelation 10:8-10) had visions of *"a roll of a book"* or *"a little book"* or scroll. In both visions the *"roll"* or scroll was eaten, and in both it was in the mouth *"as honey for sweetness."* But John adds, *"as soon as I had eaten it, my belly was bitter."*

The *"breastplate of judgment"* in Exodus 28:15 also has four colors. In Revelation 9:17 the *"breastplates of fire, and of jacinth, and brimstone"* have three colors, but the judgment of God is expressed in both cases.

Even within Revelation itself, both the phrases *"the fourth part of the earth"* (Revelation 6:8) and *"a third of the earth"* (Revelation 8:7 RSV) refer to Jerusalem. Like a kaleidoscope, the visions given are in a constant process of change; always similar but never the same; and in changing, they more accurately present the truth of the message that is being given.

Expressions Commonly Used by John in Revelation

(emphasis added by the author)

"He that sitteth on the throne" (always with slight variations) (Revelation 4:9-10; 5:1,7,13; 6:16; 7:10,15; 19:4; 20:11; 21:5) is an expression used 11 times in Revelation to refer to God.

"The Lamb" (Revelation 5:6,8,12-13; 6:1,16; 7:9-10,14,17; 12:11; 13:8; 14:1,4,10; 15:3; 17:14 (twice); 19:7,9; 21:9,14,22-23,27; 22:1,3) is used 27 times and refers to Jesus.

"The kings of the earth (or, *land*)" (Revelation 6:15; 16:14; 17:2,18; 18:3,9; 19:19; 21:24) is used eight times and refers to the emperor and his subject kings within the Roman Empire.

"The beast" (Revelation 11:7; 13:1-4,11-12,14-15,17-18; 14:9,11; 15:2; 16:2,10,13; 17:3,7-8,11-13,16-17; 19:19-20; 20:4,10) is used 34 times (twice in several of the above verses) and refers to Nero and Domitian as heads of the Roman Empire, and to the Roman Empire itself.

"The false prophet" (Revelation 16:13; 19:20; 20:10) is used three times, and refers to the College of Augures.

"The kings of the east" (or, sun-rising) (Revelation 16:12) occurs once and is used of the kings of the three former world empires: Babylonian, Medo-Persian, and Greek.

"The kings of the earth who have committed fornication" with *"the great whore"* (Revelation 17:2; 18:3,9) occurs three times, and is used of those kings within the Roman Empire who remain loyal to Rome in Rome's conflict with the beast.

"The ten horns" (Revelation 12:3; 13:1; 17:3,7,12,16; see also Daniel 7:20-21,24) is used six times in Revelation and three times in Daniel. The phrase refers to the ten kings who, with their nations and armies, leave the Roman Empire and fight alongside the beast to destroy Rome.

"The great whore" (Revelation 17:1,15-16; 19:2) or, *"woman"* (Revelation 17:3-4,6-7,9,18) is used four and six times respectively, and refers to the city of Rome, or more precisely to Roma, the goddess of Rome.

"The seven heads" of the dragon or beast (Revelation 12:3; 13:1; 17:3,7,9) occurs five times. They are *"seven kings"* (Revelation 17:10) or emperors of the Roman Empire. These are Augustus Caesar, Tiberius Caesar, Caligula Caesar, Claudius Caesar, Nero Caesar, Vespasian, and Titus. An *"eighth"* (Revelation 17:11) *"is of the seven"* was Domitian. Domitian was to have been like a Nero returned in that he would come in the persecuting spirit and power of Nero.

"Nations, and kindreds, and people, and tongues" (always with variations) (Revelation 5:9; 7:9; 10:11; 11:9; 14:6; 17:15) occurs six times and refers to the various nations and ethnic groups within the Roman Empire.

"They that dwell upon the earth" (Revelation 3:10; 6:10; 11:10 (twice); 13:8,12,14 (twice); 14:6; 17:8) occurs ten times and refers to the inhabitants of the Roman Empire.

"An hundred forty and four thousand" (Revelation 7:4; 14:1) occurs twice and refers to *"the firstfruits unto God and to the Lamb"* (Revelation 14:4), that is, the first converts to Jesus from Jerusalem. (See Acts 2:41; 4:4; 5:14; 6:1,7 for the great multitudes who came into the Jerusalem church.) The 144,000 left Jerusalem and went to Pella, a Greek city just east of the Jordan River, in A.D. 66. They were thus delivered from the agonies of the Roman-Jewish War of A.D. 66–70. This deliverance had been prophesied by Daniel, *"and at that time thy people shall be delivered, every one that shall be found written in the book"* (Daniel 12:1b). They were also the ones to whom Jesus referred in Luke 21:18, *"But there shall not an hair of your head perish."* They had left Jerusalem in obedience to the command of Jesus, *"And when ye shall see Jerusalem compassed with armies, then know that the desolation thereof is nigh. Then let them which are in Judea flee to the mountains; and let them which are in the midst of it* [that is, of Jerusalem] *depart out; and let not them that are in the countries enter thereunto"* (Luke 21:20-21).

"A great multitude, which no man could number" (Revelation 7:9), occurs once, but this same group is seen in Revelation 12:17; 13:7; 14:2-3a,12-16; 17:6; 18:24; 19:2. These were the Gentile believers in Jesus in Rome who were martyred by Nero in A.D. 64 (as seen in Revelation 6:9-11), and also those who were prophesied to have been martyred by the *"eighth"* (Revelation 17:11) Roman emperor, who was Domitian. It was because of their unjust and cruel deaths that Rome was to have been destroyed.

"The seven spirits which are before his [God's] throne" (Revelation 1:4b; 3:1; 4:5). Angels are spirits. (Compare Acts 8:26 with 8:29,39; see also Hebrews 1:7,14.) These seven spirits are the same as *"the seven angels which stood before God"* (Revelation 8:2) who sounded forth the seven trumpets. Gabriel seems to be one of these seven (Luke 1:19).

"The seven spirits of God sent forth into all the earth" (Revelation 5:6; see also Isaiah 11:2 and Zechariah 3:9; 4:10). These are the same as the *"seven angels having the seven last plagues"* (Revelation 15:1; see also 16:1; 17:1; 21:9).

"The third part" (Revelation 8:7-9 (twice),10-12 (five times); 9:15,18; 12:4) occurs 14 times. It is from Ezekiel 5:1-5 in the Hebrew text and always refers to Jerusalem. John, in Revelation, makes many allusions to the Old Testament scriptures. Some of his allusions are from the Greek Septuagint (the LXX), and some from the Hebrew. The phrase, *"the fourth part of the earth"* (Revelation 6:8) is from the LXX, and also refers to Jerusalem.

"Small and great" (Revelation 11:18; 13:16; 19:5,18; 20:12) is an expression used by John five times, always in the same way. While the phrase *"great and small"* occurs in the Old Testament, it is not so common there as *"small and great."* By placing the word *"small"* first, John may have been identifying himself with little people.

Chapter One

Understanding
the Hebrew Idiom

Generally, when a beginning student of the Bible reads Revelation, his experience goes something like this. He reads the first verse and notes the part that reads, "*to shew unto his servants **things which must shortly come to pass**.*" Then he reads the seventh verse, "*Behold, he cometh with clouds; and every eye shall see him, and they also which pierced him: and all kindreds of the earth shall wail because of him. Even so, Amen.*" He says to himself, "Well, that certainly refers to the second coming of Jesus, but how does that fit with *'things which must shortly come to pass'?*" He continues reading, and sees the strangest picture of Jesus (Revelation 1:12-16) he could ever have imagined. He reads repeatedly of seven golden candlesticks (Revelation 1:12,20; 2:1), of seven stars (Revelation 1:16,20; 2:1; 3:1), and of the seven spirits of God (Revelation 1:4; 3:1; 4:5). He had known of only one spirit of God, and all this seems so confusing to him.

He continues reading through the scene of heaven in Revelation 4 and 5, trying to find something in which he can honestly say, "Well, I really understand this!" but it all seems so elusive. In Revelation 6:1, he may speculate who the rider on the white horse might be—perhaps Christ or Antichrist—but he generally gives up on the riders of the other horses. He reads of the martyred souls under the altar in heaven (Revelation 6:9-11), and wonders how they could all fit under an altar, and whether or not they would have to remain in such a small space for a long time. Finally, he thinks he has gotten hold of something a little more definite when he reads, *"and the sun became black as sackcloth of hair, and the moon became as blood; and the stars of heaven fell unto the earth, even as a fig tree casteth her untimely figs, when she is shaken of a mighty wind. And the heaven departed as a scroll when it is rolled together; and every mountain and island were moved out of their places"* (Revelation 6:12-14).

He looks up into the sky, and says, "Well, the heaven sure hasn't departed as a scroll yet, so all that follows this must be future!" Then he recalls the words of Revelation 1:1, *"to shew unto his servants things which **must shortly come to pass**,"* and remembers that it's been over 1900 years since this prophecy was given. Confused, he may say, "Well, *'one day is with the Lord as a thousand years, and a thousand years as one day'"* (2 Peter 3:8b), or, more likely, he will simply conclude, "I just don't see how anyone can understand Revelation!"

Actually, none of the problems in the above experience of understanding Revelation are insoluble, or even difficult. However, in order to understand Revelation, a vast change must first come in *the way we think.* That is to say, Revelation can never make sense to a person trained in a literalistic western culture. If we are willing, however, to think as those thought to whom this book originally came, then there is no problem at all. This is illustrated in *Alleged Discrepancies of the Bible* by John W. Haley, pages 14-16.[1]

> *The people of the East are fervid and impassioned in their mode of thought and expression. They think and speak in poetry. Bold metaphors and startling hyperboles abound in their writings and conversation.*
>
> *Dr. Samuel Davidson writes: "He who does not remember the wide difference between the Oriental and Occidental mind, must necessarily fall into error. The luxuriant imagination and glowing ardor of the former express themselves in hyperbolical and extravagant diction; whereas the subdued character and coolness of the latter are averse to sensuous luxuriance."*
>
> *Again, he writes, "The figures are bold and daring. Passion and feeling predominate. In the Psalms preeminently, we see the theology of the*

---

1. Note: Michaelis quotes an Arabic poet who expresses the fact that swords were drawn with which to cut the throats of enemies, thus: *"The daughters of the sheath leaped forth from their chambers, thirsting to drink in the jugular vein of their enemies."* Haley, John W., *Alleged Discrepancies of the Bible*, Baker Book House, Grand Rapids, Michigan, reprinted 1977, pg. 15.

feelings, rather than of the intellect. Logic is out of place there. Dogmas cannot be established on such a basis, nor was it ever meant to be so."

Lowth, on metaphors, writes, "The Orientals are attached to this style of composition; and many flights, which our ears—too fastidious, perhaps, in these respects—will scarcely bear, must be allowed to the general freedom and boldness of these writers."

Again, he writes of the difficulties which arise in reading authors "where everything is depicted and illustrated with the greatest variety and abundance of imagery; they must be still more numerous in such of the poets as are foreign and ancient—in the Orientals above all foreigners; they being the farthest removed from our customs and manners, and of all the Orientals, more especially in the Hebrews."

Professor Park: "More or less clandestinely, we are wont to interpret an ancient and an Oriental poet, as we would interpret a modern and Occidental essayist. The eastern minstrel employs intense words for saying what the western logician would say in tame language…the Occidental philosopher has a definite thought when he affirms that God exercises benevolence toward good men. Isaiah has essentially the same thought when he cries out: 'as the bridegroom rejoiceth over the bride, so shall thy God rejoice over thee.'"

I remember the first time I saw this truth. In Psalm 114:4-6, I read, *"the mountains skipped like rams, and the little hills like lambs. What ailed thee, O thou sea, that thou fleddest? Thou Jordan, that thou wast driven back? Ye mountains, that ye skipped like rams; and ye little hills, like lambs?"* Upon reading that, I said to myself, "You know, they didn't really talk like we would at all." Beginning with that instance, I began looking for other examples where the Hebrew expression was vastly different from our own. In Isaiah 55:12, I found, *"the mountains and the hills shall break forth before you into singing, and all the trees of the field shall clap their hands."* This is not something a westerner would have said. In Habakkuk 3:6, we read, *"and the everlasting mountains were scattered, the perpetual hills did bow,"* and Habakkuk 3:10, *"The mountains saw thee, and they trembled."*

Still, we in America will speak of it "raining cats and dogs," or of some rare event happening "only once in a blue moon," not at all intending to be taken in a literal sense. We might even say, "it will be a dark day when such and such happens," and we refer to the day of the stock market crash on October 29, 1929 as "Black Tuesday" when in physical terms it would have been no blacker than other Tuesdays. A Hebrew, however, would have been more expressive. In describing the coming wrath of God upon ancient Babylon, he might say,

For the stars of heaven and the constellations thereof shall not give their light: the sun shall be darkened in his going forth, and the moon shall not cause her light to shine (Isaiah 13:10).

Or, in describing a coming calamity upon "*Pharaoh, king of Egypt,*" he might say,

And when I shall put thee out, I will cover the heaven, and make the stars thereof dark; I will cover the sun with a cloud, and the moon shall not give her light. All the bright lights of heaven will I make dark over thee, and set darkness upon thy land, saith the Lord God (Ezekiel 32:7-8).

Joel (2:10,31; 3:15) and Amos (5:20; 8:9) often described calamities coming upon Judah, Israel, or upon neighboring nations in this way. Thus, we read of the invasion of Judah by Assyrian soldiers:

The earth shall quake before them; the heavens shall tremble: the sun and the moon shall be dark, and the stars shall withdraw their shining (Joel 2:10).

God's judgment upon those who swear by the golden calves, the gods of Dan and Beersheba, is pronounced by Amos in these words,

Shall not the day of the Lord be darkness, and not light? even very dark, and no brightness in it? (Amos 5:20).

And it shall come to pass in that day, saith the Lord God, that I will cause the sun to go down at noon, and I will darken the earth in the clear day (Amos 8:9).

Such expressions no doubt arose because events in the heavens were mysterious to the ancient peoples. An eclipse, or more likely, a sirocco (a wind heavily charged with fine dust particles) would blot out the sun, give the moon a reddish hue, or blot it out altogether, and the stars with it, and these things would be seen as a portent or a sign of dark and evil events about to take place upon their nation. Thus, these ancient peoples came to view changes in the heavens with foreboding and as signs of impending disaster.

When a prophet predicted darkness upon heavenly bodies, or stars falling, or the heavens dissolving and being rolled together as a scroll, he did not actually mean that these physical events in the heavens would take place, but that the dark and tragic events which they signified would soon occur.

This thought becomes evident as we study Isaiah 34:4-6 in regard to God's judgment upon ancient Edom.

And all the host of heaven shall be dissolved, and the heavens shall be rolled together as a scroll; and all their host shall fall down, as the leaf

falleth off from the vine, and as a falling fig from the fig tree. For my sword shall be bathed in heaven: behold, it shall come down upon Idumea, and upon the people of my curse, to judgment. The sword of the Lord is filled with blood, it is made fat with fatness, and with the blood of lambs and goats, with the fat of the kidneys of rams: for the Lord hath a sacrifice in Bozrah, and a great slaughter in the land of Idumea.

Idumea is another name for Edom. Bozrah was its chief city.

The judgment described above took place many years ago. Malachi 1:2-4 indicates that in his time the land of Edom was in ruins, and that God had "*laid his* (Esau's or Edom's) *mountains and his heritage waste for the dragons of the wilderness.*" This area is still a desolate wilderness. But what of the "*host of heaven*" being "*dissolved,*" "*and the heavens*" being "*rolled together as a scroll?*" Clearly, such poetic language was not intended to be taken literally, but was rather a figurative indication of the greatness of the judgment about to take place.

Let us place these expressions side by side with similar expressions in Revelation and ask ourselves, If these passages are clearly figurative in the Old Testament, then why should not similar expressions be viewed as figurative when used in Revelation?

The earth shook, *the heavens also dropped at the presence of God, even Sinai itself was moved at the presence of God, the God of Israel* (Psalm 68:8).

And I beheld when he had opened the sixth seal, and lo, **there was a great earthquake** (Revelation 6:12).

The sun **shall be turned into darkness**, *and* **the moon into blood,** *before the great and terrible day of the Lord come* (Joel 2:31).

and **the sun became black as** *sackcloth of hair, and the* **moon became as blood** (Revelation 6:12).

...and **all their** *(heaven's)* **host shall fall down, as the leaf falleth off from the vine, and as a falling fig from the fig tree** (Isaiah 34:4).

And the **stars of heaven fell unto the earth,** *even as a fig tree casteth her untimely figs, when she is shaken of a mighty wind* (Revelation 6:13).

And all the host of heaven shall be dissolved, and the **heavens shall be rolled together as a scroll** (Isaiah 34:4).

And the **heaven departed as a scroll** *when it is rolled together* (Revelation 6:14).

*I beheld the **mountains, and, lo, they trembled,** and all the hills moved lightly away* (Jeremiah 4:24).

*Shall not the **isles shake** at the sound of thy fall?* (Ezekiel 26:15).

*and **every mountain and island** were moved out of their places* (Revelation 6:14).

*And **they shall go into the holes of the rocks, and into the caves of the earth,** for fear of the Lord, and for the glory of his majesty, when he ariseth to shake terribly the earth* (Isaiah 2:19).

*And the kings of the earth, and the great men, and the rich men, and the chief captains, and the mighty men, and every bondman, and every free man, **hid themselves in the dens and in the rocks of the mountains*** (Revelation 6:15).

*...and they shall say to the mountains, Cover us; and to the hills, **Fall on us*** (Hosea 10:8).

*Then shall they begin to say to the mountains, **Fall on us;** and to the hills, Cover us* (Luke 23:30).

*And said to the mountains and rocks, **Fall on us,** and hide us from the face of him that sitteth on the throne, and from the wrath of the Lamb* (Revelation 6:16).

*...**who may stand** in thy sight when once thou art angry?* (Psalm 76:7b).

*For the great day of his wrath is come; and **who shall** be able to **stand?*** (Revelation 6:17)

Thus, Professor Stuart[2] writes,

> *I do not, and would not, summon them* (the books of scripture) *before the tribunal of Occidental criticism. Asia is one world; Europe and America, another. Let an Asiatic be tried before his own tribunal. To pass just sentence upon him, we must enter into his feelings, views, methods of reasoning and thinking, and place ourselves in the midst of the circumstances which surround him.*

Our experience, then, in understanding a book filled with Oriental imagery, as is Revelation, will be an experience in entering into the culture and thought forms of an ancient people. Fortunately, we are able to find an abundance of similar expressions in the Old Testament to help us understand this most exciting book in the New Testament.

---

2. Haley, John W., *Alleged Discrepancies of the Bible*, Baker Book House, Grand Rapids, Michigan, reprinted 1977, pg. 15

Chapter Two

Understanding
Old Testament Passages

A second major area of error which has led us away from a correct understanding of Revelation is that we have not realized that the book of Revelation makes many allusions to the Old Testament. These Old Testament passages, correctly understood, give understanding to the use of the same words and phrases in Revelation.

The coming of Christ described in Revelation 1:7 illustrates this principle, along with "the four horsemen" of Revelation 6:2-8 and "*the seven thunders*" of Revelation 10:3. Other examples of this will be given in their appropriate places in the discussion of Revelation 6–22.

The Coming of Christ

> *Behold, he cometh with clouds; and every eye shall see him, and they also which pierced him: and all kindreds of the earth shall wail because of him. Even so, Amen* (Revelation 1:7).

While the book of Revelation does not quote a single Old Testament passage verbatim, still "*from the list of 'Quotations from the Old Testament' with which the appendix to Westcott and Hort's second volume ends, it appears that of 404 verses of the Apocalypse there are 278 which contain references to the Jewish Scriptures"* (Swete, Henry Barclay, *Commentary on Revelation*, pg. cxl.). One of the references to the Old Testament that Swete lists compares Revelation 1:7 with both Daniel 7:13 and Zechariah 12:10. Using English, rather than Greek (as Swete does), the comparisons read, as follows, with bold words showing identical readings in the Greek of Revelation, Daniel, and Zechariah.

*"he comes **with...clouds**"* (Revelation 1:7).

*"lo **with the clouds...**he comes"* (Daniel 7:13).

*"if shall see him every eye, and those who him **pierced, and shall mourn over** him all the Tribes of the land"* (Revelation 1:7).

*"they shall look upon me, whom they have **pierced, and shall mourn over him**...and the land shall mourn (wail, lament) in separate tribes (families)"* (Zechariah 12:10-12).

This is the theme of Revelation. It is the grand climax toward which all else builds. Thus, in Revelation 11:14-19 this theme is returned to, and Revelation 16:17 through 22:5 is an expansion of Revelation 11:14-19. The comparison below illustrates this relationship.

Christ's coming revealed	Revelation 11:15-17	Revelation 19:11-16
Nations angry	Revelation 11:18	Revelation 19:17-21
God's wrath comes	Revelation 11:18	Revelation 20:11-15
Dead judged	Revelation 11:18	Revelation 20:4; 21; 22
Prophets, saints rewarded	Revelation 11:18	Revelation 19:11-21; 20:7-10

Revelation 1:7 also compares closely with Matthew 24:30, *"And then shall appear the sign of the Son of man in heaven: and then shall all **the tribes of the earth mourn**, and they shall see the Son of man coming in the clouds of heaven with power and great glory."* Here, again, the underlined words indicate that the Greek words used in Matthew are identical to the Greek used in Revelation. There is an intended relationship between the passages

referred to in Daniel, Zechariah, and Matthew with Revelation. Thus, by understanding these Old Testament passages and those of Matthew, we should be able to better understand Revelation 1:7.

Daniel 7:13,14 reads, "*I saw in the night visions, and, behold, one like the Son of man came with the clouds of heaven, and came to the Ancient of days, and they brought him near before him. And there was given him dominion, and glory, and a kingdom, that all people, nations, and languages, should serve him: his dominion is an everlasting dominion, which shall not pass away, and his kingdom that which shall not be destroyed.*" This is a vision of the Son of man coming to the Ancient of days—God—to receive a kingdom, and all people would serve him.

In Zechariah 12:10 we see, following a great victory of Judah and Jerusalem over all the nations of the world, that "*I will pour upon the house of David, and upon the inhabitants of Jerusalem, the spirit of grace and of supplications: and they shall look upon me whom they have pierced, and they shall mourn for him, as one mourneth for his only son, and shall be in bitterness for him, as one that is in bitterness for his firstborn.*" When we understand these passages from Daniel and Zechariah, we will be helped in our understanding of Revelation 1:7.

It should be noted, too, that Matthew 24, Mark 13, and Luke 21 cover the same material as Revelation, but Revelation expands on this prophecy to reveal more precisely the way in which these prophetic developments would occur. Basically, Matthew 24:1-29, Mark 13:1-25, Luke 21:5-26, and Revelation 6 through 9 all refer to the events preceding the destruction of Jerusalem and the actual destruction itself. The coming of Jesus, as told in Matthew 24:30, Mark 13:26, and Luke 21:27, was to have come soon after the destruction upon both Jerusalem and Rome, and upon the entire kingdom of the beast (Revelation 16; 19, entire chapters). We will cover this in the next chapter on "The Last Days."

The Four Horsemen

First, we will quote in full both Zechariah 1:8-11 and more importantly, Zechariah 6:1-8. In doing so we hope to illuminate the account of the four horses of Revelation 6:2-8.

> *I saw by night, and behold a man riding upon a red horse, and he stood among the myrtle trees that were in the bottom; and behind him were there red horses, speckled, and white. Then said I, O my lord, what are these? And the angel that talked with me said unto me, I will shew thee what these be. And the man that stood among the myrtle trees answered and said, These are they whom the Lord hath sent to*

*walk to and fro through the earth. And they answered the angel of the Lord that stood among the myrtle trees, and said, We have walked to and fro through the earth, and, behold, **all the earth sitteth still, and is at rest*** (Zechariah 1:8-11).

*And I turned, and lifted up mine eyes, and looked, and behold, there came four chariots out from between two mountains; and the mountains were mountains of brass. In the first chariot were red horses; and in the second chariot black horses; And in the third chariot white horses; and in the fourth chariot grisled and bay horses. Then I answered and said unto the angel that talked with me, **What are these my lord?** And the angel answered and said unto me, **These are the four spirits of the heavens,** which go forth from standing before the Lord of all the earth. The black horses which are therein go forth into the north country; and the white go forth after them; and the grisled go forth toward the south country. And the bay went forth, and sought to go that they might walk to and fro through the earth...So they **walked to and fro through the earth.** Then cried he upon me, and spake unto me, saying, Behold, these that go toward the north country **have quieted my spirit** in the north country* (Zechariah 6:1-8).

In both of these passages we have variously colored horses, three colors in Zechariah 1 and four colors in Zechariah 6. In both passages the horses were "*to walk to and fro through the earth*" (Zechariah 1:10; 6:7). The results of the horses patrolling the earth were similar: "*behold, all the earth sitteth still, and is at rest*" (Zechariah 1:11), and, "*Behold, these that go toward the north country have quieted my spirit in the north country*" (Zechariah 6:8). The purposes of the horses, in both cases, seem to have been to patrol and quiet the areas to which they had been sent.

In both passages Zechariah asks the question we are also asking in regard to the four horses of Revelation, "*What are these, my lord?*" (Zechariah 1:9: 6:4), and in Zechariah 6:5 we have the answer, "*These are the four **spirits** of the heavens which go forth from standing before the Lord of all the earth.*" So the horses are ***spirits!***

However, in Deuteronomy 28:63 we read that if the Jews turn away from the Lord,

It shall come to pass, that as the Lord rejoiced over you to do you good, and to multiply you; so the Lord will rejoice over you to destroy you, and to bring you to naught.

But since God now rejoices over the Jews to destroy them, even as He had once rejoiced over them to do them good, these four spirits that go forth from standing before the Lord of the earth no longer are sent to patrol and to quiet. Now it's just the opposite: to incite and to inflame those actions that produce destruction! The contrast, then, between the spirit horses of Zechariah and those of Revelation is evident. With this in mind, we will look at the passage regarding the white horse.[3]

> *And I saw, and behold a white horse: and he that sat on him had a bow; and a crown was given unto him: and he went forth conquering, and to conquer* (Revelation 6:2).

White horses were commonly ridden by a conquering hero, thus the color of the horse emphasized the type of spirit horse this was. There is also a relationship between the four beasts of Revelation 4:7 and the horses being introduced by them. The lion represents dominion; the calf, strength; the man, intellect; and the flying eagle, omnipresence. (Lamsa, *New Testament Commentary*, pg. 562). The first beast—the lion, symbol of dominion—introduced the conquering horse.

This spirit horse may be named, "The Conquering Spirit." "*He that sat on him had a bow.*" This would indicate that this spirit would stir the Jews as the Romans were not known to be adept in archery. The Romans generally used Arabians and employed Asiatic mercenaries for archery (see *Wars of the Jews* (Bella Judaica) or *Wars*, III, V, 2).

"*And a crown was given unto him.*" There are two Greek words, *stephanos* and *diadem*, which most translations render with the single English word "crown." *Stephanos* and *diadem* are not synonymous, however. *Diadem* is the crown a king would wear, the symbol of kingly rule. The word *diadem* is used in Revelation 12:3, 13:1, and 19:12. In Revelation 6:2, we have *stephanos*, a victor's crown, or wreath, won in a contest. It also appears in Revelation 2:10; 3:11; 4:4,10; 6:2; 9:7; 12:1; and 14:14.

In Revelation 6:2 we have a divine forecasting of the event that began the Jewish-Roman War in A.D. 66. The Roman general, Cestius, acting on orders from Nero Caesar, surrounded Jerusalem, just as Jesus, our Lord, had prophesied (Luke 21:20). However, after about six days, Cestius withdrew his troops. Jewish militants, who had been looking for a way to escape entrapment within Jerusalem, now rushed out of the city and began cutting down the Roman army in great numbers. It was a tremendous victory of the Jews over Roman might. "The Conquering Spirit" can be clearly seen in the following passage, quoted previously, from Josephus, "*Now the Jews, after they had beaten Cestius, were so much elevated with their unexpected success, that they could not govern their zeal, but, like people blown up into a flame by their good fortune, carried the war to*

---

3. A table at the end of this section helps explain the beasts, the horsemen, and their meanings.

remoter places." A better description of "The Conquering Spirit" at work could hardly have been written!

Revelation 6:3-4 reads,

> *And when he had opened the second seal, I heard the second beast say, Come and see. And there went out another horse that was red: and power was given to him that sat thereon to take peace from the earth, and that they should kill one another: and there was given unto him a great sword.*

The "second beast," the "calf" (Revelation 4:7), a symbol of strength, beckoned John to see the red horse. I have titled this "The Spirit of Civil Strife," but it could as well be titled, "The Spirit of Murder." Red is the symbol of blood, and thus the color of this horse pictures the purpose for which it is sent. Josephus describes repeatedly the strife and murder that developed and grew to intensity among the Jewish forces in Judea, and most of all, in Jerusalem. The following quotes will reveal the spirit of the red horse—the Spirit of Civil Strife, the Spirit of Murder—as it stirred the Jews after the Spirit of Conquest, or The Conquering Spirit.

> *There were besides disorders and civil wars in every city; and all those that were at quiet from the Romans turned their hands one against another. There was also a bitter contest between those that were fond of war, and those that were desirous of peace (Wars, IV, III, 2).*

If you have the writings of Josephus available, you may want to read further than is quoted here as Josephus devotes several pages to these disorders. In *Wars*, V, V, 2, we read of the Idumeans in Jerusalem. "*But the rage of the Idumeans was not satiated by these slaughters; but they now betook themselves to the city, and plundered every house, and slew everyone they met.*" We also read, "*Now after these were slain, the zealots and the multitude of the Idumeans fell upon the people as upon a flock of profane animals, and cut their throats*" (*Wars*, V, V, 3). Of the Galileans, Josephus wrote, they "*drew their swords from under their finely dyed cloaks and ran everybody through whom they alighted upon*" (*Wars*, IV, IX, 10). The following quote expands on this, but also reveals how the spirit of the red horse of civil strife and murder was followed by the black horse spirit of famine.

> *And now there were three treacherous factions in the city, the one parted from the other. Eleazar and his party, that kept the sacred first-fruits, came against John in their cups. Those that were with John plundered the populace, and went out with zeal against Simon. This Simon had his supply of provisions from the city, in opposition to the seditious. When, therefore, John was assaulted on both sides, he made*

his men turn about, throwing his darts upon those citizens that came up against him, from the cloisters he had in his possession, while he opposed those that attacked him from the temple by his engines of war; and if any time he was freed from those that were above him, which happened frequently, from their being drunk and tired, he sallied out with a great number upon Simon and his party; and this he did always in such parts of the city as he could come at, till he set on fire those houses that were full of corn, and of all other provisions. The same thing was done by Simon, when, upon the other's retreat, he attacked the city also; as if they had, on purpose, done it to serve the Romans, by destroying what the city had laid up against the siege, and by thus cutting off the nerves of their own power. Accordingly, it so came to pass, that all the places that were about the temple were burnt down, and were become an intermediate desert space, ready for fighting on both sides, and that almost all the corn was burnt, which would have been sufficient for a siege of many years. So they were taken by the means of the famine, which it was impossible they should have been, unless they had thus prepared the way for it by this procedure (Wars, V, I, 4).

The following passage describes this spirit of the black horse of famine:

And when he had opened the third seal, I heard the third beast say, Come and see. And I beheld, and lo a black horse; and he that sat on him had a pair of balances in his hand. And I heard a voice in the midst of the four beasts say, A measure of wheat for a penny, and three measures of barley for a penny; and see thou hurt not the oil and wine (Revelation 6:5-6).

In the previous quote from Josephus we saw the word "corn." This doesn't refer to maize, what we call "corn" in this country. "Corn" in this passage would be better translated "grain" and includes both wheat and barley. In England (where William Whiston, the one who translated *The Works of Josephus* into English, lived), "corn" commonly refers to wheat. Thus, the phrase in Revelation 6:6—"*a measure of wheat for a penny, and three measures of barley for a penny*"—finds its direct fulfillment in the famine conditions that prevailed in Jerusalem in A.D. 70. The phrase, "*and see thou hurt not the oil and the wine*" (Revelation 6:6), no doubt has reference to John of Gischala. After this John had taken over the temple from Eleazar and his army (*Wars*, V, III, 1), he melted down many of the sacred utensils, and then "*he emptied the vessels of that sacred wine and oil which the priests kept to be poured on the burnt offerings* (the firstfruits and the tithes, as in Nehemiah 10:37-39), *and which lay in the inner court of the temple, and distributed it among the multitude, who, in their anointing themselves and drinking, used (each of them) above a hin* (1.62 gallons) *of them*" (*Wars*, V, XIII, 6). This "oil and wine" had been given to God and not to John of Gischala. In this passage, John of Gischala was in this passage put on notice that he did not have God's permission to steal and to waste it!

But why did "the third beast" (Revelation 6:5), that "had a face as a man" (Revelation 4:7), introduce this black horse spirit of famine? The "face of a man" symbolizes intelligence, and to destroy one's own food supply seems an incredibly stupid thing to do. Still, Josephus describes John of Gischala, who first began to destroy the food supplies of his rivals in Jerusalem, thus: "*He was a cunning knave*," "*very sagacious in bringing about what he hoped for*" (*Wars*, IV, II, 1). "*He was a man of great craft*"(*Wars*, IV, III, 13). "*...for he was a shrewd man*" (*Wars*, IV, VII, Sect.1). Josephus also writes of John's escape from Gischala to Jerusalem, in which he "deluded" Titus (*Wars*, IV, II, 5), "*Now this was the work of God, who therefore preserved this John, that he might bring on the destruction of Jerusalem*" (*Wars*, IV, II, 3). And so, John's cunning and intelligence was used of God to serve his (John's) enemies, as a brilliant man is said, at times, to "outsmart himself." But how can we even identify the black horse with the "Spirit of Famine"? In Matthew 20:2 we see that a penny (or *denarius*) was a day's wages. A quart (Greek, *choenix*, about a pint and a half) of wheat was a slave's provision of food for one day. The idea here is that the labor of an entire day would be required for a slave's ration for oneself, with nothing remaining for one's family.

The final section in this passage, Revelation 6:7-8, reads as follows:

> *And when he had opened the fourth seal, I heard the voice of the fourth beast say, Come and see. And I looked, and behold a pale horse: and his name that sat on him was Death, and Hell followed with him. And power was given unto them over the fourth part of the earth, to kill with sword, and with hunger, and with death, and with the beasts of the earth.*

The fourth beast, that "*was like a flying eagle*" (Revelation 4:7), a symbol of omnipresence, introduced the fourth horse, the Spirit of Death. Eagles were rare in the Middle East, and the eagle referred to here would best be translated "a griffon vulture," although the same Hebrew word "*neser*" was used of both birds. (See *The International Standard Bible Encyclopedia*, Vol. 2, pg. 1.) While there are many similarities between the eagle and the griffon vulture (size, strength, longevity, lofty flight, nesting patterns, and feeding habits) the vulture is more a symbol of death as a scavenger bird wheeling over a dying victim. Thus, the *Concordant Literal New Testament* translates Revelation 4:7 as "*like a flying vulture.*" This vulture, a symbol of death, introduces the Spirit of Death in this passage, and with that spirit rides "Hell," or more literally, Hades, the Spirit of the Abode of the Dead, garnering to himself those fallen in death. The phrase, "*to kill with sword, and with hunger, and with death, and with the beasts of the earth,*" reminds one of the plagues given in Jeremiah 15:2-3 and in Ezekiel 5:12. Deuteronomy 28:49-68 was also literally fulfilled at this time.

Josephus records cannibalism (*Wars*, VI, III, 4-5) at this time in Jerusalem, and writes thus of the famine:

> *Now of those that perished by famine in the city, the number was prodigious, and the miseries they underwent were unspeakable; for if so much as the shadow of any kind of food did anywhere appear, a war was commenced presently; and the dearest friends fell a fighting one with another about it, snatching from each other the most miserable supports of life* (*Wars*, VI, III, 3).

Josephus also records of the Jews that "*the severity of the famine made them bold in thus going out*" of Jerusalem, looking for food. Caught, "*they were first whipped, and then tormented with all sorts of tortures before they died, and were then crucified before the wall of the city.*" The Romans "*caught every day five hundred Jews*" (*Wars*, V, XI, 1).

> *So all hope was now cut off from the Jews, together with their liberty of going out of the city. Then did the famine widen its progress, and devoured the people by whole houses and families: the upper rooms were full of women and children that were dying by famine; and the lanes of the city were full of the dead bodies of the aged; the children also and the young men wandered about the marketplaces like shadows, all swelled with the famine, and fell down dead wheresoever their misery seized them* (*Wars*, V, XII, 3).

> *Thus did the miseries of Jerusalem grow worse and worse every day, and the seditious were still more irritated by the calamities they were under, even while the famine preyed upon themselves, after it had preyed upon the people. And indeed the multitude of carcasses that lay in heaps upon one another, was a horrible sight, and produced a pestilential stench, which was a hindrance to those that would make sallies out of the city to fight the enemy* (*Wars*, VI, I, 1).

From A.D. 66 to 70, these four horses were present in Jerusalem and in Judea: the Spirit of Conquest, the Spirit of Civil Strife (or Murder), the Spirit of Famine, and the Spirit of Death. No wonder Jesus said, "*Daughters of Jerusalem, weep not for me, but weep for yourselves, and for your children*" (Luke 23:28).

By understanding properly the Old Testament passage from Zechariah that these horses were spirits, we were able to understand this entire passage as it unfolded in Jerusalem.

	Introducing Beast		Horse and Rider	
	Symbol	Meaning	Symbol	Meaning
First	Lion	Dominion	White horse, Bow, Victor's crown	Conquering Spirit
Second	Calf	Strength	Red horse, power to take peace	Spirit of Murder or Civil Strife
Third	Man	Intelligence	Black horse, Balances, Weighing bread	Spirit of Famine
Fourth	Eagle/Vulture	Omnipresence	Pale (green) horse, Death, Hell	Spirit of Death

The Seven Thunders

In Revelation 10:1 we read:

> *And I saw another mighty angel come down from heaven, clothed with a cloud: and a rainbow was upon his head, and his face was as it were the sun, and his feet as pillars of fire.*

The significance here is that this angel's message is fresh from the throne of God. Thus, the phrases, "*clothed with a cloud,*" "*a rainbow was upon his head,*" and "*his face was as it were the sun, and his feet as pillars of fire*" are given to support the basic thought that this angel has just emerged from God's presence, and therefore has God's latest message. "Clouds" were symbols of God's presence and glory, since those who saw Him in vision (Isaiah 6:4 "*smoke*"; Daniel 7:13), or who prophesied of Him (Isaiah 19:1), or who wrote glorifying Him (Leviticus 16:2; Exodus 16:10; 40:38; Psalm 104:3) often referred to Him as being in or on clouds. In like manner the rainbow is associated with God's glory (Ezekiel 1:28; Revelation 4:3). The faces of those who have just come from God's presence shine with glory (Moses, Exodus 34:29; an angel, *"his face was as the appearance of lightning,"* Daniel 10:6). His *"feet as pillars of fire"* remind one of the feet of Jesus in Revelation 1:15, *"his feet like unto fine brass, as if they burned in a furnace."*

"And he had in his hand a little book open; and he set his right foot upon the sea, and his left foot on the earth" (Revelation 10:2). This thought of *"the little book"* is found in Ezekiel (2:8-10; 3:1-3). The significance here is that *"the little book"* contained *"lamentations, and mourning, and woe"* (Ezekiel 2:10). But for whom? The prophecies concerning the fall of Judah and Jerusalem have been completed. Revelation 10 begins to prepare us, then, for a change in direction, as God's wrath is about to be pronounced upon others.

"And cried with a loud voice, as when a lion roareth: and when he had cried, (the) seven thunders uttered their voices" (Revelation 10:3). In Amos 3:4 we read, *"Will a lion roar in the forest, when he hath no prey? will a young lion cry out of his den, if he have taken nothing?"* The angel's loud voice, as a lion's roar, is a cry of victory. The picture here is that God has been in a conflict—a war—with Judah and Jerusalem, and has emerged victor and this cry—His victory cry—sets the tone for the seven thunders that follow. (It may seem strange to us in the Western world to describe God's power as the roar of a lion, but in the Old Testament this usage is common. See Isaiah 31:4; 42:13; Jeremiah 25:30; Hosea 11:10; Joel 3:16; Amos 1:2.)

The Greek here reads not *"seven thunders,"* but **"the seven thunders,"** as though John would have known what these *"seven thunders"* were. Ancient peoples thought of thunder as the voice of God. We read of this many times in Scripture. (See 2 Samuel 22:14-16; Job 37:5; 38:34; 40:9; Psalm 81:7) and the two identical verses in Jeremiah (10:13 and 51:16; also John 12:27-29.) Thus, *"God thundereth marvelously with his voice"* (Job 37:5), " *canst thou thunder with a voice like him* (God)?" A passage in *Rulers of New Testament Times*, page 47, illustrates this thought:

> *At the beginning of his spectacular career, Caligula announced that he was a god, fully equal to Jupiter. He then ordered the heads on the statues of the gods to be removed and to be replaced with replicas of his own head. Next, he had a thunder machine constructed, and answered "Jove's thunder" with his own, peal for peal. But sometimes the natural thunder was too much for him. On such occasions he crawled whimpering under the bed.*

In Psalm 29, which is known as "The Psalm of the Thunderstorm," we see a picture of a great thunderstorm coming in from the Mediterranean Sea and moving with great force against the northern forest (cedars of Lebanon, vs. 5) and against the southern desert (wilderness of Kadesh, vs. 8). *In this psalm the words "the voice of the Lord" occur seven times.* This is the passage in the Old Testament to which *"the seven thunders"* of Revelation refers. The emphasis in Psalm 29 is not on what the seven thunders said, however but upon their manifestation of God's awesome power.

"And when the seven thunders had uttered their voices, I was about to write: and I heard a voice from heaven saying unto me, Seal up those things which the seven thunders uttered, and write them not" (Revelation 10:4). *"The seven thunders"* also represented God's victory shout, but He wants us to know that even though He has manifested His great power in His triumph over Christ-rejecting Judah and Jerusalem, it is too early to record His victory shout, as there is another enemy in the field of battle. God must deal first with another enemy that had persecuted His children before the seven thunders can sound their praises to His mighty power.

As we can see, the book of Revelation is full of allusions to Old Testament scriptures and is understood only by those with an understanding of the rest of Scripture. This should be expected for a book written to a first-century church which was very familiar with the Old Testament. For us to understand, we need to look at the book through the idioms and literary references these people would have used to understand it in their time. The next chapter draws us further into their mind-set as we understand the meaning of "The Last Days."

Chapter Three

The Last Days

In our times it is common for Christians, especially prophecy teachers, to state that we are living in "the end times." This phrase means that we are in the last days before the return of Jesus, and the setting up of His kingdom on earth. But it may come as a mental shock for many to realize that Jesus, Matthew, Mark, Luke, John, Paul, James, Peter, Jude, and the writer of the Epistle to the Hebrews also believed that they were in the final generation just before God's kingdom would come upon the earth. It may also come as a shock to the thinking of many to realize that a clear understanding of this truth is necessary to understanding the book of Revelation.

The following passages of Scripture are given so that we may carefully and prayerfully consider the extent to which Jesus and every writer of the New Testament held to this belief.

Jesus said,

> *There be some standing here, which shall not taste of death, till they see the Son of man coming in his kingdom* (Matthew 16:28; see also Mark 9:1; Luke 9:27).

Then, after telling of His soon return, He said,

This generation shall not pass, till all these things be fulfilled. Heaven and earth shall pass away, but my words shall not pass away (Matthew 24:34-35; see also Mark 13:30-31; Luke 21:32-33).

Those who wrote the New Testament did not take Jesus' words lightly; rather they believed Him devoutly. They believed that they themselves were living in the last times—the times just before Jesus would return to earth to establish His heavenly kingdom.

Thus, Paul wrote,

And that, knowing the time, that now it is high time to awake out of sleep: for now is our salvation nearer than when we believed. The night is far spent, the day is at hand (Romans 13:11-12a).

But this I say, brethren, the time is short (1 Corinthians 7:29a).

...for the fashion of this world passeth away (1 Corinthians 7:31b).

Now all these things happened unto them for ensamples: and they are written for our admonition, upon whom the ends of the world are come (1 Corinthians 10:11).

Let your moderation be known unto all men. The Lord is at hand (Philippians 4:5).

Also, in 2 Timothy 3:1-5, "*the last days*" of which Paul wrote to Timothy, in which "*men shall be lovers of their own selves, covetous, boasters, proud,*" must refer to the days in which Timothy was then living since he was warned to "*turn away*" "*from such*" people.

The writer of the Epistle to the Hebrews wrote,

God, who at sundry times and in divers manners spake in time past unto the fathers by the prophets, Hath in these last days spoken unto us by his Son...(Hebrews 1:1-2a).

For then must he often have suffered since the foundation of the world: but now once in the end of the world hath he appeared to put away sin by the sacrifice of himself (Hebrews 9:26).

Not forsaking the assembling of ourselves together, as the manner of some is; but exhorting one another: and so much the more, as ye see the day approaching (Hebrews 10:25).

For yet a little while, and he that shall come will come, and will not tarry (Hebrews 10:37).

James wrote,

Ye have heaped treasure together for (Greek, *en*, in) *the last days* (5:3b).

Be patient therefore, brethren, unto the coming of the Lord (5:7a).

Be ye also patient; stablish your hearts: for the coming of the Lord draweth nigh (5:8).

Peter wrote,

...you, Who are kept by the power of God through faith unto salvation ready to be revealed in the last time (1 Peter 1:4b-5).

Christ...Who verily was foreordained before the foundation of the world, but was manifest in these last times for you (1 Peter 1:20).

But the end of all things is at hand: be ye therefore sober, and watch unto prayer (1 Peter 4:7).

Jude wrote that "*there should be mockers in the last time*" (Jude 18). Since the "*mockers*" of which he wrote were living then, it is evident that he was referring to his days as "*the last time.*"

And John wrote,

Little children, it is the last time: and as ye have heard that antichrist shall come, even now are there many antichrists; whereby we know that it is the last time (1 John 2:18).

The Revelation of Jesus Christ, which God gave unto him, to shew unto his servants things which must shortly come to pass (Revelation 1:1a).

...for the time is at hand (Revelation 1:3b).

Behold, he cometh with clouds; and every eye shall see him, and they also which pierced him (Revelation 1:7a).

In the above passage we see that those who "*pierced*" Jesus would yet be alive to see Him when he returned in glory. This must be true, since the unrighteous dead will not be raised at Jesus' second coming. (See 1 Corinthians 15:21-24; Philippians 3:11; 1 Thessalonians 4:13-17; Revelation 20:4-6.)

And he said unto me, These sayings are faithful and true: and the Lord God of the holy prophets sent his angel to shew unto his servants the things which must shortly be done (Revelation 22:6).

He which testifieth these things saith, Surely I come quickly. Amen. Even so, come, Lord Jesus (Revelation 22:20).

Besides the above Scripture passages, there are others that bear witness to the fact that the writers of the New Testament expected Jesus to return in their lifetimes. Thus, in 2 Timothy 4:1, the King James Version, and nearly all modern English versions of the Bible, fail to translate the Greek word *mellontos* (about) which appears here in the Greek text. With *mellontos* translated into English, the King James Version should have read, "*I charge thee therefore before God, and the Lord Jesus Christ, who is about* (mellontos) *to judge the quick* (or living) *and the dead at his appearing and his kingdom*" (2 Timothy 4:1).

Since *mellontos* (about) is not a disputed reading in the Greek texts, there does not appear to be a proper reason for its not being translated. This is added evidence that those who wrote the New Testament believed that they were living in the last days just before the return of Jesus.

Other passages of Scripture that indicate a belief of living in the last times are found by comparing carefully the "*seal the book*" and the "*seal not*" phrases of Daniel 12:4,9 and Revelation 22:10, as follows:

But thou, O Daniel, shut up the words, and seal the book, even to the time of the end...And he said, Go thy way, Daniel: for the words are closed up and sealed till the time of the end. (Daniel 12:4,9).	*And he saith unto me, Seal not the sayings of the prophecy of this book: for the time is at hand* (Revelation 22:10).

We see from the above comparison that Daniel was to "*seal the book*" because the fulfillment of the events prophesied was so far in the future, whereas John was to leave Revelation unsealed because the fulfillment of the events prophesied was so close at hand.

But the time since John received this revelation in A.D. 70 until now has been 1900 plus years. This is far, far longer than the 608 years between Daniel's prophecy and the destruction of Jerusalem in A.D. 70, about which Daniel prophesied (9:26; 12:1,7). How can this be?

Clearly, the prophecies of Revelation were intended to be fulfilled in much less than 608 years. In fact, as we shall soon see, they were intended to be fulfilled soon after they were given.

A final passage on this subject is from Revelation 17:10-11.

> *And there are seven kings: five are fallen, and one is, and the other is not yet come; and when he cometh, he must continue a short space. And the beast that was, and is not, even he is the eighth, and is of the seven, and goeth into perdition.*

This passage will be examined more thoroughly in our chapter on "Dating the Revelation." For now, we will simply state that the five kings who had fallen were Augustus, Tiberius, Caligula, Claudius, and Nero. The "*one*" who "*is*" was Vespasian. The "*other*" who "*is not yet come*," but who "*must continue a short space*" was Titus. Titus would be ruling the Roman Empire just two years. The "*eighth*" king would have been Domitian who was to have been "*of the seven*," or "*one of the seven*." (See Greek, "ek ton hepta esti," "*out of the seven is*"). He was to have been like the fifth "*king*" who was Nero.

Domitian was scheduled, then, to be the beast of Revelation, and Jesus would have returned to earth in His second coming and cast Domitian "*alive into a lake of fire burning with brimstone*" (Revelation 19:20).

Since Domitian's reign was from A.D. 81-96, *then Jesus must have originally been scheduled to come during that time!*

Thus, the critical importance of the passages of Scripture in this chapter is that they reveal clearly, from every writer in the New Testament—and most importantly, from Jesus Himself—that we do not have 19 wide centuries and countless events to which we may labor to apply the prophecies of Revelation. Rather, the prophecies of Revelation up to, and including the second coming of Jesus, were all meant to be fulfilled in the first century A.D.

From the giving of Revelation in the early months of A.D. 70 to the death of Domitian on September 18, A.D. 96 is about 26 1/2 years. Within that brief period of time all the prophecies of Revelation were meant to have been fulfilled, except for the ones related to the millennium, the judgment, and those that follow after Revelation 19.

The next chapter, "Does God Ever Change His Plans?" will give biblical reasons as to why some of the prophecies of Revelation were fulfilled in A.D. 70, while others, which were meant to be fulfilled in the reign of Domitian, were instead thrown far into the future.

Chapter Four

Does God Ever Change His Plans?

In Malachi 3:6 we read, "*For I am the Lord, I change not*" and in 1 Samuel 15:29 Samuel, the prophet, told King Saul, "*And also the Strength of Israel will not lie nor repent: for he is not a man, that he should repent.*" These passages are no doubt true where the character of God is concerned.

Still, a number of Scriptural passages indicate that God does change His plans either to judge, or to bless, His children, when either repentance or moral failure occurs.

In our previous chapter we showed, through numerous passages of Scripture that Jesus and the writers of the New Testament believed devoutly that He would return to earth in their generation to set up His heavenly kingdom. This was the first truth to be learned in our understanding of the book of Revelation.

In this chapter the truth that God does change His plans in response to prayer and repentance, on the one hand, and moral failure, on the other, will also be documented in Scripture, and becomes a second truth to be learned in understanding the book of Revelation.

The scriptural principle for this truth is stated in Jeremiah 18:7-10. In the opinion of this author, this reference is so important that it should be memorized by every teacher of Bible prophecy. In this passage God says,

> At what instant I shall speak concerning a nation, and concerning a kingdom, to pluck up, and to pull down, and to destroy it; If that nation, against whom I have pronounced, turn from their evil, I will repent of the evil that I thought to do unto them. And at what instant I shall speak concerning a nation, and concerning a kingdom, to build and to plant it; If it do evil in my sight, that it obey not my voice, then I will repent of the good, wherewith I said I would benefit them.

A number of scriptural passages are referred to below to illustrate the above principle.

In Jonah 3:4 Jonah spoke the word of the Lord, saying, "Yet forty days, and Nineveh shall be overthrown." But "the people of Nineveh believed God, and proclaimed a fast, and put on sackcloth, from the greatest of them even to the least of them" (Jonah 3:5). "And God saw their works, that they turned from their evil way; and God repented of the evil, that he had said that he would do unto them; and he did it not" (Jonah 3:10).

But was the judgment of God against Nineveh canceled or was it postponed? Several passages of Scripture indicate that the judgments of God are postponed when repentance takes place, and that they are visited upon a people when a moral lapse occurs. Thus, the judgments of God may be postponed, but not canceled.

In the case of Nineveh, 150 years after Jonah, the prophet Nahum wrote, "The burden of Nineveh" (Nahum 1:1). In his proclamation of judgment against Nineveh, Nahum declared that God would "make an utter end" of it (Nahum 1:9), and that the people seeing it would say, "Nineveh is laid waste" (Nahum 3:7). In this instance, since there was no evidence of repentance, the prophecy came true as given, and Nineveh was destroyed by the armies of Babylon.

Thus the prophecy of Jonah that Nineveh would be overthrown did occur, but at a later time. This truth becomes clearer in other passages.

In Daniel 4:5-17 we read of a dream given to King Nebuchadnezzar that Daniel interpreted (Daniel 4:19-27). In his interpretation Daniel saw terrible things that would happen to King Nebuchadnezzar, including that he would be driven from among men, would eat grass as oxen, and would be wet with the dew of heaven until seven times (or seven years) passed over him (Daniel 4:25). Then Daniel said to Nebuchadnezzar, "Wherefore, O king, let my counsel be acceptable unto thee, and break off thy sins by *righteousness, and thine iniquities by showing mercy to the poor; if it may be a lengthening of thy tranquility"* (Daniel 4:27).

In this passage Daniel knew that God's judgment upon Nebuchadnezzar would not be canceled, but that Nebuchadnezzar's tranquility could be lengthened, or postponed, by repentance.

In 1 Kings 21 we read that Jezebel arranged the murder of Naboth, and gave her husband, King Ahab, Naboth's vineyard which Ahab had coveted. Because of this, God sent the prophet Elijah to pronounce a judgment of doom upon Ahab, his wife, and his household (1 Kings 21:19-23). *"And it came to pass, when Ahab heard those words, that he rent his clothes, and put sackcloth upon his flesh, and fasted, and lay in sackcloth, and went softly. And the word of the Lord came to Elijah the Tishbite, saying, Seest thou how Ahab humbleth himself before me? Because he humbleth himself before me, I will not bring the evil in his days: but in his son's days will I bring the evil upon his house"* (1 Kings 21:27-29).

Here again, we see that through Ahab's repentance, God's judgment was postponed—but not canceled!

In 2 Chronicles 32:24-26 we read an account in the life of Hezekiah, king of Judah, which reinforces this same point.

> *In those days Hezekiah was sick to the death, and prayed unto the Lord: and he spake unto him, and he gave him a sign. But Hezekiah rendered not again according to the benefit done unto him; for his heart was lifted up: therefore there was wrath upon him, and upon Judah and Jerusalem. Notwithstanding Hezekiah humbled himself for the pride of his heart, both he and the inhabitants of Jerusalem, so that the wrath of the Lord came not upon them in the days of Hezekiah.*

Here, again, God's wrath was postponed—but not canceled!

Manasseh, the most wicked king that Judah ever had, was captured by the Assyrians, bound with fetters, and taken to Babylon (2 Chronicles 33:2-13). *"And when he was in affliction, he besought the Lord his God, and humbled himself greatly before the God of his fathers, And prayed unto him: and he was entreated of him, and heard his supplication, and brought him again to Jerusalem into his kingdom"* (2 Chronicles 33:12-13a). Then when Manasseh was restored to his throne, he sought to undo the evil he had done (2 Chronicles 33:15-16). Nevertheless, two kings later, in the reign of the good king Josiah, we read, *"Notwithstanding the Lord turned not from the fierceness of his great wrath, wherewith his anger was kindled against Judah, because of all the provocations that Manasseh had provoked him withal"* (2 Kings 23:26; see also Jeremiah 15:4).

Manasseh's repentance, then, had only postponed the coming judgment which came in the reign of King Zedekiah (2 Chronicles 36:11-19). Nebuchadnezzar, the king of Babylon, came against Jerusalem with his army and destroyed Jerusalem and the temple of God, and took many Jews into captivity.

But what does all this have to do with our study of the book of Revelation? In time, we will show that Revelation prophesies God's judgments against two cities—Jerusalem and Rome. Jerusalem did not repent, and God's prophesied judgment came upon Jerusalem in A.D. 70. But a great repentance came to Rome in the first century A.D., and God's judgment was postponed. We'll study that further in another chapter.

Other scriptural passages that support the theme of this chapter that God does change His mind are:

Numbers 14:30-34

1 Samuel 13:13-14

Deuteronomy 31:3 (contrast with Judges 2:21)

2 Chronicles 34:28; 35:23

Numbers 16:21,24

2 Samuel 12:14,16

1 Kings 9:3

2 Kings 22:20

1 Kings 11:36,38

Jeremiah 18:11, compare with 22:3-4; 26:3,13

Jeremiah 36:3,7

Genesis 19:20-21

Ezekiel 4:12,15

Deuteronomy 28:68

Genesis 19:2-3,22

Deuteronomy 23:3 (David's great-grandmother was Ruth the Moabite.)

Amos 7:3,6

Luke 24:28-29

Jeremiah 26:18-19 (See also Micah 3:12)

Jeremiah 42:10

Chapter Five

Why God Spared Rome

God spared Rome from the judgment He had pronounced against it for the same reason He spared Nineveh. Rome, like Nineveh, repented and turned to God.

Nineveh's judgment was to have come in *"forty days"* (Jonah 3:4). Rome's judgment was to have come in the reign of the *"eighth"* Roman king, or emperor (Revelation 17:11,16), who would have been Domitian. Domitian reigned from A.D. 81-96, and since Domitian was the prophesied *"beast"* who, with *"ten kings,"* was to have burned Rome with fire (Revelation 17:16), Rome's judgment was to have come within the time period of Domitian's reign.

Jonah 3:1-10 gives the details of Nineveh's repentance, and of God's turning from His fierce anger against that city. But the details of Rome's repentance are largely, though not altogether, outside the pages of Scripture.

Here are the facts of this strange, but marvelous development, as the common people of Rome and of the Roman Empire turned in faith to Jesus Christ.

1. Scriptural evidences of Rome's turning to Jesus Christ.

Paul wrote to the Roman Christians, "*First, I thank my God through Jesus Christ for you all, that your faith is spoken of throughout the whole world*" (Romans 1:8). Something was happening in Rome that was causing notice of their faith throughout the Roman Empire. In Acts 18:2, we discover something of that development. There we read that "*Claudius had commanded all Jews to depart from Rome.*" But why? The Roman historian, Suetonius, in commenting on this decree, about A.D. 52, wrote, "*Since the Jews were continually making disturbances at the instigation of Chrestus, he* [Claudius] *expelled them from Rome.*" Apparently, the furor between the Jews who believed in Jesus, and those in Rome who did not believe in Him, was getting the gospel known within that city. We see this also in Acts 28:22. Paul had called "*the chief of the Jews together*" (Acts 28:17), and they had told Paul, "*But we desire to hear of thee what thou thinkest: for as concerning this sect, we know that everywhere it is spoken against.*"

This tells us that the gospel of Jesus was not unknown in Rome in the first century A.D.

Paul had also told the Roman Christians that "*the preaching of Jesus Christ*" was "*made known to all nations for the obedience of faith*" (Romans 16:25-26), and to the Colossians, Paul maintained that the gospel "*was preached to every creature that is under heaven*" (Colossians 1:23).

Again, Paul writing to the Philippian Christians while in bonds in Rome explains, "*that the things which happened unto me have fallen out rather unto the furtherance of the gospel; So that my bonds in Christ are manifest in all the palace, and in all other places*" (Philippians 1:12-13). Did Paul really mean that the gospel had gone into the "palace" of Nero? Apparently so, for he concludes this letter with the words, "*All the saints salute you, chiefly they that are of Caesar's household*" (Philippians 4:22). Certainly the gospel was having an amazing penetration in the first century A.D.

2. Other historical evidences of Rome's turning to Jesus Christ.

In his *History of Christianity*, Kenneth Scott LaTourette titles one chapter, "The Sweep of Christianity Across the Graeco-Roman World." At the beginning of this chapter LaTourette writes:

> One of the most amazing and significant facts of history is that within five centuries of its birth Christianity won the professed allegiance of the overwhelming majority of the population of the Roman Empire and even the support of the Roman state. Beginning as a seemingly obscure sect of Judaism, one of scores, even hundreds of religions and religious

groups which were competing within that realm, revering as its central figure one who had been put to death by the machinery of Rome, and in spite of having been long proscribed by that government and eventually having the full weight of the state thrown against it, Christianity proved so far the victor that the empire sought alliance with it and to be a Roman citizen became almost identical with being a Christian...[4]

LaTourette, in detailing this remarkable transformation, writes, *"Christianity quickly moved out of the Jewish communities and became prevailingly non-Jewish."*[5]

Then, after giving the early persecutions of imperial Rome against the church, he writes, *"In what must have seemed an unequal contest between naked, ruthless force and unarmed passive resistance, it was not the imperial government but Christianity which emerged victor."*[6] He then gives the reasons for this amazing empire-wide conversion, and summarizes his answer, *"Whence came these qualities which won for Christianity its astounding victory? Careful and honest investigation can give but one answer, Jesus."*[7]

These Romans who turned to Jesus were not perfect, but they were committed. They truly desired to make Jesus the Lord of their lives. God honored their commitment, forgave their sins, and spared the Roman Empire from the judgment He had pronounced against it.

In our day the area of the old Roman Empire is turning from Christ, and is sinking again into the paganism it once rejected. For this reason only, the time is short for the appearance of the one described in Revelation as the "*beast.*" He will be as a modern-day Roman emperor, will rule from Rome, and will, no doubt, be the head of the European Community. Eventually, he will turn against Christians and will take the lead in persecuting and destroying them. His "*war with the saints*" will continue "*forty and two months*" (Revelation 13:5,7), then he will be confronted and destroyed by the returning Jesus!

But still, even as repentance among the Roman people kept Domitian from being the beast he was prophesied to be, we, too, could through our repentance and through our turning to Jesus put off the days of the "*beast*" for a thousand years. God does not look at prophecy charts to decide what He is going to do next! He looks upon the condition of our hearts, and acts toward us accordingly.

---

4. LaTourette, Kenneth Scott, *A History of Christianity*, pg. 65

5. ibid, pg. 75

6. ibid, pg. 91

7. ibid, pg. 107

Chapter Six

Dating the Revelation

Another major error which has led students away from a correct under-standing of Revelation is that we have misdated the book, and then, remembering the words of God's angel to John, "*to shew unto his servants things which must shortly come to pass*" (Revelation 1:1), we have looked into history and found nothing to which the words of Revelation could consistently apply. This has led to confusion.

The date for Revelation is generally put at A.D. 95 or 96. This dating has been based largely, though not entirely, upon the words of Iranaeus (about A.D. 180), a disciple of Polycarp, who was a disciple of the apostle John.

Iranaeus' quotation regarding either Revelation, or the apostle John, is given in Eusebius' *Ecclesiastical History*, page 188, as follows:

> *And a little further on he (that is, Iranaeus) speaks of the same John:* "We, therefore," *says he,* "do not venture to affirm any thing with certainty respecting the name of antichrist. For were it necessary that his name should be clearly announced to the present age, it would have been declared by him who saw the revelation. For it has not been long since (it or he) was seen, but almost in our own generation, about the end of Domitian's reign."

Thus, by reading "it" rather than "he" in the above quotation, the view gained in prominence that the Revelation was seen "*about the end of Domitian's reign,*" rather than John, was seen then.

In any case this dating of Revelation at A.D. 95 or 96 cannot be allowed, because

(1) It contradicts the "*one is*" phrase of Revelation 17:10 as to the time in which Revelation was written, and

(2) Significant internal evidence points to an earlier date.

In Revelation 17:10 we read, "*And there are seven kings: five are fallen, and one is, and the other is not yet come; and when he cometh, he must continue a short space.*"

Obviously, if we are able to identify the five kings that are fallen, and especially the "*one*" that "*is*," we should be able to arrive at an approximate date for the receiving and writing of Revelation.

The five kings that are fallen are easily identified as the first five emperors of Rome. However, in the colloquial language of the common people, they were not referred to as "emperors," but as "kings." Thus, in Scripture, the word "emperor" does not appear, but we read, "*We have no king but Caesar*" (John 19:15) or, "*Submit…to the king, as supreme*" (1 Peter 2:13).

These five kings were then

Augustus Caesar	31 B.C. to A.D. 14
Tiberius Caesar	A.D. 14 to A.D. 37
Caligula Caesar	A.D. 37 to A.D. 41
Claudius Caesar	A.D. 41 to A.D. 54
Nero Caesar	A.D. 54 to A.D. 68

It may be objected that Julius Caesar is not included in this list. But Julius Caesar was offered the position of king just before he was killed on the Ides (15th) of March, 44 B.C., and he rejected the kingship. Therefore, he was a dictator, but not a king or emperor of Rome, and thus was not one of the kings that had fallen.

So what king or emperor answers to the "*one is*" phrase of Revelation 17:10? Actually, there were three emperors reigning in Rome in rapid succession after Nero. Josephus gives their names and the lengths of their reigns as:

Galba	7 months, 7 days
Otho	3 months, 2 days
Vitellius	8 months, 5 days

However, because of the brevity of their reigns, and because their reigns were successfully contested, none of these three emperors was recognized as emperor in the provinces. In this connection, there may be some significance in the fact that Ptolemy's Canon (a list of ancient rulers and the length of their reigns, written from Alexandria, Egypt) skips over the reigns of Galba, Otho, and Vitellius altogether.

Because none of these three emperors was recognized as such in the Roman provinces, neither the apostle John nor his fellow countrymen in the province of Asia would have so recognized them. The next king or emperor that John and his fellow countrymen in the Roman province of Asia would have recognized would have been Vespasian. Thus we have for the sixth and seventh kings of Revelation 17:10 the "*one*" who "*is*" and the "*other*" who "*is not yet come*" as follows:

Vespasian   A.D. 69 to A.D. 79

Titus   A.D. 79 to A.D. 81

Revelation must, then, have been received and written during the reign of the "*one*" who "*is*," that is, during the reign of Vespasian. But, if this is correct, then how are we to account for a rather persistent tradition that Revelation was written when Domitian reigned in Rome. Eusebius quoted a rather ambiguous statement from Clement of Alexandria (about A.D. 200) to that effect. Victorinus, bishop of Pettow, toward the close of the third century expressly states this, as does Jerome in the fourth century.

A little-known fact that Josephus points out, however, is that after Vespasian's general, Mucianus, had defeated the forces of Vitellius, "*He then produced Domitian and recommended him to the multitude, until his father* (Vespasian) *should come himself*" (*Wars*, IV, XI, 4). This is a most important clue in the dating of Revelation. Because Scripture has Revelation written during the reign of Vespasian, and tradition has Revelation written under Domitian, both could be correct. That is, John received and wrote the Revelation in the reign of Vespasian, during which Vespasian's younger son, Domitian, served as regent in place of his father, until his father could come.

Domitian was but an eighteen-year-old boy at the time. He did not reign in his own right until 81 to A.D. 96. Vespasian was in Alexandria, Egypt, waiting for the winter storms to subside before coming to Rome. Thus, Domitian ruled in Rome from December 15, A.D. 69 until June A.D. 70, and the facts available to us point to Revelation being written during this time.

However, we may be able to pinpoint the date of the receiving and the writing of Revelation closer than that. There is yet another passage in Revelation that relates to its date.

In Revelation 1:10, we read, "*I was in the Spirit on the Lord's day*." On this matter a quote from A. T. Robertson, *Word Pictures in the New Testament*, Volume VI, page 290, is helpful.

> *Deissmann has proven (Bible Studies, p. 217f.; Light, etc., p.357ff.) from inscriptions and papyri that the word kuriakos (lord) was in common use for the sense "imperial" as imperial finance and imperial treasury and from papyri and ostraca that hemera Sebaste (Augustus Day) was the first day of each month, Emperor's Day on which money payments were made.*

The Lord's day of which John wrote was an important day to the Roman guards, and also to the prisoners who were on the Roman penal colony on the island of Patmos. It was the first day of the month, a day in honor of Augustus Caesar. (Later the Christians would use this same term as relating to the first day of the week, but John was speaking in the common term of the penal colony.) On this day the Roman guards on Patmos and throughout the Roman Empire would receive their pay and, no doubt, pay the debts that they had incurred. For the prisoners the atmosphere would be freer, and very likely their forced labor would be relaxed on this one day while their guards were engaged elsewhere. John, in referring to "*the Lord's day*" is simply explaining why he could even have received a revelation, and why he would have the time to write it down. Ordinarily, there would have been no time for such activity while he was bound in slave labor. So John writes, "*I was in the Spirit on the Lord's day*."

On some first day of some month between January 1, A.D. 70 and June 1, A.D. 70 the Revelation was given. But the Roman battle for Jerusalem recommenced under Titus on the Passover (about May 1), A.D. 70.

This Roman-Jewish War had begun in A.D. 66 under Nero Caesar, and with Vespasian, the Roman general. But after Nero's suicide on June 9, A.D. 68, the war came to a halt during the reigns of Galba and Otho, and recommenced briefly under Vitellius, only to halt again while Vespasian's forces contested those of Vitellius for the Roman throne. Thus, for a year and a half, there was very little military activity. Then, about May 1, A.D. 70 the war recommenced with Vespasian the emperor, but with Domitian acting in Rome as his regent, and with Titus now the Roman general. Titus gathered his forces together at Caesarea preparing for his assault upon Jerusalem.

This eliminates both June 1, A.D. 70 and May 1, A.D. 70 as possible dates for the receiving and writing of Revelation, since one must conclude that, having come so close to this most significant Divine judgment in the previous half a millennium for the Jews, this must be included in the judgments about which Revelation prophesied. Also, now we must consider the place that the destruction of Jerusalem had in the heart and mind of Jesus. He wept over the city (Luke 19:41), and four times had warned Jerusalem of her coming destruction (Luke 13:34-35; 19:41-44; 21:20-23; 23:27-31). Surely, Jesus in heaven was the same Jesus as He was on earth, and His feelings about Jerusalem had not changed.

Thus, because the battle for Jerusalem started about May 1, A.D. 70, the Revelation must have been given before that, or we would be dealing with history instead of prophecy.

So, this leaves us with January 1, February 1, March 1, or April 1, of A.D. 70 as possible dates for John to have received the Revelation. But April 1 is only one month away from the time when this awesome judgment is to begin, and this Revelation must be carried across 70 miles of sea from Patmos to Ephesus, then by road to the six other churches on the circular road that connects their seven cities to each other in the Roman province of Asia. Because the Revelation is to be read in the seven churches at their weekly gatherings, it would require seven weeks to accomplish this, unless it were recopied by hand, or unless special meetings were called—not an easy task where travel and communications are difficult and where some of the congregation are slaves. The date of April 1 hardly gives time for this.

Let's look then at January 1, A.D. 70. As we read in Acts 27:9, the waters of the Mediterranean Sea became violent and impassable in winter. "*Now when much time was spent, and when sailing was now dangerous, because the fast was now already past, Paul admonished them.*" What does this mean?

The "*fast*" referred to here was the fast of the great day of the atonement. It came on the tenth day of the month Tishri, which answers to a part of September and a part of October. The Roman military writer, Vegetius, tells us that navigation was considered dangerous after September 15, and ceased for the winter from November 11 to March 10.

This was not an absolute rule, however, as this very journey by Paul was continued "*after three months*" (Acts 28:11) at Malta, which would have been near the end of January or the first of February.

Thus, it appears that January 1 is too unlikely for Revelation to have been received, written, and sent by ship to Ephesus, due to the reluctance of ship owners to commit their ships to the stormy seas.

Thus, either February 1, or March 1, of A.D. 70 offers the best possibilities. There is no need to pin the date down further. Very likely, on one of those dates, John, on *"the Lord's day,"* entered a cave on the isle of Patmos, came to be in the Spirit, and received and wrote the Revelation.

In just two or three months the Romans would open their campaign to take Jerusalem. Truly, *"the time"* was *"at hand"* (Revelation 1:3).

We mentioned earlier that "significant internal evidence" within Revelation also "points to an earlier date" than the usually given A.D. 95 or 96 dating. One of the interesting things about truth is that once it is recognized in one area, other areas become instantly illuminated.

So, in this instance, these bits of internal evidence were just waiting to be found, when we were able to come to a correct dating of Revelation.

(1) In the letters to two of the seven churches of Asia—Smyrna and Philadelphia—we read of *"the blasphemy of them which say they are Jews, and are not, but are the synagogue of Satan"* (Revelation 2:9), and *"Behold, I will make them of the synagogue of Satan, which say they are Jews, and are not, but do lie; behold, I will make them to come and worship before thy feet, and to know that I have loved thee"* (Revelation 3:9). These passages indicate a substantial problem in these two churches with the unbelieving Jews. This problem existed due to the fact that before the destruction of Jerusalem, the break between Judaism and Christianity was not yet complete.

This is not to suggest that the Jews who believed in Jesus, and those Jews who disbelieved in Jesus, were often together in the same synagogue in A.D. 70. Because the synagogues were repeatedly split under Paul's preaching (as in Antioch of Pisidia—Acts 13:14,42-45, Iconium—Acts 14:1-4, Thessalonica—Acts 17:1-5, Berea—Acts 17:10-13, Corinth—Acts 18:1,4,6, Ephesus—Acts 18:19; 19:8-9), such an occurrence as their being together must have been rare.

However, the Jewish believers in Jesus at this time did not see themselves as "Christians," but simply as true Jews in that they had received their Messiah. The term "Christian" was needed to designate Gentile believers in Jesus, and it was first given in Antioch, a Gentile city. But the Jewish believers in Jesus did not need this name. They needed only to see themselves as true Jews, and this is the view we see in Revelation. By A.D. 95 or 96 the break between Judaism and Christianity was complete, and the three great feasts of Passover, Pentecost, and Tabernacles no longer brought the two groups together as they formerly had. (See Acts 20:16; 21:20; 1 Corinthians 16:8).

(2) It would be absolutely amazing, even unthinkable, that no mention would have been made in Revelation of the destruction of Jerusalem and of the holy temple if Revelation had been written in A.D. 95 or 96.

(3) The most persuasive internal evidence, however, is how quickly the pieces of this puzzle fall into place when the correct date is accepted.

To illustrate this, an outline of the prophetic parts of Revelation will follow this chapter, with brief evidences included, so that the reader may get a panoramic view, as it were, of what Revelation is all about.

Verse by Verse Through Revelation 6–22

Revelation 6

The Seven Seals

The seven seals are the first of two visions connected by one message. The seven trumpets are the second of the two-vision series. Both of these visions contain detailed prophecies, given in sequential order, of the coming destruction of Jerusalem, fulfilled in A.D. 70. Both also contain less specific *allusions* to the destruction of Rome. The detailed and sequential prophecies against Jerusalem are given twice "*because the thing is established by God, and God will shortly bring it to pass*" (Genesis 41:32*)*.

Concerning Rome, we have in these two visions, only allusions or hints of her destruction, but we do have one, *detailed* prophecy—the seven bowls of God's wrath (Revelation 16:1-21). The two detailed prophecies of the destruction of Jerusalem, and the one detailed prophecy of the destruction of Rome are given to suggest (Genesis 41:32 again) that Rome could repent and avert, or postpone, her fate, while Jerusalem could not, as Jerusalem's fate was "*established by God*" and He would "*shortly bring it to pass.*"

Four Spirit Horses (see Zechariah 6:1-8, esp. vs. 5) Bring God's Wrath upon Jerusalem.

Note: There is more discussion of this passage in the chapter on "Understanding Old Testament Passages."

1 And I saw when the Lamb opened one of the seals, and I heard, as it were the noise of thunder, one of the four beasts saying, Come and see.

2 And I saw, and behold a white horse: and he that sat on him had a bow; and a crown was given unto

Spirit of Conquest, symbolized by a white horse.

(1) The Roman general, Cestius, acting on orders from Nero Caesar, surrounded Jerusalem, just as Jesus, our Lord, had prophesied (Luke 21:20). However, after about six days, Cestius withdrew his troops. Jewish militants, who had been looking for a way to escape entrapment within Jerusalem, now rushed out of the city and began cutting down the Roman army in great numbers. It was a tremendous victory of the Jews over Roman might.

him: and he went forth conquering, and to conquer (Revelation 6:1-2).

(2) *"A bow."* This would indicate that this spirit would stir the Jews as the Romans were not known to be adept in archery. The Romans generally used Arabians and employed Asiatic mercenaries for archery (see *Wars*, III, V, 2).

(3) *"A crown* (Greek *stephanos*, wreath) *was given unto him."* This refers not to a kingly crown but to a victor's wreath, indicating that Titus—at the time this Revelation was given—had already won military victories. (He had fought alongside his father, Vespasian, at Jotapata and Gamala, and he had directed the battles against Taricheea and Gischala.)

(4) *"He went forth conquering, and to conquer."* Titus had been conquering, and would continue to conquer, until Jerusalem itself would be conquered.

3 And when he had opened the second seal, I heard the second beast say, Come and see.

4 And there went out another horse that was red: and power was given to him that sat thereon to take peace from the earth (Greek, ge, earth, or land), and that they should kill one another: and there was given unto him a great sword (Revelation 6:3-4).

Spirit of Murder, symbolized by a red horse.

(1) Three Jewish armies within Jerusalem fought furiously among themselves as Titus and 80,000 Roman soldiers approached the city. The leaders of these Jewish armies were Simon bar Giora, the main leader; John of Gischala; and Eleazar, the captain of the temple, who also was in charge of keeping the firstfruits, that is, the sacred oil and wine which had been given to God.

(2) *"That they should kill one another."* This phrase indicates the fierce civil war within Jerusalem as the Romans approached. John of Gischala wrested control of the temple from the forces of Eleazar during the Passover, thus reducing the Jewish armies within Jerusalem to two. He also took possession of the sacred firstfruits of oil and wine.

(3) *"There was given unto him a great sword."* This indicates that the murder within Jerusalem would be great.

Bread by Weight

And when I have broken the staff of your bread, ten women shall bake your bread in one oven, and they shall deliver you your bread again by weight: and ye shall eat and not be satisfied (Leviticus 26:26).

Moreover he said unto me, Son of man, behold, I will break the staff of bread in Jerusalem: and they shall eat **bread by weight**, *and with care; and they shall drink water by measure, and with astonishment* (Ezekiel 4:16).

5 And when he had opened the third seal, I heard the third beast say, Come and see. And I beheld, and lo a black horse; and he that sat on him had a pair of balances in his hand.

6 And I heard a voice in the midst of the four beasts say, A measure of wheat for a penny (Greek, denarion, denarius), and three measures of barley for a penny; and see thou hurt not the oil and the wine[8] *(Revelation 6:5-6).*

Spirit of Mourning and Famine, symbolized by a black horse.

(1) *"A pair of balances."* These balances, which were used for weighing food, were a symbol of scarcity and famine. "Bread by weight" always implies scarcity. (See Leviticus 26:26; Ezekiel 4:10,16-17.) Thus, in the bitter warfare between the Jewish armies within Jerusalem, John of Gischala destroyed the houses of grain under the control of Simon bar Giora, and then Simon bar Giora destroyed the houses of grain under the control of John of Gischala. (*Wars*, V, I, 4) In this way, these Jewish armies brought the famine upon Jerusalem.

(2) *"A measure of wheat for a penny* (denarius), *and three measures of barley for a penny* (denarius)." Wheat was scarcer than barley, and three times as expensive. Barley bread was the common food of the poor. Thus, during this siege of Jerusalem in A.D. 70, Josephus writes that *"Many there were indeed who sold what they had for one measure; it was of wheat, if they were of the richer sort, but of barley, if they were poorer."* (*Wars*, V, X, 2)

---

8. Note: The "chamber of oil" where the oil and wine were stored was situated in the southwest corner of the Court of the Women, according to Emil Schurer, in his work, *The History of the Jewish People in the Age of Jesus Christ*, Vol. I, page 505.

(3) *"See thou hurt not the oil and the wine."*
After John of Gischala had taken over the
temple from Eleazar and his army (*Wars*, V,
III, 1), John melted down many of the
sacred utensils, and then *"he emptied the
vessels of that sacred wine and oil which the
priests kept to be poured on the burnt offerings* (the firstfruits and the tithes, as in
Nehemiah 10:37-39), *and which lay in the
inner court of the temple, and distributed it
among the multitude, who, in their anointing
themselves and drinking, used (each of them)
above a hin* (hin, 1.62 gallons) *of them."*
(*Wars*, V, XIII, 6) This *"oil and wine"* had
been given to God and not to John of
Gischala who—in this passage—was put on
notice that he did not have God's permission to steal and to waste it!

The Fourth Part of the Land

(Compare Ezekiel 5:1-5, as translated from the Hebrew text with the
Septuagint Version).

The King James Version
(translated from the Hebrew)

The Greek Septuagint
(translated about 285 B.C.)

*1 And thou, son of man, take thee a
sharp knife, take thee a barber's
razor, and cause it to pass upon thine
head and upon thy beard: then take
thee balances to weigh, and divide
the hair.*

*1 And thou, son of man, take thee a
sword sharper than a barber's razor;
thou shalt procure it for thyself, and
shalt bring it upon thine head, and
upon thy beard: and thou shalt take
a pair of scales, and shalt separate
the hair.*

*2 Thou shalt burn with fire a **third
part** in the midst of the city, when
the days of the siege are fulfilled: and
thou shalt take **a third part**, and
smite about it with a knife: and **a
third part** thou shalt scatter in the
wind; and I will draw out a sword
after them.*

*2 **A fourth part** thou shalt burn in the
fire in the midst of the city, at the fulfillment of the days of the siege: and
thou shalt take **a fourth part**, and
burn it up in the midst of it: **and a
fourth part** thou shalt cut with a
sword round about it: and **a fourth
part** thou shalt scatter to the wind; and
I will draw out a sword after them.*

3 Thou shalt also take thereof a few in number, and bind them in thy skirts.

3 And thou shalt take thence a few in number, and shalt wrap them in the fold of thy garment.

4 Then take of them again, and cast them into the midst of the fire; for thereof shall a fire come forth into all the house of Israel.

4 And thou shalt take of these again, and cast them into the midst of the fire, and burn them up with fire: from thence shall come forth fire; and thou shalt say to the whole house of Israel,

5 Thus saith the Lord God; **This is Jerusalem:** *I have set it in the midst of the nations and countries that are round about her.*

5 Thus saith the Lord; **This is Jerusalem:** *I have set her and the countries round about her in the midst of the nations.*

7 And when he had opened the fourth seal, I heard the voice of the fourth beast say, Come and see.

8 And I looked, and behold a pale (Greek, chloros, pale green, as in Revelation 8:7, "green grass," or Revelation 9:4, "green thing," thus, a sickly greenish color for this horse is intended) horse: and his name that sat on him was Death, and Hell (Greek, hades, Hades, personified, thus the ruler of departed spirits) followed with him. And power was given unto them

Spirit of Death, followed by the Spirit, Hades (the ruler of departed spirits), symbolized by a pale (or greenish) horse.

(1) *"The fourth part of the earth."* In Ezekiel 4:1–5:17 we read of prophecies of judgment against Jerusalem. In one of these prophecies (Ezekiel 5:1-12), Ezekiel is to shave his head and beard and to divide his hair into three parts. But in the Greek Septuagint Version (the LXX), Ezekiel is to divide his hair into four parts. In both the Hebrew and the LXX we read, *"This is Jerusalem."* Thus, strangely, both *"the fourth part"* (Revelation 6:8) and *"the third part"* (Revelation 8 and 9) entered into the thought forms of the Hebrew people as a reference to Jerusalem. Thus, the phrase *"the fourth part of the land"* refers to Jerusalem, just as much as the phrase *"the third part"* also refers to Jerusalem.

(2) Death by war, famine, pestilence, and wild beasts. Five hundred Jews each day were beaten and crucified by the Romans during the siege. Jews seeking to escape Jerusalem were caught and disemboweled to see if they had swallowed gold. Great piles of carcasses produced a pestilential stench in Jerusalem.

over the fourth part of the earth (Greek, *ge,* earth or land), *to kill with sword, and with hunger, and with death* (such as, "pestilence," as in Ezekiel 14:21), *and with the beasts of the earth* (Revelation 6:7-8).

More than one million died in the siege. (*Wars*, VI, IX, 3)

9 And when he had opened the fifth seal, I saw under the altar the souls of them that were slain for the word of God, and for the testimony which they held (Revelation 6:9).

Christians *"slain for the word of God"* by Nero Caesar Await God's Vengeance upon Rome

"*I saw **under the altar** the souls of them that were slain.*" The phrase, "*under the altar,*" may be understood by referring to Leviticus 4:7[9]: "*And the priest…shall pour all the blood of the bullock **at the bottom** of the altar of the burnt offering.*" We must remember that these earthly things "*serve unto the example and shadow of heavenly things…*" (Hebrews 8:5). *These martyrs are pictured with their blood poured at the base of God's heavenly altar, in like manner as the blood of a bullock was poured at the base of the altar of burnt offering upon earth.* (See Leviticus 17:11: "*For the life* (Hebrew, *nephesh*; Greek LXX, *psuche*) **of the flesh is in the blood**: *and I have given it to you upon the altar to make an atonement for your* **souls** (Hebrew, *nephesh*; Greek LXX, *psuche*): *for it is the blood that maketh an atonement for the soul* (Hebrew, *nephesh*; Greek LXX, *psuche*). Thus, in both the Hebrew and in the Greek LXX, the words for "life" and "soul" are the same. Leviticus 17:11 could read, then, "*For the soul of the flesh is in the blood…*" *The souls of those martyred by Nero Caesar were in their blood which was pictured here as poured at the base of the altar of burnt offering in heaven.* See Genesis 4:10, "*The voice of thy*

---

9. Besides Leviticus 4:7, see also Leviticus 4:18, 25, 30, 34; 8:15; 9:9; also Exodus 29:12 for similar passages.

brother's blood crieth unto me from the ground." In like manner the voice of the blood of the martyrs cried to God, and God would answer with divine judgment upon Rome.

10 And they cried with a loud voice, saying, "How long, O Lord, holy and true, dost thou not judge and avenge our blood on them that dwell on the earth? (Revelation 6:10).

"How long, O Lord, holy and true, dost thou not judge and avenge our blood on them that dwell on the earth?" (Revelation 6:10). See *"Vengeance is mine; I will repay, saith the Lord"* (Romans 12:19). The phrase, *"them that dwell on the earth,"* appears often in Revelation (3:10; 6:10; 11:10; 13:14 (twice); 14:6; 17:8), and always refers to the peoples living within the Roman Empire. Another phrase, used often but having the same meaning is, *"peoples, and multitudes, and nations, and tongues"* (always with variations) (Revelation 5:9; 7:9; 10:11; 11:9; 14:6; 17:15). The phrase *"kings of the earth"* occurs six times (Revelation 17:2,18; 18:3,9; 19:19; 21:24) and always refers to the Roman emperor and to those who rule under him. The phrase *"the great city,"* with variations using the word *"great,"* as *"great Babylon,"* or *"Babylon, the great"* (Revelation 11:8; 14:8; 16:19; 17:5, 18:10,16,18-19,21), always refers to Rome. In Revelation 21:10 the word "great" in the phrase *"that **great** city"* is not in most modern English translations, nor in the oldest Greek manuscripts.

11 And white robes were given unto every one of them; and it was said unto them, that they should rest yet for a little season, until their fellow servants also and their brethren, that should be killed as they were, should be fulfilled (Revelation 6:11).

"That they should rest yet for a little season, until their fellow servants also and their brethren, that should be killed as they were, should be fulfilled" (Revelation 6:11). The persecution referred to above had been under Nero Caesar in A.D. 64. When John saw this vision in early A.D. 70, the martyrs were still waiting for God's wrath to fall on those who killed them. These martyrs were then told of another persecution that was coming that would fulfill their number. This next persecution would have occurred under *"the eighth"* king (Revelation 17:11), that is, under Domitian, and then Jesus would have returned. See Revelation 16:5-7, especially vs. 7 (*Concordant Literal New Testament*) *"And I hear the altar saying, 'Yea, Lord*

God, Almighty, true and just are Thy judgings.'" Thus, the martyrs were to have been avenged in the destruction of Rome.

12 And I beheld when he had opened the sixth seal, and, lo, there was a great earthquake; and the sun became black as sackcloth of hair, and the moon became as blood;

13 And the stars of heaven fell unto the earth, even as a fig tree casteth her untimely figs, when she is shaken of a mighty wind.

14 And the heaven departed as a scroll when it is rolled together; and every mountain and island were moved out of their places.

15 And the kings of the earth, and the great men, and the rich men, and the chief captains, and the mighty men, and every bondman, and every free man, hid themselves in the dens and in the rocks of the mountains;

16 And said to the mountains and rocks,

The Horror of God's Wrath upon Rome

(1) Rome is identified here by the phrase, "*the kings of the earth*" (Revelation 6:15). That is, since "*kings*" is plural here, and there were a number of "*kings*" reigning over the provinces in the Roman Empire, this points then to the Roman Empire and to its capital, Rome. By contrast, only one king, Herod Agrippa II, reigned over Judea.

(2) A number of idiomatic phrases are used here to describe the horror of God's wrath pouring forth upon Rome. These phrases are used elsewhere in scripture to describe *the ruin of a kingdom*: "*a great earthquake*" (Revelation 6:12; see Isaiah 29:6; Joel 2:10); "*the sun became black as sackcloth of hair, and the moon became as blood*" (Revelation 6:12; see Isaiah 13:10; Ezekiel 32:7; Joel 2:10, 31; 3:15; Amos 5:20; 8:9); "*And the stars of heaven fell unto the earth…And the heaven departed as a scroll when it is rolled together*" (Revelation 6:13, 14; see Isaiah 34:4); "*…hid themselves in the dens and in the rocks of the mountains*" (Revelation 6:15; see Isaiah 2:19-21); "*And said to the mountains and rocks, Fall on us…*" (Revelation 6:16; see Hosea 10:8; Luke 23:30). As Maimonides (1135-1204), the great Rambam of Judaism, put it, "'*The stars have fallen,*' '*The heavens are overthrown,*' '*The sun is darkened,*' '*The earth is waste and trembles,*' *and similar metaphors*" are "*frequently employed by Isaiah, and less frequently by other prophets, when they describe **the ruin of a kingdom.**"*

Fall on us,, and hide us from the face of him that sitteth on the throne, and from the wrath of the Lamb:

17 For the great day of his wrath is come; and who shall be able to stand?
(Revelation 6:12-17).

Note: This section on idiomatic phrases is more fully explained in the chapter on "Understanding the Hebrew Idiom."

Revelation 7
Identifying the 144,000

And after these things I saw four angels standing on the four corners of the earth, holding the four winds of the earth, that the wind should not blow on the earth, nor on the sea, nor on any tree.

2 And I saw another angel ascending from the east, having the seal of the living God: and he cried with a loud voice to the four angels, to whom it was given to hurt the earth and the sea,

3 Saying, Hurt not the earth, neither the sea, nor the trees, till we have sealed the servants of our God in their foreheads.

4 And I heard the number of them which were sealed: and there were sealed an hundred and forty and four thousand of all

"The Firstfruits" Are First Converts

These (144,000) were redeemed from among men, being the firstfruits unto God and to the Lamb (Revelation 14:4b).

"When shall these things be? and what shall be the sign of thy coming, and of the end of the world?" (Matthew 24:3). Two signs: one for the destruction of Jerusalem, and one for the destruction of Rome.

(a) As to Jerusalem, her destruction will occur after the 144,000 (the Jewish believers in Jesus in Jerusalem) are sealed, or *protected*, from God's soon coming wrath.

    (1) The God who spared Noah from the flood (Genesis 7–8), and spared Lot from the destruction upon Sodom (Genesis 19), here protects the Jewish believers in Jesus who live in Jerusalem.

    (2) In A.D. 66 the Roman general, Cestius Gallus, surrounded Jerusalem. He was there for six days and then withdrew. The Jewish followers of Jesus, in obedience to the words of Jesus, left the city. (See Luke 21:20-21: *"And when ye shall see Jerusalem compassed with armies, then know that the desolation thereof is nigh. Then let them which are in Judea flee to the mountains; and let them which are in the midst of it depart out; and let not them that are in the countries enter thereinto."*)

the tribes of the children of Israel.

5 Of the tribe of Juda were sealed twelve thousand. Of the tribe of Reuben were sealed twelve thousand. Of the tribe of Gad were sealed twelve thousand.

6 Of the tribe of Aser were sealed twelve thousand. Of the tribe of Nepthalim were sealed twelve thousand. Of the tribe of Manasses were sealed twelve thousand.

7 Of the tribe of Simeon were sealed twelve thousand. Of the tribe of Levi

(3) Josephus records this departure in these words, "*After this calamity had befallen Cestius, many of the most eminent Jews swam away from the city, as from a ship when it is going to sink*" (*Wars*, II, XX, 1). Josephus apparently did not know who these people were who were leaving Jerusalem, but Eusebius tells us, "*The whole body, however, of the church at Jerusalem, having been commanded by a divine revelation, given to men of approved piety there before the war, removed from the city, and dwelt at a certain town beyond the Jordon, called Pella*" (Eusebius' *Ecclesiastical History*, pg. 86).

(4) Even after these Jewish believers in Jesus fled to Pella, the danger to their lives was not past as Roman armies would still be fighting in the proximity of Pella. But by A.D. 70 this danger was over. They were sealed, that is, protected.[10] Now God's wrath could come upon Jerusalem.

(5) In Revelation 14:4, the 144,000 are referred to as "*the firstfruits unto God and to the Lamb.*" In the New Testament firstfruits

---

10. Protective Signs in Scripture

And the Lord said unto him, Therefore whosoever slayeth Cain, vengeance shall be taken on him sevenfold. And the Lord set a mark upon Cain, lest any finding him should kill him (Genesis 4:15).

And it shall be for a sign unto thee upon thine hand, and for a memorial between thine eyes, that the Lord's law may be in thy mouth: for with a strong hand hath the Lord brought thee out of Egypt (Exodus 13:9).

And it shall be for a token upon thine hand, and for frontlets between thine eyes: for by strength of hand the Lord brought us forth out of Egypt (Exodus 13:16).

And thou shalt make a plate of pure gold, and grave upon it, like the engravings of a signet, HOLINESS TO THE LORD.
And thou shalt put it on a blue lace, that it may be upon the mitre; upon the forefront of the mitre it shall be.
And it shall be upon Aaron's forehead, that Aaron may bear the iniquity of the holy things, which the children of Israel shall hallow in all their holy gifts; and it shall be always upon his forehead, that they may be accepted before the Lord (Exodus 28:36-38).

And thou shalt bind them for a sign upon thine hand, and they shall be as frontlets between thine eyes (Deuteronomy 6:8).

Therefore shall ye lay up these my words in your heart and in your soul, and bind them for a sign upon your hand, that they may be as frontlets between your eyes (Deuteronomy 11:18).

were sealed twelve thousand. Of the tribe of Issachar were sealed twelve thousand.

8 Of the tribe of Zabulun were sealed twelve thousand. Of the tribe of Joseph were sealed twelve thousand. Of the tribe of Benjamin were sealed twelve thousand.

refers to the *first converts*[11] in a certain place. The 144,000 were the first converts for Jesus in Jerusalem.

Daniel had prophesied that the Messiah would make "*a strong covenant with many for one week*" (that is, seven years) (Daniel 9:27 RSV). Jesus' earthy ministry was three and a half years, and for the following three and a half years, until the stoning of Stephen (Acts 7:28–8:1), great multitudes came into the church at Jerusalem. (See Acts 2:41; 4:4; 5:14; 6:1,7.) After the stoning of Stephen, the Jerusalem church was scattered abroad, and we read of no more conversions within Jerusalem, and in fact, quite the opposite (Acts 22:17,18). Thus, James, in writing to "*the twelve tribes which are scattered abroad*" (James 1:1), referred to them as "*a kind of firstfruits of his creatures*" (James 1:18). While many were scattered abroad, many stayed, or returned to Jerusalem. The apostles stayed (Acts 8:1; 9:27); and prophets were there (Acts 11:27-28), and elders (Acts 15:2; 16:4; 21:18), and "*many thousands* (Greek, *murias*, ten thousands, as in Jude 14) *of Jews…which believe*" (Acts 21:20). These were the 144,000.

(6) In Revelation, especially, we see that numbers have a special meaning. Thus, 12 is the signature of Israel. A number multiplied by itself carries the same meaning, but intensified. Thus, 12 x 12 = 144, or the true Israel, because they had accepted their Messiah. (See Revelation 2:9; 3:9, where unbelieving

---

11. Firstfruits *Salute my well beloved Epaenetus, who is the firstfruits of Achaia unto Christ.* (Romans 16:5b).

I beseech you, brethren, (ye know the house of Stephanas, that it is the firstfruits of Achaia, and that they have addicted themselves to the ministry of the saints (1 Corinthians 16:15).

Jews are not even seen to be Jews.) The 144 is 144,000 because of all the believing Jews in Jerusalem of which there were "ten thousands."

(7) The 144,000 were sealed. This concept comes from Ezekiel 9, in which a "*mark*" was "*set*" "*upon the foreheads of the men that sigh and that cry for all the abominations that be done in the midst...of Jerusalem*" (Ezekiel 9:4). Those without the mark were to be slain. Thus, the mark indicated protection.

9 After this I beheld, and, lo, a great multitude, which no man could number, of all nations (Greek, ethnos, nations or Gentiles), and kindreds, and people, and tongues, stood before the throne, and before the Lamb, clothed with white robes (as in Revelation 6:11: "And white robes were given unto every one of them..."), and palms in their hands;

10 And cried with a loud voice, saying, Salvation to our God which sitteth upon the throne, and unto the Lamb.

(b) As to Rome, her destruction will occur when the number of martyrs is completed who are to be killed by a returning Nero, the "*eighth*" king, who would have been Domitian.

(1) In the Aramaic language—the earthly language of Jesus and the apostle John—the letters of the alphabet are also numbers. Thus, the letters in Nero Caesar add up to the 666 of Revelation 13:18.

(2) Three times the angel told John that "*the beast was, and is not*" (Revelation 17:8 (twice), 11). Thus, at the time John received the Revelation, Nero was dead. He committed suicide on June 9, A.D. 68.

(3) "*And the beast that was, and is not, even he is the eighth, and is of the seven and goeth into perdition*" (Revelation 17:11). The "*eighth*" king, Domitian, would be "*of the seven*"[12] or "*one of the seven.*" He would be like a Nero returned. That is, Domitian would come in the spirit and power of Nero.

(4) In Revelation 7:1-8 the 144,000 were Jews. In Revelation 7:9-17 we read of *Gentiles*, "*a great multitude, which no man could*

---

12. Of The Seven: The phrase "*is of the seven*" (Gr. *Ek ton hepta*) is translated "*one of the seven*" in Acts 21:8 even though the Greek is the same.

11 And all the angels stood round about the throne, and about the elders and the four beasts, and fell before the throne on their faces, and worshiped God,

12 Saying, Amen: Blessing, and glory, and wisdom, and thanksgiving, and honour, and power, and might, be unto our God for ever and ever. Amen.

13 And one of the elders answered, saying unto me, What are these which are arrayed in white robes? And whence came they? (Revelation 7:9-13).

14 And I said unto him, Sir, thou knowest. And he said to me, These are they which came out of great tribulation, and have washed their robes, and made them white in the blood of the Lamb.

15 Therefore are they before the throne of God, and serve him day and night in his temple: and he that sitteth on the throne

*number, of all **nations**, and kindreds, and people, and tongues"* (Revelation 7:9). The word, *"nations,"* is translated from the Greek word, *"ethnos,"* which the King James translators rendered 64 times in the New Testament as *"nation,"* and 93 times as *"Gentiles."* Thus, the *"great multitude"* was Gentile.

(5) This great multitude *"stood before the throne, and before the Lamb, clothed with white robes, and palms in their hands"* (Revelation 7:9b). This passage, and Revelation 7:15-17, indicate that they were in heaven.

(6) This great multitude *"came out of great tribulation, and have washed their robes, and made them white in the blood of the Lamb"* (Revelation 7:14). This, and Daniel 7:21; Revelation 13:7, and Revelation 14:2-3 compared with Revelation 15:2-3, indicate that these were martyred.

(7) By comparing Revelation 7:14 with Revelation 6:9-11 we learn that *"the*

shall dwell among them.

16 They shall hunger no more, neither thirst any more; neither shall the sun light on them, nor any heat.

17 For the Lamb which is in the midst of the throne shall feed them, and shall lead them unto living fountains of waters: and God shall wipe away all tears from their eyes (Revelation 7:14-17).

great multitude" "fulfilled" the number of martyrs in preparation for their blood to be avenged on those who dwell on the earth. It was necessary for the number of martyrs to be completed before the vials (or bowls) of the wrath of God would be poured out upon Rome, and upon the beast. (See Revelation 16:1-21; compare especially Revelation 16:6-7 with Revelation 6:9-11.)

Revelation 8
The Seven Trumpets

And when he had opened the seventh seal, there was silence in heaven[13] about the space of half an hour.

2 And I saw the seven angels[14] which stood before God; and to them were given seven trumpets (Revelation 8:1-2).

The Seventh Seal

(a) The seventh seal does more than introduce the seven trumpets. Its purpose is to tie the seals and the trumpets together so that the reader will recognize that *these two judgments are one message*, much like the two dreams of Genesis 41:1-7 were one message. Like the first four of the seal judgments, which gave specific details regarding the coming destruction of Jerusalem, the first five and one-half of the seven trumpet judgments will do the same.

These five and one-half trumpet judgments will describe

---

13. Silence in Heaven *Woe unto him that saith to the wood, Awake; to the dumb stone, Arise, it shall teach! Behold, it is laid over with gold and silver, and there is no breath at all in the midst of it. But the Lord is in his holy temple: let all the earth keep silence before him* (Habakkuk 2:19-20).

   Hold thy peace at the presence of the Lord God: for the day of the Lord is at hand: for the Lord hath prepared a sacrifice, he hath bid his guests (Zephaniah 1:7).

14. The Names of *"the seven angels which stood before God"* In the ancient book of 1 Enoch, from which the General Epistle of Jude quotes (Jude 14-15 quotes 1 Enoch II., XXVI. 2), six *"angels who watch"* are named. These are Uriel; Raphael; Raguel; Michael; Sarakiel (another edition has "Sariel" here, see page 84 in *The Legacy of Zion*); and Gabriel (1 Enoch XX. 1-7). Another edition of *The Legacy of Zion* adds "Remiel" here, making seven holy angels who watch.

   In 1 Enoch LXX. 4, we read, "And Michael, one of the archangels..." This may imply that the other five named above are archangels, or chief angels, as well.

   Repeatedly, we read in 1 Enoch of Michael, Raphael, Gabriel, and Phanuel (1 Enoch XL. 8, 9; LIII. 6; LXX. 11, 16), which could indicate that Phanuel also is an archangel.

   In the apocryphal book of Tobit (Tobit 12:15) we read, *"I am Raphael, one of the seven angels who stand in attendance on the Lord and enter his glorious presence"* (New English Bible). This passage tells us that seven angels stand in God's presence, which we see confirmed in Revelation 8:2.

   A similar passage occurs in Luke 1:19 (New English Bible), *"I am Gabriel; I stand in attendance upon God, and I have been sent to speak to you (Zacharias) and bring you this good news."*

   Apparently, then, these seven angels had names that were known. Anna the prophetess was the daughter of Phanuel, who may have received his name from the archangel, Phanuel (Luke 2:36).

(1) the warfare against Jerusalem, which started in the spring when the grass was green, and ended in late summer when "*all green grass was burnt up*" (Revelation 8:7);

(2) the fall of Jerusalem;

(3) the fall of the main Jewish military leader, Simon bar Giora, and the death of the "*many men*" (Revelation 8:11) who followed him;

(4) the exact length of the Roman campaign to take Jerusalem will be given (that is, "*five months*" (Revelation 9:5,10);

(5) the many Jewish slaves who were protected from death for those five months, only to be tormented with scorpion stings (Roman whips) in their slavery to Rome (Revelation 9:3-5, 10);

(6) the "*golden crowns*" (Greek, *stephanoi*, wreaths), which Titus gave to his soldiers who performed great exploits in this war (*Wars*, VII. I. 3);

(7) the 97,000 Jews captured by the Romans who were required to entertain their captors by their deaths; these and other details are described in the first five and a half of the trumpet judgments.

(b) "*There was silence in heaven about the space of half an hour*" (Revelation 8:1). God's actions in judgment are often introduced by a reference to silence. (See Habakkuk 2:19-20; Zephaniah 1:7; Zechariah 2:13[15]). The silence emphasizes the ominous fierceness of God's wrath about to descend. Like the stillness before the storm, in this instance, the contrast emphasizes that the storm of God's wrath is about to fall.

---

15. *Be silent, O all flesh, before the Lord: for he is raised up out of his holy habitation* (Zechariah 2:13).

And another angle came and stood at the altar, having a golden censer; and there was given unto him much incense, that he should offer it with the prayers of all saints upon the golden altar which was before the throne.

4 And the smoke of the incense, which came with the prayers of the saints, ascended up before God out of the angel's hand.

5 And the angel took the censer, and filled it with fire of the altar, and cast it into the earth: and there were voices, and thunderings, and lightnings, and an earthquake.

6 And the seven angels which had the seven trumpets prepared themselves to sound (Revelation 8:3-6).

*The first angel sounded, and there followed hail and fire mingled with blood, and they were cast upon the **earth*** (Greek, *ge,* earth, or

The seven trumpets restate and carry forward in symbolic language the themes of the seven seals. "*Another angel*" (Revelation 8:3) is performing the priest's function. The golden altar of incense on earth is a type of this one in heaven (as in Hebrews 8:5). On earth, a priest burned incense on the golden altar every morning and evening. David wrote, "*Let my prayer be set forth before thee as incense; and the lifting up of my hands as the evening sacrifice*" (Psalm 141:2). Also, in Luke 1:10 we read, "*And the whole multitude of the people were praying without at the time of incense.*" Thus, the prayers of God's people ascended with the smoke of the incense before God. In this case the prayers of the suffering saints, both Jews and Gentiles, are in view. The "*peals of thunder, loud noises, flashes of lightning, and an earthquake*" (Revelation 8:5b, RSV) indicate the storm of divine retribution coming in answer to their prayers.

The First Four Angels Sound Trumpets of Doom for Jerusalem

Trumpets, in scripture, were used in various ways, including the announcement of divine judgment[16] (Jeremiah 6:1,17; Ezekiel 33:3-6; Joel 2:1,15), as they are in these passages.

---

16. Trumpets Announce Divine Judgment

Blow ye the trumpet in Zion, and sound an alarm in my holy mountain: let all the inhabitants of the land tremble: for the day of the Lord cometh, for it is nigh at hand (Joel 2:1).

land): and the third part of trees was burnt up, and all green grass was burnt up (Revelation 8:7).

There is a relationship, also, between these trumpet judgments and the plagues upon Egypt. See Deuteronomy 28:63: "*And it shall come to pass, that as the Lord rejoiced over you to do you good, and to multiply you; so the Lord will rejoice over you to destroy you, and to bring you to nought; and ye shall be plucked from off the land whither thou goest to possess it.*"

(a) **The First Trumpet Sounds,** followed by hail and fire mingled with blood (Revelation 8:7). Hail and fire were prominent in the seventh plague in Egypt (Exodus 9:22-26). "*Hail*" relates to the large boulders flung from the Roman catapults that crashed against the walls of Jerusalem, and that fell within the city of Jerusalem in A.D. 70. These stones were "*the weight of a talent*" (*Wars*, V. VI. 3), that is 114 lbs., "*and were carried two furlongs* (Greek, *stadion,* 607 feet; thus two stadia is 1214 feet) *and farther*" (*Wars*, V. VI. 3). "*Fire*" relates to the fires used by both sides, and "*blood*" to the blood shed by both sides in the Roman attack upon Jerusalem.

"*A third of the earth was burnt up*" (Revelation 8:7, RSV). "*A third of,*" or "*the third part of*" (KJV) is used 15 times (14 in KJV) in five and a half trumpet judgments, and also once in Revelation 12:4. The phrase always refers to Jerusalem. This is *because Ezekiel 5:2 has* "*a third part*" three times, and these **third parts all relate to Jerusalem!** (See Ezekiel 5:5, "*This is Jerusalem.*") Thus, "*the third part*" in Revelation also refers to Jerusalem.

"*The third part of trees was burnt up*" (Revelation 8:7). Thus, "*for all the trees that were about the city had been already cut down for the making of the former banks*" (*Wars*, V. XII. 4). These banks prevented the Jews within Jerusalem from going without the city to look for food. "*And all green grass was burnt up*" (Revelation 8:7). Green grass was known in Judea only in the spring. It became green with the latter, or spring, rain, which fell in March or April. Thereafter, it became scorched and burnt by the sun's heat. "*The kings and armies of the East,*" says Chardin, "*do not march but when there is grass, and when they can encamp, which is in April.*" (See also 2 Samuel 11:1.) The "*green grass,*" which was in Judea when Titus began his campaign against Jerusalem, "*was burnt up*" when Titus completed his conquest of Jerusalem in September, A.D. 70.

And the second angel sounded, and as it were a great mountain burning with fire was cast into the sea: and the third part of the sea became blood;

9 And the third part of the creatures which were in the sea, and had life, died; and the third part of the ships were destroyed
(Revelation 8:8-9).

(b) **The Second Trumpet Sounds;** and a great mountain burning with fire is cast into the sea. In Jeremiah 51:25 we see the passage to which this refers. "*Behold, I am against thee, O destroying mountain, saith the Lord, which destroyest all the earth: and I will stretch out mine hand upon thee, and roll thee down from the rocks, and will make thee a burnt mountain.*" In this passage, we see three figures used of "*Babylon*" (Jeremiah 51:24):

(1) The government of Babylon is referred to as a "*mountain,*" a "*destroying mountain*";

(2) The figure of Babylon losing altitude, being rolled "*down from the rocks,*" indicates its loss of power and strength; and

(3) The figure of Babylon being "*a burnt mountain*" indicates that it was to be destroyed.

In Revelation 8:8 we also see

(1) a mountain,

(2) losing altitude, "*cast into the sea,*"

(3) being burnt, "*burning with fire.*"

Mountains in Scripture are used as symbols of force or strength unified and built into an awesome power. In Jeremiah 51:25 the mountain referred to Babylon. In Revelation 8:8 it refers to Jerusalem. The meaning of the symbol of a mountain burning with fire and cast into the sea was that Jerusalem was to be destroyed.

But why was the mountain cast into the sea? In Isaiah 57:20 we read, "*But **the wicked are like the troubled sea**, when it cannot rest, whose waters cast up mire and dirt.*" The "*sea*" is a symbol of the "*wicked*." The Roman peoples, being idolaters, were viewed as especially wicked, and thus are symbolized by "*the sea*" into which Jerusalem symbolically was cast. In Revelation 17:1 and 17:15, we see "*the great whore (Rome) that sitteth upon many waters.*" "*The waters*" are the "*peoples, and multitudes, and nations, and tongues*" of the Roman Empire.

"*And the third part of the creatures which were in the sea, and had life, died; and the third part of the ships were destroyed*" (Revelation 8:9).

"*Creatures*" in Scripture often refer to men, even to the exclusion of other animal life[17] (Mark 16:15; Romans 8:19; Colossians 1:15). The "*creatures which were in the sea*" here would be the Jews, surrounded by Roman soldiers.

"*The sea.*" In scripture,[18] overflowing waters are pictured as enemy armies (Isaiah 8:7; 54:19b,

---

17. "*Creatures*" in Scripture often refer to men, even to the exclusion of other animal life.

   If ye continue in the faith grounded and settled, and be not moved away from the hope of the gospel, which ye have heard, and which was preached to every creature which is under heaven; whereof I Paul am made a minister (Colossians 1:23).

   And he said unto them, Go ye into all the world, and preach the gospel to every creature (Mark 16:15).

18. In Scripture, overflowing waters are pictured as enemy armies.

   Now, therefore, behold, the Lord bringeth up upon them the waters of the river, strong and many, even the king of Assyria, and all his glory: and he shall come up over all his channels, and go over all his banks (Isaiah 8:7).

   When the enemy shall come in like a flood, the Spirit of the Lord shall lift up a standard against him (Isaiah 59:19b).

   The sorrows of death compassed me, and the floods of ungodly men made me afraid (Psalm 18:4).

   And after threescore and two weeks shall Messiah be cut off, but not for himself: and the people of the prince that shall come shall destroy the city and the sanctuary: and the end thereof shall be with a flood, and unto the end of the war desolations are determined (Daniel 9:26).

   Thus, the rising tide of the sea is also pictured as an enemy army.

   The sea is come up upon Babylon: she is covered with the multitude of the waves thereof (Jeremiah 51:42).

Psalm 18:4), and in Jeremiah 51:42, the rising tide of the sea is pictured as an enemy army. Since the "*wicked*" were the Romans, and the overflowing waters were soldiers, Jerusalem fell into a "*sea*" of Roman soldiers.

"*Ships*" in Scripture[19] picture those who are proud and lofty (Isaiah 2:11-17). Those Jerusalem Jews in positions of privilege would be destroyed with the fall of Jerusalem.

The basic thought in Revelation 8:9 is that of total destruction within the area of "*the third part*," that is, within Jerusalem.

The Third Trumpet Sounds

And the third angel sounded, and there fell a great star from heaven, burning as it were a lamp, and it fell upon the third part of the rivers, and upon the fountains of waters;

11 And the name of the star is called Wormwood: and the third part of the waters became wormwood; and many men died of the waters, because they were made bitter (Revelation 8:10-11).

A great star fell from heaven (Revelation 8:10, 11).

A star is the symbol of a person who is highly placed. Even in our society we may speak of a movie star or a football star. In Isaiah 14:12 we read the following in the King James Version, "*How art thou fallen from heaven, O Lucifer, son of the morning! how art thou cut down to the ground, which didst weaken the nations!*" To fall from heaven would, of course, be to lose one's highly placed position. But "*Lucifer*" is not a translation of the Hebrew word, *heylel*, which is placed here in the Hebrew text. *Heylel* is translated as follows in other versions: "*shining star*" (Moffat), "*shining one*" (Rotherham), "*day star*" (Amplified), "*star of the morning*" (American Standard), "*day star*" (Jerusalem Bible), and "*Day Star*" (Revised Standard Version). Only the King James version

---

19. "*Ships*" in Scripture picture those who are proud and lofty.
The lofty looks of man shall be humbled, and the haughtiness of men shall be bowed down, and the Lord alone shall be exalted in that day.
For the day of the Lord of hosts shall be upon every one that is proud and lofty; and upon every one that is lifted up, and he shall be brought low:
And upon all the cedars of Lebanon that are high and lifted up, and upon all the oaks of Bashan,
And upon all the high mountains, and upon all the hills that are lifted up,
And upon every high tower, and upon every fenced wall,
And upon all the ships of Tarshish, and upon all pleasant pictures.
And the loftiness of man shall be bowed down, and the haughtiness of men shall be made low: and the Lord alone shall be exalted in that day (Isaiah 2:11-17).

and the Roman Catholic Douay Version translate "*heylel*" by the word, "*Lucifer*" as Lucifer was the name that the ancients gave to the planet Venus. Pliny says, "*Before the sun revolves, a very large star...when in advance and rising before the dawn receives the name of Lucifer, and being another sun and bringing the dawn...*" Jerome, in the fourth century, was the first who translated "*heylel*," that is, "*day star*" or "*morning star*," by the word "*Lucifer*." The translators of both the King James and the Douay Versions followed Jerome's lead. But the apostle John, who lived centuries before Jerome, would not have understood the "*heylel*" of Isaiah 14:12 to have been "*Lucifer*." Isaiah 14:4 reads, "*That thou take up this proverb against the king of Babylon...*" Thus, the original one to whom *heylel* referred was Nebuchadnezzar, king of Babylon. This is not to question the fact that the occult significance of Venus, whether by the name of Lucifer or any other name, symbolizes Satan, and as a double-reference prophecy, we may apply this passage to Satan. But its original reference was to Nebuchadnezzar.

Thus, in Revelation 8:10 the "*great star*" would have been the most prominent person in Judea, the main leader of the Jewish rebellion in the Jewish-Roman War of A.D. 66 to 70. Josephus gives this one as *Simon bar Giora* (*Wars*, V. VI. 1). Simon's seizure by the Romans after the fall of Jerusalem (*Wars*, VII. II. 1), and his death, in Rome before the temple of Jupiter (*Wars*, VII. V. 6) are given in great detail by Josephus. But if all this is true, then how does Simon bar Giora obtain the name "*Wormwood*" (Revelation 8:11)? In Deuteronomy 29:18-19[20] Moses, in writing of any whose heart turns away "*from the Lord our God,*" declares, "*lest there should*

---

20. *Lest there should be among you man, or woman, or family, or tribe, whose heart turneth away this day from the Lord our God, to go and serve the gods of these nations; lest there should be among you a root that beareth gall and wormwood;*
   And it come to pass, when he heareth the words of this curse, that he bless himself in his heart, saying, I shall have peace, though I walk in the imagination of mine heart, to add drunkenness to thirst: The Lord will not spare him, but then the anger of the Lord and his jealousy shall smoke against that man, and all the curses that are written in this book shall lie upon him, and the Lord shall blot out his name from under heaven (Deuteronomy 29:18-20).

*be among you a **root** that beareth gall and **wormwood**, And it come to pass, when he heareth the words of this curse, that **he** bless himself in his heart, saying...*" Here, the *root of wormwood* is identified *as a person.* This person says (New American Standard Bible), "*I have peace though I walk in the stubbornness of my heart in order **to destroy the watered land** with the dry.*" The "*watered land*" in this passage, and "*the rivers, and...the fountains* (or *springs) of waters*" of Revelation 8:10 reveal an identifying relationship between these passages, as do the "**root** that *beareth gall and* **wormwood**" of Deuteronomy 29:18, and the "*Wormwood*" of Revelation 8:11.

Wormwood in the natural is bitter, but not poisonous, but this wormwood, Simon bar Giora, *was* poisonous, as demonstrated by all those who were killed who drank of, or followed, him.

The Fourth Trumpet Sounds

And the fourth angel sounded, and the third part of the sun was smitten, and the third part of the moon, and the third part of the stars; so as the third part of them was darkened, and the day shone not for a third part of it, and the night likewise.

13 And I beheld, and heard an angel flying through the midst of heaven, saying with a loud voice, Woe, woe, woe, to the inhabiters of the earth by reason of the other voices of the trumpet of the

Three woes are forecasted. One and a half woes for Jerusalem; one and a half woes for Rome (Revelation 8:12).

This passage shows the impossibility of taking Revelation literally. We have here the sun, moon, and stars being smitten in a heaven that has departed as a scroll. Also, scientifically, if a third of the sun, moon, and stars were smitten, it would not have the effect of making the day and night dark a third of the time; it would only make for less light for the same time period. But the passage was meant to be understood figuratively, not literally. Thus, the principal emphasis here is not the darkening of a third of the sun, moon, and stars, but rather the darkness that was to come upon Jerusalem—darkness being a symbol of approaching gloom, distress, and woe.

The word "*angel*" in our text is not well supported in the manuscripts. Most translations read "*eagle.*"

three angels, which are yet to sound (Revelation 8:12-13).

Still, eagles were rare in the Middle East, and what is referred to here as an "*angel*" or an "*eagle*" would best be translated "*vulture*," although the same Hebrew word, "*neser*," was used of both birds. (See *The International Standard Bible Encyclopedia*, Vol. 2, Pg. 1.) The "*vulture*" would be the Griffon Vulture, and while there are many similarities between the eagle and the Griffon Vulture (size, strength, longevity, lofty flight, nesting patterns, and feeding habits), the Griffon Vulture is more a symbol of death and woe, as a scavenger bird wheeling over a dying victim. Thus, the *Concordant Literal New Testament* reads "*vulture*" in this passage (Revelation 8:13).

The "*vulture*," then, announces three woes that are about to descend—one and a half of these woes for Jerusalem (Revelation 9:1-19), and one and a half for Rome (Revelation 11:3-19). An interlude (Revelation 9:20–11:2) is to prepare us for the change from Jerusalem to Rome.

Revelation 9
The Locusts

And the fifth angel sounded, and I saw a star fall from heaven unto the earth: and to him was given the key of the bottomless pit.

2 And he opened the bottomless pit; and there arose a smoke out of the pit, as the smoke of a great furnace; and the sun and the air were darkened by reason of the smoke of the pit (Revelation 9:1-2).

The Fifth Trumpet Sounds

The first woe begins as Roman soldiers force Jewish survivors into slavery.

Throughout Revelation (Revelation 9:1-2,11; 11:7; 17:8; 20:1,3), "*the bottomless pit*" refers to Rome.[21] This is because of the vileness and corruption of Rome. In fact, one of the Hebrew words for "*pit*" is "*shachath,*" which is translated in the King James Version as "*pit*" 14 times, and as "*corruption*" four times. Thus, Tacitus, the Roman historian (c. 60–120), wrote (Annales, xv. 44), "*...Rome, that receptacle for everything that is sordid and degrading from every quarter of the world.*" The picture in Revelation 9:2 is that of a volcanic

---

21. Every reference to "*The Bottomless Pit*" in Revelation fits, or has a special meaning for the vileness and corruption of Rome

Roman soldiers came from Rome. (See Revelation 9:1-2 above.)

The destroying angel, who leads the Roman soldiers, comes from Rome.
And they had a king over them, which is the angel of the bottomless pit, whose name in the Hebrew tongue is Abaddon (Hebrew, *destruction*), *but in the Greek tongue hath his name Apollyon* (Greek, *destroyer*) (Revelation 9:11).

Domitian rises out of the vileness and corruption of Rome.
And when they shall have finished their testimony, the beast that ascendeth out of the bottomless pit shall make war against them, and shall overcome them, and kill them (Revelation 11:7).

The beast that thou sawest was, and is not; and shall ascend out of the bottomless pit, and go into perdition: and they that dwell an the earth shall wonder, whose names were not written in the book of life from the foundation of the world, when they behold the beast that was, and is not, and yet is (Revelation 17:8).

Revelation 17:11 is also conclusive in identifying this beast as Domitian:
And the beast that was, and is not, even he is the eighth, and is of the seven, and goeth into perdition.

Satan is imprisoned beneath the ruined and desolate city of Rome.

And I saw an angel come down from heaven, having the key of the bottomless pit and a great chain in his hand.
And he laid hold on the dragon, that old serpent, which is the Devil, and Satan, and bound him a thousand years,

eruption with locusts spewed forth like smoke. (Locusts filling the air have the appearance of smoke.) *Out of the corruption of Rome* these locusts descend upon Jerusalem.

Locusts were the most dreaded and destructive creatures of the ancient world.[22] In the Old Testament they were used as symbols of desolation and destruction. The Hebrew word *"arbeh"* is translated *"grasshopper"* four times and *"locust"* 20 times, in the King James Version. In Judges 6:3-6 and 7:12, and in Nahum 3:15,17, enemy soldiers are described as being like locusts.

In Joel 1:4 we read, *"That which the palmerworm hath left hath the locust eaten; and that which the locust hath left hath the cankerworm eaten; and that which the cankerworm hath left hath the caterpillar eaten."* Dake's Annotated Bible, (page 890), translates this, *"Gnawers remnant, Swarmer eats; Swarmers remnant, Devourer eats; Devourers remnant, Consumer eats."* Thus, 12 Hebrew words condense the whole thought. The Revised Standard Version translates this verse, *"What the cutting locust left, the swarming locust has eaten. What the swarming locust left, the hopping locust has eaten, and what*

And cast him into the bottomless pit, and shut him up, and set a seal upon him, that he should deceive the nations no more, till the thousand years should be fulfilled: and after that he must be loosed a little season (Revelation 20:1-3).

See also the following comparison between the "angels with trumpets" and the "angels with bowls of wrath," which is taken from Revelation 15:1 of this outline. Note the 5th angels in the outline below. This *comparison is consistent only if "the bottomless pit" relates to Rome.*

Angels With Trumpets	Angels	Angels With Bowls Of Wrath
"cast upon the earth" (8:7)	1st	"poured...upon the earth" (16:2)
"cast into the sea" (8:8)	2nd	"poured...upon the sea" (16:3)
"upon the...rivers, and upon the fountains of waters" (8:10)	3rd	"poured out...upon the rivers and fountains of waters" (16:4)
"the sun," "the moon," "the stars" (8:12)	4th	"poured out...upon the sun" (16:8)
"the bottomless pit" (that is, the pit, or seat of corruption, of *Rome*) (9:1)	5th	"Poured out...upon the seat of the beast (that is, *Rome*) (16:10)
"the great river Euphrates" (9:14)	6th	"poured out...upon the great river Euphrates" (16:12)
"voices in heaven" (11:15)	7th	"poured out...into the air" (16:17)

22. *"Along with them went a motley host like a swarm of locusts, countless as the dust of the earth"* (Judith 2:20).

the hopping locust left, the destroying locust has eaten." These were, then, but four stages of the locust, and these locusts were used to describe successive incursions of enemy soldiers against Judah and Jerusalem (Joel 3:6,20). Some of the ways that scholars have used to identify these locusts as enemy soldiers are

(1) The figure had been used this way before (Judges 7:12), and it was common to identify soldiers with locusts in Joel's time (Jeremiah 46:23).

(2) The "*locust*" plague is called the "*northern army*" (Joel 2:20), while real locusts would have come from the south.

(3) The "*locusts*" do what real locusts do not do, but what soldiers do. "*A fire devoureth before them; and behind them a flame burneth*" (Joel 2:3). They march in rank like soldiers (Joel 2:7), and assault cities (Joel 2:9).[23]

(4) Those familiar with the idiom of the Hebrew people interpreted these "*locusts*" to be soldiers. Thus, *The International Standard Bible Encyclopedia*, Vol. 2, page 1079, reads, "*an allegorical-historical interpretation, in which the plague is seen as an allegory **for historical human invaders**, is found already in the Targum* (a translation of Hebrew scripture from Hebrew to Aramaic) *and early Christian writers.*"

With this in mind, let us consider these parallels between the "*locusts*" (enemy soldiers) of Joel, and the "*locusts*" of Revelation 9.

*For a nation is come up upon my land, strong, and without number, **whose teeth are the teeth of a lion**, and he hath the cheek teeth of a great lion* (Joel 1:6).	*...and their **teeth were as the teeth of lions*** (Revelation 9:8).

---

23. Biederwolf, William E., *The Second Coming Bible*, page 248.

The appearance of them is as the **appearance of horses; and as horse-** *men, so shall they run* (Joel 2:4).	*"And the shapes of the locusts* **were** *like unto horses prepared unto bat-* *tle…*(Revelation 9:7).
Like the **noise of chariots** *on the tops of mountains shall they leap* (Joel 2:5).	*…and the sound of their wings was as the* **sound of chariots** *of many horses running to battle* (Revelation 9:9).

Thus, by identifying the "*locusts*" of Joel the way early Christian writers identified them—that is, as enemy soldiers—we can see from the above comparisons that the "*locusts*" of Revelation 9 should be identified the same way. The "*locusts*" of Revelation 9 were, then, enemy soldiers, and coming as they did from Rome, they were Roman soldiers!

This knowledge will help us in understanding the remainder of this passage, that is, Revelation 9:3-11.

For instance, we see repeatedly that these "*locusts*" have tails like scorpions (Revelation 9:3,5,10). This takes us back to Rehoboam's answer to Israel in 2 Chronicles 10:14: "*My father chastised you with whips, but I will chastise you with* **scorpions.**" Here we see "*whips*" and "*scorpions*" used as a means of chastisement. Roman whips were horrible instruments of torture. Their ends were interwoven with sharp nails—"*tails like unto scorpions*" (Revelation 9:10). Woe to the man who should ever come under the lash!

And there came out of the smoke locusts upon the earth: and unto them was given power, as the scorpions of the earth have power.

4 And it was commanded them that they should not hurt the grass of the earth, neither any green thing, neither any tree; but only those men which have not the seal of God in their foreheads (Revelation 9:3-4).

Josephus tells us of the following event, which occurred after the fall of Jerusalem, "*And as for the rest of the multitude that were above seventeen years old, he* (Titus) *put them into bonds, and sent them to the Egyptian mines…but those that were under seventeen years of age were sold for slaves*" (*Wars*, VI. IX. 2). Thus, forced labor and slavery were the lot of these who were kept alive.

These slaves were those, then, who were in "*bonds*" and lashed with the Roman whips. They sought death, but did not find it. They desired to die, and death fled from them.

Since the "*locusts*" were Roman soldiers, it is easy to see why they would not "*hurt the grass of the earth, neither any green thing, neither any tree.*" These were the normal food of real locusts, but these "*locusts*" of Revelation, being Roman soldiers, would not be eating them. Also, we can now see why they would hurt "*only those men which have not the seal of God in their foreheads*" (Revelation 9:4b). Those with the "*seal of God*" were the 144,000, the Jewish believers in Jesus from Jerusalem who went to Pella, and while there were protected during this entire war.

And to them it was given that they should not kill them, but that they should be tormented five months: and their torment was as the torment of a scorpion, when he striketh a man.

6 And in those days shall men seek death, and shall not find it; and shall desire to die, and death shall flee from them.

7 And the shapes of the locusts were like unto horses prepared unto battle; and on their heads were as it were crowns like gold, and their faces were as the faces of men.

8 And they had hair as the hair of women, and their teeth were as the teeth of lions.

9 And they had

But how do we interpret this verse? "*And to them* (the "*locusts*" or Roman soldiers) *it was given that they should not kill them, but that they should be tormented five months: and their torment was as the torment of a scorpion, when he striketh a man*" (Revelation 9:5).

The normal life span of a locust was five months, from May to September. The length of the Roman effort to take Jerusalem was also five months, and also from May to September.

The Roman soldiers had not been permitted by God to kill these many Jews who were taken slaves. Some were taken captive at the beginning, others at the middle of the five months. But at the end of the five months of conflict, the Roman soldiers returned to Rome, and the Jewish slaves went to Egyptian mines and other places.

The "*locusts*" being like horses (Revelation 9:7) shows that the Roman soldiers rode horses, "*the sound of chariots*" shows that the Roman soldiers had chariots. The "*breastplates of iron*" describe the Roman armor (Revelation 9:9). These "*locusts*" had the "*faces of men*" (Revelation 9:7), because that's what they really were. They had "*the teeth of lions*"—a symbol of the great destruction that they wrought.

But what of the "*hair as the hair of women*"[24] (Revelation 9:8)? The *Encyclopedia of Religion and*

---

24. *Doth not even nature itself teach you, that, if a man have long hair, it is a shame unto him? But if a woman have long hair, it is a glory to her: for her hair is given her for a covering* (1 Corinthians 11:14-15).

Note: See Deuteronomy 32:42 (The Amplified Bible), which may refer to this practice.

"*I will make My arrows drunk with blood, and My sword shall devour flesh with the blood of the slain and the captives, from the long-haired heads of the foe.*" See also Psalm 68:21.

breastplates, as it were breastplates of iron; and the sound of their wings was as the sound of chariots of many horses running to battle.

10 And they had tails like unto scorpions, and there were stings in their tails: and their power was to hurt men five months (Revelation 9:5-10).

And they had a king over them, which is the angel of the bottomless pit, whose name in the Hebrew tongue is Abaddon, but in the Greek tongue hath his name Apollyon.

12 One woe is past; and, behold, there come two woes more hereafter (Revelation 9:11-12).

Ethics, Volume 6, page 474, gives the following information. Ancient peoples believed that "*hair must not be cut during times of special danger…Travelers did not cut their hair until the end of their journey.*" Hair and nails, when cut, may fall into the hands of an enemy who could use them for working magic against the person, and for this reason they were left uncut.

Thus, the Roman soldiers in John's vision had long hair, that is, "*hair as the hair of women.*" (See 1 Corinthians 11:15.)

But what can the phrase mean? "*…and on their heads…were crowns like gold…*" A quote from Josephus will explain this one. "*Hereupon Titus ordered those whose business it was, to read the list of all that had performed great exploits in this war, whom he called to him by their names, and commended them before the company, and rejoiced in them…He also put on their heads crowns of gold…*" (*Wars*, VII. I. 3).

Before we leave this section, we need to write regarding Abaddon (Hebrew, *destruction*), or Apollyon (Greek, *destroyer*).[25]

(1) He is the king of the "*locusts*," and the angel of "*the bottomless pit*" (Revelation 9:11). Agur wrote, "*The locusts have no king*" (Proverbs 30:27), but that statement would not apply here because these Roman soldiers were not true locusts.

(2) Abaddon is not an angel of Satan, as he is the one who binds Satan "*a thousand years*" (Revelation 20:1-2). In both Revelation 9:1 and 20:1, we read that he has "*the key of the*

---

25. "*Abaddon*" and "*Apollyon*"

"*As for the Greek name Apollyon, in the* LXX *Abaddon is regularly rendered as* Apoleia, "*destruction,*" *so that Apollyon (Apolluon) is essentially the Greek equivalent of the Hebrew. Because of the similarity, some see in this a slighting reference to the god Apollo and through him to the claims of the emperors to divine status, since Augustus considered himself to be under the protection of Apollo, even calling himself his son, and successors of Augustus thought of themselves as being closely related to the sun god. Abaddon, however, is an angel not of Satan but of God, performing his work of destruction at God's bidding*" (*The Interpreter's Bible*, Vol. 12, p. 434).

bottomless pit." He is, therefore, an angel of God.[26]

(3) This destroying angel is recorded several times in scripture.

> (a) Exodus 12:23, "*the destroyer*" was sent of God to smite the firstborn of Egypt. (See also Hebrews 11:28, "*he that destroyed.*")

> (b) Numbers 14:27-37 compared with 1 Corinthians 10:10—"*the destroyer*" destroyed by means of a "*plague*" (Numbers 14:37); the ten men who brought back an evil report and all Israel (except Joshua and Caleb) for murmuring.

> (c) 2 Samuel 24:16, "*the angel that destroyed the people.*" 1 Chronicles 21:12-15,20,27: "*the angel of the Lord destroying throughout all the coasts of Israel*" (vs. 12).

> (d) 2 Kings 19:35; 2 Chronicles 32:21; Isaiah 37:36—the angel of the Lord smote 185,000 Assyrians.

But the best-remembered time in which this destroying angel was seen, was when he smote the firstborn of Egypt. Now the same angel, who worked then to deliver the Jews from Egypt, leads the Roman soldiers to destroy them.[27]

---

26. The Destroying Angel in Scripture

For the Lord will pass through to smite the Egyptians; and when he seeth the blood upon the lintel, and on the two side posts, the Lord will pass over the door, and will not suffer the destroyer to come in unto your houses to smite you (Exodus 12:23).

Neither murmur ye, as some of them also murmured, and were destroyed of the destroyer (1 Corinthians 10:10).

And when the angel stretched out his hand upon Jerusalem to destroy it, the Lord repented him of the evil, and said to the angel that destroyed the people, It is enough: stay now thine hand. And the angel of the Lord was by the threshingplace of Araunah the Jebusite (2 Samuel 24:16).

And it came to pass that night, that the angel of the Lord went out, and smote in the camp of the Assyrians an hundred fourscore and five thousand: and when they arose early in the morning, behold, they were all dead corpses (2 Kings 19:35).

27. Behold therefore the goodness and severity of God

"And it shall come to pass, that as the Lord rejoiced over you to do you good, and to multiply you; so the Lord will rejoice over you to destroy you, and to bring you to nought; and ye shall be plucked from off the land whither thou goest to possess it (Deuteronomy 28:63).

This section deals with a further woe upon Jerusalem after the Roman soldiers (the locusts) had taken 97,000 young Jews as slaves. At this time Jerusalem has been destroyed, the temple is in ruins and the Jews are now leaderless and totally disorganized.

And the sixth angel sounded, and I heard a voice from the four horns of the golden altar which is before God.

14 Saying to the sixth angel which had the trumpet, Loose the four angels which are bound in the great river Euphrates (Revelation 9:13-14).

The Sixth Trumpet Sounds

The second woe begins, as Jews captured in the fall of Jerusalem are required to entertain their captors by their deaths. "*The four horns of the golden altar which is before God*" (Revelation 9:13). This is the altar of incense in heaven.[28] The earthly tabernacle was patterned after the one in heaven, as we learn from Hebrews 9:11,24. On earth there were two altars, a brazen altar and a golden altar. The brazen altar was the altar of burnt offerings. The golden altar was the altar of incense. The golden altar, or the altar of incense, is referred to here to show that this judgment is God's response to the anguished prayers and cries of His persecuted children (see Revelation 5:8; 8:3-5).

"*Loose the four angels which are bound in the great river Euphrates*" (Revelation 9:14). The Euphrates River was the boundary of the Roman Empire.

"*Loose the four angels…*" These are destroying angels, held until this very time. These destroying angels were bound by the Euphrates River. Since they were prepared for this, we learn that this particular destructive force could not be unleashed until this time. This eliminated the possibility that this force could have been the Roman army. This is rather a force that could not arise until Judea, the "*great mountain burning with fire*" (Revelation 8:8), had

---

28. Heaven's patterns of earth's tabernacle with its furnishings

Who serve unto the example and shadow of heavenly things, as Moses was admonished of God when he was about to make the tabernacle: for, See, saith he, that thou make all things according to the pattern shewed to thee in the mount (Hebrews 8:5).

But Christ being come an high priest of good things to come, by a greater and more perfect tabernacle, not made with hands, that is to say, not of this building (Hebrews 9:11).

It was therefore necessary that the patterns of things in the heavens should be purified with these; but the heavenly things themselves with better sacrifices than these.
For Christ is not entered into the holy places made with hands, which are the figures of the true; but into heaven itself, now to appear in the Presence of God for us (Hebrews 9:23-24).

fallen; until the main Jewish leader, Simon bar Giora, the "*great star from heaven*" named "*wormwood*" (Revelation 8:10-11), had fallen; until the Roman soldiers, the "*locusts*" (Revelation 9:1-11) had completely taken over Judea; and the young and the strong of the Jews had either been killed or reduced to slavery. To "*slay the third part of men*" is meant here to slay men in the third part of the Roman Empire, principally Judea. That is, the Roman Empire was about to permit and encourage something not previously allowed. Before this time they had prevented the various nations within the empire from destroying one another. Now the captives who were taken with the fall of Jerusalem were taken to theatres throughout the Roman Empire where they were burnt with flames of fire, set upon by wild beasts, and forced to fight and kill one another for the entertainment of the peoples of the nations who were loyal to Rome.

And the four angels were loosed, which were prepared for an hour, and a day, and a month, and a year, for to slay the third part of men (Revelation 9:15).

"...*which were prepared for an hour, and a day, and a month, and a year*" (Revelation 9:15). This dreadful judgment could not begin until a specific time. That specific time was when the final conquest of Jerusalem was completed. The year was A.D. 70. The month was the Jewish month of Elul, corresponding to August and September. The day was the eighth day of Elul (*Wars*, VI. X. 1). The "hour" was the hour when Jewish resistance collapsed. The Roman soldiers continued killing the surviving Jews until they were tired of it, and then Titus commanded them to take the remainder alive.

Those taken alive were divided into these categories:

(1) The 700 who were the tallest and most handsome, including Simon bar Giora and John of Gischala, were kept for the triumphal procession in Rome.

(2) Many of those above 17 years of age were put in bonds (chains) and sent to forced labor in Egyptian mines.

(3) Many of those below 17 years of age were sold as slaves.

(4) "*Titus also sent a great number into the provinces, as a present to them, that they might be destroyed upon their theatres, by the sword and by wild beasts*" (*Wars*, VI. IX. 2).

Those in categories (2) and (3) above were kept alive for their forced, or slave, labor. Their fate was described in Revelation 9:1-11. The captives in category (4) are those that Revelation 9:13-19 pictures. They were to entertain their captors by their deaths. Josephus writes of them that Titus "*exhibited all sorts of shows*" at Caesarea Philippi, "*and here a great number of captives were destroyed, some being thrown to wild beasts, and others in multitudes forced to kill one another, as if they were enemies*" (*Wars*, VII. II. 1). Also, at "*Caesarea which was on the seaside,*" Titus celebrated his brother Domitian's birthday (October 24) by inflicting death on the Jews "*for the number of those that were now slain in fighting with the beasts, and were burnt, and fought with one another, exceeded two thousand five hundred*" (*Wars*, VII. III. 1). Also, at *Berytus*, a Roman colony in Phoenicia, Titus celebrated his father's birthday (November 17), "*so that a great multitude of the captives were here destroyed after the same manner as before*" (*Wars*, VII. III. 1).

"*...for to slay the third part of men*" (Revelation 9:15). These captives, and those sent to the provinces for the same purpose of entertaining their victorious spectators by their violent deaths, are those described in scripture as "the *third part of men*"; "*the third part*" being a phrase signifying Jerusalem. These were those captured upon the fall of Jerusalem.

Josephus records, "*Now the number of those that were carried captive during this whole war was collected to be ninety-seven thousand*" (*Wars*, VI. IX. 3).

And the number of the army of the horsemen were two hundred thousand thousand (Greek, duo muriades muriadon, two myriads of myriads): and I heard the number of them (Revelation 9:16).

The *"two hundred thousand thousand"* horsemen is literally *"two myriads of myriads."* The number "two" is the signature of strength; the *"myriads of myriads"* suggests an innumerable overwhelming force. There would be no possible way that these captives could escape with their lives. The force against them was just too numerous, too bloodthirsty, and much too strong.

But what force could have possibly arisen all at once, and under the noses of the Roman Army, which was already there? We quote here from *Gospel Light*, by George Lamsa (page 134), on "Carcass and Eagles," from Matthew 24:28.

> *Christ foretold the destruction of the Jewish state by Rome: Jerusalem was to fall and the temple which was the pride and center of the nation was to be demolished.* **When Rome was through with her task, other small nations around Judea would take their turn and gather like eagles over the defeated nation to devour it.** *After the fall of Jerusalem, Jewish enemies would multiply and national calamity would be great. There is an Oriental proverb, "When an ox is tied up and led down to slaughter, the knives to cut off his head are plentiful." The Jews were not only defeated by the Roman army who were like wolves, but they were to be humiliated at the hands of neighboring peoples who were like eagles waiting to descend upon the desolate city which was the carcass. This prophecy was fulfilled when Jerusalem was conquered by Titus, the Roman general, and the Jews were scattered throughout the world.*

This same thing had happened earlier when Judea had been destroyed by Nebuchadnezzar, king of Babylon. The nations round about Judea had made successive incursions against Judea, after Babylon had destroyed it. (See Lamentations 1:2-3,7,10,17,21; 2:15-17; 3:46,59-63; 4:19; 5:2-6.) Thus the Ammonites (Ezekiel 25:3), Edom

And thus I saw the horses in the vision, and them that sat on them, having breastplates of fire, and of jacinth (Greek, huakinthinos, hyacinth-like, or dark blue), and brimstone: and the heads of the horses were as the heads of lions; and out of their mouths issued fire and smoke and brimstone (Revelation 9:17).

(Ezekiel 25:12-14), Moab and Seir (Ezekiel 25:8-10), Philistia (Ezekiel 25:15), Tyrus, or Tyre (Ezekiel 26:1-21), Zidon, or Sidon (Ezekiel 28:20-26), and Egypt (Ezekiel 32:11) were all said to have attacked Judea after the Babylonians had destroyed it. In this same way, Judea was about to be pillaged again by these peoples who were round about Judea, after it was destroyed by the Romans.

"Horses" were described in Habakkuk (1:8) as *"swifter than leopards, and…more fierce than the evening wolves."* The horses of Babylon had been described as *"swifter than eagles"* (Jeremiah 4:13), and Babylon itself had been described as a *"lion"* *"come up from his thicket"* (v.7) when it was about to attack Jerusalem. These nations coming to attack Judea and Jerusalem are thus described in the same way.

"…having breastplates of fire, and of jacinth, and brimstone…" (Revelation 9:17a).

"Breastplates" in Scripture are of different kinds, but the thought is always that they make one impervious to attack. Thus, a breastplate of righteousness (Isaiah 59:17; Ephesians 6:14) would make one able to withstand an attack from Satan. A breastplate of *"faith and love"* (1 Thessalonians 5:8) would do the same. In Exodus 28:15,29-30, we read of a *"breastplate of judgment"*[29] which Aaron was to wear *"upon his heart."* The colors of this *"breastplate of*

---

29. The different kinds of "breastplates" in Scripture

For he put on righteousness as a breastplate, and an helmet of salvation upon his head; and he put on the garments of vengeance for clothing, and was clad with zeal as a cloak (Isaiah 59:17).

Stand therefore, having your loins girt about with truth, and having on the breastplate of righteousness (Ephesians 6:14).

But let us, who are of the day, be sober, putting on the breastplate of faith and love; and for an helmet, the hope of salvation (1 Thessalonians 5:8).

Aaron's "breastplate of judgment"
(Notice the colors of this breastplate.)

And thou shalt make the breastplate of judgment with cunning work; after the work of the ephod thou shalt make it; of gold, of blue, and of purple, and of scarlet, and of fine twined linen, shalt thou make it. -Exodus 28:15

And Aaron shall bear the names of the children of Israel in the breastplate of judgment upon his heart, when he goeth in unto the holy place, for a memorial before the Lord continually (Exodus 28:29).

And thou shalt put in the breastplate of judgment the Urim and the Thummim; and they shall be upon Aaron's heart, when he goeth in before the Lord: and Aaron shall bear the judgment of the children of Israel upon his heart before the Lord continually (Exodus 28:30).

judgment" seem similar to the colors of fire, jacinth, and brimstone given in the above passage from Revelation.

There is a correlation intended here between the colors of "*the breastplate of judgment*" and "*the breastplates of fire, and of jacinth, and brimstone.*" (The "*jacinth*" in the King James Version is not a translation, but a meaningless transliteration of *huakinthinos, hyacinthine,* or *hyacinth-like,* that is, having the color of hyacinth, which is dark blue.)

This, then, was a "*breastplate of judgment*" against the people of Jerusalem and Judea, but those nations attacking them were impervious from any attack upon themselves. The phrase "*out of their mouths issued fire and smoke and brimstone*" reminds us of the total destruction by fire and smoke and brimstone upon the cities of the plain (Genesis 19:24, 28). Smoke is an Aramaic idiom for disaster, according to the note in Lamsa's *Holy Bible* for Isaiah 14:31.

The Amplified Bible correctly gives the sense here, as "*the riders wore breastplates the color of fiery red and sapphire blue and sulphur (brimstone) yellow.*" The hyacinth was a dark blue sapphire stone as this translation indicates.

There is also a correlation between "*the breastplate of judgment,*" "*the breastplates of fire, and of jacinth, and brimstone,*" and the colors of "*fire and smoke and brimstone*" that issued from the mouths of the lion-headed horses. The import here is that the "*fire and smoke and brimstone*" which slay "*the third part of men,*" are the judgments of God.

"...*the heads of the horses were as the heads of lions*" (Revelation 9:17b); "...*their tails were like unto serpents*" (Revelation 9:19b). Like the horses described by Habakkuk (1:8), which were "*swifter than the leopards, and...more fierce than the evening wolves,*" so these horses are both swift and fierce. In Jeremiah 4:7-13 we see the

Babylonian army compared to both a lion and to horses.[30]

The meaning here of the horses with heads as the heads of lions and tails like unto serpents is that this figure describes in a colorful way the three means by which the Jewish captives were killed.

Having been caught by the Roman soldiers, and unable to escape because of the speed of their horses, they then had to fight a losing battle with lions or other wild beasts, or they were burnt in flames of fire. If the wild beasts or the fire didn't get them, there remained the *"tails like unto serpents."* In Scripture, people are sometimes compared to serpents.[31] (See Psalm 58:3-4; Ecclesiastes 10:11; Isaiah 14:29-31; Jeremiah 8:5-17.) This seems to refer to their battles in the theatres with fellow Jews. But it was the *"fire and smoke and brimstone"*—the judgment of God—that killed them! Thus, those who had escaped the rampant murder of the rival Jewish armies, the famine, the murder by the Romans when Jerusalem fell, and the forced labor in Egyptian mines and being sold into slavery, were here killed for the entertainment of their captors! No wonder Jesus wept over the city (Luke 19:41).

18 By these three was the third part of men killed, by the fire, and by the smoke, and by the

Like the tails of Samson's 300 foxes (Judges 15:4), their power to hurt was in their tails. The thought may be that in both approaching and leaving, these marauding bands attacked and plundered the Jews.

---

30. The Babylonian army compared to a lion, and to horses

   The lion is come up from his thicket, and the destroyer of the Gentiles is on his way; he is gone forth from his place to make thy land desolate; and thy cities shall be laid waste, without an inhabitant. Behold, he shall come up as clouds, and his chariots shall be as a whirlwind: his horses are swifter than eagles. Woe unto us! for we are spoiled (Jeremiah 4:7,13).

31. In Scripture, people are sometimes compared to serpents

   The wicked are estranged from the womb: they go astray as soon as they be born, speaking lies. Their poison is like the poison of a serpent: they are like the deaf adder that stoppeth her ear (Psalm 58:3-4).

   Surely the serpent will bite without enchantment; and a babbler is no better (Ecclesiastes 10:11).

   Rejoice not thou, whole Palestina, because the rod of him that smote thee is broken: for out of the serpent's root shall come forth a cockatrice (Hebrew, basilisk, adder, viper), and his fruit shall be a fiery flying serpent (Isaiah 14:29).

brimstone, which issued out of their mouths.

19 For their power is in their mouth, and in their tails: for their tails were like unto serpents, and had heads, and with them they do hurt (Revelation 9:18-19).

And the rest of the men which were not killed by these plagues yet repented not of the works of their hands, that they should not worship devils, and idols of gold, and silver, and brass, and stone, and of wood: which neither can see, nor hear, nor walk (Revelation 9:20).

The five and one-half trumpet judgments and the one and a half woes that were prophesied to come against Jerusalem end here. Because of these judgments, Jerusalem was destroyed. All buildings and houses were torn down, with the exception of three towers which were left standing to show how great the city had been. Also, the "western wall" was spared to provide a camp for the tenth Roman legion, which would remain stationed there. Thus, the prophecies of Revelation in regard to the destruction of Jerusalem were completely fulfilled!

Those *"Not Killed by These Plagues"*

The revelation here begins a transition. Our attention is turned in another direction. One and a half of the trumpet woes remain.

These last two verses begin to prepare us for God's awesome judgments against Rome. The Amplified Bible renders Revelation 9:20, *"And the rest of humanity, who were not killed by these plagues, even then did not repent…"*

Up to this point in the trumpet judgments we have read the phrase *"the third part"* repeatedly (see Revelation 8:7-12; 9:15,18). We will not read that phrase again in these remaining trumpet judgments, which conclude with Revelation 11:19. *"The third part"* was a reference to Jerusalem, and the prophecy against Jerusalem has been completed. But if *"the third part"* were killed, then what of the two-thirds that remained alive?

"…The rest of the men which were not killed by these plagues" (Revelation 9:20a) would refer to the nations within the Roman Empire. They had seen God's terrible judgments against the Jews, and yet they did not become fearful of God and did not consider that they, too, needed to repent of those things that He hates for His human children to do.

"...*by these plagues yet repented not...*" (Revelation 9:20a). The "*yet...not*" in this phrase is from the Greek word "*oude*," translated as follows in the Amplified and the New International Versions:

"*And the rest of humanity, who were not killed by these plagues, even then did not repent...*" (Amplified).

"*The rest of mankind that were not killed by these plagues still did not repent...*" (New International Version).

The thought here is that God's judgment against Jerusalem was so massive, so complete, so awesome that those not judged should have repented out of fear, but did, or would, not. However, since the people of Rome did repent, this prophecy and those related to Rome have been thrown into the future.

(For the details of Rome's repentance, see the chapter, "Why God Spared Rome.")

It should be pointed out here that the sins to be repented of were not primarily "Jewish" sins, but rather typical "Roman" sins. The statement, "*that they should not worship devils* (Greek, *daimonia*, demons)*, and idols of gold, and silver, and brass, and stone, and of wood: which neither can see, nor hear, nor walk*" does not describe what a Jew would do. Whatever faults a Jew would have, bowing down to a graven image was not one of them, but the Romans did do these things.

The final verse lends additional support to the fact that Romans, rather than Jews, are in view here.

"*Neither repented they of their murders, nor of their sorceries, nor of their fornication, nor of their thefts*" (Revelation 9:21).

While the Jews were certainly guilty of "*murders,*" "*fornication,*" and "*thefts,*" still "*sorceries*" would not have been a typical "Jewish" sin.

In the passages of Revelation that follow, we will see continuing evidences that Rome is more and more the subject of the prophecy.

Revelation 10
An Interlude within the Sixth Trumpet; The Second Woe

This chapter is an interlude to prepare us for a change of direction. God's awesome wrath has been seen prophetically as coming upon Messiah-rejecting Jerusalem. Now the prophecy is to move against the "*many peoples, and nations, and tongues, and kings*" (Revelation 10:11) that made up the Roman Empire, and especially against Rome itself because of its rejection of Christ, for murdering Him, and for the persecution and murder of God's servants, the Christians.

"And I saw another mighty angel come down from heaven, clothed with a cloud: and a rainbow was upon his head, and his face was as it were the sun, and his feet as pillars of fire" (Revelation 10:1).

"*Another mighty angel*" (Revelation 10:1). The description of this angel is to make known to us that he has just emerged from the presence of God. He has, therefore, God's latest message.

These descriptive characteristics showing that this angel has just come from God's presence may be recognized by comparing these characteristics with the scriptures given below.

This "*mighty angel*" was "*clothed with a cloud,*" as clouds symbolize majesty and glory[32] (Isaiah 19:1; Daniel 7:13). "*A rainbow was upon his head.*" The glory of the Lord had appeared to Ezekiel as a rainbow (Ezekiel 1:28). "*His face was as it were the sun,*" that is, like Moses, whose face shone from being in the presence of God[33] (Exodus 34:29);

---

32. Clouds in Scripture are seen as vehicles, or as clothing, for spirit beings

    The burden of Egypt. Behold, the Lord rideth upon a swift cloud, and shall come into Egypt: and the idols of Egypt shall be moved at his presence, and the heart of Egypt shall melt in the midst of it (Isaiah 19:1).

33. Like the angel in Revelation 10:1, Moses' face also shone from being in God's presence

    And it came to pass, when Moses came down from mount Sinai with the two tables of testimony in Moses' hand, when he came down from the mount, that Moses wist not that the skin of his face shone while he talked with him.

    And when Aaron and all the children of Israel saw Moses, behold, the skin of his face shone; and they were afraid to come nigh him (Exodus 34:29-30).

also, when John saw Jesus, in Revelation (1:16), "*his countenance was as the sun shineth in his strength…And his feet as pillars of fire.*" In Revelation 1:15, Jesus' feet were seen as "*like unto fine brass, as if they burned in a furnace.*" John's description of this "*mighty angel*" is similar to Daniel's description of an angel (Daniel 10:5-6), who also had just come from the presence of God.[34]

And he had in his hand a little book open: and he set his right foot upon the sea, and his left foot on the earth (Revelation 10:2).

The "*little book,*" like the "*roll of a book*" in Ezekiel, would contain "*lamentations, and mourning, and woe.*"

"*And when I looked, behold, an hand was sent unto me; and, lo, a roll of a book was therein; And he spread it before me; and it was written within and without: and there was written therein **lamentations, and mourning, and woe***" (Ezekiel 2:9-10).

"*And he had in his hand a little book* (Greek, *biblaridion,* a little scroll) *open: and he set his right foot upon the sea, and his left foot on the earth*" (Revelation 10:2). This thought of "*a little scroll*" comes from Ezekiel (2:8-10; 3:1-3). The significance is that "*the little scroll*" contained "*lamentations, and mourning, and woe*" (as in Ezekiel 2:10). But for whom? The prophecies concerning the fall of Jerusalem have been completed. "*The little scroll*" open in the hand of the "*mighty angel*" contained a message of "*lamentations, and mourning, and woe*" for Rome. In Daniel 10:21, an angel showed Daniel "*that which is noted in the scripture of truth.*" Daniel was then permitted to know in advance coming events in the histories of the great world empires. These foretold events covered the time period from Daniel's time to the destruction of Jerusalem (Daniel 11–12). In the same way John was given "*the little scroll*" so he, too, would know in advance the nature of the woes that would yet come upon

---

34. John's description of the angel in Revelation 10:1 is similar to Daniel's description of an angel, who also had just come from the presence of God

Then I lifted up mine eyes, and looked, and behold a certain man clothed in linen, whose loins were girded with fine gold of Uphaz:

His body also was like the beryl, and his face as the appearance of lightning, and his eyes as lamps of fire, and his arms and his feet like in color to polished brass, and the voice of his words like the voice of a multitude (Daniel 10:5-6).

Rome. The "*scroll*" would be "*little*" because these were the last times just before the reign of King Jesus, and history was coming to a close. These "*woes*" upon Rome from "*the little scroll*" are those given in Revelation 11:3-13 regarding the plagues that the two witnesses were to have brought upon Rome, and also those given in Revelation 11:14-19, regarding God's wrath upon the nations (vs. 18), which—had this been fulfilled in that time, as first intended—would have necessarily meant the nations within the Roman Empire, the nations loyal to Rome.

And cried with a loud voice, as when a lion roareth: and when he had cried, (the) seven thunders uttered their (own) voices (Revelation 10:3).

"*And cried with a loud voice, as when a lion roareth.*"

Often in the Old Testament God's power is described as the roar of a lion[35] (Isaiah 31:4; 42:13; Jeremiah 25:30; Hosea 11:10; Joel 3:16; Amos 1:2), but in this passage the "*mighty angel's*" power is described in this way. In Amos 3:4 we read, "*Will a lion roar in the forest, when he hath no prey? will a young lion cry out of his den, if he have taken nothing?*" The mighty angel's loud voice, as a lion's roar, is, then, a cry of victory! "*...and when he hath cried, (the) seven thunders uttered their* (own) *voices*" (Revelation 10:3b). The Greek reads here, not "*seven thunders,*" but "***the** seven thunders,*" as though John would have known what, or who, these seven thunders were.

Ancient peoples thought of thunder as the voice of God![36] Many scriptures indicate this. (See 2

---

35. Often, in Scripture, God's power is described as the roar of a lion

For thus hath the Lord spoken unto me, Like as the lion and the young lion roaring on his prey, when a multitude of shepherds is called forth against him, he will not be afraid of their voice, nor abase himself for the noise of them: so shall the Lord of hosts come down to fight for mount Zion, and for the hill thereof (Isaiah 31:4).

The Lord also shall roar out of Zion, and utter his voice from Jerusalem; and the heavens and the earth shall shake: but the Lord will be the hope of his people, and the strength of the children of Israel (Joel 3:16).

And he said, the Lord will roar from Zion, and utter his voice from Jerusalem: and the habitations of the shepherds shall mourn, and the top of Carmel shall wither (Amos 1:2).

36. Ancient peoples thought of thunder as the voice of God

The Lord thundered from heaven, and the most High uttered his voice (2 Samuel 22:14).

God thundereth marvelously with his voice; great things doeth he, which we cannot comprehend (Job 37:5).

Samuel 22:14,16; Job 37:5; 38:34; 40:9; Psalm 81:7; and the two identical verses in Jeremiah 10:13 and 51:16; also John 12: 27-29.) In Psalm 29, which is known as "the Psalm of the Thunderstorm," we see a picture of a great thunderstorm coming in from the Mediterranean Sea, and moving with great force against the northern forest (*"the cedars of Lebanon,"* vs.5) and against the southern desert (*"the wilderness of Kadesh,"* vs.8). In this psalm, the words, *"the voice of the Lord,"* occur seven times.

This psalm is the passage in the Old Testament to which *"the seven thunders"* of Revelation 10 refers. As A.T. Robertson in *Word Pictures in the New Testament,* Vol. VI, pg. 371, points out, the Greek construction in Revelation 10:3b means that *"the seven thunders uttered their own voices."* This ascribes personality, and the ability to take intelligent action to *"the seven thunders."* Like *"the arm of the Lord"* (See John 12:36-41; compared with Isaiah 51:9; 53:1; Psalm 44:3), which also shows personality and intelligence to Jesus, so *"the seven thunders"*—while the seven voices of God—here utter their own voices. Like the mighty angel's cry of victory, so also the seven thunders give forth a victory

---

Hast thou an arm like God? or canst thou thunder with a voice like him? (Job 40:9).

*Thou calledst in trouble, and I delivered thee; **I answered thee in the secret place of thunder:** I proved thee at the waters of Meribah. Selah* (Psalm 81:7).

Psalm 29

Give unto the Lord, O ye mighty, give unto the Lord glory and strength.
2 Give unto the Lord the glory due unto his name; worship the Lord in the beauty of holiness.
*3 **The voice of the Lord** is upon the waters: the God of glory thundereth: the Lord is upon many waters.*
*4 **The voice of the Lord** is powerful; **the voice of the Lord** is full of majesty.*
*5 **The voice of the Lord** breaketh the cedars; yes, the Lord breaketh the cedars of Lebanon.*
6 He maketh them also to skip like a calf; Lebanon and Sirion like a young unicorn.
*7 **The voice of the Lord** divideth the flames of fire.*
*8 **The voice of the Lord** shaketh the wilderness; the Lord shaketh the wilderness of Kadesh.*
*9 **The voice of the Lord** maketh the hinds to calve, and discovereth the forests: and in his temple doth every one speak of his glory.*
10 The Lord sitteth upon the flood; yea, the Lord sitteth King for ever.
11 The Lord will give strength unto his people; the Lord will bless his people with peace.

Count the number of times we read the phrase *"the voice of the Lord."* We will count this phrase seven times! The *"seven thunders"* is from this passage.

In the following passages, where the King James and other versions read "thunder(s)" or "thunderings," the Hebrew reads "voices" (Exodus 9:23,28-29,33-34; 19:16; 20:18; 1 Samuel 7: 10; 12:17-18; Job 28:26; 38:25).

shout of sevenfold triumph over Christ-rejecting Jerusalem!

4 And when the seven thunders had uttered their voices, I was about to write: and I heard a voice from heaven saying unto me, Seal up those things which the seven thunders uttered, and write them not (Revelation 10:4).

"*Seal up those things which the seven thunders uttered, and write them not*" (Revelation 10:4b). Clearly, it was too early to record the seven thunders' voices of victory. There remained yet another enemy on the field of battle. True, Jerusalem was prophetically seen as fully destroyed. But Rome had also persecuted and killed God's children, and it, too, must be destroyed before the seven thunders could sound their own praises to God's complete victory over His enemies.

Thus, the same angel that prophesied the destruction of Jerusalem in Daniel 12:7 now returns after 608 years to declare again that that prophecy is about to be completed. His voice is "*as when a lion roareth*" (Revelation 10:3a). God is seen prophetically as taking Jerusalem prey. But while Jerusalem is seen as destroyed, John must eat "*the little scroll*" containing "*lamentations, and mourning, and woe*" for the "*many peoples, and nations, and tongues, and kings*" (Revelation 10:11) which make up the Roman Empire.

But why could the "*mighty angel*" give a cry of victory "*like the roar of a lion*" while the voices of "*the seven thunders*" were sealed? The "*mighty angel*" gave a *single* shout, or cry of victory and that was correct since Jerusalem was seen prophetically as destroyed: But *seven* is the number, or signature, of *completeness*, and God's victory would not be complete until Rome also was destroyed. Thus, "*the seven thunders*" were premature in sounding forth complete victory, and their words were sealed until Rome, too, would be destroyed.

The theme of seven representing completeness will be explored further and from another standpoint in our study of Revelation 11.

This angel who "*set his right foot upon the sea, and his left foot upon the earth*" (Revelation 10:2), reminds us somewhat of the three angels in Daniel 12:5-7,[37] two on the banks on either side of the river, and one of on the waters of the river. Thus, this angel that John saw stood upon both sea and earth.

5 And the angel which I saw stand upon the sea and upon the earth lifted up his hand to heaven,

In Daniel's vision, the angel upon the waters of the river lifted both hands to heaven and "*sware by him that liveth for ever*" (Daniel 12:7).

In John's vision, the "*mighty angel*" lifted one hand to heaven, and also "*sware by him that liveth for ever and ever*" (Revelation 10:6), though this angel's oath was recorded as longer in content than the angel in Daniel 12:7.

6 And sware by him that liveth for ever and ever, who created heaven, and the things that therein are, and the earth, and the things that therein are, and the sea, and the things which are therein, that there should be time no longer:

Still, the similarities between the angel in Daniel who stood upon the waters of the river, and the "*mighty angel*" in Revelation are impressive and may be intended to suggest that these are the same angel.

"*And the angel which I saw stand upon the sea and upon the earth lifted up his hand to heaven, and sware by him that liveth forever and ever, who created heaven…and the earth…and the sea…that there should be time no longer*" (Revelation 10:5-6). There is a clear and intended connection between this angel and the angel in Daniel 12:7. "*And I heard the man clothed in linen, which was upon the waters of the river, when he held up his right hand and his left hand unto heaven, and sware by him that liveth for ever that it shall be for a time, times and an half; and when he shall have accomplished to scatter the power of the holy people, all these things shall be finished*" (Daniel 12:7). This angel of Daniel 12:7 had appeared about 530 years before this and had prophesied this very destruction upon the Jews,

7 But in the days of the voice of the seventh angel, when he shall begin to sound, the mystery of God should be finished, as he hath declared to his servants the prophets (Revelation 10:5-7).

---

37. John's angel (Revelation 10) compared with Daniel's angels

Then I Daniel looked, and, behold, there stood other two, the one on this side of the bank of the river, and the other on that side of the bank of the river.

And one said to the man clothed in linen, which was upon the waters of the river, How long shall it be to the end of these wonders?

And I heard the man clothed in linen, which was upon the waters of the river, when he held up his right hand and his left hand unto heaven, and sware by him that liveth for ever that it shall be for a time, times, and an half; and when he shall have accomplished to scatter the power of the holy people, all these things shall be finished (Daniel 12:5-7).

which came in A.D. 70. But that angel had told Daniel, "*Go thy way, Daniel: for the words are closed up and sealed till the time of the end*" (Daniel 12:9). That which Daniel's angel told him was "*sealed*," has in Revelation been *unsealed*!

Both Daniel's angel and John's angel gave prophecies regarding time. Daniel's angel gave the length of the Roman Jewish War as "*a time, times, and an half*" (Daniel 12:7), or three and one half years, which proved to be correct in A.D. 66 to 70, over 600 years later. John's angel proclaimed that "*there should be time* (or delay) *no longer*" (Revelation 10:6), "*but in the days of the voice of the seventh angel, when he shall begin to sound, the mystery of God should be finished*" (Revelation 10:7). Since the seventh angel prophesied concerning God's wrath upon the nations that were angry (the nations of the Roman Empire), this passage indicates that there would be no delay in the matter of proceeding to destroy Rome.

Is this "*mighty angel*" of Revelation 10 the same angel as the one who stood upon the waters of the river in Daniel 12? It certainly seems so.

8 And the voice which I heard from heaven spake unto me again, and said, Go and take the little book which is open in the hand of the angel which standeth upon the sea and upon the earth.

9 And I went unto the angel, and said unto him, Give me the little book. And he said unto me, Take it, and eat it up; and it shall make thy belly bitter, but it shall be in thy

When John ate "*the little scroll*" it was in his mouth "*sweet as honey,*" and what could be sweeter than to be personally chosen to speak forth God's words! But when he had eaten it, his belly was bitter, since the message within him was a bitter message—a message of "*lamentation, and mourning, and woe,*" a message of doom for Rome. This bitter message of "*the little scroll*" is given in Revelation 11. It made John sick to carry such woe within.

mouth sweet as honey.

10 And I took the little book out of the angel's hand, and ate it up; and it was in my mouth sweet as honey: and as soon as I had eaten it, my belly was bitter.

11 And he said unto me, Thou must prophesy again before many peoples, and nations, and tongues, and kings (Revelation 10:8-11).

Revelation 11
The Little Scroll Predicts Woe for Rome

And there was given me a reed like unto a rod: and the angel stood, saying, Rise, and measure (or, anoint) the temple of God, and the altar, and them that worship therein.

2 But the court which is without the temple leave out, and measure (or, anoint) it not; for it is given unto the Gentiles: and the holy city shall they tread under foot forty and two months
(Revelation 11:1-2).

In Revelation 11:1 John is told to "*Rise, and measure the temple of God, and the altar, and them that worship therein.*" In the Aramaic language the word *meshakh* means both "to measure" and "to anoint." The Aramaic language was the language that John spoke. In this instance, *meshakh* probably meant "to anoint," the thought being that God preserves those who receive anointing (as in Psalm 18:50; 20:6; 89:20-23).

The temple (Greek, *naos*, sanctuary) of God refers to the believers in Jesus. "*The altar*" refers to the altar of burnt offering. It was in the court of the priests, but here is a reference to the sacrifice of Jesus on the cross. "*We have an altar...*" (Hebrews 13:10a), and "*Christ our passover is sacrificed for us*" (1 Corinthians 5:7b).

The meaning of Revelation 11:1-2 is clear: the Jewish believers in Jesus from Jerusalem are pictured here as the temple of God. Those in "*the court which is without the temple*" (Revelation 11:2a) were those Jerusalem Jews outside of Christ. They are not even considered as Jews in this revelation, because they have rejected their Messiah.[38] (See Revelation 2:9; 3:9.)

Thus, they were in the Court of the Gentiles.

---

38. Jews who have rejected Jesus as their Messiah, are not considered as Jews in this revelation

I know thy works, and tribulation, and poverty, (but thou art rich) and I know the blasphemy of them which say they are Jews, and are not, but are the synagogue of Satan (Revelation 2:9).

Behold, I will make them of the synagogue of Satan, which say they are Jews, and are not, but do lie; behold, I will make them to come and worship before thy feet, and to know that I have loved thee (Revelation 3:9).

Those anointed were protected.[39] These were the 144,000, the Jewish followers of Jesus who left Jerusalem in A.D. 66 and went to Pella, a city beyond the Jordan River. They were protected then, and also later as Roman armies fought near Pella. But those who were not anointed were not protected. These were the unbelieving Jews who had remained in Jerusalem, *"and the holy city shall they* (the Gentiles) *tread under foot forty and two months"* (Revelation 11:2b). John's prophecy proved correct! The *"forty and two months"* is three and one-half years, and was the time period of the Roman-Jewish War of A.D. 66-70. But, we may ask, why does Revelation 11:1-2 take up such matters as God's protection of the Jerusalem Jews who believed in Jesus, God's judgment on the Jerusalem Jews who rejected Jesus, and *"the holy city"* of Jerusalem being trodden underfoot by the Gentiles? Had not John adequately covered all these matters previously in prophecy? Was not John commissioned now to be prophesying about the *"many peoples, and nations, and tongues, and kings"* (Revelation 10:11) that made up the Roman Empire?

The above questions reveal an accurate but limited understanding of Revelation. In Revelation, numbers are important, and this is especially true of the number seven which represents completeness, and also of the number 3 1/2, which is the signature of incompleteness, being one-half of seven.

Three and a half years, in Revelation, or Daniel, may be worded in various ways, but the meaning of incompleteness is always intended. For instance, three and a half years may be given as *"forty and two*

---

39. God preserves those who are *"His anointed"*

Great deliverance giveth he to his king; and sheweth mercy to his anointed, to David, and to his seed for evermore (Psalm 18:50).

Now know I that the Lord saveth his anointed; he will hear him from his holy heaven with the saving strength of his right hand (Psalm 20:6).

I have found David my servant; with my holy oil have I anointed him: With whom my hand shall be established: mine arm also shall strengthen him.
The enemy shall not exact upon him; nor the son of wickedness afflict him.
And I will beat down his foes before his face, and plague them that hate him (Psalm 89:20-23).

months," "*a thousand two hundred and threescore days*," or "*a time, and times, and half a time*." Thus, all the above phrases indicate incompleteness, and a prophecy containing such phrases is, by itself, an incomplete prophecy.

The following time periods, which were prophesied in both Daniel and Revelation regarding Jerusalem and Rome, will illustrate that two three-and-a-half-year periods are needed to make up a complete prophetic period of seven years.

Incomplete Prophetic Time Periods from Daniel and Revelation Regarding Jerusalem and Rome

Jerusalem

"*a time, times, and an half*"..."*to scatter the power of the holy people*" (Daniel 12:7).

"*and the holy city shall they* (the Gentiles) *tread under foot forty and two months*" (Revelation 11:2).

"*And the woman fled into the wilderness, where she hath a place prepared of God, that they should feed her there a thousand two hundred and threescore days*" (Revelation 12:6).

"*And to the woman were given two wings of a great eagle, that she might fly into the wilderness, into her place, where she is nourished for a time and times, and half a time, from the face of the serpent*" (Revelation 12:14).

Rome

"*...and they* (the saints) *shall be given into his hand until a time and times and the dividing of time*" (Daniel 7:25).

"*and they* (the two witnesses) *shall prophesy a thousand two hundred and threescore days, clothed in sackcloth*" (Revelation 11:3).

"*And there was given unto him* (the beast) *a mouth speaking great things and blasphemies; and power was given unto him to continue forty and two months*" (Revelation 13:5).

Thus, in Daniel 12:7, the "*holy people*," the Jews, would have their power scattered (or shattered) in three and a half years (the length of the Roman-Jewish War of A.D. 66-70), while in Daniel 7:25 the "*saints*," or Christians, would be given into the hand of the "*little horn*," the beast, for three and a half years.

In Revelation 11:2, the first three and a half years is the time in which "*the holy city*" (Jerusalem) is trodden down by the Gentiles, while the second three and a half years is the time when "*the great city*" (Rome) is buffeted by the plagues sent by the two witnesses (Revelation 11:3).

In Revelation 12:6,14 the first three and a half years is the time in which "*the woman*," the Jewish believers in Jesus from Jerusalem, "*fled into the wilderness*," to Pella, while the second three and a half years is the time in which the Gentile Christians would be "*overcome*" by the beast.

In each of these three pairs of examples, the two three-and-a-half-year periods make up the seven years—the complete prophetic picture. Even the two witnesses are prophesied as dead for three and a half days—but three and a half days multiplied by the two witnesses gives a total of *seven*—a complete prophetic picture.[40]

Thus, Revelation 11:1-2 refers back to Jerusalem to show that the "*forty and two months*" in which Jerusalem would be trodden down of the Gentiles, is completed by the "*thousand two hundred and threescore days*" in which the plagues brought by the two witnesses would bring woe upon Rome.

By bringing together the prophecies related to Jerusalem and to Rome into one complete prophetic unit of seven years, and with three and a half years given to bring about the destruction of Jerusalem, and three and a half years in which the two witnesses bring woe upon Rome, the thought suggests that the fulfillment of both parts is soon and certain. With this in mind we proceed to the discussion of the two witnesses.

And I will give power unto my two witnesses, and they shall prophesy a thousand two hundred and threescore days, clothed in sackcloth (Revelation 11:3).

"Clothed in Sackcloth"

"*Sackcloth*" (Greek, *sakkos*, a warm garment made of goat's or camel's hair, and thus of a dark color.) Sackcloth was used for mourning, especially because of sins, and expressed a need for repentance. Prophets, such as John the Baptist, wore rough clothing (Matthew 3:4; Mark 1:6), and a "*rough garment*" was common apparel for one who was a prophet. (See Zechariah 13:4.)

---

40. The Two Witnesses are prophesied as dead for three and a half days—but three and a half days multiplied by the two witnesses gives a total of seven (days)—a complete prophetic picture.

And they of the people and kindreds and tongues and nations shall see their dead bodies three days and an half, and shall not suffer their dead bodies to be put in graves (Revelation 11:9).

And after three days and an half the Spirit of life from God entered into them, and they stood upon their feet; and great fear fell upon them which saw them (Revelation 11:11).

In Revelation 11:3-13, we look further into *"the little scroll"* that John ate, but whose contents are given in Revelation 11. This passage (Revelation 11:3-13) completes the time period of the sixth trumpet, and of *"the second woe."*

Let us compare the descriptive language in Revelation 11:4-7 with similar language elsewhere to help us interpret it.

*These are **the two olive trees, and the two candlesticks** standing before the God of the earth* (Revelation 11:4).

*And said unto me, What seest thou? And I said, I have looked, and behold **a candlestick** all of gold, with a bowl upon the top of it, and his seven lamps thereon, and seven pipes to the seven lamps, which are upon the top thereof: And **two olive trees** by it, one upon the right side of the bowl, and the other upon the left side thereof. Then said he, These are the two anointed ones, that stand by the Lord of the whole earth* (Zechariah 4:2-3,14).

*And if any man will hurt them, **fire proceedeth out of their mouth, and devoureth their enemies:** and if any man will hurt them, he must in this manner be killed* (Revelation 11:5).

*Wherefore thus saith the Lord God of hosts, Because ye speak this word, behold, I will make my words **in thy mouth fire,** and this people wood, **and it shall devour them*** (Jeremiah 5:14).

And Elijah answered and said to the captain of fifty, If I be a man of God, then let fire come down from heaven, and consume thee and thy fifty. And there came down fire from heaven, and consumed him and his fifty (2 Kings 1:10).

These have power to shut heaven, that it rain not in the days of their prophecy: and have power over waters to turn them to blood, and to smite the earth with all plagues, as often as they will (Revelation 11:6).

*And Elijah the Tishbite, who was of the inhabitants of Gilead, said unto Ahab, As the Lord God of Israel liveth, before whom I stand, **there shall not be dew nor rain these years,** but according to my word* (1 Kings 17:1).

*And Moses and Aaron did so, as the Lord commanded; and he lifted up the rod, and smote the waters that were in the river, in the sight of Pharaoh, and in the sight of his servants; **and all the waters that were in the river were turned to blood*** (Exodus 7:20).

And when they shall have finished their testimony, the beast that ascendeth out of the bottomless pit shall make war against them, and shall overcome them, and kill them (Revelation 11:7).

*The beast that thou sawest was, and is not; and **shall ascend out of the bottomless pit**, and go into perdition...* (Revelation 17:8a).

Our basic questions regarding the *"two witnesses"* include such matters as,

(1) Who are they?

(1) Where will they prophesy? and

(1) What will be the nature of their mission?

Who are they?

At various times in the history of the Hebrew people, two witnesses arose.[41] Moses and Aaron were the two witnesses for their time, and together brought the plagues upon Egypt. In turning the waters of Egypt to blood, Moses obeyed God's command to tell Aaron to lift his rod and to

---

41. At various times in the history of the Hebrew people, two witnesses arose

Moses and Aaron: And the Lord spake unto Moses, Say unto Aaron, Take thy rod, and stretch out thine hand upon the waters of Egypt, upon their streams, upon their rivers, and upon their ponds, and upon all their pools of water, that they may become blood; and that there may be blood throughout all the land of Egypt, both in vessels of wood, and in vessels of stone.
And Moses and Aaron did so, as the Lord commanded; and he lifted up the rod, and smote the waters that were in the river, in the sight of Pharaoh, and in the sight of his servants; and all the waters that were in the river were turned to blood (Exodus 7:19-20).

Joshua and Caleb: Surely none of the men that came up out of Egypt, from twenty years old and upward, shall see the land which I sware unto Abraham, unto Isaac, and unto Jacob; because they have not wholly followed me:
Save Caleb the son of Jephunneh the Kenezite, and Joshua the son of Nun: for they have wholly followed the Lord (Numbers 32:11-12).

Elijah and Elisha: And it came to pass, when the Lord would take up Elijah into heaven by a whirlwind, that Elijah went with Elisha from Gilgal.
And it came to pass, as they still went on, and talked, that, behold, there appeared a chariot of fire, and horses of fire, and parted them both asunder; and Elijah went up by a whirlwind into heaven. And when the sons of the prophets which were to view at Jericho saw him, they said, The spirit of Elijah doth rest on Elisha. And they came to meet him, and bowed themselves to the ground before him (2 Kings 2:1,11,15).

Zerubbabel and Joshua, the high priest: In the second year of Darius the king, in the sixth month, in the first day of the month, came the word of the Lord by Haggai the prophet unto Zerubbabel the son of Shealtiel, governor of Judah, and to Joshua the son of Josedech, the high priest, saying... (Haggai 1:1).

smite "*the waters that were in the river*" "*and all the waters that were in the river were turned to blood*" (Exodus 7:19-20).

Joshua and Caleb were mentioned together in several passages of Scripture and were, no doubt, seen as God's two witnesses for their time (Numbers 14:6,30,38; 32:12; Deuteronomy 1:36-38; Joshua 14:6,13).

Elijah and Elisha were also mentioned together in Scripture, and would have been the two witnesses for their time (1 Kings 19:15-21; 2 Kings 2:1-15; 3:11).

Zerubbabel and Joshua, the high priest, were also mentioned together repeatedly in Scripture, and were God's two witnesses for their time (Ezra 2:2; 3:2,8; 4:3; 5:2; Nehemiah 7:7; 12:1; Haggai 1:1,12,14; 2:2,4; Zechariah 3:1-10 (Joshua, the high priest); 4:1-13 (Zerubbabel).

In the early church, Peter and Paul were mentioned most prominently, especially in the book of Acts. Both were killed about the same time under orders of Nero Caesar. They were, no doubt, seen as the two witnesses for their time. However, since Nero was dead when Revelation was given, it was not Peter or Paul who were the two witnesses of whom John was writing as they were both dead.

If the prophecy regarding the two witnesses had been fulfilled in the first century A.D., as originally intended, the two witnesses would have given their testimony in Rome before the eighth king, or emperor, who would have been Domitian. (Compare Revelation 11:7 with 17:11.) Using the examples of the various two witnesses named above, it would appear that in every case they were God's two leaders of Israel for their times.

But who would have been "*the two witnesses*" if repentance had not thrown these prophecies far into the future, even beyond our own times? The following quotations from Eusebius' *Ecclesiastical History*, pgs. 101-102, will help us to identify them.

> "*Domitian had issued orders, that the descendants of David should be slain.*" "*Some of the heretics accused the descendants of Judas, as the brother of our Saviour, according to the flesh.*" These "*were brought to Domitian by the Evocatus. For this emperor was as much alarmed at the appearance of Christ as Herod. He put the question, whether they were of David's race, and they confessed that they were. He then asked them what property they had, or how much money they owned. And* **both of them** *answered, that they had between them only nine thousand denarii, and this they had not in silver, but in the value of a piece of land, containing only thirty-nine acres; from which they raised their taxes and supported themselves by their own labour. Then they also*

*began to show their hands, exhibiting the hardness of their bodies, and the callosity formed by incessant labour on their hands, as evidence of their own labour. When asked also, respecting Christ and his kingdom, what was its nature, and when and where it was to appear, they replied, 'that it was not a temporal nor an earthly kingdom, but celestial and angelic; that it would appear at the end of the world, when coming in glory he would judge the quick and the dead, and give to every one according to his works.' Upon which, Domitian despising them, made no reply; but treating them with contempt, as simpletons, commanded them to be dismissed, and by a **decree ordered the persecution to cease**. Thus delivered, **they ruled the churches**, both as witnesses and relatives of the Lord."*

These were two. They were "witnesses." They were taken to Rome where they stood before "*the eighth*" king, Domitian, who was the prophesied beast (Revelation 17:11). "*They ruled the churches.*" Another source gives their names as *James and Sokker.*[42] They were, without doubt, the prophesied "*two witnesses*" of Revelation 11:3-13.

As James and Sokker stood before Domitian, many prayers were ascending to God for their lives. God Himself heard, and answered, and delivered them from death.

This, then, was the climax—the very point in time in which this prophecy regarding James and Sokker, the two witnesses, and the prophecies regarding Domitian, the beast, and the prophecies regarding the fall of Rome, and the return of Jesus—yes, all these were at this very point thrown into the future!

This must be true, since "*the two witnesses*" must be here when the beast is here, as he ascends "*out of the bottomless pit*" (Rome) to "*kill them*" (Revelation 11:7). And the beast must be here when Rome is destroyed, because he and the ten kings "*hate the whore*" (Rome), "*and shall burn her with fire*" (Revelation 17:16). Also, the beast and the false prophet must be here when Jesus returns, because Jesus will fight against them (Revelation 19:19), and He will capture them and cast them alive into "*a lake of fire*" (Revelation 19:20). Thus, all these events, being interconnected, were thrown together into the future.

When Domitian "*by a decree ordered the persecution to cease,*" he prevented himself from being the beast he was prophesied to be, the beast of Revelation (!), and God threw the above prophecies at least 1900 years into the future! What an event!

---

42. Schonfield, Dr. Hugh J., *The Passover Plot*, pg. 245.

The days of the beast are moving close again! But widespread repentance and prayer and a turning to Christ could even yet change the course of history *God turned from His wrath before, and He can do it again*!

Our second basic question regarding *"the two witnesses"* is,

Where Will They Prophesy?

While most commentators on Revelation have placed the prophesying of *"the two witnesses"* in Jerusalem, this simply is not the case. The accumulated evidence for their prophesying in Rome is overwhelming. In documenting this evidence it would be impractical to restate all that has been previously written. The reader is advised to re-read the appropriate sections to review the substance of each argument.

(1) The phrase *"the rest of the men which were not killed by these plagues"* (Revelation 9:20) indicates a different group of men from *"the third part of men"* who were killed (Revelation 9:15,18). Since *"the third part"* was a reference to Jerusalem, *"the rest of the men which were not killed by these plagues"* would indicate that the subjects of the prophecy were of Rome,

(2) The sins of idolatry and sorceries (Revelation 9:20-21), being more "Roman" sins than "Jewish" sins, indicate that it is Rome that is now to be prophesied against.

(3) The sealing of the things that *"the seven thunders"* uttered (Revelation 10:4) indicates that God's awesome judgment upon Jerusalem would not be a complete victory over all His enemies, as Rome had also persecuted and killed His children. This indicates that a further prophecy of judgment must come now against Rome.

(4) The phrase in which John was told *"Thou must prophesy again before many peoples, and nations, and tongues, and kings"* (Revelation 10:11) constitutes strong evidence in favor of Rome. It could in no way apply to Jerusalem. Why would God tell John this and then send *"the two witnesses"* to prophesy against Jerusalem?

(5) Revelation 11:1-2 as we have previously shown, is to show that the *"forty and two months"* or three and a half years in which the Gentiles tread under foot *"the holy city"* of Jerusalem constitutes an incomplete prophecy. The complete seven years is when *"the two witnesses...prophesy a thousand two hundred and threescore days"* (or another three and a half years) to *"the great city."* Jerusalem, in

Scripture, is never called "*the great city*." It is "*the holy city*"[43] (Nehemiah 11:1,18; Isaiah 48:2; 52:1; Daniel 9:24; Matthew 4:5; 27:53; Revelation 11:2). The phrase "*the great city*" is a clear reference to Rome. See footnote "e" in The Jerusalem Bible, page 329, for Revelation 11:8. "*The 'Great City' or 'Babylon' in this book is Rome whose actions were identified with Sodom's rejection of God's messengers and Egypt's oppression of God's people.*"

(6) The beast ascends out of "*the bottomless pit*" which, as we pointed out previously, was a reference to Rome.

(7) "*They of the people and kindreds and tongues and nations*" (Revelation 11:9) is a strong reference to the peoples of the Roman Empire, particularly Rome.

(8) "*They that dwell upon the earth*"—a phrase used twice in this verse—(Revelation 11:10) is also a reference to the peoples of the Roman Empire, especially Rome.

(9) Besides all this, since the prophecies of the seven seals began with Jerusalem and ended with Rome, we must expect the seven trumpets to follow the same pattern.

NOTE: This is not to say that "*the two witnesses*" will never prophesy in Jerusalem.

As God's two leaders for Israel for their times, they must surely live and prophesy in Jerusalem far more than in Rome.

But this three-and-a-half-year scene in Revelation 11:3-13 takes place in Rome.

---

43. Jerusalem, in Scripture, is never called "*the great city*." It is "*the holy city*."

And the rulers of the people dwelt at Jerusalem: the rest of the people also cast lots, to bring one of ten to dwell in Jerusalem the holy city, and nine parts to dwell in other cities (Nehemiah 11:1).

All the Levites in the holy city were two hundred fourscore and four (Nehemiah 11:18).

For they call themselves of the holy city, and stay themselves upon the God of Israel; the Lord of hosts is his name (Isaiah 48:2).

Awake, awake; put on thy strength, O Zion; put on thy beautiful garments, O Jerusalem, the holy city: for henceforth there shall no more come into thee the uncircumcised and the unclean (Isaiah 52:1).

Seventy weeks are determined upon thy people and upon thy holy city, to finish the transgression, and to make an end of sins, and to make reconciliation for iniquity, and to bring in everlasting righteousness, and to seal up the vision and prophecy, and to anoint the most Holy (Daniel 9:24).

Then the devil taketh him up into the holy city, and setteth him on a pinnacle of the temple (Matthew 4:5).

And came out of the graves after his resurrection, and went into the holy city, and appeared unto many (Matthew 27:53).

But the court which is without the temple leave out, and measure it not; for it is given unto the Gentiles: and the holy city shall they tread under foot forty and two months (Revelation 11:2).

Each of these nine reasons are conclusive proof that *"the two witnesses"* were to have confronted Domitian, the *"eighth"* king, in Rome. And that is, in fact, exactly what James and Sokker did.

However, against this array of reasons, one verse—Revelation 11:8, particularly the last phrase—has been urged as a reason for believing that the two witnesses were to testify for their 3 1/2 years against Jerusalem.

*8 And their dead bodies shall lie in the street of **the great city**, which spiritually is called Sodom and Egypt, **where also our** (Greek, auton, their)* **Lord was crucified.**

In scripture, Sodom is a symbol of wickedness (Deuteronomy 32:32; Ezekiel 16:46,55), and Egypt was a symbol of oppression (Exodus 1-15). Also, Sodom had rejected God's two witnesses, the two angels (Genesis 19:1-28), and Egypt had also rejected God's two witnesses, Moses and Aaron. Thus, both of these symbols could apply to Rome.

*9 And they of **the people and kindreds and tongues and nations** shall see their dead bodies three days and an half, and shall not suffer their dead bodies to be put in graves.*

Of course, Jesus was crucified outside of Jerusalem. But there is a sense in which Jesus was crucified in Rome when Peter was crucified there, because whatever people do to Jesus' followers, they do also to Him! When Jesus said to Saul of Tarsus, *"Saul, Saul, why persecutest thou Me?"* He did not mean that Saul of Tarsus had entered into heaven and was seeking to kill Jesus there! He meant that Saul's persecution of His followers was a persecution of Him! In Matthew 25:40, Jesus

*10 And **they that dwell upon the earth** shall rejoice over them, and make merry, and shall send gifts one to another; because these two prophets tormented **them that dwelt on the earth.***

said, *"Inasmuch as ye have done it unto one of the least of these my brethren, ye have done it unto me."* So when Peter and Paul, and other Christians were killed in Rome, Jesus was *"crucified"* there as well.[44]

A poem I learned years ago in college expresses this thought. It went like this:

---

44. Does the ancient legend of "Quo Vadis?" relate to the phrase in Revelation 11:8, "...*where also their Lord was crucified*"?

This ancient legend was recorded in Acta Petr. (Acts of Peter) 35. It tells of the Apostle Peter attempting to leave Rome to save his life.

As he (Peter) went out of the gate he saw the Lord entering Rome; and when he saw him he said, 'Lord, whither (goest thou) here?' And the Lord said to him, 'I am coming to Rome to be crucified.' And Peter said to him, 'Lord, art thou being crucified again?' He said to him, 'Yes, Peter, I am being crucified again.'

In this passage, Jesus was coming to Rome to be crucified again. But Peter, ashamed of his cowardice, reversed himself, and was crucified head down.

11 and after three days and an half the Spirit of life from God entered into them, and they stood upon their feet; and great fear fell upon them which saw them.

12 And they heard a great voice from heaven saying unto them, Come up hither. And they ascended up to heaven in a cloud; and their enemies beheld them.

13 And the same hour was there a great earthquake, and the tenth part of the city fell, and in the earthquake were slain of men seven thousand: and the remnant were affrighted, and gave glory to the God of heaven (Revelation 11:8-13).

In the above scriptures, all references to Rome, or to the Roman Empire, are in bold.

Christ Is Crucified Anew

Not only once, and long ago,
There on Golgotha's rugged side,
Has Christ, the Lord been crucified
Because He loved a lost world so.
But hourly souls, sin-satisfied,
Mock His great love, flout His commands,
And drive deep nails into His hands,
And thrust the spear within His side.

John Richard Moreland

Rome, in killing the two witnesses, had also *"crucified" "their Lord."*[45]

In *Visions Beyond the Veil*, by H. A. Baker, we read of visions given to the children of the Adullam Rescue Mission in Yunnanfu, Yunnan Province, in China, sometime before the Communist takeover.

*During the reign of this super-man (the Antichrist) in his God-defying power, the saints of God were standing true and bearing faithful testimony in spite of every hardship and danger. **They saw the two witnesses in Jerusalem,** and they saw the saints, as well as these two, endued with mighty supernatural power to fight with and to resist the power of darkness in that awful time, the like of which has never been upon the earth—the time when the devil and all his angels and demons will be turned loose upon the earth, having great wrath, knowing their time is short…They had visions of preaching the gospel in the midst of great persecution; but they were given such power that by a word from*

---

45. The Martyrdom *of "the Two Witnesses"* (who are also called *"the two prophets"*) as Seen in Other Passages of Revelation.

Besides Revelation 11:3-13, *"the two witnesses"* or *"two prophets"* are seen as martyred also in the following passages:

For they (the people of Rome) *have shed the blood of saints and prophets, and thou hast given them blood to drink; for they are worthy* (Revelation 16:6).

Rejoice over her, thou heaven, and ye holy apostles (Peter and Paul) *and prophets* (the two witnesses); *for God hath avenged you on her* (Revelation 18:20).

And in her (that is, Rome) *was found the blood of prophets, and of saints, and of all that were slain upon the earth* (Revelation 18:24).

them, enemies were smitten by plagues or death. This power seemed to issue from within and came out of their mouths; with it they rebuked and slew their enemies.

In some cases, after giving testimony in a town that rejected them and having left it at a distance, fire from heaven descended and destroyed the wicked place, even as Sodom and Gomorrah were swept away. When persecution was bitter, they were sometimes caught away bodily by the Holy Spirit as was Philip and as the prophets supposed Elijah had been (II Kings 2:16). They were thus by the Spirit carried away to a place of safety. In time of hunger and need, food was miraculously provided—manna, fruit, and other food" (pg 102-103).

Thus, the normal residence of the two witnesses would, no doubt, be in Jerusalem. They may also have a wide ministry in other towns, before they come to Rome to fulfil Revelation 11:3-13.

Our third basic question in regard to the two witnesses is,

What Will Be the Nature of Their Mission?

Revelation 11:3 tells us that the "*two witnesses*" shall "*prophesy,*" and Revelation 11:10 refers to them as the "*two prophets.*" We are not told what the two witnesses will say in their prophecy, but because Revelation 9:12–11:14 is in the period of "*the second woe,*" it would be a prophecy of God's impending wrath about to come upon Rome.

The two witnesses not only prophesy God's soon coming wrath upon Rome, but are also instruments for bringing forth that wrath.

It is interesting to note that in this section (Revelation 11:3-13), the beast defends Rome from the plagues brought by the two witnesses by killing them (Revelation 11:7), but later, in another vision, this same beast "*shall hate the whore*" (Rome) and, with ten kings, "*burn her with fire*" (Revelation 17:16).

14 The second woe is past; and, behold, the third woe cometh quickly.

15 And the seventh angel sounded; and there were great voices in heaven, saying, The kingdoms of this world are become the kingdoms of our Lord, and of his Christ; and he shall reign for ever and ever.

16 And the four and twenty elders which sat before God on their seats, fell upon their faces, and worshipped God,

17 Saying, We give thee thanks, O Lord God Almighty, which art, and wast, and art to come; because thou hast taken to thee thy great power, and hast reigned (Revelation 11:14-17).

And the nations were angry, and thy wrath is come, and the time of the dead, that they should be judged, and that

The Second Woe

As "*the second woe*" comes to a close, we are able to piece together a chronology of events, such as:

1. The "*war*" against the two witnesses (Revelation 11:7), and,

2. The "*war with the saints*" (Revelation 13:7).

These two—the war against the two witnesses and the war with the saints—were both of a three-and-one-half-year duration (Revelation 11:3; 13:5; see also Daniel 7:25).

As we shall shortly see, these two events were also to have occurred in the same three-and-one-half-year time period. This is so, since there was to have been one three-and-a-half-year period in which the Jews were scattered, Jerusalem trodden down, and in which "*the woman*," that is, true Israel, fled into the wilderness (Daniel 12:7; Revelation 11:2; 12:6,14). Then there was to be a second three-and-one-half-year period in which the saints were given into the hand of "*the fourth beast*"—the Roman Empire (Daniel 7:25), and the beast of Revelation makes war with the two witnesses and continues to blaspheme and have power (Revelation 11:3,7; 13:5). These two three-and-a-half-year periods are necessary to a complete prophetic time period of seven years. Thus, "*the blood of saints and prophets*" (the "*prophets*" being "*the two witnesses*"—Revelation 11:10) are given together in Revelation 16:6 and 18:24. In this "*second woe*," the beast and "*the great whore*" (Rome) would kill the Christians, and then in "*the third woe*" the wrath of God will come upon both Rome and the beast.

"The Third Woe"
"The Mystery of God Is Finished"

"*The third woe*," as given in Revelation 11:14-19, is given again in an expanded form in Revelation 16–18. This "*third woe*" includes the "*seven golden vials* (or bowls) *full of the wrath of God*" (Revelation

thou shouldest give reward unto thy servants the prophets, and to the saints, and them that fear thy name, small and great; and shouldest destroy them which destroy the earth (Revelation 11:18).

15:7; 16:1-21), which come first upon Rome and then upon the beast, the false prophet, and the kings from the sun-rising and their armies.

Thus the phrase, *"the nations were angry"* (Revelation 11:18) will reveal the anger of the nations with each other in the civil war that is to erupt and that ends when the beast and the ten kings destroy Rome by fire (Revelation 17:16). Then the nations were also to be angry *"against the Lord, and against his anointed"* (Psalm 2:2) at the return of Jesus when He comes to fight against the beast, and the kings of the earth and their armies (Revelation 19:11-21). The phrase, *"thy wrath is come"* (Revelation 11:18), refers specifically to the seven vials, or bowls, of God's wrath. The seventh bowl of God's wrath includes events that occur at the time of Jesus' return, in which Jesus brings destruction, not only to the armies and cities of the Roman Empire but upon the armies and cities of the three previous world empires as well. Thus the phrase *"the cities of the nations fell"* (Revelation 16:19b) must include not only the cities of the Roman Empire, but also those in the remnants of the Babylonian, Medo-Persian, and Greek empires as Revelation correlates closely with Daniel. Daniel 2:31-45 and 7:1-27, as well as Revelation 16:12, *"the kings of the east* (or *from the sun-rising)"*, indicates that these three former empires were also included.

But while *"the third woe"* brought doom for the Roman Empire, for the three former world empires, for the beast, and the kings of the earth and their armies, *it was clearly not a "woe" for Christians!* This is indicated by the phrase given within the period of *"the third woe...that thou shouldest give reward unto thy servants the prophets* (the two witnesses again), *and to the saints, and them that fear thy name, small and great"* (Revelation 11:18d).

Those faithful to Christ will have *"power over the nations"* and will *"rule them with a rod of iron"*

(Revelation 2:26-27). We are to live and reign with Christ "*a thousand years*" (Revelation 20:4-6). We are to live in "*the holy city, New Jerusalem,*" which comes down from God out of heaven, and we are to be "*prepared as a bride adorned for her husband*" (Revelation 21:2).

The phrase, "*and the time of the dead, that they should be judged*" (Revelation 11:18) is also within the period of "*the third woe*" and is referred to further in Revelation 20:11-15. In this passage John writes, "*And I saw the dead, small and great, stand before God; and the books were opened: and another book was opened, which is the book of life: and the dead were judged out of those things which were written in the books, according to their works*" (Revelation 20:12).

"*The third woe,*" which was to come against those who rejected Jesus, continues through the millennium (Revelation 20:4-6), and through the great war that follows it (Revelation 20:7-10), through the judgment of the "*great white throne*" (Revelation 20:11), continues eternally in "*the lake of fire*" (Revelation 20:15).

It might be well, then, to note here the following difference between the time period encompassed by the seventh trumpet (Revelation 11:15-19), and the time period encompassed by the seventh vial, or bowl, or God's wrath. The seventh trumpet, which covers the period from Revelation 16:1–22:5, covers many more events and a far longer period of time than does the seventh bowl of God's wrath. The seventh trumpet encompasses all the bowls of God's wrath, but far more. The seventh bowl of God's wrath occurs along with, and just after, the return of Jesus (Revelation 19:11-21), which is indicated by the words of God, "*It is done*" (Revelation 16:17).

The return of Jesus is, then, a part of "*the third woe,*" as He brings to a final end the Babylonian, Medo-Persian, Greek, and Roman Empires. He levels their cities (Revelation 16:18-19) and destroys their armies (Revelation 19:17-21).

But during this "*third woe*" for the enemies of Jesus, His followers are not suffering any woe at all. We are to be blessed by "*the tree of life*" to serve God and the Lamb (Revelation 22:2-3). We will see the face of God (see also Matthew 5:8) and of Jesus. God's name, the new name of Jesus, and the name of the New Jerusalem will be written in our foreheads (Revelation 3:12; 22:4).

So "*the third woe*" is not for the servants of God and of Jesus.

The final phrase in Revelation 11:18 is "…*and shouldest destroy them which destroy the earth.*" The Greek word used in this passage for "*destroy*" is "*diaphtheiro,*" which carries the double meaning of both *destroy* and *corrupt.* (In the King James version "*diaphtheiro*" is translated "*corrupt*" or "*corrupteth*" in 1 Timothy 6:5 and in Luke 12:33, "*destroyed*" or "*destroy*" in Revelation 8:9; 11:18; and "*perish*" in 2 Corinthians 4:16.)

In Revelation 19:2, it is "*the great whore*" (Rome), which did "*corrupt* (Greek, *ephtheire,* from *phtheiro, corrupt* or *destroy*) *the earth.*" Those who corrupt the earth will be destroyed!

And the temple of God was opened in heaven, and there was seen in his temple the ark of his testament: and there were lightnings, and voices, and thunderings, and an earthquake, and great hail (Revelation 11:19).

The concluding verse of this vision, Revelation 11:19, tells of "*the temple of God*" being "*opened in heaven,*" and "*seen*" therein was "*the ark of his testament,*" the heavenly ark from which the one on earth had been patterned (see Hebrews 8:5). The one on earth had been lost after the destruction of Jerusalem by Nebuchadnezzar, though an account in 2 Maccabees 2:4-8 states that Jeremiah, prompted by a divine message, took the Tent of Meeting and the ark to the mountain from which Moses saw God's promised land. There Jeremiah saw a cave-dwelling. He carried the tent, the ark, and the incense-altar into it, and then blocked up the entrance.

Jeremiah is said to have prophesied, "*The place shall remain unknown, until God finally gathers His people together and shows mercy to them. Then the Lord will bring these things to light again, and the glory of the Lord will appear with the cloud, as it was seen both in the time of Moses and when Solomon prayed that the shrine might be worthily consecrated"* (2 Maccabees 2:7-8, The New English Bible).

Be that as it may, "*the ark of His testimony*" in heaven was safe, even though the one on earth was lost.

The final phrase gives a heavenly array of awesome wonders to the eyes and ears. It would be interesting to compare this final passage concluding the seventh trumpet with similar passages, including those at the end of the seventh seal and of the seventh bowl (or vial) of God's wrath.

One should take notice in these comparisons of the increase in both the number of events and their intensity as we come closer to the prophesied event.

"*And out of the throne proceeded **lightnings** and **thunderings**, and **voices**.*" -Revelation 4:5a

(Notice three heavenly sights or sounds.)

"*And the angel took the censer, and filled it with fire of the altar, and cast it into the earth: and there were **voices**, and **thunderings**, and **lightnings**, and an **earthquake***" (Revelation 8:5).

(Notice four heavenly sights or sounds, an increase of one.)

"*And the temple of God was opened in heaven, and there was seen in his temple the ark of his testament: and there were **lightnings**, and **voices**, and **thunderings**, and an **earthquake**, and **great hail**''* (Revelation 11:19).

(Notice five heavenly sights or sounds, an increase of one over Revelation 8:5.)

"*And the seventh angel poured out his vial (bowl) into the air; and there came a great voice out of the temple of heaven, from the throne, saying, It is done. And there were **voices**, and **thunders**, and **lightnings**; and there was a **great earthquake** such as was not since men were upon the earth, so mighty an earthquake, and so great. And the great city was divided into three parts, and the cities of the nations fell: and great Babylon came in remembrance before God, to give unto her the cup of the wine of the fierceness of his wrath. And **every island fled away and the mountains were not found**. And there fell upon men a **great hail** out of heaven, every stone about the weight of a* *talent: and men blasphemed God because of the plague of the hail; for the plague thereof was exceeding great*" (Revelation 16:17-21).

(Notice six heavenly sights or sounds, also an increase in intensity over Revelation 11:19.)

Thus, the last verse of the seventh seal (Revelation 8:5) the last verse of the seventh trumpet (Revelation 11:19), and the last verses of the seventh bowl (or vial) of God's wrath (Revelation 16:17-21) blend together, building into a crescendo so that as we come closer to this final event, the picture of God's awesome wrath becomes more fearsome!

Through these awesome judgments, "*great Babylon*" (Rome) (Revelation 16:19) was fully destroyed as Daniel also had prophesied (Daniel 2:44; 7:26-27), and the time had come for the establishment of the kingdom of God.

Concluding Remarks

Revelation contains seven prophetic units.[46] Revelation 6:1–11:19, was one prophetic unit. Revelation 12:1–13:18 is another prophetic unit. It presents some of the same themes as we saw in Revelation 6:1–11:19, but in a different way. New material is also included. For instance, the Jewish believers in Jesus from Jerusalem were presented in Revelation 6:1–11:19 as the 144,000 who were sealed, or protected. In Revelation 12:1–13:18 these same ones are presented as a woman (true Israel) who gives birth to Jesus and who flees into the wilderness (Pella) for three and a half years, the length of the Roman-Jewish War.

The "*war in heaven*" (Revelation 12:7-12) is new material and speaks of an amazing war that took place in heaven in A.D. 66, but *which was viewed from earth*. This war was first prophesied by Daniel (12:1), and is reported and interpreted here by John. It was also recorded by two ancient historians—Josephus, a Jew, and Tacitus, a Roman—both of whose quotations regarding this momentous event will be given in our outline on Revelation 12:1–13:18.

We also will find in this next prophetic unit the beast's "*war with the saints*" (Revelation 13:7), which we saw presented in a different way in

---

46. The seven prophetic units of Revelation are:

    (1)   Revelation 6:1 to 11:19
    (2)   Revelation 12:1 to 13:18
    (3)   Revelation 14:1-20
    (4)   Revelation 15:1 to 16:21
    (5)   Revelation 17:1 to 19:10
    (6)   Revelation 19:11 to 21:8
    (7)   Revelation 21:9 to 22:5

Revelation 7:9-17. New material comes in the form of the false prophet (compare Revelation 13:11 with 16:13 and 19:20), the *"image of the beast,"* and the beast's identification number of *"six hundred threescore and six"* (Revelation 13:18).

In this next chapter, we will not only see how the events of Revelation 12 were fulfilled in the past, but we will also begin to understand how Revelation 13 would have been fulfilled then, had it not been thrown into the future by a massive repentance in Rome. This will help us to gain some insights as to how these events will be fulfilled in the future!

Revelation 12
The Woman Clothed with the Sun

One of the interesting things we notice as we move from vision to vision in Revelation is that some of the same themes are presented again and again in the various visions. But these themes may be presented in different ways and expanded upon, with new material being added. This is true in the present vision.

And there appeared a great wonder in heaven; a woman clothed with the sun, and the moon under her feet, and upon her head a crown of twelve stars:

2 And she being with child cried, travailing in birth, and pained to be delivered (Revelation 12:1-2).

(a) The woman identified (Revelation 12:1). Several important identifying characteristics are given in this verse by which this woman can be positively identified. We read, "*And there appeared a great wonder in heaven; a woman clothed with the sun, and the moon under her feet, and upon her head a crown of twelve stars.*"

The above passage refers to the dream of Joseph in Genesis 37:9. "*And he* (Joseph) *dreamed yet another dream, and told it his brethren, and said, Behold, I have dreamed a dream more; and behold, the sun and the moon and the eleven stars made obeisance to me.*

Joseph told this dream to his father, who correctly understood its meaning: "*Shall I and thy mother and thy brethren indeed come to bow down ourselves to thee to the earth?*" (Genesis 37:10b). In Joseph's dream, Jacob, his father, *is represented by the sun.* Leah is here called Joseph's mother—since Rachel, his real mother, was now dead (Genesis 35:16-18)—and *is represented by* the moon, and *each of Joseph's brothers is represented by a star.*

These symbols—the sun, the moon, and the stars—are in Revelation 12:1 to identify this "*woman*" as Israel! But she is not unbelieving Israel. That doesn't fit, and besides Jesus tells John of those "*which say they are Jews and are not, but are the synagogue of Satan*" (Revelation 2:9; 3:9). This "*woman*" is the true believing Israel; the Jews from Jerusalem who follow Jesus. In this passage, this woman refers to the very same group as the 144,000 (Revelation 7:4-8), and her flight into the wilderness was the flight of the Jerusalem church to Pella.

(b) The woman in travail (Revelation 12:2-6). Israel was sometimes pictured in the Old Testament as a woman in travail (Isaiah 26:17; 66:7-8; Micah 4:10).[47] In these passages, the "*child,*" or "*man child,*" is an obvious reference to Jesus (see Revelation 12:5).

And there appeared another wonder in heaven; and behold a great red dragon, having seven heads and ten horns, and seven crowns upon his heads.

The "*great red dragon*" (Revelation 12:3) is Satan, but he looks much like the "*beast*" of Revelation 13:1 in that both have "*seven heads*" and "*ten horns,*" though the dragon has seven crowns, and the beast, ten.

4 And his tail drew the third part of the stars of heaven, and did cast them to the earth: and the dragon stood before the woman which was ready to be delivered, for to

The dragon is here represented as operating through the Roman Empire, and as doing two things.

(1) "*His tail drew the third part of the stars of heaven, and did cast them to the earth*" (Revelation 12:4a).

"*The third part*" relates to Jerusalem. "*The stars of heaven*" refer to persons highly

---

47. *Like as a woman with child, that draweth near the time of her delivery, is in pain, and crieth out in her pangs; so have we been in thy sight, O Lord* (Isaiah 26:17).

Be in pain, and labour to bring forth, O daughter of Zion, like a woman in travail: for now shalt thou go forth out of the city, and thou shalt dwell in the field, and thou shalt go even to Babylon; there shalt thou be delivered; there the Lord shall redeem thee from the hand of thine enemies (Micah 4:10).

*devour her child as
soon as it was born.*

*5 And she brought
forth a man child,
who was to rule all
nations with a rod of
iron: and her child
was caught up unto
God, and to his throne*
(Revelation 12:3-5).

placed.[48] (See Daniel 8:9, 10 in The Living Bible, or the Amplified Bible, where "*stars*" refer to the exalted or highly placed persons which Antiochus Epiphanes overthrew. Also, as we have previously noted, in Isaiah 14:12, the "*heylel*" in the Hebrew text should be rendered "*day star*" or "*morning star*," rather than "*Lucifer*." The "*day star*" referred to a person highly placed, that is, in this instance to Nebuchadnezzar,[49] "*king of Babylon*" (Isaiah 14:4).) *Satan, operating through the Roman Empire, was seen prophetically as having thrown down the highly placed Jews in Jerusalem.* Thus, the Jewish Council, or Sanhedrin, a body of 71 members having both religious and civil authority, was destroyed in the fall of Jerusalem.

(2) "*The dragon stood before the woman which was ready to be delivered, for to devour her child as soon as it was born*" (Revelation 12:4b). This passage referred to Herod's attempt to *kill Jesus in His infancy.* (See Matthew 2:1-18, especially verse 16.)

Note: Satan had often tried to kill key persons in God's program in order to

---

48. *And [in my vision] this horn grew great, even against the host of heaven [God's true people, the saints], and some of the host and of the stars [priests] it cast down to the ground and trampled on them* (Daniel 8:10 The Amplified Bible).

And it waxed great, even to the host of heaven; and it cast down some of the host and of the stars to the ground, and stamped upon them (Daniel 8:10 King James Version).

He fought against the people of God and defeated some of their leaders (Daniel 8:10 The Living Bible).

"*Interestingly, stars can stand for exalted creatures* (no doubt because of their brilliance and glory), *either foes of God or his servants.*" *The International Standard Bible Encyclopedia*, Volume Four, "Star," page 612.

Also an "*angel*" is seen as a "*star*" (compare Revelation 9:1 with Revelation 9:11).

49. Nebuchadnezzar, "*king of Babylon*," was seen as a star

How are you fallen from Heaven, O light-bringer and day-star, son of the morning! How you are cut down to the ground, you who weakened and laid prostrate the nations [O blasphemous, satanic king of Babylon!] (Isaiah 14:12 The Amplified Bible).

frustrate God's divine plan. For example, Satan tried to kill *Moses* by Pharaoh (Exodus 1:16); *David* by Saul (1 Samuel 19); *Joash* (David's seed) by Queen Athaliah (2 Kings 11:1-2); *King Ahaz* (David's seed) by the kings of Israel and Syria (Isaiah 7:6); *Esther* and the *Jews* by Haman (Esther 3:13); *Jesus* by Herod (Matthew 2:1-18); and in the future, *the Christians* by the beast (Daniel 7:21-22; Revelation 13:7).

6 And the woman fled into the wilderness, where she hath a place prepared of God, that they should feed her there a thousand two hundred and threescore days (Revelation 12:6).

7 And there was war in heaven: Michael and his angels fought against the dragon; and the dragon fought and his angels,

8 And prevailed not; neither was their

"*The woman fled into the wilderness*" (Revelation 12:6a). The Jewish believers in Jesus in Jerusalem fled into the wilderness, "*where she hath a place prepared of God*" (that is, Pella), "*that they should feed her there a thousand two hundred and threescore days*" (Revelation 12:6b). (This was the length of the Roman-Jewish War from A.D. 66-70.)

(c) "*And there was war in heaven*" (Revelation 12:7). *Which* heaven? There are three heavens (2 Corinthians 12:2).[50] In Jewish theology, there was one which we see *by day* (the first, or lowest heaven, where the birds fly); one which we see *by night* (the second heaven, where the stars are); and one which we see *by faith* (the third heaven, where the throne of God is). Since Satan is "*the prince of the power of the air*" (Ephesians 2:2), it is clear that this war was in the first heaven, the heaven closest to earth.

---

50. *I knew a man in Christ above fourteen years ago, (whether in the body, I cannot tell; or whether out of the body, I cannot tell: God knoweth;) such an one caught up to the third heaven* (2 Corinthians 12:2).

There cannot be a "*third heaven*" without a first heaven, and a second heaven. Thus, there are three heavens.

Also, see Ephesians 2:2, *Wherein in time past ye walked according to the course of this world, according to the prince of the power of the air, the spirit that now worketh in the children of disobedience.*

This is carefully explained in *Plains of Glory and Gloom*, by H. A. Baker. On page 48, H. A. Baker writes, "*The earth is surrounded by a series of heavenly plains...In Satan's rebellion he and the angels who rebelled with him usurped these plains in the First heaven, as well as the first perfect earth.*"

Baker's book is based upon many visions by many people whose writings confirm and explain the Scriptures.

place found any more in heaven. And the great dragon was cast out, that old serpent, called the Devil, and Satan, which deceiveth the whole world: he was cast out into the earth, and his angels were cast out with him.

10 And I heard a loud voice saying in heaven, Now is come salvation, and strength, and the king-dom of our God, and the power of his Christ: for the accuser of our brethren is cast down, which accused them before our God day and night.

11 And they overcame him by the blood of the Lamb, and by the word of their testi-mony; and they loved not their lives unto the death (Revelation 12:7-11).

Daniel had also foretold this very event: "*And at that time shall Michael stand up, the great prince which standeth for the children of thy people: and there shall be a time of trouble, such as never since there was a nation even to that same time: and at that time thy people shall be delivered, every one that shall be found written in the book*" (Daniel 12:1). It appears that God's angels were battling their way through the dragon's angels to shepherd these Jewish believers to their place of safety.

This "war in heaven" was visible from earth and both the Roman historian, Tacitus, and the Jewish historian, Josephus, record this very heavenly conflict.

Tacitus wrote,

Armies were seen to fight in the sky, and their armor looked of a bright light color, and the temple shone with sudden flashes of fire out of the clouds" (Wars, Appendix, Dissertation III; Chapter XIII).

Josephus wrote,

Besides these, a few days after that feast, on the one-and-twentieth day of the month Artemisius (Jyar), a certain prodigious and incredible phenomenon appeared; I suppose the account of it would seem to be a fable, were it not related by those that saw it and were not the events that followed it of so considerable a nature as to deserve such signals: for, before sun-setting, chariots and troops of soldiers in their armor were seen running about among the clouds, and surrounding of cities (Wars, VI. V. 3).

Josephus dates this "*war in heaven*" on the 21st of Artemisius, according to the Syro-Macedonian calendar (May, A.D. 66, by our calendar). About 5 1/2 months later, on the 8th of Dius (October-November, A.D. 66), the Roman general, Cestius Gallus, suffered a devastating defeat by the Jews shortly after he broke off his siege of Jerusalem. Immediately, the Jerusalem Jews who believed in Jesus left the city and went to Pella. (See Luke 21:20-21.) In February, A.D. 67, the Roman general, Vespasian, arrived and the Roman-Jewish War began in earnest.

Daniel (12:1) had prophesied of this "*war in heaven*," and Tacitus and Josephus had recorded it. But John explained it from God's point of view—by revelation!

12 Therefore rejoice, ye heavens, and ye that dwell in them. Woe to the inhabitants of the earth and of the sea! for the devil is come down unto you, having great wrath, because he knoweth that he hath but a short time.

"*A short time*" (Revelation 12:12b). The dragon (Satan) wanted to persecute the true Israel, but had only three and a half years to accomplish this.

(d) The woman received "*two wings of a great eagle, that she might fly into the wilderness*" (Revelation 12:14).

This figure of speech comes from the message that God gave Moses for Israel in Exodus 19:4. "*Ye have seen what I did unto the Egyptians, and how I bare you on eagle's wings, and brought you unto myself.*" Actually, in both instances (Exodus 19:4; Revelation 12:14) they walked the distances involved, but the "*eagle's wings*" indicated God's divine protection as in Psalm 91:4: "*He shall cover thee with his feathers, and under his wings shalt thou trust.*"

13 And when the dragon saw that he was cast unto the earth, he persecuted the woman which brought forth the man child.

14 And to the woman were given two wings of a great

(e) The serpent casts out of his mouth water as a flood after the woman (Revelation 12:15-17a).

In Scripture, invading armies are sometimes compared to the waters of a flood.[51] (See espe-

51. See Scriptures listed in Notes to Revelation 16:3 and also the following passages.

"*When the enemy shall come in like a flood, the Spirit of the Lord shall lift up a standard against him*" (Isaiah 59:19b).

"*Who is this that cometh up as a flood, whose waters are moved as the rivers?*
Egypt riseth up like a flood, and his waters are moved like the rivers; and he saith, I will go up, and will cover the earth; I will destroy the city and the inhabitants thereof.
Come up, ye horses; and rage, ye chariots; and let the mighty men come forth; the Ethiopians and the Libyans that handle the shield; and the Lydians, that handle and bend the bow.
For this is the day of the Lord God of hosts, a day of vengeance, that he may avenge him of his

continued on next page

eagle, that she might fly into the wilderness, into her place, where she is nourished for a time, and times, and half a time, from the face of the serpent.

15 And the serpent cast out of his mouth water **as a flood** *after the woman, that he might cause her to be carried away* **of the flood.**

16 And the earth helped the woman, and the earth opened her mouth, and **swallowed up the flood** *which the dragon cast out of his mouth.*

17 And the dragon was wroth with the woman, and went to make war with the remnant of her seed, which keep the commandments of God, and have the testimony of Jesus Christ (Revelation 12:12-17).

cially Isaiah 8:7-8; Jeremiah 46:7-9; 47:2-3.) Thus, the Roman-Jewish War was fought within a few miles of Pella, the city to which the Jerusalem Jews who believed in Jesus had fled. The Roman army went through Sythopolis, eight miles NE of Pella; and later it destroyed Gerasa, 21 miles SW of Pella, and also Gadera, 15 miles N of Pella, but stopped short of Pella itself.

Thus "*the earth helped the woman*" (Revelation 12:16). When the Roman armies stopped short of the city in which the followers of Jesus from Jerusalem had taken refuge, Satan was frustrated in his evil designs against them. Then "*the dragon* (Satan)*…went to make war with* **the remnant of her seed**." The bold words refer to *the Gentile believers.* These are the remnant of the seed of the woman "*which keep the commandments of God, and have the testimony of Jesus Christ*" (Revelation 12:17b).

Revelation 13 now proceeds to explain how "*the dragon*" would persecute these Gentile believers in Jesus.

---

adversaries: and the sword shall devour, and it shall be satiate and made drunk with their blood: for the Lord God of hosts hath a sacrifice in the north country by the river Euphrates" (Jeremiah 46:7-10).

"The word of the Lord that came to Jeremiah the prophet against the Philistines, before that Pharaoh smote Gaza.
Thus saith the Lord; Behold, waters rise up out of the north, and shall be an overflowing flood, and shall overflow the land, and all that is therein; the city, and them that dwell therein: then the men shall cry, and all the inhabitants of the land shall howl.
At the noise of the stamping of the hoofs of his strong horses, at the rushing of his chariots, and at the rumbling of his wheels, the fathers shall not look back to their children for feebleness of hands" (Jeremiah 47:1-3).

Revelation 13
The Dragon's War Against the Gentile Church

The dragon, unable to destroy Jesus who ascended into heaven, and unable to destroy the Jews from Jerusalem who believe in Jesus, becomes infuriated and seeks to destroy the Gentile Church (see Revelation 13).

The thoughts of Revelation 13:1-10 are found in Daniel 7. These two passages are placed side by side in the columns below.

Daniel 7:1,4-8,21,24-25

*1 And four great beasts **came up from the sea**, diverse one from another.*

4 The first was like a lion, and had eagle's wings: I beheld till the wings thereof were plucked, and it was lifted up from the earth, and made stand upon the feet as a man, and a man's heart was given to it.

5 And behold another beast, a

Revelation 13:1-10

*1 And I stood upon the sand of the sea, and saw a **beast rise up out of the sea**, having seven heads and ten horns, and upon his horns ten crowns, and upon his heads the name of **blasphemy**.*

*2 And the beast which I saw was like unto a **leopard**, and his feet were as the feet of a **bear**, and his mouth as the mouth of a*

In Revelation 13:1, the term "*beast*" refers to the Roman Empire, but it also sometimes refers to the head of the Roman Empire (as in Revelation 13:14; 16:13; 17:8,11; 19:20). This "*beast*," the Roman Empire, has "*seven heads*" and "*ten horns, and upon his horns ten crowns.*" The "*seven heads*" were the seven mountains, or hills of Rome (Revelation 17:9), but they were also "*seven kings*" (Revelation 17:10), and in this passage it is the "*seven kings*" that are in view (Revelation 13:3). The "*ten horns*" with "*ten crowns*" are also ten kings that had received no kingdom at John's writing, but would receive power as kings "*one hour*" (a brief period of time) with the beast (Revelation 17:12). We see the "*ten horns*" also in Daniel 7:7,20,24. In Daniel, the "*beast*" of Revelation is referred to as the "*little horn.*" (See Daniel 7:8,11,20,24-26.)

"*The name of blasphemy*" (Revelation 13:1b) refers to the practice of the Roman emperors claiming to be a

second, like to a **bear**, *and it raised up itself on one side, and it had three ribs in the mouth of it between the teeth of it: and they said thus unto it, Arise, devour much flesh.*

6 After this I beheld, and lo another, like a **leopard**, *which had upon the back of it four wings of a fowl; the beast had also four heads; and dominion was given to it.*

lion: *and the dragon gave him his power, and his seat, and great authority.*

"god." (See 2 Thessalonians 2:4; also Daniel 7:8, 20, 25.) The description of the "*beast*" is not intended to give his actual appearance, but is to portray certain ideas about him.

In Revelation 13:2, the "*beast,*" the Roman Empire, has the combined strength of the Greek, Medo-Persian, and Babylonian empires. The Roman Empire would be as swift as "*a leopard*" (Greek Empire, see Daniel 7:6); and would have strength as "*the feet of a bear*" (Medo-Persian Empire, see Daniel 7:5); and would have the voracious appetite of "*the mouth of a lion*" (Babylonian Empire, see Daniel 7:4).

"*And the dragon gave him his power, and his seat, and great authority*" (Revelation 13:2b). "*The dragon's…power*" was the brute force of the Roman army. His "*great authority*" was his ironhanded rule over the wide area that Rome ruled. "*The dragon's…seat*" was Rome (see Revelation 17:7,9,18). Rome will be the seat of the coming beast, just as it was the seat of the beast of the past:

7 After this I saw in the night visions, and behold a fourth beast, dreadful and terrible, and strong exceedingly; and it had great iron teeth: it devoured and brake in pieces, and stamped the residue

3 And I saw one of his heads as it were wounded to death; and his deadly wound was healed: and all the world wondered after the beast.

"*And I saw one of his heads as it were wounded to death; and his deadly wound was healed…*" (Revelation 13:3a). One of the first seven heads, or kings, of Rome was to receive a deadly wound, but this deadly wound was to have been healed. This thought is restated briefly in Revelation 13:12 ("*the first beast, whose deadly wound was healed*"), and is stated more fully in Revelation 13:14 ("*the beast, which had the* **wound by a sword**, *and did live*"). The Amplified Bible translates these words, "*…the beast which was wounded* **by the (small) sword** *and still lived.*"

with the feet of it: and it was diverse from all the beasts that were before it; and it had ten horns.

The Greek language has two words for sword. *Vine's Expository Dictionary of New Testament Words*, pg. 1123, gives these words as *machaira*, "*a short sword or dagger*," and *rhomphaia*, "*a Thracian weapon of large size*." The word used in Revelation 13:14 is *machaira*, "*a short sword or dagger*."

This passage, Revelation 13:14, refers, no doubt, to the fact that Nero, the fifth Roman emperor, or king, attempted suicide on June 9, A.D. 68, by pushing a short sword, or dagger, into his throat. But he was unable to accomplish the task on his own and so summoned his servant, Epaphroditis, to push the blade deeper. It was this action to which Revelation 13:3a, 12b, and 14b refer.

While Caligula was also killed with a sword, two factors show that these references indicate Nero:

(1) Caligula was killed with a large sword. Nero was killed with a *machaira*, "*a short sword or dagger*."

(2) The number 666 (Revelation 13:18) is the number of Nero Caesar in the Aramaic language. It is not the number of Caligula.

"*His deadly wound was healed*" (Revelation 13:3a). This passage, together with other passages (Revelation 11:7; 17:8,10-11) teaches that *Nero would return*—that is, his persecuting spirit would return, *in the person of the "eighth"* (Revelation 17:11) *Roman king, Domitian.*

8 I considered the horns, and, behold, there came up

5 And there was given unto him a **mouth speak-**

"*And they worshipped the dragon which gave power unto the beast: and they worshipped the beast*" (Revelation 13:4a). Domitian required the worship of his

among them another little horn, before whom there were three of the first horns plucked up by the roots: and, behold, in this horn were eyes like the eyes of man, and a mouth speaking great things. 4 And they worshipped the dragon which gave power unto the beast: and they worshipped the beast, saying, Who is like unto the beast? Who is able to make war with him?

ing great things and blasphemies; and power was given unto him to continue forty and two months.

6 And he opened his mouth in blasphemy against God, to blaspheme his name, and his tabernacle, and them that dwell in heaven.

subjects.[52] This was practiced by worshiping one of his statues, or images, with incense and wine. Domitian did not claim to be simply a god—but God! He required officials to refer to him in their documents as "*Dominos et Deus Noster*"—"our Lord and God." He filled Rome with statues of himself, and at Ephesus, Domitian's own temple stood with a colossal cult-statue. As God-monarch of the Roman Empire, he was the first to require his subjects to swear by his genius, and he tested their loyalty to him by the sacrifice they offered to his image. Those refusing were charged with atheism and then slain. Dio Cassius notes an increasing number of trials for this offense in Domitian's last years (*Dio* LXVII, 14, 1, 2). Domitian organized a new order of priests, the Flaviales, to tend to his worship.

Domitian was hated by the Roman senate, but because he increased the pay of the Roman army by a third, he had their loyalty! Thus, the question "*who is able to make war with him?*" (Revelation 13:4b) would evoke the answer, "No one!"

Both Domitian's "*blasphemy*" (Revelation 13:5-6) and the "*forty and two months*" (Revelation 13:5b) were prophesied in Daniel 7:25, and in both places refer to the length of his persecution against the saints.

---

52. "*Who is like unto the beast?*"

This question is both a parody of the name Michael (Revelation 12:7) which, in the Hebrew, means, "Who is like God?," and also a parody of Exodus 15:11, Psalm 35:10; and Psalm 113:5.

Who is like unto thee, O Lord, among the gods? Who is like thee, glorious in holiness, fearful in praises, doing wonders? (Exodus 15:11).

All my bones shall say, Lord, who is like unto thee, which deliverest the poor from him that is too strong for him, yea, the poor and the needy from him that spoileth him? (Psalm 35:10).

Who is like unto the Lord our God, who dwelleth on high (Psalm 113:5).

21 I beheld, and the same horn made **war with the saints, and prevailed against them;**

24 And the ten horns out of this kingdom are ten kings that shall arise: and another shall rise after them; and he shall be diverse from the first, and he shall subdue three kings.

25 And he shall speak **great words against the most High,** and shall wear out the saints of the most High, and think to change times and laws: and

7 And it was given unto him to make **war with the saints, and to overcome them:** and power was given him over all[53] kindreds, and tongues, and nations.

8 And all that dwell upon the earth shall worship him, whose names are not written in the book of life of the Lamb slain from the foundation of the world.

9 If any man have an ear, let him hear.

10 He that leadeth into captivity shall go into captivity: he that killeth with the sword

"And it was given unto him to make war with the saints, and to overcome them" (Revelation 13:7). Daniel wrote, "I beheld, and the same horn made war with the saints, and prevailed against them" (Daniel 7:21). Domitian was also to have made "war" against the two witnesses (Revelation 11:7). It is not stated whether the "war" against the two witnesses, and the "war with the saints" was to have taken place at the same time, but the time period of both wars was three and a half years (Revelation 11:3; 13:5), and because, as we have previously shown, this time period for Rome was to complete a prophetic time period of seven years' duration, this seems to suggest that the war against the two witnesses, and the war against the saints took place during the same three and a half years.

The statement, "He that leadeth into captivity shall go into captivity" (Revelation 13:10), is a rendering not well supported in our best manuscripts. A better reading is, "He that is for captivity, shall go into captivity" and this thought comes from Jeremiah 15:2, "…and such as for the captivity, to the captivity." John may have been reminded of his current captivity on Patmos. Resistance would have been hopeless, and so John receives inspiration to write, "He that killeth with the sword must be killed with the sword" (Revelation 13:10b). John had seen the futility of resistance to Roman might, not only for

---

53. "…And power was given him over all kindreds, and tongues, and nations"

A study of the use of the word "all" in Scriptures will show that the Hebrews did not necessarily use the word "all" in a literal sense.

"…and all the cattle of Egypt died…" (Exodus 9:6).

But the cattle of Egypt still receive plagues, as "a boil breaking forth upon man, and upon beast (Hebrew, behemah, cattle), throughout all the land of Egypt" (Exodus 9:9), and "hail" (Exodus 9:19-21). Also, when God slew "all the firstborn of the land of Egypt," this included "all the first-born of cattle." (Exodus 12:29).

they shall be | *must be killed* | himself but also for other captured
given into his | *with the* | Christians. He must have recalled the
hand until a | *sword.*[54] *Here is* | words of Jesus, *"...all they that take the*
time and times | *the patience* | *sword shall perish with the sword"*
and the divid- | *and the faith of* | (Matthew 26:52).
ing of time. | *the saints.*

And I beheld another | *"And I beheld another beast* **coming up out of the**
beast coming up out of | **earth"** (Revelation 13:11a). This beast seems to be
the earth;[55] *and he* | contrasted with the first beast, *"I...saw a beast* **rise**
had two horns like a | **up out of the sea"** (Revelation 13:1). These two
lamb, and he spake as | phrases come from Daniel 7:3 and 7:17. But in
a dragon (Revelation | Daniel 7:3 we read of *"four great beasts"* which
13:11). | *"came up* **from the sea,"** while in Daniel 7:17 the
| same *"great beasts"* **"shall arise out of the earth."**

In Daniel, then, these two phrases do not seem to
have a significant difference as both phrases apply
to the same four great beasts. But the contrast in
Revelation between the two phrases suggests that
to John a distinction is here in Revelation to be
made. The *"sea*[56]*"* like the *"many waters"* (of
Revelation 17:1) would be *"peoples, and multitudes, and nations, and tongues"* (as in Revelation
17:15). Thus the first beast, the Roman Empire, is
said *to rise up from many peoples.*

The second beast John saw *"coming up out of the
earth."* This thought suggests that this beast had
previously been in a space under the earth. The
concept is similar in meaning to the phrase,

---

54. *And it shall come to pass, if they say unto thee, Whither shall we go forth? then thou shalt tell them,
    Thus saith the Lord; Such as for death, to death; and such as are for the sword, to the sword; and
    such as are for the famine, to the famine; and such as are for the captivity, to the captivity*
    (Jeremiah 15:2).

    *And when he cometh, he shall smite the land of Egypt, and deliver such as are for death to death; and
    as are for captivity to captivity; and such as are for the sword to the sword* (Jeremiah 43:11).

55. *And I stood upon the sand of the sea, and saw a beast rise up out of the sea, having seven heads
    and ten horns, and upon his horns ten crowns, and upon his heads the name of blasphemy*
    (Revelation 13:1).

    And four great beasts came up from the sea, diverse one from another (Daniel 7:3).

    These great beasts, which are four, are four kings, which shall arise out of the earth (Daniel 7:17).

56. The *"sea"* also symbolizes the *"wicked."* See Isaiah 57:20, *"But the wicked are like the troubled sea."*
    So the meaning of the word *"sea"* in Revelation 17:1 is the sea of wicked multitudes from many
    peoples.

"...*ascendeth out of the bottomless pit*" (Revelation 11:7; see also 9:1-2,11; 17:8; 20:1,3).

An ancient quotation put it, "*If there be a hell, Rome is built above it; it is an abyss from which all sins proceed*" (*Barnes' Notes*, Revelation, pg. 272). In a similar sense, in Revelation, "*the bottomless pit*" was thought of as beneath the city of Rome. *So in "coming up out of the earth," the second beast rose up out of the vileness and corruption of Rome!*

"*And he had two horns like a lamb, and he spake as a dragon*" (Revelation 13:llb). This passage was not given to describe the actual appearance of this beast, but rather to convey certain ideas about him. Because the first beast was primarily a system, rather than a person, we may expect this second beast to be a system, rather than a person, as well. And because this second beast has "*two horns like a lamb,*" he clearly assumes a religious character. But "*he spake as a dragon!*" He is, then, of Satan! In later passages in Revelation this second beast is referred to as "*the false prophet*" (Revelation 16:13; 19:20).

And he exerciseth all the power of the first beast before him, and causeth the earth (Greek, *ge, the earth, or land*) *and them which dwell therein to worship the first beast, whose deadly wound was healed* (Revelation 13:12).

One prominent identifying characteristic of this second beast,[57] "*the false prophet,*" is that he has no power (Greek, *exousia*, authority) except when he is in the presence of the first beast. Thus, "*he exerciseth all the power* (authority) *of the first beast before him*" (Revelation 13:12a); "*And deceiveth them that dwell on the earth by the means of those miracles which he had power* (authority) *to do in the sight of the beast*" (Revelation 13:14a); "*And the beast was taken, and with him the false prophet that wrought miracles before him*" (Revelation 19:20a).

---

57. This second "*beast*" which "*had two horns like a lamb,*" but "*spake as a dragon*" (Revelation 13:11b) is elsewhere called "*the false prophet.*"

And I saw three unclean spirits like frogs come out of the mouth of the dragon, and out of the mouth of the beast, and out of the mouth of the false prophet (Revelation 16:13).

And the beast was taken, and with him the false prophet that wrought miracles before him, with which he deceived them that had received the mark of the beast, and them that worshipped his image. These both were cast alive into a lake of fire burning with brimstone (Revelation 19:20).

And the devil that deceived them was cast into the lake of fire and brimstone, where the beast and the false prophet are, and shall be tormented day and night for ever and ever (Revelation 20:10).

This identifying characteristic points clearly to the *College of Augures* as *"the false prophet"* of Revelation.

The word, "augures," from "augur," means to predict, to prophesy, or to divine the future by the use of omens. Originally, the College of Augures consisted of three members, but before Domitian's time it consisted of 16 members. They used as omens the flight, singing, and feeding of birds; the appearance of the entrails of sacrificial animals; and other portents.

Their predictions were to discern whether the gods did, or did not, approve of an action, and their decisions affected all state business, including the appointment of priests, the consecration of temples, the reaping of crops, the meeting of assemblies for the election of magistrates, and the passing of laws.

But the College of Augures had no governmental authority of their own, and could not even report their own predictions except to presiding state officials, who were said to "possess the auspices." Thus, *"the false prophet"* (the College of Augures) could act only in the presence of the first beast, the governing authorities of the Roman realm.

"And causeth the earth and them which dwell therein to worship the first beast, whose deadly wound was healed" (Revelation 13:12b). *"The false prophet,"* the College of Augures—as they were seen muttering over the color of the entrails of a sacrificial animal—appeared to have a mysterious and divine power in that they seemed to have the ability to discern the minds of the gods. This caused people to feel that a mysterious and divine power was behind the Roman Empire, and thus they gave their worship to its head *"whose deadly wound was healed,"* that is, to Domitian.

And he doeth great wonders, so that he maketh fire come

"And he doeth great wonders, so that he maketh fire come down from heaven on the earth in the sight of men" (Revelation 13:13). This passage serves to

down from heaven on the earth in the sight of men.

14 And deceiveth them that dwell on the earth by the means of those miracles which he had power to do in the sight of the beast; saying to them that dwell on the earth, that they should make an image to the beast, which had the wound by a sword, and did live.

15 And he had power to give life (Greek, pneuma, a spirit) unto the image of the beast, that the image of the beast should both speak, and cause that as many as would not worship the image of the beast should be killed (Revelation 13:13-15).

remind us of the prophet Elijah who, on Mount Carmel, also brought fire "*down from heaven on the earth in the sight of men*" (as in 1 Kings 18:38).[58] The passage is not intended to suggest that the College of Augures actually brought fire down from heaven. It is rather given so that by recalling to mind the same incident in the life of Elijah we might identify this second beast in the role of a prophet. But since "*he spake as a dragon,*" that is, his inspiration came from Satan, he is a "*false prophet.*"

This 13th chapter of Revelation—having previously introduced the first beast (the Roman Empire) with its seven heads, or kings, and the second beast, or "*false prophet*" (the College of Augures)—now introduces the "*image to the beast, which had the wound by a sword, and did live*" (Revelation 13:14b). This refers, of course, to the images, or statues, of Domitian.

"*The false prophet*" "*had power to give life* (Greek, *pneuma*, a spirit) *unto the image of the beast*" (Revelation 13:15a).

"*Life*" is not a translation of the Greek word "*pneuma*" which appears here in the Greek text. Most other translations have "*give breath*" here, but they also fail to communicate the meaning intended. The literal translations (Young's; Concordant; Rotherham's) correctly render pneuma as "*spirit.*"

Out of 381 times in which *pneuma* is translated in the King James New Testament, this passage in Revelation 13:15 is the *only* time in which "*pneuma*" is rendered "*life.*" The King James translators rendered

---

58. The phrase, "*he maketh fire come down from heaven on the earth in the sight of men*" recalls a similar incident in the life of Elijah the prophet

And it came to pass at the time of the offering of the evening sacrifice, that Elijah the prophet came near, and said, Lord God of Abraham, Isaac, and of Israel, let it be known this day that thou art God in Israel, and that I am thy servant, and that I have done all these things at thy word.
Hear me, O Lord, hear me, that this people may know that thou art the Lord God, and that thou hast turned their heart back again.
Then the fire of the Lord fell, and consumed the burnt sacrifice, and the wood, and the stones, and the dust, and licked up the water that was in the trench.
And when all the people saw it, they fell on their faces: and they said, The Lord, he is the God; the Lord, he is the God (I Kings 18:36-38).

"*pneuma*" as "*ghost*" or "*Ghost*" *(with* "Holy") 91 times, and as "*spirit*" or "*Spirit*" (with "*Holy*") 288 times. One time (1 Corinthians 14:12) "*pneuma*" is rendered "*spiritual (gifts).*"

The Greek word for "*life*" is not "*pneuma,*" but "*bios,*" "*zoe,*" or "*psuche.*"

Young's Literal Translation of the Bible correctly renders this phrase, "*and there was given to it* (to the second beast, "*the false prophet*") *to give a spirit to the image of the beast…*" (Revelation 13:15a).

Giving "*life*" to an image, or idol, was not a biblical concept! Habakkuk (2:19) wrote of the idol, "*there is no breath at all in the midst of it.*" Jeremiah insisted concerning idols, in two identical passages (Jeremiah 10:14; 51:17), "*Every man is brutish in his knowledge: every founder is confounded by the graven image: for his molten image is falsehood, and **there is no breath in them**.*" In Psalm 135:15-17 we read, "*The idols of the heathen are silver and gold, the work of men's hands. They have mouths, but they speak not; eyes have they, but they see not; They have ears, but they hear not; neither is there any breath in their mouths.*" These passages did not suddenly become untrue with the arrival of Domitian's statues.

No, *the image of the beast was still dead*, but "*a spirit,*" or demon, was given to it, which may have spoken as a ventriloquist would with a "dummy." Demons are capable of speech. Images are not. False prophets, being themselves inspired by deceiving spirits, were able to use those same spirits to deceive others (1 John 4:1). The College of Augures, "*the false prophet,*" seemed to give an unnatural and demonic power to the images of Domitian. Spirits, or demons, generally hover about images, and are attracted by them. Both Moses (Deuteronomy 32:16-17) and Paul (1 Corinthians 10:19-20) teach that the worship given to idols is actually given to demons.[59] In the case of Domitian's images it was clearly an idolatrous, domineering, and murderous spirit that the College of Augures gave to it to "*cause that as many as would not worship the image of the beast should be killed*" (Revelation 13:15b).

16 And he causeth all, both small and great, rich and poor, free and bond, to receive a mark in their right hand, or in their foreheads:

The Greek word for "*mark*" is "*charagma.*" It denotes a stamp, or impress, or to engrave, and is the same word translated "*graven*" in Acts 17:29.

Because it was to be used in buying and selling, it would not have been invisible as was the "*mark*" of Ezekiel 9:4, nor "*the seal of the living God*" in Revelation 7:2.

17 And that no man might buy or sell, save he that had the mark, or the name of the beast, or the number of his name.

Inasmuch as slaves and prostitutes were branded on the forehead with the mark of their owner (See Jeremiah 3:3, "*a whore's forehead*"), this mark may also suggest ownership by the beast.

No known ancient writer has told us of a "666" mark being branded into the skin of the right hands or foreheads of the peoples of the Roman Empire. Thus, we may conclude that this development had not yet taken place when these prophecies were thrown into the future.

18 Here is wisdom. Let him that hath understanding count the number of the beast: for it is the number of a man; and his number is Six hundred threescore and six (Revelation 13:16-18).

This is the number of Nero Caesar in the Aramaic language, the earthly language of both Jesus and John, and the language, no doubt, in which Revelation was given.

In that language the alphabet served also as their numeral system. Thus, in Aramaic, Nero Caesar is NRON KSR, and the 666 is figured as follows:

---

59. *They provoked him to jealousy with strange gods, with abominations provoked they him to anger. They sacrificed unto devils, not to God; to gods whom they knew not, to new gods that came newly up, whom your fathers feared not* (Deuteronomy 32:16-17).

What say I then? that the idol is any thing, or that which is offered in sacrifice to idols is any thing? But I say, that the things which the Gentiles sacrifice, they sacrifice to devils (Greek, *daimonion, demons*), *and not to God: and I would not that ye should have fellowship with devils* (Greek, *daimonion, demons*) (1 Corinthians 10:19-20).

And they served their idols: which were a snare unto them.
Yea, they sacrificed their sons and their daughters unto devils,
And shed innocent blood, even the blood of their sons and of their daughters, whom they sacrificed unto the idols of Canaan: and the land was polluted with blood (Psalm 106:36-38).

And they shall no more offer their sacrifices unto devils, after whom they have gone a whoring (Leviticus 17:7).

N	50
R	200
O	6
N	50
K	100
S	60
R	200
	666

A few ancient manuscripts read "616," rather than "666."

The reason for this change is apparent. In Rome, where the Latin language predominated, Nero was written without the final "N." Because "N" was equivalent to 50, the sum of the letters would be 616 without it.[60]

Someone in Rome had changed the figure from 666 to 616, so that no one would miss the fact that that number pointed to Nero as the beast!

In *Redating the New Testament*, by John A.T. Robinson, pages 235, 236, we quote the following:

> *Further, for the naming of Nero as "the beast" there is the interesting parallel, quoted by Edmundson, from Philostratus' Apollonius of Tyana. Apollonius is represented as saying on his arrival in Rome at this time:*
>
>> *In my travels, which have been wider than ever man yet accomplished, I have seen many, many wild beasts of Arabia and India; but this beast, that is commonly called a Tyrant, I know not how many heads it has, nor if it be crooked of claw, and armed with horrible fangs. However, they say it is a civil beast, and inhabits the midst of cities; but to this*

---

60. Both The Living Bible and the Revised Standard Version Contain Notes on Revelation 13:18 (the 666 passage). These state, "Some manuscripts read '616.'" (TLB). "Other ancient authorities read six hundred and sixteen." The New American Standard Version also notes, "Some mss. read, 616."

The manuscripts containing this reading are: C (a manuscript located in Paris and dated from the 5th century); also, according to Iranaeus there was a manuscript (z) written in Old Latin containing this reading. Tyconius (AD 380) also refers to this.

extent it is more savage than the beasts of mountain and forest, that whereas lions and panthers can sometimes by flattery be tamed and change their disposition, stroking and petting this beast does but instigate it to surpass itself in ferocity and devour at large. And of wild beasts you cannot say that they were ever known to eat their own mothers, but Nero has gorged himself on this diet.

Revelation 14
144,000 Firstfruits to God

An interesting feature of these visions is the manner in which both Jerusalem and Rome are referred to in them. In the first vision (Revelation 6:1–11:19), Jerusalem was mostly in view. In the second vision (Revelation 12:1–13:18), *"the woman,"* the messianic Jews from Jerusalem, and Rome receive about equal attention. In the third vision (Revelation 14:1-20), and the fourth vision (Revelation 15:1–16:21), the emphasis upon the "144,000" from Jerusalem is receding as the emphasis centers more upon the persecutions and destruction of Rome. The fifth vision (Revelation 17:1–19:10) centers upon Rome altogether.

When Jerusalem returns to view in the sixth vision (Revelation 19:11–21:8), it is *"the holy city, New Jerusalem"* (Revelation 21:2) that we see.

In the seventh vision (Revelation 21:9–22:5), Rome is forever eclipsed, as the *"holy Jerusalem"* is presented in her glory.

And I looked, and, lo, a Lamb stood on the mount Sion, and with him an hundred forty and four thousand, having his Father's name written in their foreheads.

2 And I heard a voice from heaven, as the voice of many waters, and as the voice of a great thunder: and I heard the voice of harpers harping with their harps:

The 144,000 With The Lamb On Mount Zion

"And I looked, and, lo, a Lamb stood on the mount Sion, and with him an hundred forty and four thousand, having his Father's name written in their foreheads" (Revelation 14:1). The Jerusalem church would return in safety to Mount Zion in Jerusalem after the Roman-Jewish War, thus demonstrating God's protection of His firstfruits. This would demonstrate that *"the seal of the living God"* *"in their foreheads"* (Revelation 7:2-3) had truly protected them from physical death. Also, as a matter of historical fact, these Jerusalem Jews who believed in Jesus did return to Jerusalem, and to that section of Jerusalem which was known as "Zion." This information comes to us from Epiphanius, a bishop in the fourth century, who

3 And they sung as it were a new song before the throne, and before the four beasts, and the elders: and no man could learn that song but the hundred and forty and four thousand, which were redeemed from the earth.

4 These are they which were not defiled with women; for they are virgins. These are they which follow the Lamb whithersoever he goeth. These were redeemed from among men, being

stated that these Jews who believed in Jesus returned from Pella, and established themselves on "Zion" (Epiphanius, *De Mens. et Pond.* xiv - xv).[61] Eusebius also lists 14 bishops of the church "*at Jerusalem*," after the Roman-Jewish War of A.D. 66-70 (Eusebius' *Ecclesiastical History*, pgs. 117,131).[62]

"*The hundred and forty and four thousand, which were* **redeemed from** (Greek, *apo, by means of*) *the earth*" (Revelation 14:3b). The bold words have been misunderstood to mean that the 144,000 were in heaven. This misunderstanding has been because

1. the Greek word, *apo*,[63] which is translated "*from*" in our text, has not been correctly understood, and

2. those attempting to understand Revelation have not seen the connection between this phrase ("*redeemed from the earth*") and Revelation 12:16, "*And the earth helped the woman, and the earth opened her mouth, and swallowed up the flood which the dragon cast out of his mouth.*"

Thus, these 144,000 were "*redeemed* (apo) *by means of the earth.*"

---

61. "*And he (Aquila) found the temple of God trodden down and the whole city devastated save for a few houses and the church of God, which was small...For there it had been built, that is, in that portion of Zion which escaped destruction...So Aquila, while he was in Jerusalem, also saw the disciples of the disciples of the apostles flourishing in the faith and working great signs, healings and other miracles. For they were such as had come back from the city of Pella to Jerusalem*" (Epiphanius, quoted from Bar Kokhba, Yigael Yadin, p. 259 from "Treatise on Weights and Measures," *De Mensuris et Ponderibus*, xiv - xv).

62. "*Simeon died as a martyr, who, we have shown, was appointed the second bishop of the church at Jerusalem*" (pg. 117).

"*The first, then, was James called the brother of our Lord*" (this one was before the Roman-Jewish War of A.D. 66-70 (pgs. 77-78); the others were bishops of Jerusalem after that war, and until the second Roman-Jewish War in A.D. 132-135); "*after whom, the second was Simeon*" (who continued to the reign of the emperor Trajan (pg. 117)), "*the third Justus, the fourth Zaccheus, the fifth Tobias, the sixth Benjamin, the seventh John, the eighth Matthew, the ninth Philip, the tenth Seneca, the eleventh Justus, the twelfth Levi, the thirteenth Ephres, the fourteenth Joseph*" (William Whiston, who translated the works of Josephus into English, devoted much space to show that this Joseph was the famous historian, Josephus (see Josephus, *Antiquities*, Vol. IV, pages 422, 427, 429, 430).) "*and finally, the fifteenth Judas. These are all the bishops of Jerusalem that filled up the time from the apostles until the aforementioned time, all of the circumcision*" (Eusebius' *Ecclesiastical History*, Baker Book House, Grand Rapids, Michigan, pg. 131).

63. The Meanings of "*apo*"

apo prep. with gen. from; away from; *by means of*; of; because of; as a result of; since; ever since; about; for; with; apo mias pantes one after another, one and all (Luke 14:18).

the firstfruits unto God and to the Lamb.

5 And in their mouth was found no guile: for they are without fault before the throne of God (Revelation 14:1-5).

The Vatican manuscript, No. 1160, attempted to correct the misunderstanding here by changing the wording to read, "*redeemed on the earth.*" Thus, these 144,000 were not seen to be in heaven, but upon the earth.

"*These are they which were not defiled with women; for they are virgins*" (Revelation 14:4a). In Scripture, adultery and whoredoms often carry the meaning of idolatry, witchcraft, or, in other words, traffic with evil spirits.[64]

In the same way, a "*virgin*" would indicate a person, or group, who would be free of seduction by evil spirits.

Thus, Nahum (3:4) was inspired to call Nineveh "*the wellfavoured harlot*" in referring to her witchcraft or her use of evil spirits to control the lives of others. "*Because of the multitude of the whoredoms of the wellfavoured harlot, the mistress of witchcrafts, that selleth nations through her whoredoms, and families through her witchcrafts.*" (See also Ezekiel 16:15-36; 23:36-39.)

The apostle Paul also wrote to the Corinthians: "*For I am jealous over you with godly jealousy: for I have espoused you to one husband, that I may present you as a chaste virgin to Christ*" (2 Corinthians 11:2). Being "*a chaste virgin*" would be to be committed only to Jesus Christ and to be indwelt only by His Holy Spirit, and consequently

---

64. *Lest thou make a covenant with the inhabitants of the land, and they go a whoring after their gods, and do sacrifice unto their gods, and one call thee, and thou eat of his sacrifice;*
And thou take of their daughters unto thy sons, and their daughters go a whoring after their gods, and make thy sons go a whoring after their gods (Exodus 34:15-16).

And they shall no more offer their sacrifices unto devils, after whom they have gone a whoring. This shall be a statute for ever unto them throughout their generations (Leviticus 17:7).

Then I will set my face against that man, and against his family, and will cut him off, and all that go a whoring after him, to commit whoredom with Molech, from among their people.
And the soul that turneth after such as have familiar spirits, and after wizards, to go a whoring after them, I will even set my face against that soul, and will cut him off from among his people (Leviticus 20:5-6).

And the Lord said unto Moses, Behold, thou shalt sleep with thy fathers; and this people will rise up, and go a whoring after the gods of the strangers of the land, whither they go to be among them, and will forsake me, and break my covenant which I have made with them (Deuteronomy 31:16).

For other references on this subject, see Judges 2:17; 8:27, 33; 1 Chronicles 5:25; Psalm 73:26-27; 106:39; Ezekiel 6:9; 16:36; 23:1-4, 36-39; Hosea 4:12; 9:1.

being uninfluenced by demonic spirits either in doctrine, or in one's thoughts and behavior. Thus, Paul continued writing to the Corinthians: *"For if he that cometh preacheth **another Jesus**, whom we have not preached, **or if ye receive another spirit, which ye have not received**, or **another gospel**, which ye have not accepted, ye might well bear with him"* (2 Corinthians 11:4).

The church of Jerusalem, after its return from Pella, *was described twice by Hegesippus* (who wrote about A.D. 160-180) as a *"virgin."* Thus, Hegesippus is quoted by Eusebius, as writing, *"But after James the Just had suffered martyrdom as our Lord had for the same reason, Simeon, the son of Cleophas our Lord's uncle, was appointed the second bishop, whom all proposed, as the cousin of our Lord. Hence **they called the church as yet a virgin**, for it was not yet corrupted by vain discourses"* (Eusebius' *Ecclesiastical History*, pg. 157). Also, after the martyrdom of Simeon, Eusebius quotes in another place from Hegesippus, who described *"the church at Jerusalem"* as follows: *"**the church continued until then as a pure and uncorrupt virgin**"* (Eusebius' *Ecclesiastical History*, pg. 118).

*"These were redeemed from among men, **being the firstfruits unto God and to the Lamb**"* (Revelation 14:4b). The *"firstfruits"*—the first ingathering of crops—were offered to God (Exodus 23:19; Leviticus 2:12; Nehemiah 10:35). These *"firstfruits"* were, in a special sense, God's own possession.[65]

Because of this special sense of being God's Own, Israel was seen as *"firstfruits."* Thus, *"Israel was holiness unto the Lord, and the **firstfruits** of his increase; all that devour him shall offend; evil shall come upon them, saith the Lord"* (Jeremiah 2:3).

---

65. *And to bring the firstfruits of our ground, and the firstfruits of all fruit of all trees, year by year, unto the house of the Lord:*
Also the firstborn of our sons, and of our cattle, as it is written in the law, and the firstlings of our herds and of our flocks, to bring to the house of our God, unto the priests that minister in the house of our God:
And that we should bring the firstfruits of our dough, and our offerings, and the fruit of all manner of trees, of wine and of oil, unto the priests, to the chambers of the house of our God; and the tithes of our ground unto the Levites, that the same Levites might have the tithes in all the cities of our tillage (Nehemiah 10:35-37).

In the New Testament the term *"firstfruits"* was used of those who were the first converts of a certain area, and who were, therefore, God's special possession. Thus, we read, *"Salute my wellbeloved Epaenetus, who is the **firstfruits** of Achaia unto Christ"* (Romans 16:5b). Also, *"I beseech you, brethren, (ye know the house of Stephanas, that it is the **firstfruits** of Achaia, and that they have addicted themselves to the ministry of the saints)"* (1 Corinthians 16:15).

Since *"the firstfruits unto God, and to the Lamb"* were the first converts to Jesus and were especially God's own, they were protected by Him, when His wrath was being poured forth upon their enemies. It was in reference to these very ones that Jesus declared prophetically, *"But there shall not a hair of your head perish"* (Luke 21:18).

We read further of these *"firstfruits unto God, and to the Lamb"* in the book of Acts. Let's read about them:

"Then they that gladly received his word were baptized: and the same day there were added unto them about three thousand souls" (Acts 2:41).

"Howbeit many of them which heard the word believed; and the number of the men was about five thousand" (Acts 4:4).

"And believers were the more added to the Lord, multitudes both of men and women" (Acts 5:14).

"In those days, when the number of the disciples was multiplied..." (Acts 6:1).

"And the word of God increased; and the number of the disciples multiplied in Jerusalem greatly; and a great company of the priests were obedient to the faith" (Acts 6:7).

Here they were, the *"firstfruits,"* that is, the first converts among the Jews to Jesus. They were the 144,000. These 144,000 were not the whole church, however. They were only the *"firstfruits"* of the great gospel harvest.

"And I heard a voice from heaven, as the voice of many waters, and as the voice of a great thunder: and I heard the voice of harps harping with their harps: And they sung as it were a new song before the throne, and before the four beasts, and the elders: and no man could learn that song but the hundred and forty and four thousand, which were redeemed from (or by means of) the earth" (Revelation 14:2-3).

The Martyred Gentile Christians Sing a New Song in Heaven.

These Gentile Christians, which are here seen in heaven, are the same as those described more carefully in Revelation 7:9-17.[66] These are those with whom *"the little horn"* of Daniel (7:8,21), and those with whom the *"beast"* of Revelation (13:7) *"made war."* It is because of their unjust and cruel deaths that Rome must be destroyed.

Because of the continuous repetition of the various themes in Revelation, it becomes obvious that their *"new song"* is *"the song of Moses the servant of God, and the song of the Lamb,"* which is given in full in Revelation 15:3-4.

---

66. These martyred Gentiles (who are seen in Revelation 14:2-3a) are described more fully in Revelation 7:9-17, and in Daniel 7:8, 21 and Revelation 13:7

After this I beheld, and, lo, a great multitude, which no man could number, of all nations, and kindreds, and people, and tongues, stood before the throne, and before the Lamb, clothed with white robes, and palms in their hands;

And cried with a loud voice, saying, Salvation to our God which sitteth upon the throne, and unto the Lamb.

And all the angels stood round about the throne, and about the elders and the four beasts, and fell before the throne on their faces, and worshipped God,

Saying, Amen: Blessing, and glory, and wisdom, and thanksgiving, and honour, and power, and might, be unto our God for ever and ever. Amen.

And one of the elders answered, saying unto me, What are these which are arrayed in white robes? and whence came they?

And I said unto him, Sir, thou knowest. And he said to me, These are they which came out of great tribulation, and have washed their robes, and made them white in the blood of the Lamb.

Therefore are they before the throne of God, and serve him day and night in his temple: and he that sitteth on the throne shall dwell among them.

They shall hunger no more, neither thirst any more; neither shall the sun light on them, nor any heat.

For the Lamb which is in the midst of the throne shall feed them, and shall lead them unto living fountains of waters: and God shall wipe away all tears from their eyes (Revelation 7:9-17).

I considered the horns, and, behold, there came up among them another little horn, before whom there were three of the first horns plucked up by the roots: and, behold, in this horn were eyes like the eyes of man, and a mouth speaking great things....

I beheld, and the same horn made war with the saints, and prevailed against them (Daniel 7:8,21).

And it was given unto him to make war with the saints, and to overcome them: and power was given him over all kindreds, and tongues, and nations (Revelation 13:7).

And I saw another angel fly in the midst of heaven, having the everlasting gospel to preach unto them that dwell on the earth, and to every nation, and kindred, and tongue, and people.

7 Saying with a loud voice, Fear God, and give glory to him; for the hour of his judgment is come: and worship him that made heaven, and earth, and the sea, and the fountains of waters (Revelation 14:6-7).

The Angel with the Everlasting Gospel

This gospel went to *"them that dwell on the earth,"* and *"to every nation, and kindred, and tongue, and people"* which are phrases indicating the peoples of the Roman Empire. (Though in Daniel, similar phrases referred to the Babylonian [Daniel 3:4,7,29; 4:1; 5:19] or to the Medo-Persian [Daniel 6:25] empires.)

This gospel announced that *"the hour of his* (God's) *judgment is come,"* which prepares us for the following verses concerning God's judgment upon Babylon (Rome), and upon those who take the mark of the beast.

These two verses were considered fulfilled when Romans (A.D. 57-58) and Colossians (A.D. 58-62) were written.[67] (See Romans 10:18; 16:26; Colossians 1:5-6a,23.) *And there followed another angel, saying, Babylon is fallen, is fallen, that great city, because she made all nations drink of the wine of the wrath of her fornication* (Revelation 14:8).

"Babylon is fallen, is fallen"

The *"judgment"* of the previous verse is here revealed. It is the fall of Babylon (Rome). This fall of Rome was not that which took place under Alaric and his Goths on August 24, A.D. 410, since the fall of Rome that was prophesied was to be accomplished by the beast and the ten kings allied with him (Revelation 17:16, 17), and the beast must be here when Jesus returns (Revelation 19:19).

This fall of Rome is, then, yet future!

---

67. *Now to him that is of power to stablish you according to my gospel, and the preaching of Jesus Christ, according to the revelation of the mystery, which was kept secret since the world began,*
But now is made manifest, and by the scriptures of the prophets, according to the commandment of the everlasting God, made known to all nations for the obedience of faith (Romans 16:25-26).

For the hope which is laid up for you in heaven, whereof ye heard before in the word of truth of the gospel;
Which is come unto you, as it is in all the world; and bringeth forth fruit, as it doth also in you, since the day ye heard of it, and knew the grace of God in truth (Colossians 1:5-6).

If ye continue in the faith grounded and settled, and be not moved away from the hope of the gospel, which ye have heard, and which was preached to every creature which is under heaven; whereof I Paul am made a minister (Colossians 1:23).

And the third angel followed them, saying with a loud voice, If any man worship the beast and his image, and receive his mark in his forehead, or in his hand,

10 The same shall drink of the wine of the wrath of God, which is poured out without mixture into the cup of his indignation; and he shall be tormented with fire and brimstone in the presence of the holy angels, and in the presence of the Lamb:

11 And the smoke of their torment ascendeth up for ever and ever: and they have no rest day nor night, who worship the beast and his image, and whosoever receiveth the mark of his name (Revelation 14:9-11).

Here is the patience of the saints: here are they that keep the commandments of God, and the faith of Jesus.

13 And I heard a voice from heaven

The Torment of Those Who Worship the Beast and His Image, or Who Receive His Mark

The "judgment" announced in Revelation 14:7 continues. The "*fire and brimstone*" (14:10) seem to be the same as the "*lake of fire burning with brimstone*" of Revelation 19:20; also 20:10,14. The body of the beast was the Roman Empire (Revelation 13:1-3), but sometimes the "beast" is seen more as one of the seven heads of the Roman Empire, in particular as the fifth head, Nero, returned to life (Revelation 17:8,11; see also 13:14; 16:13; 19:20), who would have been Domitian, but is now the head of the Roman Empire yet to come.

"Blessed Are the Dead Which Die in the Lord from Henceforth"

This prepares us for the reaping in Revelation 14:14-16 which follows. Those who are to be reaped are those who have been martyred for their faith.

saying unto me, Write, Blessed are the dead which die in the Lord from henceforth: Yea, saith the Spirit, that they may rest from their labours; and their works do follow them (Revelation 14:12-13).

And I looked, and behold a white cloud, and upon the cloud one sat like unto the Son of man, having on his head a golden crown, and in his hand a sharp sickle.

15 And another angel came out of the temple, crying with a loud voice to him that sat on the cloud, Thrust in thy sickle, and reap: for the time is come for thee to reap; for the harvest of the earth (or *land*) *is ripe* (Greek, *xeraino*, dry).

16 And he that sat on the cloud thrust in his sickle on the earth; and the earth was reaped (Revelation 14:14-16).

The Harvest of the Son of Man

"*A white cloud*" (14:14) is used in Scripture as a vehicle for Deity. (See Isaiah 19:1; Daniel 7:13; Matthew 24:30; 26:64; Acts 1:9; 1 Thessalonians 4:17.)

"*Like unto the Son of man.*" See the same wording in Revelation 1:13 where this phrase refers to Jesus. Jesus referred to Himself as "*the son of man*" 75 times in the Gospels. The "*golden crown*" (Greek, *stephanos*, wreath) (14:14) symbolizes Jesus' victory over Satan. It is a victor's wreath that is won.

Compare these two passages.

"*Thrust in thy sickle, and reap: for the time is come for thee to reap; for the harvest of the earth is ripe*" (Revelation 14:15).

"*Thrust in thy sharp sickle, and gather the clusters of the vine of the earth; for her grapes are fully ripe*" (Revelation 14:18b).

The King James Version, and most other translations, translate two Greek words in the above passages, by the single English word, "*ripe.*"

Thus in Revelation 14:15, we read, "*...for the harvest of the earth is **ripe***." But the Greek word translated "*ripe*" in this passage is *xeraino*, to dry up or wither. We could more accurately translate this, "*for the harvest of the earth is dry.*"

In Revelation 14:18, we read, *"for her grapes are fully ripe."* The Greek word here is *akmazo* (to be at the prime point of ripeness), thus *"fully ripe"* in this instance is a good translation.

In Joel 3:13,[68] we see two harvests contrasted. These are the wheat harvest and the vintage (or grape) harvest. And these are the same two harvests being contrasted in Revelation. (Revelation 14:14-16 refers to the wheat harvest, while Revelation 14:17-20 refers to the vintage harvest.) Wheat, in Scripture, refers to those in a right relationship with God[69] (Matthew 9:37-38; 13:30,38-39; Mark 4:29; Luke 10:2; John 4:35); thus, *"the good seed (wheat) are the children of the kingdom"* (Matthew 13:38).

So in the correct translation of Revelation 14:15 (*"the harvest of the earth is dry"*), the meaning is that the wheat, that is, the Christians, are dead, as the wheat is dead when it is dry. (The figure is accurate since, even when wheat is dry, it can spring forth to renewed life, and so a Christian also lives after the body is dead.)

The wheat, in this instance, are the Christians who have been martyred by Rome for their refusal to receive the mark of the beast, or the name of the beast, or the number of his name. They are being harvested by Jesus, that is, Jesus is taking those who have been killed to His heavenly granary.[70]

---

68. *"Put in the sickles, for the harvest is ripe; go in, tread down; for wheat pits are full and the wine presses overflow; for their wickedness is great"* (Joel 3:13 The Holy Bible, by George M. Lamsa).

69. *Another parable put he forth unto them, saying, The kingdom of heaven is likened unto a man which sowed good seed* (wheat) *in his field:*
But while men slept, his enemy came and sowed tares among the wheat, and went his way....
Let both grow together until the harvest: and in the time of harvest I will say to the reapers, Gather ye together first the tares, and bind them in bundles to burn them: but gather the wheat into my barn....
He answered and said unto them, He that soweth the good seed is the Son of man;
The field is the world; the good seed are the children of the kingdom; but the tares are the children of the wicked one;
The enemy that sowed them is the devil; the harvest is the end of the world; and the reapers are the angels (Matthew 13:24-25,30,37-39).

Whose fan is in his hand, and he will thoroughly purge his floor, and gather his wheat into the garner; but he will burn up the chaff with unquenchable fire" (Matthew 3:12).

70. Job 5:26 compares a man's coming to his *"grave in a full age,"* *"as a shock of corn* (wheat) *cometh in in his season."*

And another angel came out of the temple which is in heaven, he also having a sharp sickle. And another angel came out from the altar, which had power over fire; and cried with a loud cry to him that had the sharp sickle, saying, Thrust in thy sharp sickle, and gather the clusters of the vine of the earth; for her grapes are fully ripe. And the angel thrust in his sickle into the earth, and gathered the vine of the earth, and cast it into the great winepress of the wrath of God (Revelation 14:17-19).

And the winepress was trodden without the city, and blood came out of the winepress, even unto the horse bridles, by the space of a thousand and six hundred furlongs (Revelation 14:20).

The Vintage Harvest; A Judgment upon the Enemies of Christ

"*Another angel came out of the temple*" (Revelation 14:17), that is, immediately from the presence of God. See the same wording in verse 15.

"*Another angel came out from the altar, which had power over fire*" (Revelation 14:18a), that is, power to send fire from the heavenly altar to the earth in judgment, as in Revelation 8:5. This was done in response to the prayers of the persecuted saints. (See Revelation 6:9-10; 8:3-5.)

"*Thrust in thy sharp sickle, and gather the clusters of the vine of the earth*" (Revelation 14:18). The vintage followed the wheat harvest in Judea (Deuteronomy 16:9-13), so John is given a vision that applies this truth of nature in a symbolic way.

"*The great winepress of the wrath of God*" (Revelation 14:19b). The grape clusters, symbolizing the enemies of God (as in Joel 3:13b), are thrown into the great winepress of God's wrath. The winepress symbolizes God's wrath on a horrid battlefield.[71] (See Isaiah 63:1-6; Lamentations 1:15.)

"*And the winepress was trodden **without the city…***" (Revelation 14:20a). The ancient wine-presses were in the vineyards, not in the cities. This fact was symbolic of the fact that opposing and defending armies fought outside the city under attack. But which city, and which armies?

"*The city*" was the city mentioned previously in this vision as the one coming under God's judg-ment. (See Revelation 14:8, "*Babylon* (that is, Rome) *is fallen, is fallen.*")

It is "*the city*" that was to have perpetrated the martyrdoms warned of in Revelation 14:13 ("*Blessed are the dead which die in the Lord from henceforth…*"), and which were seen prophetically

---

71. *The Lord hath trodden under foot all my mighty men in the midst of me: he hath called an assembly against me to crush my young men: the Lord hath trodden the virgin, the daughter of Judah, as in a winepress* (Lamentations 1:15).

as accomplished in Revelation 14:15b ("...*for the harvest of the earth is dry.*")

It was "*the city*" that was then reigning "*over the kings of the earth*" (Revelation 17:18), and was thus capable of such strong, independent, and murderous action. It was "*the city*" that was "*drunken with the blood of the saints, and with the blood of the martyrs of Jesus*" (Revelation 17:6).

God's prophetic pronouncement of judgment upon Jerusalem had at this point in Revelation been completed! Thus, this "city" is not Jerusalem! It is Rome!

The "*winepress*" "*without the city*" is a metaphor for a battlefield. This winepress is another way of describing the action of "*the third angel*" in Revelation 16:4-7 in which, as we shall later see, attacking and defending armies fight outside Rome, just before its fall.

"*For true and righteous are his judgments: for he hath judged the great whore, which did corrupt the earth with her fornication, **and hath avenged the blood of his servants at her hand**" (Revelation 19:2).

But which armies were prophesied to bring about this destruction of Rome? In Revelation 17:16-17 (RSV) we read, "*And the **ten horns** that you saw, **they and the beast will hate the harlot;** they will make her desolate and naked, and devour her flesh **and burn her up with fire,** for God has put it into their hearts to carry out his purpose by being of one mind and giving over their royal power to the beast, until the words of God shall be fulfilled.*"

Thus, it was the armies of the beast (who would have been Domitian), and the ten horns (or kings) allied with him, which were to be used of God to destroy Rome. Defending Rome would, no doubt, have been the armies loyal to Rome, though this is not stated, but without them there would have been no "*winepress.*"

The phrase in Revelation 14:20, "*and blood came out of the winepress, even unto the horse bridles,*" pictures a very large winepress. It is so large that it is no longer men with bare feet who tread the grapes of this winepress, but now horses (and no doubt warriors have fallen slain from their backs, since they have "*bridles*"). Instead of juice, we read of "*blood*" as the metaphor of the winepress changes to the horror of a battlefield, and a lake of blood produced by a terrible slaughter.[72]

Revelation 14:20 talks about "*…the space of a thousand and six hundred furlongs*" ("*Furlongs*," Greek, *stadion,* 607 ft.) This would be equal to about 184 miles.

But this is a symbolic number. 1600 is 40 x 40. Forty (40) is the number of divine punishment.[73] (See Exodus 16:35; Numbers 14:33; 32:13; Joshua 5:6; Judges 13:1; Psalm 95:10; Ezekiel 29:11-13; Hebrews 3:9-17). *A number multiplied by itself carries the same meaning, but intensified.* Thus, *40 times 40 is the symbol of a most horrible divine punishment!* It is the special punishment reserved for Rome, which will be destroyed "*with fire*" by the beast and the ten kings allied with him

---

72. In the Hebrew mind, the juice of the grape was so akin to blood, that it was called "*the blood of grapes*" (Genesis 49:11; Deuteronomy 32:14).

73. *And your children shall wander in the wilderness forty years, and bear your whoredoms, until your carcasses be wasted in the wilderness* (Numbers 14:33).

   And the Lord's anger was kindled against Israel, and he made them wander in the wilderness forty years, until all the generation, that had done evil in the sight of the Lord, was consumed (Numbers 32:13).

   And the children of Israel did evil again in the sight of the Lord; and the Lord delivered them into the hand of the Philistines forty years (Judges 13:1).

   Forty years long was I grieved with this generation, and said, It is a people that do err in their heart, and they have not known my ways:
   Unto whom I sware in my wrath that they should not enter into my rest (Psalm 95:10-11).

   And the land of Egypt shall be desolate and waste; and they shall know that I am the Lord: because he hath said, The river is mine, and I have made it.
   Behold, therefore I am against thee, and against thy rivers, and I will make the land of Egypt utterly waste and desolate, from the tower of Syene even unto the border of Ethiopia.
   No foot of man shall pass through it, nor foot of beast shall pass through it, neither shall it be inhabited forty years (Ezekiel 29:9-11).

   Wherefore (as the Holy Ghost saith, To-day if ye will hear his voice,
   Harden not your hearts, as in the provocation, in the day of temptation in the wilderness:
   When your fathers tempted me, proved me, and saw my works forty years.
   Wherefore I was grieved with that generation, and said, They do alway err in their heart; and they have not known my ways.
   So I sware in my wrath, They shall not enter into my rest) (Hebrews 3:7-11).

(Revelation 17:16). Rome will then also be destroyed by "*a great earthquake*" and by enormous hailstones (Revelation 16:18-19,21).

In the future, it would appear that when the leader of the European Community (the revived Roman Empire) takes up his residence in Rome, the events prophesied concerning Rome will begin to unfold.

Revelation 15
Seven Angels Having Seven Bowls

In Revelation, we see *two groups* of seven spirits, or angels. In Scripture, the words *"angel"* and *spirit"* are used interchangeably[74] (see Acts 8:26, compared with Acts 8:29, 39, also Hebrews 1:13,14), and this concept holds true in Revelation (as in Revelation 14:13 and 22:17).

The first group of seven angels, or spirits, in Revelation, are represented by seven lamps of fire burning before the throne of God (Revelation 4:5), which suggests that these angels, or spirits, also, are constantly positioned there (Revelation 1:4; 8:2).

Thus, when these seven angels are given trumpets by which they announce God's judgments, there is no suggestion that they move from their places, or that they go anywhere.

The second group of seven angels, or spirits, is represented by the seven eyes of the Lamb, that is, of Jesus. These *"seven eyes" "run to and fro through the whole earth"* (Zechariah 3:9; 4:10), and this suggests that these spirits, or angels are *"sent forth into all the earth"* (Revelation 5:6).

Thus, when this second group of angels, or spirits, are to bring forth the wrath of God upon Babylon (Rome), and upon the beast, they are told to *"Go your ways"* (Revelation 16:1), and they *"went"* (Revelation 16:2)! This second group of seven spirits, or angels, is described further in Isaiah 11:2.[75]

---

74. In Scripture, all angels are spirits, though spirits aren't always angels.

Thus, in Acts 8:26, we read, *"And the angel of the Lord spake unto Philip..."* But, in Acts 8:29, when this angel is referred to again, we read, *"...the Spirit said unto Philip...,"* and in Acts 8:39, *"...the Spirit of the Lord caught away Philip..."*

In Hebrews 1:13-14, *"angels"* are referred to as *"ministering spirits."* We may also see the words *"angel"* and *"spirit"* used interchangeably in Revelation 22:16, *"I Jesus have sent mine angel,"* and in Revelation 22:17, *"And the Spirit and the bride say, Come."*

Also, in Isaiah 63:9-10, *"The angel of his presence"* is identified as *"his holy Spirit"* (see also Isaiah 63:11). This is also seen in Exodus 32:34, *"...behold, mine angel shall go before thee,"* while in Exodus 33:14 we read, *"My presence shall go with thee, and I will give thee rest."*

75. King James Version
"And the spirit of the Lord shall rest upon him, the spirit of wisdom and understanding, the spirit of counsel and might, the spirit of knowledge and of the fear of the Lord:.."

The Septuagint Version
"...and the Spirit of God shall rest upon him, the spirit of wisdom and understanding, the spirit of counsel and strength, the spirit of knowledge and godliness shall fill him;

3 the spirit of the fear of God."

It is this second group of seven angels, or spirits, that we read of in Revelation 15 and 16.

And I saw another sign in heaven, great and marvelous, seven angels having the seven last plagues; for in them is filled up the wrath of God (Revelation 15:1).

Seven Angels Having *"the Seven Last Plagues"*

These *"the seven last plagues"* (Revelation 15:1) were to have come upon Rome and upon the beast soon after the destruction of Jerusalem, and then Jesus would have returned. But God could not bless the Jews with His wonderful kingdom while they were unrepentant, and He could not curse Rome with destruction when they were turning to Him. However, these prophecies will yet be fulfilled!

There is a close correlation between the events described in the trumpets judgments, and the events described in the bowls of wrath judgments, as follows

Angels with Trumpets	Angels	Angels with Bowls Of Wrath
*"cast upon **the earth**"* (8:7)	1st	*"poured…upon **the earth**"* (16:2)
*"cast into **the sea**"* (8:8)	2nd	*"poured…upon **the sea**"* (16:3)
*"upon the…**rivers**, and upon the **fountains of waters**"* (8:10)	3rd	*"poured out…upon the **rivers** and **fountains of waters**"* (16:4)
*"**the sun**," "**the moon**," "**the stars**"* (8:12)	4th	*"poured out…upon the **sun**"* (16:8)
*"**the bottomless pit**"* (that is, the pit, or seat of corruption, of *Rome*) (9:1)	5th	*"Poured out…upon the seat of the beast* (that is, *Rome*) (16:10)
*"the **great river Euphrates**"* (9:14)	6th	*"poured out…upon the **great river Euphrates**"* (16:12)
*"voices in **heaven**"* (11:15)	7th	*"poured out…**into the air**"* (16:17)

2 And I saw as it were a sea of glass mingled with fire: and them that had gotten the victory over the beast, and over his image, and

But what does this obvious correlation between the trumpets judgments and the bowls of wrath mean? The God who would soon prove His power to destroy Jerusalem, would with similar, but worse, and more extensive plagues, prove His power to destroy Rome, the beast, and all others who persecute and kill His beloved children!

over his mark, and over the number of his name, stand on the sea of glass, having the harps of God.

*"And I saw as it were **a sea of glass mingled with fire**: and them that had gotten the victory over the beast, and over his image, and over his mark, and over the number of his name, stand on the sea of glass, having the harps of God"* (Revelation 15:2).

In Revelation 4:6, there was *"before the throne...a sea of glass like unto crystal,"* but here in Revelation 15:2, the *"sea of glass"* is *"mingled with fire."* This is to indicate the fiery deaths through which these Christians were to pass. They would be victorious because they would choose death with victory, rather than life with defeat, when faced with the idolatrous demands of the beast.

3 And they sing the song of Moses the servant of God, and the song of the Lamb, saying (Revelation 15:2-3a).

In Revelation 14:1-3, we saw two groups who were to be able to sing this song—the 144,000 Jerusalem Jews who believed in Jesus, and the great multitude of Gentile Christians who were to have been martyred by Domitian, the prophesied beast of Revelation.

The *"song"* is to be a song of victory. The 144,000 had a victory such as the victory of Moses at the Red Sea, in which they, like Moses, were delivered from death. The Gentile Christians, on the other hand, would have a victory such as Jesus had on the cross when He, as the Lamb of God, was victorious *through* death. Thus, these two groups would experience victory, either like Moses, or like the Lamb, and thus, this song would have a *special meaning* for both.

While there are actually two songs in the Old Testament called the song of Moses (Exodus 15:1-19; Deuteronomy 32:1-43), this song in Revelation 15:3-4 bears no resemblance to either of them. This song is rather a string of Old Testament phrases brought together into a meaningful song. The 144,000 Jerusalem Jews who believed in Jesus had been delivered from death when they went to Pella under the reign of Nero Caesar. The great multitude of Gentile Christians were to have been delivered *through* death in the reign of a second Nero,[76] Domitian. But this has been thrown even into our future. Who among us will qualify to sing this song of victory?

The Song of Moses the Servant of God, and the Song of the Lamb

Other Scriptures That Support the Same Thoughts

Great	*"The works of the Lord are great"* (Psalm 111:2).	God's *"works"* were both *"great and marvelous"* because He had brought both groups to a victory, but a victory of a different kind!
and marvelous are thy works,	*marvelous are thy works* (Psalm 139:14).	
	"I would seek unto God, and unto God would I commit my cause: Which doeth great things and unsearchable; marvelous things without number" (Job 5:8-9).	
Lord God Almighty;	*"Lord God"* (Genesis 15:2 and many places)	
	"God Almighty" (Genesis 28:3; 35:11 and elsewhere) *"Lord God Almighty"* (Revelation 4:8; 11:17; 16:7).	
	"…Lord God Almighty…" is a phrase used in Amos 4:13 in the	

---

76. In the "faith chapter" of the Bible (Hebrews 11), we see the contrast between those saved *from* death, and those saved *through* death and suffering

Those saved *from* death:

"By faith they passed through the Red Sea as by dry land: which the Egyptians assaying to do were drowned.
By faith the walls of Jericho fell down, after they were compassed about seven days.
By faith the harlot Rahab perished not with them that believed not, when she had received the spies with peace.
And what shall I more say? for the time would fail me to tell of Gideon, and of Barak, and of Samson, and of Jephthah: of David also, and Samuel, and of the prophets:
Who through faith subdued kingdoms, wrought righteousness, obtained promises, stopped the mouths of lions,
Quenched the violence of fire, escaped the edge of the sword, out of weakness were made strong, waxed valiant in fight, turned to flight the armies of the aliens.
Women received their dead raised to life again…"

Those saved *through* death and suffering:

"…and others were tortured, not accepting deliverance; that they might obtain a better resurrection.
And others had trial of cruel mockings and scourgings, yea, moreover of bonds and imprisonment;
They were stoned, they were sawn asunder, were tempted, were slain with the sword; they wandered about in sheepskins and goatskins; being destitute, afflicted, tormented;
(of whom the world was not worthy:) they wandered in deserts, and in mountains, and in dens and caves of the earth" (Hebrews 11:29-38).

Greek Septuagint version (LXX), quoted below:

"For, behold, I am he that strengthens the thunder, and creates the wind, and proclaims to men his Christ, forming the morning and the darkness, and mounting on the high places of the earth, The Lord God Almighty is his name" (Amos 4:13 LXX).

just (Greek, *dikaiai*, righteous) *and true are thy ways,*

"…for the ways of the Lord are right" (Hosea 14:9).

"The judgments of the Lord are true and righteous altogether" (Psalm 19:9b).

"The Lord is righteous in all his ways, and holy in all his works" (Psalm 145:17).

"He is the Rock, his work is perfect: for all his ways are judgment: a God of truth and without iniquity, just and right is he" (Deuteronomy 32:4).

This contrasts with the Roman beast who demanded their worship, but whose ways were neither true nor righteous, but were rather ways of forced idolatry.

thou King of saints (other manuscripts read, *"ages"* or *"nations"* rather than *"saints"*).

"Who would not fear thee, O King of nations?" (Jeremiah 10:7a).

"God is greatly to be feared in the assembly of the saints, and to be had in reverence of all them that are about him" (Psalm 89:7).

4 Who shall not fear thee, O Lord,

"Fear ye not me? saith the Lord: will ye not tremble at my presence…" (Jeremiah 5:22).

and glorify thy name?

"All nations whom thou hast made shall come and worship before thee, O Lord; and shall glorify thy name" (Psalm 86:9).

"Ye that fear the Lord, praise him; all ye the seed of Jacob, glorify him; and fear him, all ye the seed of Israel" (Psalm 22:23).

The Roman beast had demanded that the Christians fear and glorify him, but God would soon show who was the real *"King of nations"* and who

for thou only art holy:

"*There is none holy as the Lord...*" (1 Samuel 2:2).

"*But thou art holy, O Thou that inhabitest the praises of Israel*" (Psalm 22:3).

"*Exalt ye the Lord our God, and worship at his footstool; for **he is holy**"* (Psalm 99:5).

"*Exalt the Lord our God, and worship at his holy hill; for **the Lord our God is holy**"* (Psalm 99:9).

for all nations shall come and worship before thee;

"*All nations whom thou hast made shall come **and worship before thee**"* (Psalm 86:9).

"*O praise the Lord, all ye nations: praise him, all ye people*" (Psalm 117:1).

"*All the ends of the world shall remember and turn unto the Lord: and **all the kindreds of the nations shall worship** before thee*" (Psalm 22:27).

for thy judgments are made manifest (Revelation 15:3-4).

"*His righteousness hath he openly shewed in the sight of the heathen*" (Psalm 98:2).

"*He is the Lord our God: **his judgments are in all the earth**"* (Psalm 105:7).

was worthy of the fear and glory of all men!

In spite of the fact that the Roman beast has the enforced worship of these many nations now, it will not always be so. God's righteous judgments will soon be manifested!

5 And after that I looked, and, behold, the temple (Greek, *naos,* sanctuary) *of the tabernacle of the testimony in heaven*

Bowls of God's Wrath from His Heavenly Tabernacle

The "*temple of the tabernacle of the testimony in heaven*" is not a heavenly pattern for the temple in Jerusalem. A more accurate wording here would be "*the **sanctuary** of the tabernacle of the testimony in*

was opened
(Revelation 15:5).

heaven." It refers to the heavenly pattern for the sanctuary of the tabernacle, or tent of witness (or testimony) on earth (Numbers 9:15; 17:7). It was opened so that the seven angels could stream forth on their divinely appointed mission of bringing the wrath of God upon Rome, upon the beast, and upon those who were to have submitted to his idolatrous demands.

6 And the seven angels
came out of the temple
(Greek, naos, sanctu-
ary), having the seven
plagues, clothed in
pure and white linen,
and having their
breasts girded with
golden girdles.

Angels are usually described in Scripture as being dressed in bright white garments (Matthew 28:3; Mark 16:5). The garments of these angels are similar, if not identical, to the garment of the glorified Jesus who was "*clothed with a garment down to the foot, and girt about the paps with a golden girdle*" (Revelation 1:13). The angel in Daniel 10:5 was also clothed with linen and gold.

7 And one of the four
beasts gave unto the
seven angels seven
golden vials (Greek,
chrusas, saucers or
bowls) full of the
wrath of God, who
liveth for ever and ever.

These "*chrusas*" are not long slender vials such as a pharmacist would use, but rather are shallow bowls, or saucers, such as those in which incense was burned every morning and evening upon the golden altar of incense (Exodus 30:7-8; 1 Chronicles 28:17; 2 Chronicles 4:8).

But these bowls, which were given to the seven angels, were not filled with incense as in Revelation 5:8, but rather were full of the wrath of God!

8 And the temple was
filled with smoke from
the glory of God, and
from his power; and
no man (Greek,
oudeis, no one) was
able to enter into the
temple, till the seven
plagues of the seven

We read of a similar occurrence in 1 Kings 8:10-11: "*And it came to pass, when the priests were come out of the holy place, that the cloud filled the house of the Lord, So that the priests could not stand to minister because of the cloud: for the glory of the Lord had filled the house of the Lord.*"

In the same way, these seven angels could not enter the heavenly sanctuary of the tabernacle, because of the glory of the Lord that was within it.[77]

---

77. In Scripture, "*The glory of the Lord*" is often seen as a cloud

"*And it came to pass, as Aaron spake unto the whole congregation of the children of Israel, that they looked toward the wilderness, and behold, the glory of the Lord appeared in the cloud*" (Exodus 16:10).

"*And the glory of the Lord abode upon mount Sinai, and the cloud covered it six days: and the seventh day he called unto Moses out of the midst of the cloud*" (Exodus 24:16).

angels were fulfilled (Revelation 15:6-8). In Revelation 6:10, God had been asked, "*How long, O Lord, holy and true, dost thou not judge and avenge our blood on them that dwell on the earth?*" But now, the number of martyrs was to have been fulfilled, and the wrath of God upon their murderers was to have been pushed to its limit. Now no one can enter the sanctuary to intercede with God for a change, or a delay! Even those in right relationship with Him are not to be close, until His righteous fury is poured out in full measure upon Rome, and upon the beast, and upon all who have killed His servants.[78] Truly, "*the great day of his wrath is come; and who shall be able to stand?*" (Revelation 6:17).

"*Then a cloud covered the tent of the congregation, and the glory of the Lord filled the tabernacle. And Moses was not able to enter into the tent of the congregation, because the cloud abode thereon, and the glory of the Lord filled the tabernacle*" (Exodus 40:34-35).

"*And the Lord said unto Moses, Speak unto Aaron thy brother, that he come not at all times into the holy place within the veil before the mercy seat, which is upon the ark; that he die not: for I will appear in the cloud upon the mercy seat*" (Leviticus 16:2).

"*Then the glory of the Lord went up over the cherub, and stood over the threshold of the house; and the house was filled with the cloud, and the court was full of the brightness of the Lord's glory*" (Ezekiel 10:4).

NOTE: A number of passages will refer to fire, also, as being associated with the cloud in manifesting God's glory. But this study was exclusively upon the cloud. (See Exodus 13:21; 14:24; 24:17; 40:38; Numbers 9:16; 2 Chronicles 7:1-3 for examples of fire in manifesting the glory of the Lord.)

78. The pouring forth of God's wrath and fury

"*Pour out thy wrath upon the heathen that have not known thee, and upon the kingdoms that have not called upon thy name.*
For they have devoured Jacob, and laid waste his dwelling place" (Psalm 79:6-7).

"*Therefore wait ye upon me, saith the Lord, until the day that I rise up to the prey: for my determination is to gather the nations, that I may assemble the kingdoms, to pour upon them mine indignation, even all my fierce anger; for all the earth shall be devoured with the fire of my jealousy*" (Zephaniah 3:8).

Revelation 16
Seven Bowls of Wrath

These seven bowls of God's wrath explain, and expand upon, the phrase of Revelation 11:18a, *"And the nations were angry, and thy wrath is come."*

In fact, Revelation 16:1–22:5 is an explanation, and expansion upon *"the seventh trumpet"* or *"the third woe"* of Revelation 11:15-19.

And I heard a great voice out of the temple saying to the seven angels, Go your ways, and pour out the vials of the wrath of God upon the earth.[79]

2 And the first went, and poured out his vial (or bowl) **upon the earth; and there fell a noisome and grievous sore** (Greek, *helkos,* a sore or ulcer, primarily a wound) *upon the men which had the mark of the beast, and upon them which*

The First Plague: Sores (wounds) upon those who took the mark of the beast, and who worshiped his image

"And I heard a great voice out of the temple (Greek, *naos,* sanctuary)*..."* (Revelation 16:la). (See also Revelation 16:17, *"...and there came a great voice out of the temple* (or sanctuary) *of heaven, from the throne..."*). Obviously, in both instances, this was the voice of God.

"...the men which had the mark of the beast, and upon them which worshipped his image" (Revelation 16:2). This passage proves that the eighth Roman ruler, Domitian, was to have been here on earth, when these plagues were to have come.

But what does it mean, when the first angel went and poured out his bowl *"upon the earth"*? Since the phrase *"they that dwell upon the earth"* refers to the peoples dwelling within the Roman Empire,[79]

---

79. The phrase, *"upon the earth"* (Revelation 16:1-2), is a part of the phrase so commonly used in Revelation, *"they that dwell upon the earth"* (Revelation 3:10; 6:10; 11:10 (twice); 13:8,12,14 (twice); 14:6; 17:8). This phrase, *"they that dwell upon the earth"* is from Daniel 4:1 and Daniel 6:25, where we read, in both passages, *"...that dwell in all the earth."* In Daniel 4:1, this phrase referred to the peoples dwelling within the Babylonian empire, while in Daniel 6:25, this same phrase referred to the peoples dwelling within the Medo-Persian empire.

Thus, by a very natural transference, when the Roman Empire arose, this phrase, *"they that dwell upon the earth,"* which is so close to the similar phrase in Daniel 4:1 and 6:25, came to refer to the peoples dwelling within the Roman Empire,[79]

worshipped his image (Revelation 16:1-2).

the word "*earth*" in this phrase, must refer to the Roman Empire itself.[80]

Because Rome was to have been destroyed (burned) by the beast (Domitian) and the ten kings allied with him (Revelation 17:11,16), this suggests the outbreak of *civil war* within the boundaries of the Roman Empire; the "*sores*" being the wounds received in battle.[81]

Domitian was unpopular in Rome. The Roman senate and the leaders of Rome hated him. The Roman army was loyal to Domitian, however, as he had increased their pay by one third!

The phrase "*upon the earth*" would seem to indicate that the fighting erupted in the Roman provinces. A likely scenario would be that Domitian was expelled from Rome and then, rallying his army, he would have begun to fight back. He appears to have the support of the College of Augures (the false prophet) in his attempt (Revelation 16:13). Christians would not have been involved in this civil war, as they would have left Rome in obedience to God's Word (Revelation 18:4).[82]

3 And the second angel poured out his vial upon the sea; and it became as the blood of a dead man: and every living soul died in the sea (Revelation 16:3).

The Second Plague: The sea becomes blood–and brings death

"*And the second angel poured out his vial* (bowl) *upon the sea; and it became as the blood of a dead man* (or, it became blood as of a dead man); *and every living soul died in the sea*" (Revelation 16:3).

In the trumpets judgments, "*the third part of the creatures which were in the sea, and had life, died*"

---

80. In Revelation, the Greek word *ge* has several meanings. It may mean (1) the entire earth; (2) land, as dirt, soil, or ground; (3) a nation, or empire, as Judea, or the Roman Empire; or (4) a large land area, as the area of the Roman Empire and of the three previous world empires. In Revelation 12:16 (twice) and in Revelation 14:3, "*the earth*" is a specific reference to Pella where the Jewish believers in Jesus fled in A.D. 66.

81. "*Sore*" (Greek, *helkos*), as rendered by *Vine's Expository Dictionary of New Testament Words*, pg. 1075.

Helkos, "*a sore or ulcer (primarily a wound), occurs in Luke 16:21; Revevelation 16:2,11.*"

82. "*And I heard another voice from heaven, saying, Come out of her, my people, that ye be not partakers of her sins, and that ye receive not of her plagues*" (Revelation 18:4).

(Revelation 8:9a). In that instance the judgment was limited to Jerusalem. In this one, the judgment engulfs the entire Roman Empire.

But again, what does it mean, when the second angel poured out his bowl *"upon the sea?"* In Revelation 17:1, we read of *"the great whore that sitteth upon many waters,"* and in Revelation 17:15 these *"many waters"* are defined: *"And he saith unto me, **The waters** which thou sawest, where the whore sitteth, **are peoples, and multitudes, and nations, and tongues."** The "peoples"* within the Roman Empire are *"the sea."*

In Revelation 8:8-9, *"the sea"* was interpreted to mean *"enemy armies,"* in that instance, *"Roman soldiers."* But this was because Jerusalem had fallen into *"the sea,"* and the overflowing waters, in Scripture, are compared to enemy armies (as in Isaiah 8:7; 17:12-13; 59:19b; Jeremiah 46:7-8; Daniel 9:26; 11:22). But because Rome is not pictured here as sinking below the surface of the waves (as Jerusalem was in Revelation 8:8-9), the symbol is different. *"The sea,"* in Revelation 16:3, is the *"peoples"* within the Roman Empire.

The *"blood"* is a way of expressing conflict.[83] The civil war, being murderous, destroys the multitudes throughout the Roman Empire. The *"blood as of a dead man"* is coagulated and clotted, foul and putrefying. The picture is of large numbers of corpses lying in their blood

---

83. *"And when all the kings of the Moabites heard that the kings were come up to fight against them, they gathered all that were able to put on armour, and upward, and stood in the border.*
And they rose up early in the morning, and the sun shone upon the water, and the Moabites saw the water on the other side as red as blood:
And they said, This is blood: the kings are surely slain, and they have smitten one another: now therefore, Moab, to the spoil" (2 Kings 3:21-23).

"And David said to Solomon, My son, as for me, it was in my mind to build an house unto the name of the Lord my God.
But the word of the Lord came to me, saying, Thou hast shed blood abundantly, and hast made great wars: thou shalt not build an house unto my name, because thou hast shed much blood upon the earth in my sight" (1 Chronicles 22:8-9).

"Their blood have they shed like water round about Jerusalem; and there was none to bury them" (Psalm 79:3).

"Then whosoever heareth the sound of the trumpet, and taketh not warning; if the sword come, and take him away, his blood shall be upon his own head" (Ezekiel 33:4).

throughout the Roman Empire, to such an extent that "*every living soul died in the sea*" (Revelation 16:3b).

And the third angel poured out his vial upon the rivers and fountains of waters; and they became blood.

5 And I heard the angel of the waters say, Thou art righteous, O Lord, which art, and wast, and shalt be, because thou hast judged thus.

6 For they have shed the blood of saints and prophets, and thou hast given them blood to drink; for they are worthy.

7 And I heard another out of the altar say, Even so, Lord God Almighty, **true and righteous are thy judgments**[84] (Revelation 16:4-7).

The Third Plague: Rivers, fountains of waters, become blood

"*And the third angel poured out his vial (bowl) upon the rivers and fountains of waters; and they became blood*" (Revelation 16:4).

The "*fountains of waters*" refer to the sources of the rivers, such as the tributaries of the Tiber River which flows through Rome.

The action of "*the third angel*" is both similar and dissimilar to that of "*the second angel*"—similar in that both poured out their bowls upon water, and in both instances the water turned to blood. Their actions are dissimilar in that "*the sea*" is much more water than "*the rivers and fountains of waters.*"

Another similarity is that the actions of both angels involve "*many waters,*" that is, the "*peoples, and multitudes, and nations, and tongues*" (Revelation 17:15) of the Roman Empire. And dissimilar in that this conflict moves from the larger body of water (the Roman Empire, apparently) to the smaller tributaries (obviously Rome, then).

In the warfare between the beast and his armies, and the armies defending Rome, the battle has moved from the Roman provinces to Rome.

The action of "*the third angel*" fits the scene in Revelation 14:18-20 of a most horrible divine punishment upon Rome. The slaughter is so great that the martyrs who, in Revelation 6:10, cried, "*How long, O Lord, holy and true, dost thou not judge and avenge our blood on them that dwell on the earth?,*" yes, these same martyrs and many more besides, are saying, "*Even so, Lord God Almighty, true and righteous are thy judgments*" (Revelation 16:7). This shows they have now been avenged.

---

84. "*The fear of the Lord is clean, enduring for ever: the judgments of the Lord are true and righteous altogether*" (Psalm 19:9).

Thus, in Revelation 16:4-7, the armies defending Rome have been defeated by the armies of the beast. The "*great city*" of Rome stands powerless before the beast (who would have been Domitian), whose intent is to wreak his vengeance upon the city.

"*And I heard* **the angel of the waters** *say, Thou art righteous, O Lord, which art, and wast, and shalt be, because thou hast judged thus. For they have shed the blood of saints and prophets*[85] (for instance, "*the two witnesses*" who are also called "*two prophets*" in Revelation 11:10), *and thou hast given them blood to drink; for they are worthy*" (Revelation 16:5-6).

"*The angel of the waters.*" We have read previously of "*the angel of the bottomless pit*" (Revelation 9:11); "*another angel...which had power over fire*" (Revelation 14:18); "*four angels...holding the four winds of the earth*" (Revelation 7:1); and "*the four angels which are bound in the great river Euphrates*" (Revelation 9:14). A quote on this matter may help. "*The Rabbinic writers speak of an angel set over the earth, and of another who is prince of the sea; every element, every form of created life, has its angel-counterpart.*" (Yalkut Ruben, f.7.1 quoted from Swete, *Commentary on Revelation*, pg. 202 under verse 5.)

The phrases, "*the angel of the waters*" and "*thou hast given them blood to drink,*" seem to indicate that these waters were not only figurative, but also literally true, and that the Tiber River, which flows through Rome, and nearby streams would be polluted with the blood of the slain.

---

85. A reference to Psalm 105:15, "*Touch not mine enointed, and do my prophets no harm.*"

"*Now he which stablisheth us with you in Christ, and hath anointed us, is God;
Who hath also sealed us, and given the earnest of the Spirit in our hearts*" (2 Corinthians 1:21-22).

"*But the anointing which ye have received of him abideth in you, and ye need not that any man teach you: but as the same anointing teacheth you of all things, and is truth, and is no lie, and even as it hath taught you, ye shall abide in him*" (1 John 2:27).

Because all God's saints were anointed, this was a clear violation of God's Word, and God would be avenging this violation.

8 And the fourth angel poured out his vial upon the sun; and power was given unto him to scorch men with (Greek, en, in) fire.

9 And men were scorched with great heat, and blasphemed the name of God, which hath power over these plagues: and they repented not to give him glory (Revelation 16:8-9).

The Fourth Plague: Men are *"scorched"* with fire

The *"fourth angel"* now pours out his bowl upon the sun, the symbol or representative of fire, and *"men were scorched with great heat."* The ancients, including the Hebrews, thought of the sun, the moon, and the stars as having personality. The sun was masculine, and the moon was feminine.[86] There are clear statements in Revelation that Rome is to be burned by fire: *"she shall be utterly burned with* (or in) *fire"* (Revelation 18:8); and this burning is to be done by the beast and by the ten kings allied with him (Revelation 17:16).

Thus, after the beast and his allies (the ten kings) have defeated those defending Rome, the city is at his mercy. He and those with him, then set fire to Rome, and this is the meaning of the fourth plague.

Those being scorched would include those bewildered and defeated soldiers who had retreated into the city; those refugees who had previously flooded into Rome, and also, the residents of Rome.

But the Greek here does not say that men were scorched *"with fire,"* but *"in fire."* This suggests that terrible flames were burning all about them, and

---

86. *"...as the sun when he goeth forth in his might"* (Judges 5:31).

"His (the sun's) *going forth is from the end of heaven, and his circuit unto the ends of it; and there is nothing hid from the heat thereof"* (Psalm 19:6).

"He appointed the moon for seasons: the sun knoweth his going down" (Psalm 104:19).

"The sun also ariseth, and the sun goeth down, and hasteth to his place where he arose" (Ecclesiastes 1:5).

"For the stars of heaven and the constellations thereof shall not give their light: the sun shall be darkened in his going forth, and the moon shall not cause her light to shine" (Isaiah 13:10).

"Then the moon shall be confounded, and the sun ashamed when the Lord of hosts shall reign in mount Zion, and in Jerusalem, and before his ancients gloriously" (Isaiah 24:23).

"And when I shall put thee out, I will cover the heaven, and make the stars thereof dark; I will cover the sun with a cloud, and the moon shall not give her light" (Ezekiel 32:7).

"Immediately after the tribulation of those days shall the sun be darkened, and the moon shall not give her light, and the stars shall fall from heaven, and the powers of the heavens shall be shaken" (Matthew 24:29).

"...as the sun shineth in his strength" (Revelation 1:16).

"They fought from heaven; the stars in their courses fought against Sisera" (Judges 5:20).

"...in the sight of this sun" (2 Samuel 12:11).

"When the morning stars sang together, and all the sons of God shouted for joy?" (Job 38:7).

"Praise ye him, sun and moon; praise him, all ye stars of light" (Psalm 148:3).

were so close that they could not fully escape their heat. This, then, is the prophetic picture being presented by this fourth plague.

These Romans would blaspheme the name of God, but even though their city was being destroyed, still they would not repent and give Him glory.

10 And the fifth angel poured out his vial upon the seat (Greek, thronon, throne) of the beast; and his kingdom was full of darkness; and they gnawed their tongues for pain,

11 And blasphemed the God of heaven because of their pains and their sores (or wounds), and repented not of their deeds (Revelation 16:10-11).

The Fifth Plague: *"The seat of the beast"* (Rome) receives bowl of God's wrath; beast's kingdom is in darkness

The *"seat"* or *"throne"* of the beast was in Rome. Because Babylon (Rome) is to be destroyed by the beast and the ten kings allied with him (Revelation 17:16), then *Babylon (Rome) must be destroyed before the beast is destroyed by the returning* Jesus. This fact clearly supports our finding that places the destruction of Rome by fire during the fourth plague. Also, the fact that, in the following sixth plague, the beast and his armies are no longer in the vicinity of Rome, but rather are at Armageddon, indicates that the burning of Rome is over at that time. Later, Rome would be dealt a final blow by God Himself, in the form of an enormous earthquake and hailstones (Revelation 16:19,21).

Because Rome has by this time been destroyed by fire, the *"darkness"*[87] of this fifth plague would have been produced by *"the smoke of her burning"* so prominently mentioned in Revelation 18:9,18. (See also 19:3.[88])

---

87. This *"smoke"* which is to darken the Roman provinces may seem somewhat insignificant, but darkness is a symbol of gloom, distress, and woe. In this instance (Revelation 16:10-11) it is because Rome ("*Babylon*") is to have fallen.

To review the symbolic meaning of darkness, see Chapter One, Understanding the Hebrew Idiom.

This *"smoke"* which darkens the Roman provinces in this fifth bowl of God's wrath (Revelation 16:10-11) is then a portent, or prophetic omen, of the further destruction that occurs during the seventh bowl of God's wrath (Revelation 16:17-21) when Rome is struck by *"so mighty an earthquake"* that *"the great city was divided into three parts, and the cities of the nations fell,"* and *"a great hail"* falls upon the people of Rome, as God remembers *"great Babylon."*

88. *"And the kings of the earth, who have committed fornication and lived deliciously with her, shall bewail her, and lament for her, when they shall see the smoke of her burning"* (Revelation 18:9).

"And cried when they saw the smoke of her burning, saying, What city is like unto this great city!" (Revelation 18:18).

"And again they said, Alleluia. And her smoke rose up for ever and ever" (Revelation 19:3).

Revelation 18 gives a picture of the extent of this darkness, or smoke, as kings (18:3,9), merchants (18:3,11,15), and shipmasters and sailors (18:17) bewail her and see the smoke of her ruin. Thus as columns of smoke billow forth from the smoldering ruins of Rome, they darken the kingdom that Rome had ruled. Death and destruction are everywhere. *"BABYLON THE GREAT [ROME] IS FALLEN, IS FALLEN..."*

The first five plagues of the bowls of wrath give the successive steps by which Rome would have been destroyed in the reign of Domitian, and by which it will be destroyed in the future. These steps, which we have seen pictured in these first five plagues, are:

(1) Civil war breaks out within the Roman Empire;

(2) The murderous civil war destroys multitudes throughout the Roman Empire;

(3) The slaughter of civil war has moved from the Roman provinces to Rome;

(4) Rome is burned by the beast and his allies;

(5) The smoke from Rome's burning rises and darkens the Roman provinces.

Inasmuch as Rome has now been seen prophetically as destroyed, we are ready for the sixth plague. This plague prepares the beast and all those allied with him, also the kings from the sun-rising, for their destruction.

And the sixth angel poured out his vial upon the great river Euphrates; and the water thereof was dried up,[89] *that the*

The Sixth Plague: The beast meets the kings from the sun-rising at Armageddon

The *"kings from the sun-rising"* identified: In identifying the *"kings from the sun-rising"* it is necessary to refer to the prophecies of Daniel, regarding the

---

89. *"'The water thereof was dried up" is an Eastern saying which means that the armies were large and powerful. When a large and thirsty army encamps by a stream or a river, it uses a great quantity of water. Then again, when the campaigns of a successful general are related, it is said that the rivers dried up before him'"* (*New Testament Commentary*, George Lamsa, pg. 588).

Thus, for the *"great river Euphrates"* to be *"dried up"* would figuratively suggest very large armies, armies so large that they could figuratively drink the entire river, and dry it up.

Other passages of Scripture related to this are:

continued on next page

way of the kings of the east (Greek, *apo ana-toles heliou, from risings of sun) might be prepared* (Revelation 16:12).

four great empires that were to come upon the earth, and that were to be supplanted by the kingdom of God.

In Daniel 2:1-45, we read of Nebuchadnezzar's great dream which Daniel interpreted. Later, another dream, with different symbols, but with the same meanings, was given to Daniel (see 7:2-28).

In these two dreams, four great world empires were predicted. These were the Babylonian, the Medo-Persian, the Greek, and the Roman Empires. These four empires, or kingdoms, were to be supplanted on earth by the victorious kingdom of God!

Daniel is clear that the coming kingdom of God would not only supplant the Roman Empire, but that it would also supplant the Babylonian, the Medo-Persian, and the Greek empires *at the same time*! The following passage, studied in its context, indicates this.

"Then was the iron, the clay, the brass, the silver, and the gold, broken to pieces together, and became like the chaff of the summer threshingfloors; and the wind carried them away, that no place was found for them: and the stone that smote the image became a great mountain, and filled the whole earth" (Daniel 2:35).

"A sword is upon the Chaldeans, saith the Lord, and upon the inhabitants of Babylon, and upon her princes, and upon her wise men...
A drought is upon her waters; and she shall be dried up: for it is the land of graven images, and they are mad upon their idols" (Jeremiah 50:35,38).

"Therefore thus saith the Lord; Behold, I will plead thy cause, and take vengeance for thee; and I will dry up her sea, and make her springs dry" (Jeremiah 51:36).

"Thus saith the Lord God; I will also make the multitude of Egypt to cease by the hand of Nebuchadnezzar king of Babylon.
He and his people with him, the terrible of the nations, shall be brought to destroy the land: and they shall draw their swords against Egypt, and fill the land with the slain.
And I will make the rivers dry, and sell the land into the hand of the wicked: and I will make the land waste, and all that is therein, by the hand of strangers: I the Lord have spoken it" (Ezekiel 30:10-12).

Also, Joel 1:2-20 is a picture of successive enemy incursions into Judah and Jerusalem to such an extent that *"the rivers of water are dried up"* (Joel 1:20), figuratively producing a great famine. (See also Isaiah 19:4-10).

It needs also to be noted that the Babylonian, Medo-Persian, and Greek empires occupied, for the most part, the same land areas, whereas the Roman Empire, for the most part, occupied a different land area, though all four empires reigned over the land of Judea.

But the Babylonian, Medo-Persian, and Greek empires were not to be completely destroyed until they and the Roman Empire were destroyed together by the coming kingdom of God! As we read in Daniel 7:12 (which again needs to be studied in its context), *"As concerning the rest of the beasts, they had their dominion taken away: yet their lives were prolonged for a season and time."*

These three former world empires—the Babylonian, the Medo-Persian, and the Greek—became a part of a loose confederation of states and mini-states called by the Greeks, "the Parthian empire," though there is no evidence that those living there referred to themselves as "Parthians."

This "empire," according to Pliny (latter first century A.D.), consisted of eleven "upper" kingdoms and seven "lower" kingdoms. These eighteen kingdoms were the nations and peoples which had previously been parts of the Babylonian, Medo-Persian, and Greek empires, and which were here in Revelation 16:12 described as *"the kings from the sun-rising."*

Thus, Daniel had prophesied that the kingdom of God would *"break in pieces and consume all these kingdoms"* (Daniel 2:44), while Revelation shows more precisely just how this was to happen.

Accordingly, in Revelation 16:12-16, we see the kings of the nations which made up these three former world empires gathering at Armageddon, together with the beast and his armies, while in Revelation 19:11-21, we see the defeat by Jesus and His army, of the beast, and of the kings of the earth who led the remnants of the three former great world empires.

We do not know at what point the Roman beast and *"the kings from the sun-rising"* became aware that they were gathering to fight against Jesus, and that His kingdom would supplant all of theirs, but Revelation 16:13-14 suggests that this was to be the work of the *"three unclean spirits like frogs."*

And I saw three unclean spirits like frogs come out of the mouth of the dragon, and out of the mouth of the beast, and out of the mouth of the false prophet.

14 For they are the spirits of devils (Greek, *daimonion,* demons), *working miracles, which go*

The *"three unclean spirits like frogs"* (Revelation 16:13-14) explained: Frogs remind us of the second plague against Egypt (Exodus 8:1-15). Spirits, good and bad, sometimes take the form of animals,[90] as horses (see Zechariah 1: 8-11; 6:1-8, especially vs. 5, *"These are the four spirits of the heavens…"*), a *"python spirit"* (Acts 16:16, Greek, *pneuma puthonos,* spirit of python), also a *"goat demon"* (Leviticus 17:7, NASV). Thus, these spirits appeared as frogs.

Frogs were an unclean creature (see Leviticus 11:10, where frogs are described, but not named), and were thought to spread corruption, such as

---

90. New American Standard
"And they shall no longer sacrifice their sacrifices to the goat demons with which they play the harlot. This shall be a permanent statute to them throughout their generations" (Leviticus 17:7).

The Amplified Bible
"So they shall no more offer their sacrifices to goatlike gods or demons or field spirits, after which they have played the harlot. This shall be a statute for ever to them throughout their generations" (Leviticus 17:7).

The Septuagint Version (LXX)
*"I saw by night, and behold a man mounted on a red horse, and he stood between the shady mountains; and behind him were red horses, and grey, and piebald, and white.
And I said, What are these, my lord? And the angel that spoke with me said to me, I will shew thee what these things are.
And the man that stood between the mountains answered, and said to me, These are they whom the Lord has sent forth to go round the earth.
And they answered the angel of the Lord that stood between the mountains, and said, We have gone round all the earth, and behold, all the earth is inhabited, and is at rest"* (Zacharias 1:8-11 LXX).

*"And I turned, and lifted up mine eyes, and looked, and behold, four chariots coming out from between two mountains; and the mountains were brazen mountains
In the first chariot were red horses; and in the second chariot black horses;
And in the third chariot white horses; and in the fourth chariot piebald and ash-coloured horses.
And I answered and said to the angel that talked with me, What are these, my lord? And the angel that talked with me answered and said, These are the four winds* (Greek, *anemos,* wind from the Hebrew, *ruach,* spirit or wind) *of heaven, and they are going forth to stand before the Lord of all the earth.
As for the chariot in which were the black horses, they went out to the land of the north; and the white went out after them; and the piebald went out to the land of the south.
And the ash-coloured went out, and looked to go and compass the earth: and he said, Go, and compass the earth. And they compassed the earth.
And he cried out and spoke to me, saying, Behold, these go out to the land of the north, and they have quieted mine anger in the land of the north"* (Zacharias 6:1-8 LXX).

forth unto the kings of the earth and of the whole world, to gather them to the battle of that great day of God Almighty (Revelation 16:13-14).

disease and pollution (see Psalm 78:45, in a reference to the second plague upon Egypt, "...*and frogs which destroyed* (Hebrew, *shachath*, to mar, *corrupt*, destroy) or, **corrupted** *them*").

These three frog spirits are pictured as especially unclean, because they come from the most unclean places imaginable, that is, "*out of the mouth of the dragon, and out of the mouth of the beast, and out of the mouth of the false prophet*" (Revelation 16:13). Also, "*they are the **spirits of devils** (Greek, pneumata daimonion, **spirits of demons**)*" (Revelation 16:14a).

These "*spirits of demons*," "**working miracles**" (Greek, *poiounta semeia*, *doing signs*) "*go forth unto the kings* ("*of the earth*" in the King James Version is an interpolation here, though this same phrase, "*the kings of the earth*," is correct in Revelation 19:19) *of the whole world* (Greek, *oikoumenas holas*, *habitable whole*), *to gather them to the battle of that great day of God Almighty*" (Revelation 16:14).

This "*battle of the great day of God Almighty*" is further referred to in Revelation 17:14; 19:19.

"*These* (ten kings) *shall make war with the Lamb, and the Lamb shall overcome them...*" (Revelation 17:14a).

"*And I saw the beast, and the kings of the earth, and their armies, gathered together to make war against him that sat on the horse, and against his army*" (Revelation 19:19).

The phrase, "*habitable whole*," translated "*the whole world*" in Revelation 16:14 (KJV), needs to be understood in the light of other passages of Scripture.

Thus, in Daniel 2:38, Daniel told king Nebuchadnezzar that "*wheresoever the children of men dwell, the beasts of the field and the fowls of the heaven hath he given into thine hand, and **hath made thee ruler over them all**.*" Daniel then told the king that after him would arise "*another kingdom inferior to thee, and another third kingdom of brass, **which shall bear rule over all the earth**"* (Daniel 2:39).

In Daniel 7:23, we read the following regarding the area to be ruled by the Roman Empire: "*The fourth beast shall be the fourth kingdom upon the earth, which shall be diverse from all kingdoms, **and shall devour the whole earth**, and shall tread it down, and break it in pieces.*"

Yet, none of these four kingdoms reigned in North or South America, Australia, New Zealand, or Southeast Asia, and they reigned in only a small part of Africa. Then what does the scripture mean by such phrases as "*all the world,*" "*all the earth,*" and "*hath made thee ruler over them all?*" Clearly these phrases described an area much less than modern man would mean by the same phrases, and this would be true of the phrase "*kings of the habitable whole*" and "*of the whole world*" which we find in Revelation 16:14. These phrases indicated a large land area. Nothing more. Even the land area of Judea is referred to as "*all the world*" (Acts 11:28).[91] In Revelation 16:14 and 19:19 the phrases obviously include "*the kings from the sun-rising,*" that is, the area known in history as

---

91. "*And in these days came prophets from Jerusalem unto Antioch.*
And there stood up one of them named Agabus, and signified by the spirit that there should be great dearth throughout all the world: which came to pass in the days of Claudius Caesar.
Then the disciples, every man according to his ability determined to send relief unto the brethren Which dwelt in Judea:
Which also they did, and sent it to the elders by the hands of Barnabas and Saul" (Acts 11:27-30).

"Chapter XII - Helen, Queen of the Osrhoenians.

*About this time it happened that the great famine **took place in Judea**, in which also queen Helen having purchased grain from Egypt, with large sums, distributed to the needy. You will also find this statement in accordance with that in the Acts of the Apostles, where it is said, that according to the ability of the disciples at Antioch, they determined, each one, to send to the assistance of those in Judea. Which also they did, sending to the elders by the hands of Barnabas and Paul. Of this same Helen, mentioned by the historian, splendid monuments are still to be seen in the suburbs of the city (Jerusalem) now called Aelia. But she is said to have been queen of the Adiabeni*" (Eusebius' Ecclesiastical History, page 62).

"*Now her* (Helena, queen mother of Adiabene, who had embraced Judaism) *coming was of very great advantage to the people of Jerusalem; for whereas a famine did oppress them at that time, and many people died for want of what was necessary to procure food withal, queen Helena sent some of her servants to Alexandria with money to buy a great quantity of corn, and others of them to Cyprus, to bring a cargo of dried figs; and as soon as they were come back, and brought those provisions, which was done very quickly, she distributed food to those that were in want of it, and left a most excellent memorial behind her of this benefaction, which she bestowed on our whole nation; and when her son Izates* (the king of Adiabene, who had also embraced Judaism) *was informed of this famine, he sent great sums of money to the principal men in Jerusalem. However, what favors this queen and king conferred upon our city Jerusalem, shall be further related hereafter*" (Antiquities of the Jews, Josephus, XX. II. 5).

"the Parthian empire," as well as the area of the Roman Empire. The kings from these areas were prophesied to have been seduced by frog-like spirits of demons to assemble in the reign of Domitian for *"the battle of that great day of God Almighty."* (This prophecy, as we have stated so often before, was thrown into the future by a massive repentance throughout the Roman Empire, and also by a failure of the Jews to repent and receive the kingdom planned for them.)

Behold, I come as a thief: Blessed is he that watcheth, and keepeth his garments, lest he walk naked, and they see his shame
(Revelation 16:15).

The Watching That Is "Blessed"

Jesus' second coming is often described in Scripture as like that of a thief (Revelation 3:3; 1 Thessalonians 5:2; 2 Peter 3:10; Luke 12:39). This indicates that His coming would be sudden and unexpectedly, such as a thief's coming would be.

This verse, Revelation 16:15, contains the third of the seven blessings of Revelation. The other "blesseds" are in Revelation 1:3; 14:13; 19:9; 20:6; 22:7,14.[92]

Jesus often emphasized that we *"watch"* for His coming (Matthew 24:42; 25:13; Mark 13:33-37; Luke 12:37-43; 21:36). This *"watching"* is to help keep us morally pure (2 Peter 3:14; 1 John 3:3). There can be no doubt that there were moral requirements for entering the kingdom of God

---

92. *"Blessed is he that readeth, and they that hear the words of this prophecy, and keep those things which are written therein: for the time is at hand"* (Revelation 1:3).

"And I heard a voice from heaven saying unto me, Write, Blessed are the dead which die in the Lord from henceforth: Yea, saith the Spirit, that they may rest from their labours; and their works do follow them" (Revelation 14:13).

"Behold, I come as a thief: Blessed is he that watcheth, and keepeth his garments, lest he walk naked and they see his shame" (Revelation 16:15).

"And he saith unto me, Write, Blessed are they which are called unto the marriage supper of the Lamb. And he saith unto me, These are the true sayings of God" (Revelation 19:9).

"Blessed and holy is he that hath part in the first resurrection: on such the second death hath no power, but they shall be priests of God and of Christ, and shall reign with him a thousand years" (Revelation 20:6).

"Behold, I come quickly: blessed is he that keepeth the sayings of the prophecy of this book" (Revelation 22:7).

"Blessed are they that do his commandments, that they may have right to the tree of life, and may enter in through the gates into the city" (Revelation 22:14).

(Matthew 3:2; 4:17; Mark 1:5; Romans 14:17; 1 Corinthians 6:9-10; Galatians 5:19-21; Ephesians 5:5; 2 Thessalonians 1:5).

The *"watching"* in Revelation 16:15 is an allusion to an ancient Jewish practice. The Talmud reads, *"The Captain of the Temple visited each guard, and burning torches were carried before him...If he observed that he slept, he smote him with his stick, and he had authority to burn his dress."* (Quoted from Whittaker, H. A., *Revelation: A Biblical Approach*, pg. 203). Thus, both pain and humiliation awaited any guard who slept on duty.

In Scripture, *"garments"* refer to one's moral purity. (See Psalm 132:9a, *"let thy priests be clothed with righteousness..."*; Ecclesiastes 9:8a, *"Let thy garments be always white..."*; Revelation 7:13-14, *"What are these which are arrayed in white robes...?"* *"These...have washed their robes, and made them white in the blood of the Lamb."* Also Revelation 19:8b, *"...for the fine linen is the righteousness of saints."*)

By "watching," then, we continue to be aware of Jesus' soon coming, and with our thoughts upon Him we are able to overcome wrong thoughts and desires, and to keep our garments white.

But what about those of us who have soiled our garments? For us Jesus says, *"I counsel thee to buy of me gold tried in the fire...**and white raiment, that thou mayest be clothed, and that the shame of thy nakedness do not appear...**"* (Revelation 3:18a).

And he (or, *they,* that is, the *"three unclean spirits"*) *gathered them together into a place called in the Hebrew tongue Armageddon* (Revelation 16:16).

What and where is *"Armageddon"*?

*"And **he gathered** them **together*** (Greek, *sunagagen,* as a neuter plural with a singular verb, may be rendered *"they gathered together"*; *"they"* referring to the *"three unclean spirits"* of Revelation 16:13) *into a place called **in the Hebrew tongue** Armageddon"* (Revelation 16:16).

Because much ink has been spilt on this verse, with not much illumination, it might be well to examine more carefully the meaning of the phrase *"called in the Hebrew tongue."* It is a phrase used often in *The Antiquities of the Jews* by Josephus. Here are some passages that illustrate the usage of the phrase *"in the Hebrew tongue."*[93]

"...the Sabbath; which word denotes rest in the Hebrew tongue" (*Antiquities*, I. I. 1)

"This man was called Adam, which in the Hebrew tongue signifies one that is red, because he was formed out of the red earth" (*Antiquities*, I. I. 2).

"Now a woman is called in the Hebrew tongue Issa; but the name of this woman was Eve, which signifies the mother of all living" (*Antiquities*, I. I. 2).

"...for the Hebrews mean by the word Babel, Confusion" (*Antiquities*, I. IV. 3).

"He also commanded him to be called Israel, which in the Hebrew tongue signifies one that struggled with the divine angel" (*Antiquities*, I. XX. 2).

"Now the former of those names, Gersom, in the Hebrew tongue signifies that he was in a strange land; and Eleazer, that, by the assistance of the God of his fathers, he had escaped from the Egyptians" (*Antiquities*, II. XIII. L).

"...for Adoni in the Hebrew tongue signifies Lord" (*Antiquities*, V. II. 2).

---

93. Some New Testament scholars have felt that whenever the word *"Hebrew"* is used of the language spoken in the New Testament, we should mentally translate it *"Aramaic."* The assumption behind this notion is that the Hebrew language was no longer in use in the first century, A.D.

This view is not correct, however. The word *"Abaddon"* (Revelation 9:11), for instance, is a Hebrew word, not an Aramaic one. Also, some of the Dead Sea Scrolls, which were in current use while Jesus was yet alive, were written in Hebrew. For instance, the Habakkuk Peshur (1QpHab), the War Scroll (1QM), the Thanksgiving Hymns (1QH), and the Rule of the Community (1QH) were all written in Hebrew. However, because the Qumran Community was an isolated one, we must not consider the language patterns there as normal for Judea as a whole. Still, it can be stated with authority that Hebrew was not a dead language in the first century, A.D.

Thus, there is no need to mentally translate the word *"Hebrew"* to mean Aramaic. Hebrew means Hebrew.

However, when the apostle Paul spoke to an angry Jewish mob in Hebrew, they were quieted (Acts 21:40; 22:2). The Scriptures are clear that the Jewish people *"kept the more silence...when they heard that he spake in the Hebrew tongue to them."* This, and the following verses, indicates three things to us:

Hebrew was respected much like a sacred language, and for this reason the mob quieted;

Hebrew was an understood language, as evidenced by the fact that his Hebrew words caused them to begin again to riot (Acts 22:22-23);

continued on next page

"...they besought Deborah, a certain prophetess among them (which name in the Hebrew tongue signifies a Bee)..." (Antiquities, V. V. 1).

"Now Barak, in the Hebrew tongue, signifies Lightning" (Antiquities, V. V. 1).

"Now Naomi signifies in the Hebrew tongue happiness, and Mara, sorrow" (Antiquities, V. IX. 2).

"So Samuel gathered them together to a certain city called Mizpeh, which, in the Hebrew tongue, signifies a water-tower" (Antiquities, VI. II. L).

"Now Nabal, in the Hebrew tongue, signifies folly" (Antiquities, VI. XIII. 7).

Note in each of the above quotations that when the phrase, *"in the Hebrew tongue"* was used, it was not the *letters* of the Hebrew word but the *meaning* of the Hebrew word, that was important! This fact strongly suggests that in the phrase *"called in the Hebrew tongue Armageddon,"* the word *"Armageddon"* was intended to be translated, rather than merely transliterated as we have it in all of our English versions.

What, then, is a correct translation of the Hebrew word *"Armageddon"*? It is made up of two words:

Hebrew was not their usual language, as evidenced again by their quieting when they heard it spoken.

The evidence that Jesus (and the Palestinian Jews in the first century A.D.) spoke Aramaic is that some short quotes from Him, which were precisely remembered, are given in *Aramaic* in the Gospel according to Mark.

"And he (that is, Jesus) *took the damsel by the hand and said to her, Talitha cumi; which is, being interpreted, Damsel, I say unto thee, arise"* (Mark 5:41).

"And he (that is, Jesus) *said, Abba, Father, all things are possible unto thee; take away this cup from me: nevertheless not what I will, but what thou wilt"* (Mark 14:36).

"And at the ninth hour Jesus cried with a loud voice, saying, Eloi, Eloi lama sabachthani? which is, being interpreted, My God, my God, why hast thou forsaken me?" (Mark 15:34).

Jesus like other Palestinian Jews, normally spoke Aramaic, but He also understood, and very likely was able to speak, in Hebrew.

It needs also to be said that just as there were dialects among the Hebrews (see Judges 12:6, where the Ephraimites could not pronounce the "sh" sound), so also there were dialects in the Aramaic language.

This explains why Peter's speech gave him away (Matthew 26:73; Mark 14:70). Peter, like Jesus, spoke a Galilean, or Northern Aramaic, while the Jews who lived in Judea would have spoken a Southern Aramaic. It was for this same reason that Jesus' words on the cross, *"Eli, Eli"* were misunderstood (Matthew 27:46, 47; Mark 15:34-35) Some thought that He was calling for Elijah, when He was crying out to God. His Northern Aramaic was not easily understood in Judea, and the words for God, *Eli*, and Elijah, *Elia*, were similar.

"Ar" or *"Har,"* and *"Megiddo"* or *"Megiddon."*
"Megiddo" or *"Megiddon"* was a city on the Plain of
Jezreel (later known as the Plain of Esdraelon). The
meaning of *"Megiddo"* or *"Megiddon"* in the Hebrew
tongue was *"place of God."* (*Young's Analytical
Concordance,* pg. 652 3rd Column). But what does
the prefix *"Ar"* or *"Har"'* mean (since there is about
equal manuscript support for *"Ar"* and *"Har"* as the
prefix in this passage for *"Megiddo(n)"*)?

"Har" means *"mountain,"* and this combined with
"Megiddo" would mean *"mountain of God."*[94]

At first, *"Har"* seems more attractive than *"Ar"* as a
prefix here because it is used with a much greater
frequency in Scripture. *"Har"* is translated *"hill"* 61
times; *"hill country"* once; and *"mount"* or *"mountain"* 486 times in the King James Version.

But difficulties appear with both the literal and the
figurative usages of *"Har."*

(1) No mountain, or mountains, are named
"Megiddo."

(2) The ancient battles were not fought in the
mountains surrounding Megiddo, but rather in the
valley or plain where there was an abundance of
room for the movement of armies.

(3) The phrase, *"mountain of God"* is a scriptural
one, and is used of those mountains called Moriah
and Sinai (also called Horeb) (*"hill of God,"* Psalm
68:15; Moriah, 2 Chronicles 3:1; Sinai, or Horeb,

---

94. The terms *"the mountain* (Hebrew, *har,* mountain, mount, or hill*) of God"* (Exodus 3:1; 4:27;
18:5; 24:13; 1 Kings 19:8; Psalm 68:15), or *"the mount* (Hebrew, *har) of the Lord"* (Genesis 22:14;
Numbers 10:33; Psalm 24:3; Isaiah 2:3; 30:29; Micah 4:2; Zechariah 8:3), or *"the hill* (Hebrew,
har) of God" (Psalm 68:15; see also, *"holy hill,"* Psalm 2:6; 3:4; 15:1; 43:3; 68:16; 99:9) occur often
in Scripture.

The Hebrew word, *har,* is translated hill, 61 times, *hill country,* once, and *mount* or *mountain,* 486
times in the King James Version.

These phrases refer either to Mount Sinai (also called in Scripture, Mount Horeb), or to Mount
Moriah, though Mount Zion and Jerusalem are also used in ways that encompass Mount Moriah.

In Psalm 121:1-2, we read, "I *will lift up mine eyes unto the hills, from whence cometh my help. My
help cometh from the Lord, which made heaven and earth."* *"The hills"* in the above passage would
not have been just any hills, but the hills of Jerusalem. *"The hills"* would not be referring to just
any of the hills in Jerusalem, but to those hills—Mount Moriah and Mount Zion—which were
the ones holy to God.

Exodus 3:1), and thus could not apply to a mountain in the neighborhood of Megiddo.

The prefix "*Ar*" has not nearly so common a usage. Like "*Har*" it is a Hebrew word. It is translated "*cities*," four times; "*enemy*" once; and "*enemies*" twice in the King James Version. "Ar" is defined as follows:

1. "*A city (of busy concourse), enclosed place*" (see *Young's Analytical Concordance*, pg. 168, Col-2).

2. "*Enemy, one awake*" (see *Young's Analytical Concordance*, pg. 300, Col-2).

"*Ar*" combined with "*Megiddo*" could mean "*The place of the City of God*," or "*The enclosed place of God*." But "*the city of our God*" (Psalm 48:1) is not Megiddo, but Jerusalem. And "*the enclosed place* (or sanctuary) *of God*" would be in His temple!

Still, John saw something *very significant*, very apropos *in the meaning* of "*Armageddon*." And what could be more significant than the fact that the enemies of God had gathered at "*Armageddon*" which, in the Hebrew tongue, signified, "*THE PLACE OF THE ENEMIES OF GOD*"!

This fits! The tribe of Manasseh, under Joshua, had not been able to drive out the Canaanites at Megiddo (Judges 1:27), but it was at Megiddo that Deborah and Barak finally won the victory over that great enemy of God, Sisera, and defeated the Canaanites (Judges 5:19-20).

It was here at Megiddo that that unrighteous king of Judah, Ahaziah, (2 Chronicles 22:3) died after being smitten by the servants of Jehu (2 Kings 9:27).

And it was at Megiddo that Pharoah-Necho slew the righteous king of Judah, Josiah (2 Kings 23:29), and the mourning on that occasion was long remembered (Zechariah 12:11).

Truly, this had been "*Armageddon*," "*The Place of the Enemies of God*," and it was at this place that the *"three unclean spirits like frogs"* were gathering the armies of God's enemies for this final combat.

17 And the seventh angel poured out his vial into the air; and there came a great voice out of the temple of heaven, from the throne, saying, It is done.

The Seventh Plague: *"the Great City* (Rome) *was Divided into Three Parts, and the Cities of the Nations Fell"*

"And the seventh angel poured out his vial (bowl) *into the air..."* (Revelation 16:17a)

This seventh bowl of God's wrath does not mention the return of Jesus to confront His enemies who were last seen gathering at Armageddon. However, Jesus' coming is most definitely and clearly implied in these passages. This is because of the way that these passages are related to Daniel 2:28-45, especially verses 34, 35, and 44. That is, in Nebuchadnezzar's dream, and in Daniel's interpretation, the kingdom of God would destroy the Babylonian, Medo-Persian, Greek, and Roman Empires *at the same time.* (See Daniel 2:35, *"Then was the iron, the clay, the brass, the silver, and the*

*18 And there were voices, and thunders, and lightnings; and there was a great earthquake, **such as was not since men were upon the earth,***[95] *so*

---

95. Understanding Hebrew Time Comparisons

The above words are from Revelation 16:18, and are representative of an interesting type of Hebrew expression. It is an expression which involves a comparison of some event or creature or quality in the present, or in prophecy, with a similar event or creature or quality in the past, in which the present one, or prophesied one, is greater, and often involving a similar comparison with the future.

Here are some other examples from Scripture of Hebrew Time comparisons.

Of the locust plague in Egypt: *"Before them there were no such locusts as they, neither after them shall be such"* (Exodus 10:14).

Compare the above with the *"locust"* plague (Joel 1:4) in Joel 1 and 2.

"...there hath not been ever the like, neither shall be any more after it, even to the years of many generations" (Joel 2:2b).

Of King Hezekiah of Judah: *"He trusted in the Lord God of Israel; so that after him was none like him among all the kings of Judah, nor any that were before him"* (2 Kings 18:5).

But compare the above with King Josiah of Judah: *"And like unto him was there no king before him, that turned to the Lord with all his heart, and with all his soul, and with all his might, according to all the law of Moses; neither after him arose there any like him"* (2 Kings 23:25).

Of King Solomon's wisdom, God said, *"Behold, I have done according to thy words; lo, I have given thee a wise and an understanding heart; so that there was none like thee before thee, neither after thee shall any arise like unto thee"* (2 Kings 3:12).

But compare the above with the words of Jesus: *"The queen of the south shall rise up in the judgment with the men of this generation, and condemn them; for she came from the utmost parts of the earth to hear the wisdom of Solomon; and behold, a greater than Solomon is here"* (Luke 11:31).

Of the Passover Commemoration in the eighteenth year of King Josiah of Judah (two passages): *"Surely there was not holden such a passover from the days of the judges that judged Israel, nor in all the days of the kings of Israel, nor of the kings of Judah; But in the eighteenth year of king Josiah, wherein this passover was holden to the Lord in Jerusalem"* (2 Kings 23:22-23).

continued on next page

mighty an earthquake, and so great.

19 And the great city was divided into three parts, and the cities of the nations fell: and great Babylon came in remembrance before God, to give unto her the cup of the wine of the fierceness of his wrath.

20 And every island fled away, and the mountains were not found.

21 And there fell upon men a great hail out of heaven, every stone about the weight of a talent:

*gold, **broken to pieces together.**"*) Thus in Revelation 16:19, *"And the great city* (Rome) *was divided into three parts, and the cities of the nations fell…" "the cities of the nations"* would be the cities of the nations of the remnants of the old Babylonian, Medo-Persian, and Greek empires, and also the cities of the Roman Empire.

In this section John reveals the way Daniel's prophecies would be fulfilled in which the coming kingdom of God would destroy all of these kingdoms. Since Jesus comes in, or with, His kingdom (Matthew 16:28), He would be coming during this section when the nations are being destroyed.

In Revelation 19:11-21 we see the return of Jesus to confront the beast, the false prophet, the kings of the earth, and their armies. While Jesus is destroying them, the cities of the nations are falling, and Rome is coming under additional destruction.

"And there was no passover like to that kept in Israel from the days of Samuel the prophet; neither did all the kings of Israel keep such a passover as Josiah kept, and the priests, and the Levites, and all Judah and Israel that were present, and the inhabitants of Jerusalem. In the eighteenth year of the reign of Josiah was this passover kept" (2 Chronicles 35:18-19).

Of a certain Levite and his murdered concubine: *"And when he was come into his house, he took a knife, and laid hold on his concubine, and divided her, together with her bones, into twelve pieces, and sent her into all the coasts of Israel. And it was so, that all that saw it said, There was no such deed done nor seen from the day that the children of Israel came up out of the land of Egypt unto this day; consider of it, take advice, and speak your minds"* (Judges 19:29-30).

Of Daniel's prophecy of the distress within Jerusalem in A.D. 70: *"And at that time shall Michael stand up, the great prince which standeth for the children of thy people: and there shall be a time of trouble, such as never was since there was a nation even to that same time: and at that time thy people shall be delivered, every one that shall be found written in the book"* (Daniel 12:1).

Of Jesus' prophecy of the distress within Jerusalem in A.D. 70 (two passages): *"For then shall be great tribulation, such as was not since the beginning of the world to this time, no, nor ever shall be"* (Matthew 24:21).

"For in those days shall be affliction, such as was not from the beginning of the creation which God created unto this time, neither shall be" (Mark 13:19).

A careful reading of these Scriptures should indicate that we, in our day, take many expressions literally, which were not intended to be taken in so literal a sense among the Hebrews.

Thus, in the above scripture in Exodus 10:14, regarding the locust plague, the meaning is not that a new species of locust was prominent then which had never existed before or after that time, but simply that they had a most terrible plague of locusts.

and men blas-
phemed God
because of the
plague of the hail;
for the plague
thereof was exceed-
ing great (Revelation
16:17-21).

Appendix: Some Further Discussion on "Armageddon"

The following passages of Scripture give further support to our position
that it is the meaning of the word Armageddon that is important.

Before proceeding, however, we should note that, like Josephus (see *The*
Life of Flavius Josephus, 1, 2), the apostle John had also been a Jewish
priest. John himself tells us that he *"was known unto the high priest"* (John
18:15). Eusebius relates the following, *"Moreover, John, that rested on the*
bosom of our Lord, who was a priest that bore the sacerdotal plate, and mar-
tyr and teacher, he, also, rests at Ephesus" (Eusebius' *Ecclesiastical History*,
pg. 116). Thus, the *meanings* of Hebrew words were a part of the study of
such men. John gives the Hebrew word in five instances:

(1) *"Bethesda"* (*"house of mercy"*), John 5:2;

Both Kings Hezekiah and Josiah were devout kings of Judah, and this is the meaning intended in
the above quotations from 1 Kings 18:5 and 23:25. But to take both of those passages literally would
only lead to a pointless contradiction as to which one was the most devout.

Solomon was divinely endowed with an unusual gift of wisdom, but to take literally the words of
2 Kings 3:12 would indicate that he was the wisest man who ever lived, and would contradict the
words of Jesus in Luke 11:31 (quoted above), and would make Solomon even wiser than Jesus *"in*
whom are hid all the treasures of wisdom and knowledge" (Colossians 2:3). All that 2 Kings 3:12 actually intends to communicate is that Solomon was a very wise man.

Jesus' words in Matthew 24:21 and in Mark 13:19 (and Daniel's words in Daniel 12:1) give further
proof that we must not take these words in a literal sense.

Was not the plight of the Jews under Hitler a greater tribulation, by far, than that which the Jews
suffered in A.D. 70? It is true that Titus killed many Jews, but he did not attempt to kill every Jew,
such as Hitler did, nor did Titus have the modern means to accomplish such a design, as Hitler did,
nor were the numbers killed in Judea and Jerusalem among the Jews (1,100,000, *Wars* VI. IX. 3)
near the number of those who were killed under Hitler (6,000,000).

Jesus, like Daniel before Him, were Jews, and they both spoke as Jews speak. Their statements
regarding the coming distress in Jerusalem which came in A.D. 70 meant that that tribulation would
be a most terrible one, but not literally that none would exceed it, as we have shown in our previous
quotations.

Still, if the peoples of the Roman Empire had not repented and turned to Jesus in such large numbers as they did, then Jesus would indeed have returned in the reign of Domitian (Revelation
17:11), and the phrase, regarding the tribulation of the Jews, *"no, nor ever shall be"* (Matthew 24:21)
would have been true, as the millennial reign of Jesus would have followed (Revelation 20:4).

NOTE: For other Hebrew Time Comparisons see Exodus 9:18; Joshua 10:14; 2 Chronicles 1:12;
Ezekiel 5:8-9.

(2) *"Gabbatha"* (*"elevated place"*), John 19:13;

(3) *"Golgotha"* (*"a skull"*), John 19:17;

(4) *"Abaddon"* (*"destruction,"* i.e., *"destroyer"*), Revelation 9:11;

(5) *"Armageddon"* (*"place of the enemies of God"*), Revelation 16:16.

Of the other writers of the New Testament, only Matthew and Mark give a Hebrew word, and they only once each. In both cases that word is *"Golgotha"* (Matthew 27:33; Mark 15:22).

Let us now give further consideration to these passages of Scripture.

*"Now there is at Jerusalem by the sheep market **a pool, which is called in the Hebrew tongue Bethesda**, having five porches* (covered walks)" (John 5:2).

The *meaning* of the word, *Bethesda,* which is *"house of mercy,"* would have a special significance here both because of the previous healings that had occurred there, and now especially because of the impotent man whom Jesus healed. John, being more familiar with the Hebrew, expects his readers to know the meaning of the Hebrew words he gives without his having to reiterate them. Whereas, Matthew and Mark, as we shall see later, are careful to translate *"Golgotha"* for their readers.

*"When Pilate therefore heard that saying, he brought Jesus forth, and sat down in the judgment seat in a place that is called the Pavement, **but in the Hebrew, Gabbatha**"* (John 19:13).

John here shows the contrast between the Greek name (*lithostrotos,* pavement, or *"paved with stones"*), and the Hebrew name *"Gabbatha"* which means *"elevated place."* But no contrast is apparent unless the meaning of *"Gabbatha"* is known. John's first readers may have known such information but modern English readers do not.

"And he (that is, Jesus) *bearing his cross went forth into a place called the place of a skull* (Greek, *kranion,* a skull), *which is called in the Hebrew Golgotha"* (John 19:17).

The Hebrew word, *Golgotha,* means *"a skull,"* as does the Greek word, *kranion.* But we must know the meaning of *Golgotha* to understand the passage. Matthew and Mark are both careful to translate this word:

*"And when they were come unto a place called **Golgotha, that is to say, a place of a skull*** (Greek, *kranion,* a skull)" (Matthew 27:33).

*"And they bring him unto the place **Golgotha, which is, being interpreted, The place of a skull*** (Greek, *kranion,* a skull)" (Mark 15:22).

Luke omits giving the Hebrew word "Golgotha," but gives only its meaning!

"And when they were come to the place, which is called Calvary (Greek, *kranion,* a skull; the word '*Calvary*' is not in the Greek text, but was supplied by the King James translators from the Latin word, *Calvaria, a bare skull), there they crucified him, and the malefactors, one on the right hand, and the other on the left"* (Luke 23:33). Thus, Luke really wrote, *"And when they were come to the place, which is called the skull..."* He thus gave the meaning, rather than the Hebrew word! *"The skull,"* as a symbol of death, would have had a special significance in this passage. Thus, again, it was the *meaning* of the Hebrew word that was important.

"And they had a king over them, which is the angel of the bottomless pit, whose name in the Hebrew tongue is Abaddon, but in the Greek tongue hath his name Apollyon" (Revelation 9:11).

"Abaddon" in the Hebrew means *"destruction"; "Apollyon"* in the Greek means *"Destroyer."* Here, as in the previous three examples, the Hebrew and Greek names have no value in the passage *apart from their meanings!* Those who read the Hebrew Old Testament could read the word *"abaddon"* in Job 26:6; 28:22; Psalm 88:11; Proverbs 15:11; 27:20. In the English translation (KJV) it is always rendered *"destruction."* In Job 28:22, we read, *"Destruction* (Abaddon) *and Death say, We have heard the fame thereof with our ears."* In this passage, *"Abaddon"* is personified, that is, *"Destruction"* is presented as though it were a person. John was inspired to give the Hebrew *"Abaddon"* and the Greek *"Apollyon,"* because his readers would see how well these words "fit" with the activities of the locusts, or Roman soldiers. Their angel king bore the name *"Destruction"* or *"Destroyer,"* and thus this would typify the activities of these Roman soldiers.

In each of the above examples, the giving of the Hebrew word would have been valueless, except that the meaning of that Hebrew word was particularly significant. This confirms our position with regard to the Hebrew word *"Armageddon."*

It needs also to be noted that the word *"Armageddon"* is not found in any other passage, either in the Bible or in ancient literature, except in Revelation 16:16. Had John been interested only in giving the place of this final battle, he would have used the common word for it which was "Megiddo." But he was clearly interested in more than that.

In supplying the word *"Ar"* as a prefix to *"Megiddon,"* John was using a word which, besides meaning *"enemy"* or *"enemies,"* also carried the meaning of *"enclosed place,"* as in the following examples.

Ar, or *Ar of Moab,* a city or a region, *"the city that is in the middle of the valley,"* that is, *enclosed* within the valley (Deuteronomy 2:36; Joshua 13:9,16; 2 Samuel 24:5, NASB).

Arab, "*a court or ambushcade,*" in other words, an *enclosed* place. A city in the hill country of Judah near Hebron (Joshua 15:52).

Arabah, or *The Arabah*, "*a desert depression between areas of considerably higher ground,*" that is, *enclosed* between two mountain ranges.

Argob, a district of the kingdom of Og in Bashan. It had no less than 60 cities. It was *enclosed* between two rivers.

Aroer, "*enclosed*," an Amorite city situated on the northern rim of a canyon overlooking the Arnon River (Deuteronomy 2:36; 3:12; 4:48).

Arvad, "*refuge*," located on an island in the Mediterranean Sea, about two miles from the mainland, 125 miles north of Tyre.

Thus, *Armageddon*, "*the enclosed place of Megiddo*," was also "*The Place of the Enemies of God*," and this was what John sought to present by his use of this word!

Revelation 17
The Great Whore

And there came one of the seven angels which had the seven vials, and talked with me, saying unto me, Come hither; I will shew unto thee the judgment of the great whore that sitteth upon many waters:

2 With whom the kings of the earth have committed fornication, and the inhabitants of the earth have been made drunk with the wine of her fornication.

3 So he carried me away in the spirit into the wilderness; and I saw a woman sit upon a scarlet coloured beast, full of names of blasphemy, having seven heads and ten horns (Revelation 17:1-3).

"The Great Whore" Identified, and Her "Judgment" Described with Great Rejoicing

The purposes of Revelation 17:1-18 in this fifth prophetic unit are to identify *"the great whore"* (Revelation 17:1), or *"BABYLON THE GREAT"* (Revelation 17:5), more precisely, and also to give further details on how the destruction of *"the great whore"* (Rome) is to be accomplished. In identifying *"the great whore,"* and in understanding her *"judgment,"* it will be helpful to also identify *"the scarlet coloured beast"* (Revelation 17:3,7-8,11-13,16-17); *"the seven heads"* (Revelation 17:7,9-11); *"the ten horns,"* or *"kings"* (Revelation 17:7,12-14,16-17); and also *"the kings of the earth who have committed fornication"* with *"the great whore"* (Revelation 17:2; 18:3,9).

Revelation 18:1-24 is a song of doom made up of a string of prophetic phrases and thoughts from Isaiah, Jeremiah, and Ezekiel in their pronouncements against the ancient cities of Babylon, Tyre, and Jerusalem, and applied here against Rome. In Revelation 19:1-10, all heaven rejoices in the completion of God's judgment of *"the great whore"* (Revelation 19:1-6). Contrasted also with the destruction of *"the great whore"* (Rome) is the *"marriage of the Lamb"* and *"his wife"* (Revelation 19:7), or *"bride," "the holy city, New Jerusalem"* (Revelation 21:2,10), who is further pictured in the two later visions.

Identifying the Five Main Figures of Revelation 17

(1) *"The Great Whore"* Identified.

"The great whore" (Revelation 17:1) is referred to also as a *"woman"* (Revelation 17:3-4,6-7,18); as *"Babylon the Great"* (Revelation 17:5; 18:2), *"that great city"* (Revelation 17:18; 18:16), or *"that great city Babylon"* (Revelation 18:10). So *"the great whore"* is a city.

In Scripture, whoredom often refers to idolatry (Isaiah 23:14-17; Jeremiah 13:22,26-27; Ezekiel 16 and 23, entire chapters; Nahum 3:4-5),[96] and this is the meaning in Revelation 17:1 (and also of Babylon's *"fornication"* in Revelation 14:8; 18:3; 19:2). Nahum referred to Nineveh as a *"harlot"* (3:4), and Isaiah described Tyre as one (23:15-16), and in each of these instances their spiritual harlotry, or idolatry, was in view.

When *"the kings of the earth...committed fornication"* (Revelation 17:2) with *"the great whore,"* the meaning would be that they worshiped Roma, the goddess of Rome, and also that they became devotees of the idolatrous Roman religion.

"The great whore," or *"Babylon the great"* (Revelation 17:5), is identified as the city of Rome in the following ways:

> A. *"And the woman which thou sawest is that great city, which reigneth over the kings of the earth"* (Revelation 17:18). Only Rome reigned over *"the kings of the earth."*

---

96. *"Because of the multitude of the whoredoms of the wellfavoured **harlot**, the mistress of witchcrafts, that selleth nations through her whoredoms, and families through her witchcrafts.*
Behold, I am against thee, saith the Lord of hosts, and I will discover thy skirts upon thy face, and I will shew the nations thy nakedness, and the kingdoms thy shame" (Nahum 3:4-5).

"And it shall come to pass in that day, that Tyre shall be forgotten seventy years, according to the days of one king: after the end of seventy years shall Tyre sing as an harlot.
Take an harp, go about the city, thou harlot that hast been forgotten; make sweet melody, sing many songs, that thou mayest be remembered.
And it shall come to pass after the end of seventy years, that the Lord will visit Tyre, and she shall turn to her hire, and shall commit fornication with all the kingdoms of the world upon the face of the earth" (Isaiah 23:15-17).

See the footnote in the verse-by-verse discussion of Revelation 14:4 for additional scriptures on the subject, "In Scripture, adultery, and whoredoms, often carry the meaning of idolatry."

B. *"The seven heads are seven mountains* (Greek, *ore,* a hill, or mountain), *on which the woman sitteth"* (Revelation 17:9b). The following quote should help:

"No other city in the world has ever been celebrated, as the city of Rome has, for its situation on seven hills. Pagan poets and orators, who had no thought of elucidating prophecy, have alike characterized it as 'the seven hilled city.'" Thus Virgil refers to it: *"Rome has both become the most beautiful (city) in the world, and alone has surrounded for herself seven heights with a wall."* Propertius, in the same strain, speaks of it (adding another trait, which completes the prophetic picture) as *"The lofty city on seven hills, which governs the whole world."* Its *"governing the whole world"* is just the counterpart of the divine statement—*"which reigneth over the kings of the earth"* (Revelation 17:18). To call Rome the city *"of the seven hills"* was by its citizens held to be as descriptive as to call it by its own proper name. Hence Horace speaks of it by reference to its seven hills alone, when he addresses, *"The gods who have set their affections on the seven hills."* Martial, in like manner, speaks of *"The seven dominating mountains."* (Hislop, Alexander, *The Two Babylons,* pg. 2).

Thus, Rome, and only Rome, was famous in the ancient world for sitting upon seven hills, or mountains.

And the woman was arrayed in purple and scarlet colour, and decked with gold and precious stones and pearls, having a golden cup in her

C. Rome, because of its wealth (Revelation 18:3,15,19), was the center for imports in the first century A.D. (Revelation 18:11-17).

D. Rome, because of the *"peoples, and multitudes, and nations, and tongues"* she ruled, was described as seated *"upon many waters"* (Compare Revelation 17:1b and 15).[97]

---

97. *"And there came one of the seven angels which had the seven vials, and talked with me, saying unto me, Come hither; I will shew unto thee the judgment of the great whore that sitteth upon many waters"* (Revelation 17:1).

"And he saith unto me, The waters which thou sawest, where the whore sitteth, are peoples, and multitudes, and nations, and tongues" (Revelation 17:15).

hand full of abominations and filthiness of her fornication:

5 And upon her forehead was a name written, MYSTERY, BABYLON THE GREAT, THE MOTHER OF HARLOTS AND ABOMINATIONS OF THE EARTH.

6 And I saw the woman drunken with the blood of the saints, and with the blood of the martyrs of Jesus; and when I saw her, I wondered with great admiration.

7 And the angel said unto me, Wherefore didst thou marvel? I will tell thee the mystery of the woman, and of the beast that carrieth her, which hath the seven heads and ten horns.

8 The beast that thou sawest was, and is not; and shall ascend out of the bottomless pit, and go into perdition: and they that dwell on the earth shall wonder, whose names were not written in the book of life from the foundation of the

E. Rome, under Nero, was *"drunken with the blood of the saints, and with the blood of the martyrs of Jesus"* (Revelation 17:6). That is, Rome had killed the Christians!

F. In the literature of that day (the first century A.D.), Rome was termed "Babylon" (as in the Sibylline Oracles, 5:143) and thus, "Babylon" identified Rome.

These six identifying characteristics point clearly to the city of Rome as being *"the great whore"* of Revelation 17.

"And upon her forehead was a name written, MYSTERY, BABYLON THE GREAT, THE MOTHER OF HARLOTS AND ABOMINATIONS OF THE EARTH" (Revelation 17:5). Seneca (Rhet. I. 2. 7) and Juvenal (VI. 122f.) tell us that Roman harlots had a label upon their brows giving their names. Rome was identified in this manner also, and with a name that pictures her as an enemy of God.

(2) *"The Scarlet Coloured Beast"* (Revelation 17:3) Identified

This beast had previously appeared in Revelation 13:1, and had been fully identified there as the Roman Empire. *"The great whore"* sits upon the empire, *"having seven heads"* and *"ten horns."*

(3) The *"Seven Heads"* Identified

The *"seven heads"* have previously been identified in our chapter "The Dating of Revelation" as the first seven kings (or emperors) of the Roman Empire. These were: Augustus Caesar; Tiberius Caesar; Caligula Caesar; Claudius Caesar; Nero Caesar; Vespasian; and Titus.

An *"eighth"* (Revelation 17:11), Domitian, is *"of the seven,"* or literally *"out of the seven is."* Domitian was to have been like a Nero returned. He was to have come in the persecuting spirit and power of Nero and persecuted the Christians as Nero did.

world, when they behold the beast that was, and is not, and yet is.

9 And here is the mind which hath wisdom. The seven heads are seven mountains, on which the woman sitteth.

10 And there are seven kings: five are fallen, and one is, and the other is not yet come; and when he cometh, he must continue a short space.

11 And the beast that was, and is not, even he is the eighth, and is of the seven, and goeth into perdition (Revelation 17:4-11).

And the ten horns which thou sawest are ten kings, which have received no kingdom as yet; but receive power as kings one hour with the beast.

13 These have one mind, and shall give their power and strength unto the beast.

The word "*beast*" sometimes refers to the Roman Empire as a whole, and sometimes one of the heads, or kings, of the Roman Empire, as Nero (Revelation 13:18), or Domitian (Revelation 17:11).

Note: The phrase "*is of the seven*" (Revelation 17:11) (Greek, *ek ton hepta*) is translated in Acts 21:8, "*one of the seven*" (KJV), though the Greek (*ek ton hepta*) is the same.

(a) In the Aramaic language, the earthly language of Jesus and the apostle John, the letters of the alphabet are also numerals. Thus, the letters in *Nero Caesar* add up to the 666 of Revelation 13:18.

(b) Three times the angel told John that "*the beast was, and is not...*" (Revelation 17:8 (twice), 11). Thus, at the time John received the Revelation, *Nero was dead*. He committed suicide on June 9, A.D. 68.

(c) "*And the beast that was, and is not, even he is the eighth, and is of the seven, and goeth into perdition*" (Revelation 17:11). The "*eighth*" king, Domitian, would be "*of the seven,*" or "*one of the seven.*" He would be like Nero returned. That is, Domitian would come in the persecuting spirit and power of Nero.

(4) The "*Ten Horns*" Explained

"*And the ten horns which thou sawest are ten kings, which have received no kingdom as yet; but receive power as kings one hour with the beast*" (Revelation 17:12). The "*one hour*" here indicates a brief period of time, rather than 60 minutes, as in 1 John 2: 18, "*it is the last hour*" (RSV).

The prophetic concept of these "*ten kings*" first appears in the interpretation of the dream of the great image in Daniel 2:36-45. Since the image would have had ten toes, the ten kings are suggested.

This concept is developed more fully in Daniel 7 in the vision of the four beasts. In Daniel 7:7b, we read

14 These shall make war with the Lamb, and the Lamb shall overcome them: for he is Lord of lords, and King of kings: and they that are with him are called, and chosen, and faithful.

15 And he saith unto me, The waters which thou sawest, where the whore sitteth, are peoples, and multitudes, and nations, and tongues.

*16 And the **ten horns** which thou sawest upon the beast, these shall hate the whore, and shall make her desolate and naked, and shall eat her flesh, and burn her with fire.*

17 For God hath put in their hearts to fulfil his will, and to agree,

of the *"fourth beast"* (that is, the Roman Empire), *"and it had ten horns."*

There were 50 or more nations within the Roman Empire at the time of the reign of Domitian. *"The ten horns,"* that is, *"the ten kings,"* were not to be all of the kingdoms, or nations that made up the Roman Empire, but they were to be ten kings that would *"arise"* *"out of"* (Daniel 7:24) the Roman Empire. Revelation would be referring to the same ten horns, or kings, that Daniel saw.[98] Most of the kingdoms would remain within the body, or head, of Daniel's *"fourth beast,"* or there would have been no beast when the ten kings arose out of it.

But these ten were seen prophetically to rise out of the head, and to become distinct, or separate. Not all the kings, or kingdoms, were to arise out of the Roman Empire, but only those who give *"their power and strength unto the beast,"* who would have been Domitian. It is only these *"ten horns"* who *"hate the whore"* and *"burn her with fire"* (Revelation 17:16).

This indicates that the revived Roman Empire, the European Community, should have more than ten nations within it, but only ten of those nations would join with the beast of the future to destroy Rome.

Again, for the *"little horn"* (Daniel 7:8), who would have been Domitian, to *"rise"* (Daniel 7:24)

---

98. *"After this I saw in the night visions, and behold a fourth beast, dreadful and terrible, and strong exceedingly; and it had great iron teeth: it devoured and brake in pieces, and stamped the residue with the feet of it: and it was diverse from all the beasts that were before it; and it had ten horns. I considered the horns, and, behold, there came up among them another little horn, before whom there were three of the first horns plucked up by the roots: and, behold, in this horn were eyes like the eyes of man, and a mouth speaking great things"* (Daniel 7:7-8).

"Then I would know the truth of the fourth beast, which was diverse from all the others, exceeding dreadful, whose teeth were of iron, and his nails of brass; which devoured, brake in pieces, and stamped the residue with his feet;
And of the ten horns that were in his head, and of the other which came up, and before whom three fell; even of that horn that had eyes, and a mouth that spake very great things, whose look was more stout than his fellows" (Daniel 7:19-20).

"Thus he said, The fourth beast shall be the fourth kingdom upon earth, which shall be diverse from all kingdoms, and shall devour the whole earth, and shall tread it down, and break it in pieces. And the ten horns out of this kingdom are ten kings that shall arise: and another shall rise after them; and he shall be diverse from the first, and he shall subdue three kings" (Daniel 7:23-24).

and give their king- dom unto the beast, until the words of God shall be ful- filled.

18 And the woman which thou sawest is that great city, which reigneth over the kings of the earth (Revelation 17:12-18).

out of the *"fourth beast"* (the Roman Empire) would not mean the beginning of the reign of Domitian in A.D. 81, since if that were the case all of his predecessors (the seven kings, or emperors, over the Roman Empire) should have also been seen rising from the head of the *"fourth beast."* But rather Domitian's rising, and the rising of the *"ten horns,"* indicates that they were to come forth from the Roman Empire as separate and distinct powers.

For the future this indicates that ten of the nations (with their leaders) within the European Community will seek to leave it, and will be joined by the leader of the European Community (the future beast) in a successful attempt to destroy Rome.

According to Daniel 7:8,20-21,24, these *"ten horns"* shall arise first (as separate and distinct powers), and the *"little horn"* (Daniel 7:8), who would have been *"the eighth"* king of Revelation 17:11 (that is, Domitian), is to arise after them (as a separate and distinct power from the Roman Empire), and *"subdue three kings"* (Daniel 7:24). Domitian did, in fact, subdue Upper Germany in A.D. 89, and just before that the nation of Dacia (Romania) rose in revolt (A.D. 85-88).[99] But these prophecies were thrown into the future before Domitian was able to fulfil his part in them. Domitian's life was then cut short by a palace conspiracy on September 18, A.D. 96. He was 45 years old.

(5) *"The Kings of the Earth Who Have Committed Fornication"* with *"the Great Whore"* (Revelation 17:2; 18:3,9) **Explained**

That these *"kings of the earth who have committed fornication"* with *"the great whore"* are a separate group of kings from the *"ten kings"* referred to above is evident from the following:

A. The *"ten kings"* *"hate the whore"* (Revelation 17:16); these kings *"bewail her"* (Revelation 18:9).

---

99. The *"little horn"* of Daniel 7:8 (who would have been Domitian) would have had to have arisen as a separate and distinct power from the Roman Empire before we would begin counting the three kings which he was to have subdued.

B. The "*ten kings...eat her flesh, and burn her with fire*" (Revelation 17:16); these kings "*lament for her*" (Revelation 18:9).

C. The "*ten kings*" "*make her desolate and naked*" (Revelation 17:16); these kings "*lived deliciously with her*" (Revelation 18:9); and "*waxed rich through the abundance of her delicacies*" (Revelation 18:3).

Clearly, then, these "*kings of the earth who have committed fornication*" with "*the great whore*" were those kings who were allied with her, while the "*ten kings*" were her avowed enemies.

These "*kings of the earth who have committed fornication*" with "*the great whore*" are the subject kings who remain loyal to Rome, when Rome was to have been defeated by the beast and the ten kings.[100] Rome's defeat is to have been their defeat! When Jesus returns, He confronts the beast (Revelation 19:19), the ten kings (Revelation 17:12-14), and the "*kings from the sun-rising*" (Revelation 16:12), but not these who have already lost their kingdoms, and their power, and their glory. These "*kings of the earth*" had accepted Rome's religion and become wealthy by pandering to her idolatrous lusts. But they are now out of the picture.

The seventeenth chapter of Revelation clarifies the details of the judgment "*of the great whore.*" This "*judgment*" was described in the plagues of the bowls of God's wrath in Revelation 16. We are now ready for the rejoicing in heaven over Rome's fall, as her song of doom is given in Revelation 18.

---

100. "*The kings of the earth who have committed fornication*" with "*the great whore*" were those kings who were to have been allied with Rome, in Rome's losing war with the beast.

"*And there came one of the seven angels which had the seven vials, and talked with me, saying unto me, Come hither; I will shew unto thee the judgment of the great whore that sitteth upon many waters: With whom the kings of the earth have committed fornication, and the inhabitants of the earth have been made drunk with the wine of her fornication*" (Revelation 17:1-2).

"*For all nations have drunk of the wine of the wrath of her fornication, and the kings of the earth have committed fornication with her, and the merchants of the earth are waxed rich through the abundance of her delicacies*" (Revelation 18:3).

"*And the kings of the earth, who have committed fornication and lived deliciously with her, shall bewail her, and lament for her, when they shall see the smoke of her burning*" (Revelation 18:9).

Revelation 18
The Song of Doom

Rome's *"Judgment"* Described in a Song of Doom

This song of doom for Rome brings great rejoicing in heaven (Revelation 18:20; 19:1-6). This song is made up of a string of prophetic phrases and thoughts from Isaiah, Jeremiah, and Ezekiel in their pronouncements against the ancient cities of Babylon, Tyre, Jerusalem, and many nations, and applied here against Rome. The import of these passages, given below, is that the worst pronouncements of divine judgment from the past are now given against Rome, and that just as those ancient cities and lands were destroyed, so also Rome will be.

Old Testament Antecedents of the Song of Doom for Rome

Old Testament Reference	Revelation 18
"…and the earth shined with his glory" (Ezekiel 43:2).	*And after these things I saw another angel come down from heaven, having great power; and the earth was lightened with his glory* (18:1).
	This radiance shows that this angel has just come from the presence of God—and thus carries God's latest message.
Prophecies against ancient Babylon *"…And he answered and said, Babylon is fallen, is fallen…"* (Isaiah 21:9). *"But wild beasts of the desert shall lie there; and their houses shall be full of doleful creatures; and owls shall dwell there, and satyrs shall dance there"* (Isaiah 13:21).	*And he cried mightily with a strong voice, saying, Babylon the great is fallen, is fallen, and is become the habitation of devils (Greek, daimonon, demons), and the hold of every foul spirit, and a cage of every unclean and hateful bird* (18:2).

Prophecy against many nations *"For thus saith the Lord God of Israel unto me; Take the wine cup of this fury at my hand, and cause all the nations, to whom I send thee, to drink it. And they shall drink, and be moved, and be mad, because of the sword that I will send among them"* (Jeremiah 25:15-16).

Prophecies against ancient Babylon *"Flee out of the midst of Babylon, and deliver every man his soul: be not cut off in her iniquity; for this is the time of the Lord's vengeance; he will render unto her a recompense"* (Jeremiah 51:6. See also Jeremiah 51:45).

For all nations have drunk of the wine of the wrath of her fornication, and the kings of the earth have committed fornication with her, and the merchants of the earth are waxed rich through the abundance of her delicacies (18:3).

And I heard another voice from heaven, saying, Come out of her, my people, that ye be not partakers of her sins, and that ye receive not of her plagues (18:4).

God often calls His own to leave areas where His wrath will fall.[101] See Genesis 19:12,22 (Lot from Sodom); Numbers 16:23-27 (the congregation of Israel from Korah, Dathan, and Abiram); Jeremiah 50:8; 51:6,45; Zechariah 2:6-7 (the Jews from Babylon); Luke 21:20-21 (Jewish Christians from Judea and Jerusalem).

*"We would have healed Babylon, but she is not healed: forsake her, and let us go every one into his own country: for **her judg-***

*For her **sins have reached unto heaven**, and God hath remembered her iniquities* (18:5).

---

101. Lot from Sodom: *"And the men said unto Lot, Hast thou here any besides? son in law, and thy sons, and thy daughters, and whatsoever thou hast in the city, bring them out of this place: For we will destroy this place, because the cry of them is waxen great before the face of the Lord; and the Lord hath sent us to destroy it"* (Genesis 19:12-13).

The congregation of Israel from Korah, Dathan, and Abiram: *"And the Lord spake unto Moses, saying, Speak unto the congregation, saying, Get you up from about the tabernacle of Korah, Dathan, and Abiram. And the earth opened her mouth, and swallowed them up, and their houses, and all the men that appertained unto Korah, and all their goods"* (Numbers 16:23-24,32).

The Jews from Babylon: *"My people, go ye out of the midst of her, and deliver ye every man his soul from the fierce anger of the Lord"* (Jeremiah 51:45).

"Ho, ho, come forth, and flee from the land of the north, saith the Lord: for I have spread you abroad as the four winds of the heaven, saith the Lord.
Deliver thyself, O Zion, that dwellest with the daughter of Babylon." (Zechariah 2:6-7).

The Jewish believers in Jesus from Judea and Jerusalem:
"And when ye shall see Jerusalem compassed with armies, then know that the desolation thereof is nigh. Then let them which are in Judea flee to the mountains; and let them which are in the midst of it depart out; and let not them that are in the countries enter thereinto.
For these be the days of vengeance, that all things which are written may be fulfilled" (Luke 21:20-22).

ment reacheth unto heaven, and is lifted up even to the skies" (Jeremiah 51:9).

Prophecies against ancient Babylon
"Shout against her round about: she hath given her hand: her foundations are fallen, her walls are thrown down: for it is the vengeance of the Lord: **take vengeance upon her; as she hath done, do unto her**" (Jeremiah 50:15. See also Psalm 137:8, Jeremiah 51:24).

"And first I will recompense (to Judah) their iniquity and their sin double; because they have defiled my land, they have filled mine inheritance with the carcasses of their detestable and abominable things" (Jeremiah 16:18. See also Isaiah 40:2).

"And thou saidest, **I shall be a lady for ever...**" *Therefore hear now this, thou that art given to pleasures, that dwellest carelessly,* **that sayest in thine heart, I am, and none else beside me; I shall not sit as a widow, neither shall I know the loss of children**" (Isaiah 47:7-8).

"But these two things shall come to thee in a moment **in one day***, the loss of children and widowhood: they shall come upon thee in their perfection for the multitude of thy sorceries, and for the great abundance of thine enchantments"* (Isaiah 47:9).

Reward her even as she rewarded you,[102] *and double unto her double according to her works: in the cup which she hath filled fill to her double* (18:6).

How much she hath glorified herself, and lived deliciously, so much torment and sorrow give her; for **she saith in her heart, I sit a queen, and am no widow, and shall see no sorrow** (18:7).

Therefore shall her plagues come **in one day***, death, and mourning, and famine; and she shall be utterly burned with fire: for strong is the Lord God who judgeth her* (18:8).

---

102. *"Reward Her Even as She Rewarded You"*

"O daughter of Babylon, who art to be destroyed; happy shall he be, that rewardeth thee as thou hast served us" (Psalm 137:8).

"Call together the archers against Babylon: all ye that bend the bow, camp against it round about; let none thereof escape: recompense her according to her work; according to all that she hath done, do unto her: for she hath been proud against the Lord, against the Holy One of Israel" (Jeremiah 50:29).

"And I will render unto Babylon and to all the inhabitants of Chaldea all their evil that they have done in Zion in your sight, saith the Lord" (Jeremiah 51:24).

"As Babylon hath caused the slain of Israel to fall, so at Babylon shall fall the slain of all the earth" (Jeremiah 51:49).

Prophecies against ancient Tyre *"And it shall come to pass after the end of seventy years, that the Lord will visit Tyre, and she shall turn to her hire, and shall **commit fornication** with all the kingdoms of the world upon the face of the earth"* (Isaiah 23:17).

*"Then all the princes of the sea shall come down from their thrones and they shall take up a **lamentation for thee**"* (Ezekiel 26:16-17).

*And the kings of the earth, who have **committed fornication** and lived deliciously with her, shall bewail her, and **lament for her**, when they shall see the smoke of her burning (18:9).*

Prophecies against ancient Babylon
"Babylon is suddenly fallen and destroyed: howl for her" (Jeremiah 51:8).

"A sound of a cry cometh from Babylon, and great destruction from the land of the Chaldeans" (Jeremiah 51:54).

Standing afar off for the fear of her torment, saying, Alas, alas that great city Babylon, that mighty city! for in one hour is thy judgment come (18:10).

Prophecies against ancient Tyre

"The merchants among the people shall hiss at thee" (Ezekiel 27:36).

"...thy merchandise and all thy company in the midst of thee shall fall" (Ezekiel 27:34b).

And the merchants of the earth shall weep and mourn over her; for no man buyeth their merchandise any more (18:11).

(The merchandise brought by the nations into Tyre) (Ezekiel 27:6-24)

"...benches of ivory" (27:6); *"Fine linen with broidered work..." "...blue and purple"* (27:7); *"...silver, iron, tin, and lead"* (27:12); *"...they traded the persons of men and vessels of brass in thy market"* (27:13); *"...horses and horsemen and mules"* (27:14); *"...horns of ivory and ebony"* (27:15); *emeralds, purple, and broidered work, and fine linen, and coral, and agate"* (27:16); *"...pannag* (cakes or confections made of wheat flour), *and honey, and oil, and balm"* (27:17); *"...white wool"* (27:18); *"...bright iron, cassia, and calamus..."* (27:19); *"...pre-*

The merchandise of gold, and silver, and precious stones, and of pearls, and fine linen, and purple, and silk, and scarlet, and all thyine wood, and all manner vessels of ivory, and all manner vessels of most precious wood, and of brass, and iron, and marble (18:12).

And cinnamon, and odours, and ointments, and frankincense, and wine, and oil, and fine flour, and wheat, and beasts, and sheep, and horses, and chariots, and slaves (Greek, *somaton,* bodies), *and souls* (or, *lives*) *of men (18:13).*

cious clothes for chariots" (27:20); lambs, and rams, and goats..." (27:21); "...chief of all spices, and with all precious stones, and gold." (27:22); "...blue clothes, and broidered work, and in chests of rich apparel, bound with cords, and made of cedar..." (27:24).

"Thy riches, and thy fairs, thy merchandise, thy mariners, and thy pilots, thy calkers, and the occupiers of thy merchandise, and all thy men of war, that are in thee, and in all thy company which is in the midst of thee, shall fall into the midst of the seas in the day of thy ruin" (Ezekiel 27:27).

*And the **fruits that thy soul lusted after are departed from thee**,[103] and all things which were dainty and goodly are departed from thee, and thou shalt find them no more at all (18:14).*

Prophecies against ancient Tyre

(The mourning at the fall of Tyre, Ezekiel 27:28-34)

"The suburbs shall shake at the sound of the cry of thy pilots" (27:28).

"And all that handle the oar, the mariners, and all the pilots of the sea, shall come down from their ships, they shall stand upon the land" (27:29).

"And shall cause their voice to be heard against thee, and shall cry bitterly, and shall **cast dust upon their heads**, they

The merchants of these things, which were made rich by her, shall stand afar off for the fear of her torment, weeping and wailing (18:15).

And saying, Alas, alas that great city, that was clothed in fine linen, and purple, and scarlet,

---

103. *"And the mixt multitude that was among them fell a lusting: and the children of Israel also wept again, and said,*
    Who shall give us flesh to eat? We remember the fish, which we did eat in Egypt freely; the cucumbers, and the melons, and the leeks, and the onions, and the garlick:
    But now our soul is dried away: there is nothing at all, beside this manna, before our eyes" (Numbers 11:4-6).
    "And they sinned yet more against him by provoking the most High in the wilderness.
    And they tempted God in their heart by asking meat for their lust.
    Yea, they spake against God; they said, Can God furnish a table in the wilderness?
    Behold, he smote the rock, that the waters gushed out, and the streams overflowed; can he give bread also?
    Can he provide flesh for his people? Therefore the Lord heard this, and was wroth; so a fire was kindled against Jacob, and anger also came up against Israel;
    Because they believed not in God, and trusted not in his salvation" (Psalm 78:17-22).
    "Ye lust, and have not: ye kill, and desire to have, and cannot obtain: ye fight and war, yet ye have not, because ye ask not.
    Ye ask, and receive not, because ye ask amiss, that ye may consume it upon your lusts" (James 4:2-3).

shall wallow themselves in the ashes" (27:30).

"And they shall make themselves utterly bald for thee, and gird them with sackcloth, and they shall weep for thee with bitterness of heart and bitter wailing" (27:31).

*"And in their wailing they shall take up a lamentation for thee, and lament over thee, saying, **What city is like Tyrus,** like the destroyed in the midst of the sea?"* (27:32).

"When thy wares went forth out of the seas, thou filledst many people; thou didst enrich the kings of the earth with the multitude of thy riches and of thy merchandise" (27:33).

"In the time when thou shalt be broken by the seas in the depths of the waters thy merchandise and all thy company in the midst of thee shall fall" (Ezekiel 27:34).

<u>Prophecies against ancient Babylon</u>
"Then the heaven and the earth, and all that is therein, shall sing for Babylon: for

and decked with gold, and precious stones, and pearls! (18:16).

For in one hour so great riches is come to nought. And every shipmaster, and all the company in ships, and sailors, and as many as trade by sea, stood afar off (18:17).

And cried when they saw the smoke of her burning, saying, **What city is like unto this great city!** (18:18).

*And **they cast dust on their heads,**[104] and cried, weeping and wailing, saying, Alas, alas that great city, wherein were made rich all that had ships in the sea by reason of her costliness! for in one hour is she made desolate* (18:19).

Rejoice over her, thou heaven, and ye holy apostles (such as Peter and Paul, who were killed

---

104. "And Joshua rent his clothes, and fell to the earth upon his face before the ark of the Lord until the eventide, he and the elders of Israel, and cast dust upon their heads" (Joshua 7:6).

"And there ran a man of Benjamin out of the army, and came to Shiloh the same day with his clothes rent, and with earth upon his head" (1 Samuel 4:12).

"And Tamar put ashes on her head, and rent her garment of divers colours that was on her, and laid her hand on her head, and went on crying" (2 Samuel 13:19).

"Now in the twenty and fourth day of this month the children of Israel were assembled with fasting, and with sackclothes, and earth upon them" (Nehemiah 9:1).

"And when they lifted up their eyes afar off, and knew him not, they lifted up their voice, and wept; and they rent every one his mantle, and sprinkled dust upon their heads toward heaven" (Job 2:12).

"And shall cause their voice to be heard against thee, and shall cry bitterly, and shall cast up dust upon their heads, they shall wallow themselves in the ashes" (Ezekiel 27:30).

the spoilers shall come unto her from the north, saith the Lord" (Jeremiah 51:48).

in Rome) *and prophets* (such as the *"two witnesses,"* who were also called the *"two prophets"* [Revelation 11:10], and were prophesied to have been killed in Rome [Revelation 11:7-10]) *for God hath avenged you on her* (18:20).

Prophecies against ancient Babylon

"And it shall be, when thou hast made an end of reading this book, that **thou shalt bind a stone to it, and cast it into the midst of Euphrates:** *And thou shalt say, Thus shall Babylon sink, and shall not rise from the evil that I will bring upon her: and they shall be weary. Thus far are the words of Jeremiah"* (Jeremiah 51:63-64).

"And thou didst divide the sea before them, so that they went through the midst of the sea on the dry land; and their persecutors thou **threwest into the deeps, as a stone into the mighty waters** (Nehemiah 9:11).

God's judgment upon Tyrus (Tyre):

"For thus saith the Lord God; When I shall make thee a desolate city, like the cities that are not inhabited; when I shall bring up the deep upon thee, and great waters shall cover thee; When I shall bring thee down with them that descend into the pit, with the people of old time, and shall set thee in the low parts of the earth, in places desolate of old, with them that go down to the pit, that thou be not inhabited; and I will set glory in the land of the living; I will make thee a terror, and **thou shalt be no more though thou be sought for, yet shalt thou never be found again, saith the Lord God"** (Ezekiel 26:19-21).

And a mighty angel took up a stone like a great millstone, and cast it into the sea, saying, Thus with violence shall that great city Babylon be thrown down, **and shall be found no more at all** (18:21).

Prophecy against ancient Jerusalem
"*Moreover I will take from them the voice of mirth, and the voice of gladness, the voice of the bridegroom, and the voice of the bride, the sound of the millstones, and the light of the candle. And this whole land shall be a desolation, and an astonishment; and these nations shall serve the king of Babylon seventy years*" (Jeremiah 25:10-11).

And the voice of harpers, and musicians, and of pipers, and trumpeters, shall be heard no more at all in thee; and no craftsman, of whatsoever craft he be, shall be found any more in thee; and the sound of a millstone shall be heard no more at all in thee (18:22).

And the light of a candle shall shine no more at all in thee; and the voice of the bridegroom and of the bride shall be heard no more at all in thee: for thy merchants were the great men of the earth; for by thy sorceries were all nations deceived (18:23).

Prophecy against ancient Babylon
"*As Babylon hath caused the slain of Israel to fall, so at Babylon shall fall the slain of all the earth*" (Jeremiah 51:49).

*And in her was found the blood of prophets, and of saints, and of all that were **slain upon the earth*** (18:24).

There were two punishments against Rome that John saw clearly, and which he made clear to us in Revelation:

(1) Rome was to be burned with, or in, fire (Revelation 17:16; 18:8-9,18), and,

(2) Rome was to be permanently destroyed (Revelation 18:21,23).

These prophecies were thrown into the future by Rome's repentance, but they will yet be fulfilled.

Revelation 19

The Coming of the Lamb

The purposes of the passages in this section of Scripture are

(1) to reveal the praise in heaven to God for His judgment of "*the great whore*" (Rome) (Revelation 19:1-6); and

(2) to introduce, at this time, "*the marriage of the Lamb*" "*and his wife.*"

And after these things I heard a great voice of much people in heaven, saying, Alleluia; Salvation, and glory, and honour, and power, unto the Lord our God;

2 For true and righteous are his judgments; for he hath judged the great whore, which did corrupt the earth with her fornication, and hath avenged the blood of his servants at her hand.

3 And again they said, Alleluia. ***And her smoke rose up for ever and ever.***[105]

All Heaven Rejoices over the Judgment of "*the Great Whore*" (Rome); "*the Marriage of the Lamb*" "*and His Wife*" "*Is Come*"!

These two, "*the great whore*" and "*the wife*" of "*the Lamb,*" are both cities. The first is Rome. The second is the "*New Jerusalem*" (Revelation 21:2,9-10).

"*And after these things I heard a great voice of much people* (Greek, *ochlou pollou,* a *great crowd* or throng) *in heaven…*" (Revelation 19:la). These are the same as the "*great multitude*" (Greek, *ochlos polus,* a *great crowd* or throng) of Revelation 7:9. Here they fulfill the divine command given in Revelation 18:20, "*Rejoice over her, thou heaven, and ye holy apostles and prophets* (or, "*ye saints, and apostles and prophets*"): *for God hath avenged you on her.*" These martyrs, then, rejoice at God's command, over the destruction of "*the great whore*" (Rome) who had murdered them. They rejoice again with another, "*Alleluia,*" or "*Hallelujah,*" as they see that "*her smoke rose up for ever and ever*" (Revelation 19:3). And this same "*great multitude*" (Greek, *ochlou pollou,* a *great*

---

105. Of the land of Idumea: "*And the streams thereof shall be turned into pitch, and the dust thereof into brimstone, and the land thereof shall become burning pitch. It shall not be quenched night nor day; the smoke thereof shall go up for ever: from generation to generation it shall lie waste; none shall pass through it for ever and ever*" (Isaiah 34:9-10).

4 And the four and twenty elders and the four beasts fell down and worshipped God that sat on the throne, saying, Amen; Alleluia.

5 And a voice came out of the throne, saying, Praise our God, all ye his servants, and ye that fear him, both small and great.

6 And I heard as it were the voice of a great multitude, and as the voice of many waters, and as the voice of mighty thunderings, saying, Alleluia: for the Lord God omnipotent reigneth.

7 Let us be glad and rejoice, and give honour to him; for the marriage of the Lamb is come, and his wife hath made herself ready.

*8 And to her was granted that she should be arrayed in fine linen, clean and white: for **the fine linen is the righteousness of saints**.*[106]

crowd or throng) (Revelation 19:6) rejoices again (Revelation 19:5-7) saying, "*Alleluia* (or, *Hallelujah*): *for the Lord God omnipotent reigneth*" (Revelation 19:6b). This rejoicing prepares us for "*the marriage of the Lamb…and his wife*" (Revelation 19:7b).

The word, "*Alleluia*," or "*Hallelujah*," appears four times in this chapter (Revelation 19:1,3-4,6), but nowhere else in the New Testament. "*Hallelujah*" is a transliteration of a Hebrew word which means "*Praise ye Jah*." "*Jah*" is a form of Yahweh, or Jehovah. "*Hallelujah*" is said to be the one word that is pronounced basically the same in all languages.

"*For true and righteous are his judgments…*" (Revelation 19:2), as in Revelation 16:7. This is from Psalm 19:9b, "*…the judgments of the Lord are true and righteous altogether.*"

"And **the four and twenty elders and the four beasts** *fell down and worshipped God that sat on the throne, saying, Amen; Alleluia*" (Revelation 19:4). These elders, and "*beasts*" (or living creatures), are always shown as worshiping God (Revelation 4:4,6,10; 5:14), which is the highest act in which one may be engaged.

Since the judgment of "*the great whore*" has been completed, with the great rejoicing in heaven over her fall, we are now prepared for "*the marriage of the Lamb…and his wife*" (Revelation 19:7-9). The Lamb's wife "*hath made herself ready*" (Revelation 19:7b). This means that she is "*granted*," or permitted, to be "*arrayed in fine linen, clean and white: for the fine linen is the righteousness of saints*" (Revelation 19:8).

The wife of the Lamb, that is, the New Jerusalem, is described in greater detail in the final portion of

---

106. "*Let thy priests be clothed with righteousness; and let thy saints shout for joy*" (Psalm 132:9).

"*And one of the elders answered, saying unto me, What are these which are arrayed in white robes? and whence came they?*
And I said unto him, Sir, thou knowest. And he said to me, These are they which came out of great tribulation, and have washed their robes, and made them white in the blood of the Lamb" (Revelation 7:13-14).

9 And he saith unto me, Write, Blessed are they which are called unto the marriage supper of the Lamb. And he saith unto me, These are the true sayings of God.

10 And I fell at his feet to worship him. And he said unto me, See thou do it not; I am thy fellowservant, and of thy brethren that have the testimony of Jesus: worship God: for the testimony of Jesus is the spirit of prophecy (Revelation 19:1-10).

the sixth prophetic unit, in Revelation 21:1-8, and in the seventh prophetic unit, Revelation 21:9-22:5.

John now (Revelation 19:10a) becomes so overwhelmed by the presence of the angel that he is on the verge of worshiping him—a forbidden act (see Colossians 2:18). The angelic presence is so awesome, so overpowering that John nearly succumbs to this temptation a second time (Revelation 22:8-9).[107]

This angel refused to accept John's worship, but told John that he was a fellowservant to John, and also a fellowservant of those brethren *"that have the testimony* (Greek, *marturia*, testimony, witness, the word from which we get the word, "martyr") *of Jesus: worship God: for the testimony* (Greek, *marturia*, testimony, witness) *of Jesus is the spirit of prophecy"* (Revelation 19:10b).

John was on the penal island of Patmos *"for the testimony* (Greek, *marturios*, testimony, witness) *of Jesus"* (Revelation 1:9b). In Revelation, *marturios*, or *marturia*, seems to carry the idea or connotation of a testimony or witnessing that leads to suffering or to being killed.

---

107. Angels are such awesome beings, that they must often admonish people not to fear them. It is forbidden to worship them, however

To Gideon: *"And when Gideon perceived that he was an angel of the Lord, Gideon said, Alas, 0 Lord God! for because 1 have seen an angel of the Lord face to face. And the Lord said unto him, Peace be unto thee; fear not: thou shalt not die"* (Judges 6:22-23).

To Daniel: *"Then said he unto me, Fear not, Daniel: for from the first day that thou didst set thine heart to understand, and to chasten thyself before thy God, thy words were heard, and I am come for thy words"* (Daniel 10:12).

To Zacharias: *"And when Zacharias saw him, he was troubled, and fear fell upon him. But the angel said unto him, Fear not, Zacharias: for thy prayer is heard; and thy wife Elizabeth shall bear thee a son, and thou shalt call his name John"* (Luke 1:12-13).

To Mary: *"And the angel said unto her, Fear not, Mary: for thou hast found favour with God"* (Luke 1:30).

To the women: *"And the angel answered and said unto the women, Fear not ye: for I know that ye seek Jesus, which was crucified"* (Matthew 28:5).

To Paul: *"For there stood by me this night the angel of God, whose I am, and whom I serve, Saying, Fear not, Paul; thou must be brought before Caesar: and. lo, God hath given thee all them that sail with thee"* (Acts 27:23-24).

"Let no man beguile you of your reward in a voluntary humility and worshipping of angels, intruding into those things which he hath not seen, vainly puffed up by his fleshly mind" (Colossians 2:18).

"And I John saw these things,, and heard them. And when I had heard and seen, I fell down to worship before the feet of the angel which shewed me these things.
Then saith he unto me, See thou do it not; for I am thy fellowservant, and of thy brethren the prophets, and of them which keep the sayings of this book: worship God" (Revelation 22:8-9).

Here are some examples:

*"And from Jesus Christ, who is the faithful **witness** (Greek, martus), and the first begotten of the dead, and the prince of the kings of the earth. Unto him who loved us, **and washed us from our sins in his own blood**"* (Revelation 1:5).

*"I John, who also am your brother, and **companion in tribulation**, and in the kingdom and patience of Jesus Christ, was in the isle that is called Patmos, for the word of God, and **for the testimony** (Greek, marturion) **of Jesus Christ**"* (Revelation 1:9).

*"And when he had opened the fifth seal, I saw under the altar **the souls of them that were slain** for the word of God, and **for the testimony** (Greek, marturian) which **they** held"* (Revelation 6:9).

*"And when they shall have finished their **testimony** (Greek, marturian), the beast that ascendeth out of the bottomless pit shall make war against them, and shall overcome them, **and kill them**"* (Revelation 11:7).

"And they overcame him (Satan, the accuser of the brethren) *by the blood of the Lamb, and by the word of their **testimony** (Greek, marturias); **and they loved not their lives unto the death**"* (Revelation 12:11).

*"And the dragon was wroth with the woman, and went **to make war** with the remnant of her seed, which keep the commandments of God, and have **the testimony** (Greek, marturian) of Jesus Christ"* (Revelation 12:17. See also 13:7 following.)

"And it was given unto him (the beast) *to make war with the saints, and to overcome them: and power was given him over all kindreds, and tongues, and nations."*

The meaning of the phrase, *"for the testimony* (Greek, marturia) *of Jesus is the spirit of prophecy"* seems to be: for the testimony that brings suffering or death for Jesus is also the spirit that gives prophecy. John, as he received this revelation on

the Isle of Patmos, the Roman penal colony, had
certainly proven this statement true in his case.

This sixth prophetic unit covers such events as the triumph of Jesus over
the beast, the false prophet, and the kings of the earth and their armies,
which we last saw gathering at Armageddon in Revelation 16:12-16.
(Revelation 19:11 picks up right after Revelation 16:16, in which the beast
and the kings from the sun-rising were gathering at Armageddon.) Both
the seventh trumpet (Revelation 11:15-19) and the seventh bowl of God's
wrath (Revelation 16:17-21) reveal events occurring with the return of
Jesus (Revelation 11:15-19 covers Revelation 16:1–22:5), and thus we
should supplement our picture of Jesus' return as we find it in Revelation
19:11-21 with these other passages. Thus, at the time of Jesus' return, *"the
nations were angry, and thy wrath is come"* (Revelation 11:18a)—a statement that foretells all seven of the bowls of God's wrath. Also, as Jesus
returns, an earthquake divides *"the great city"* of Rome *"into three
parts...and the cities of the nations fell"* (Revelation 16:18-19a), these *"cities
of the nations"* being the nations of the Roman Empire, but apparently also
those of the three former world empires—the Babylonian, the
Medo-Persian, and the Greek—as these four empires were to be destroyed
together by the coming kingdom of God (see Daniel 2:34-35,44-45;
7:12).[108]

We will also see in this sixth prophetic unit: the imprisonment of Satan
(Revelation 20:1-3), the resurrection of those martyred for Jesus, and their
reigning with Him for a thousand years (Revelation 20:4-6), Satan loosed
after a thousand years from imprisonment, and his deceiving of the
nations (Revelation 20:7-8), his warfare against *"the beloved city"* of
Jerusalem, followed by his total defeat (Revelation 20:9-10), the resurrection of all the remaining dead, and their judgment before God (Revelation

---

108. The four world empires, prophesied by Daniel, were to be destroyed *together* by the coming kingdom of God.

*"Thou sawest till that a stone was cut out without hands, which smote the image upon his feet that
were of iron and clay, and brake them to pieces.*
*Then was the iron, the clay, the brass, the silver, and the gold, broken to pieces together, and became
like the chaff of the summer threshingfloors; and the wind carried them away, that no place was
found for them: and the stone that smote the image became a great mountain, and filled the whole
earth"* (Daniel 2:34-35).
*"And in the days of these kings shall the God of heaven set up a kingdom, which shall never be
destroyed: and the kingdom shall not be left to other people, but it shall break in pieces and consume
all these kingdom, and it shall stand for ever.*
*Forasmuch as thou sawest that the stone was cut out of the mountain without hands, and that it
brake in pieces the iron, the brass, the clay, the silver and the gold; the great God hath made known to
the king what shall come to pass hereafter: and the dream is certain, and the interpretation thereof
sure"* (Daniel 2:44-45).
"As concerning the rest of the beasts (the Babylonian, Medo-Persian, and Greek empires), *they had
their dominion taken away: yet their lives were prolonged for a season and time"* (Daniel 7:12).

20:11-15), a new heaven, a new earth, and the holy city, the New Jerusalem (Revelation 21:1-8).

A careful reading of this section of Revelation, and of other prophetic passages as well, indicates that *there are two phases of the coming kingdom of God.* In Revelation, we see these two phases in

(1) *"the thousand years"* (Revelation 20:2-7), and

(2) *"the holy city, New Jerusalem"* (Revelation 21:1-8).

Thus, in the first phase, Christ *"must reign, till he hath put all enemies under his feet"* (1 Corinthians 15:25). Paul does not give the length of this first phase of Christ's reign, but only indicates that Christ continues to reign till He *"shall have put down all rule and all authority and power"* (1 Corinthians 15:24a). *"The last enemy that shall be destroyed is Death"* (1 Corinthians 15:26). *"Then cometh the end, when he shall have delivered up the kingdom to God, even the Father"* (1 Corinthians 15:24a).

In the second phase, *"then shall the Son also himself be subject unto him that put all things under him, that God may be all in all"* (1 Corinthians 15:28).

Thus, in the first phase, some are raised in *"the resurrection that is out from among the dead"* (Philippians 3:11, *Concordant*), that is, *"a better resurrection"* (Hebrews 11:35), and receive *"a spiritual body"* (1 Corinthians 15:44). (See also 1 John 3:2, *"but we know that, when he shall appear, we shall be like him."*) Others, however, in this first phase of the kingdom of God will have natural human bodies. Otherwise Christ would not need to *"rebuke many people"* (Isaiah 2:4), nor could it be said, *"For all people will walk every one in the name of his god"* (Micah 4:5), nor that *"the sinner being an hundred years old shall be accursed"* (Isaiah 65:20). Those scriptures could apply only in the first phase when Christ is putting all enemies under His feet.

But in the second phase, *"flesh and blood cannot inherit the kingdom of God; neither doth corruption inherit incorruption"* (1 Corinthians 15:50).

At the present time, and in the first phase of God's kingdom, it is correct to say that *"the Father judgeth no man, but hath committed all judgment unto the Son"* (John 5:22), but when Jesus *"shall have delivered up the kingdom to God, even the Father"* (1 Corinthians 15:24a), then the Father will judge (Revelation 20:11-12).

In Matthew 13:41-43, we see these two phases of the kingdom of God. Thus,

"The Son of man shall send forth his angels, and they shall gather out of his kingdom all things that offend, and them which do iniquity." This corresponds to the first phase of the kingdom of God, that is to the *"thousand*

years" of Revelation 20:2-7, and to the phrase *"he must reign, till he hath put all enemies under his feet"* of 1 Corinthians 15:25.

"And shall cast them into a furnace of fire: there shall be wailing and gnashing of teeth" (Matthew 13:42). This corresponds to Revelation 20:15, *"And whosoever was not found written in the book of life was cast into the lake of fire."*

"Then shall the righteous shine forth as the sun in the kingdom of their Father" (Matthew 13:43). This corresponds to the second phase of the kingdom of God, and to the *"new heaven"* and *"new earth"* (Revelation 21:1), and especially to *"the holy city, New Jerusalem"* (Revelation 21:2).

And I saw heaven opened, and behold a white horse; and he that sat upon him was called Faithful and True, and in righteousness he doth judge and make war.

12 His eyes were as a flame of fire, and on his head were many crowns; and he had a name written, that no man knew, but he himself (Revelation 19:11-12).

Jesus Comes as Judge and Warrior

"And I saw heaven opened..." (Revelation 19:11a), that is, John saw into heaven as Stephen did (Acts 7:56), and as Ezekiel (1:1) did in a vision.

"...and behold a white horse" (Revelation 19:11b). A white horse was a symbol of conquest, but this is not the same white horse we saw in Revelation 6:2 as the riders are very different. The rider in Revelation 6:2 was a symbol of Titus. The rider in Revelation 19:11 is Jesus.

"...and he that sat upon him was called Faithful and True" (Revelation 19:llc). Later, in Revelation 19:13, *"...his name is called the Word of God."* Both names describe and identify this rider as Jesus. The phrases, *"the faithful witness"* (Revelation 1:5), *"he that is true"* (Revelation 3:7), and *"the faithful and true witness"* (Revelation 3:14) had already been given in reference to Jesus, and, of course, the phrase, *"The Word of God"* also identifies Jesus with certainty (John 1:14).

"...and in righteousness he doth judge and make war" (Revelation 19:11d). *Jesus is both a judge and a warrior.* He judges the beast, the kings from the sun-rising, the ten kings allied with the beast, and their armies, and He makes war upon them all.

"His eyes were as a flame of fire..." (Revelation 19:12a), as in Revelation 1:14 and 2:18. He has a piercing, discerning look.

"*...and on his head were many crowns*" (Revelation 19:12b), because He is now "*King of kings*" (Revelation 17:14; 19:16). He wears the crowns of the kings of the nations He has just defeated through the instrumentality of the beast and the ten kings (Revelation 16:1-11), "*for God hath put in their hearts to fulfil his will*" (Revelation 17:17a). His crowns were the crowns of the kings who had "*committed fornication*" with "*the great whore,*" that is, the kings of the nations loyal to Rome, who had been defeated by the beast (Revelation 17:2; 18:3,9). "*and he had a name written, that no man knew, but he himself*" (Revelation 19:12c). In Hebrew thought, to know someone's name was to have a power over that person. Thus, the meaning here is that no one could have any power over Jesus.[109]

*And he was clothed with a vesture dipped in blood; and his name is called **The Word of God**[110] (Revelation 19:13).*

"*And he was clothed with a vesture dipped in blood*" (Revelation 19:13a). Jesus' vesture, or garment, was not dipped in His own blood, but in the blood of His enemies. Also, His garment had already been "*dipped in blood*" before He defeats the beast and his allies at Armageddon. This phrase, "*he was clothed with a vesture dipped in*

---

109. Thus the angel in Genesis 32:29 would not give his name to Jacob, nor would the angel in Judges 13:17-18 give his name to Manoah, the father of Samson. (See also Revelation 2:17; 3:12; Matthew 11:27).

110. The phrase, "*the Word of God,*" identifies Jesus with certainty

"*In the beginning was the Word, and the Word was with God, and the word was God.
And the Word was made flesh, and dwelt among us, (and we beheld his glory, the glory as of the only begotten of the Father,) full of grace and truth*" (John 1:1,14).

"*That which was from the beginning, which we have heard, which we have seen with our eyes, which we have looked upon, and our hands have handled, of the Word of life;
(For the life was manifested, and we have seen it, and bear witness, and shew unto you that eternal life, which was with the Father, and was manifested unto us;)* (1 John 1:1-2).

Compare Isaiah 63:1-4 with Isaiah 61:1,2 Which Jesus Quoted at Nazareth (Luke 4:18-19).

"*And he came to Nazareth, where he had been brought up: and, as his custom was, he went into the synagogue on the sabbath day, and stood up for to read.
And there was delivered unto him the book of the prophet Esaias (Isaiah). And when he had opened the book, he found the place where it was written,
The Spirit of the Lord is upon me, because he hath anointed me to preach the gospel to the poor; he hath sent me to heal the brokenhearted to preach deliverance to the captives, and recovery of sight to the blind, to set at liberty them that are bruised,
To preach the acceptable year of the Lord.
And he closed the book, and he gave it again to the minister, and sat down. And the eyes of all them that were in the synagogue were fastened upon him.
And he began to say unto them, This day is this scripture fulfilled in your ears*" (Luke 4:16-21).

blood," is a reference to Isaiah 63:1-4 which is quoted and explained below.

"Who is this that cometh from Edom (that is, Rome[111]), *with dyed garments from Bozrah? this that is glorious in his apparel, traveling in the greatness of his strength? I that speak in righteousness, mighty to save. Wherefore art thou red in thine apparel, and thy garments like him that treadeth in the winevat? I have trodden the winepress alone; and of the people* (the Dead Sea manuscript of Isaiah has here *"my people,"* the meaning being that when Jesus treads the *"wine-press"* to destroy Rome, none of His people help Him, and thus only Jesus' vesture is *"dipped in blood"*) *there was none with me: for I will tread them in mine anger, and trample them in my fury; and their blood shall be sprinkled upon my garments, and I will stain all my raiment. For* **the day of vengeance** *is in mine heart, and the year of my redeemed is come."*

Compare the above passage with Isaiah 61:1-2 which Jesus quoted at Nazareth (Luke 4:18-19), but He quoted only the part dealing with His first coming. He stopped short of quoting *"and* **the day of vengeance of our God,"** which relates to His second coming.

"The spirit of the Lord God is upon me; because the Lord hath anointed me to preach good tidings unto the meek; he hath sent me to bind up the broken-hearted, to proclaim liberty to the captives, and the opening of the prison to them that are bound; To pro-claim the acceptable year of the Lord, and **the day of vengeance of our God"** (Isaiah 61:1-2).

But why did Edom come to identify Rome? When Herod the Great, an Edomite, was confirmed as king of the Jews by Augustus Caesar, Rome began to be called "Edom" by the Jews to avoid offense to the Roman government. In this way the Jews could speak against Rome without naming Rome and without threatening their own security.

---

111. *"The name 'Edom' is used by the Talmudists for the Roman Empire, and they applied to Rome every passage of the Bible referring to Edom or to Esau." The Jewish Encyclopedia,* Vol. 5, page 41.

In Revelation 19:13 these passages (Isaiah 63:1-4 and 61:2) are applied to Jesus who treads the winepress of the wrath of God. That is, when the beast, the ten kings, and their armies were to have destroyed Rome, Jesus was there, too, fulfilling His divine vengeance against Rome as prophesied, and figuratively, staining His garments with the blood of Rome's slain.

A further word is needed regarding the phrase, *"Who is this that cometh from Edom, with dyed garments from Bozrah?"* (Isaiah 63:1) *"Edom"* and *"Bozrah"* seem here to be used somewhat freely, or interchangeably, even though Bozrah was the chief city of Edom. This passage was *originally fulfilled* when Babylon was destroyed by the Medes and the Persians, and Edom—being a part of the Babylonian empire—was destroyed as well. But scriptures often have a *secondary fulfillment,* and as a secondary fulfillment, the "Edom" in this passage refers to Rome. This is because, in the first century B.C., and in the first century A.D., *"Edom"* was in common use as a code word for Rome, and John would have seen it in that light; that is, he would have seen Isaiah 63:1-4 as a picture of Jesus coming from Rome with blood-stained garments, though actually it would have been the armies of the beast and the ten kings that would have destroyed Rome. But this is because God uses even the wickedness of man for His purposes, as it is written, *"Surely the wrath of man shall praise thee"* (Psalm 76:10a). Thus when John sees Jesus in heaven, His garment, or *"vesture,"* was already *"dipped in blood"* (Revelation 19:13a). In His conflict with Rome, Jesus is said to have *"trodden the winepress alone; and of the* (or, *my) people there was none with me."* This means that in both the original reference to Edom, and in the double, or secondary, reference to Rome, none of His people were with Him. The Jews did not fight in Cyrus' armies against Babylon, or against Edom, and the followers of

Jesus would not, of course, have been fighting in the armies of the beast against Rome.

Isaiah 63:1-4 does not apply, however, to Jesus' conflict with the beast, the kings of the earth and their armies. In this battle, Jesus' *"people"* are with Him, and they are coming to *"reign on the earth"* (Revelation 5:10; see also 2:26-27).

And the armies which were in heaven followed him upon white horses, clothed in fine linen, white and clean (Revelation 19:14).

When Jesus returns, He will come with angels (Matthew 16:27; 25:31; Mark 8:38; 2 Thessalonians 1:7), and with saints (Zechariah 14:5; Jude 14; Revelation 17:14).[112] *"The armies which were in heaven"* included angels (Matthew 26:53), and these angels, or spirits, were known to have ridden upon spirit horses (compare 2 Kings 2:11-12 with 6:17; see also Zechariah 1:8). Angels are also dressed in *"fine linen, white and clean"* as described here (see Revelation 15:6). However, in this passage John is focusing upon the saints who are in *"the armies which were in heaven."* The saints are also *"arrayed in fine linen, clean and white: for the fine linen is the righteousness of saints"* (Revelation 19:8). However, it is Revelation 17:14 that proves it is the saints that are in view in heaven's armies. *"These* (the beast and ten kings with him) *shall make war with the Lamb, and the Lamb shall overcome them: for he is Lord of lords, and King of kings: and they **that are with him are called, and chosen, and faithful**."* These bold words remind us of the words of Jesus, *"For many are called, but few are chosen"* (Matthew 20:16). Because these words refer to saints, not angels, it

---

112. Jesus Will Come with Angels

"For the Son of man shall come in the glory of his Father with his angels; and then he shall reward every man according to his works" (Matthew 16:27).

"When the Son of man shall come in his glory, and all the holy angels with him, then shall he sit upon the throne of his glory" (Matthew 25:31).

"Whosoever therefore shall be ashamed of me and of my words in this adulterous and sinful generation; of him also shall the Son of man be ashamed, when he cometh in the glory of his Father with the holy angels" (Mark 8:38).

Jesus Will Come With Saints

"...and the Lord my God shall come, and all the saints with thee" (Zechariah 14:5b).

"And Enoch also, the seventh from Adam, prophesied of these, saying, Behold, the Lord cometh with ten thousands of his saints" (Jude 14).

"These shall make war with the Lamb, and the Lamb shall overcome them: for he is Lord of lords, and King of kings: and they that are with him are called, and chosen, and faithful" (Revelation 17:14).

seems certain that Revelation 17:14 and 19:14 do as well.

This would be in accord with Daniel 7:18 (see also 7:22,27) where we read, *"But the saints of the most High shall take the kingdom, and possess the kingdom for ever, even for ever and ever."*

And out of his mouth goeth a sharp sword, that with it he should smite the nations: and he shall rule them with a rod of iron: and he treadeth the winepress of the fierceness and wrath of Almighty God.

16 And he hath on his vesture and on his thigh a name written, KING OF KINGS, AND LORD OF LORDS (Revelation 19:15-16).

"And out of his mouth goeth a sharp sword, that with it he should smite the nations" (Revelation 19:15a).[113] This is the *"sharp two-edged sword"* of Revelation 1:16 and 2:12, and is *"the word of God"* as described in Hebrews 4:12. The *"two-edged sword"* symbolizes divine justice. The sword coming out of the mouth of Jesus indicates decisiveness. In Isaiah 11:4, we read prophetically of Jesus, *"And he shall smite the earth with the rod of his mouth, and with the breath of his lips shall he slay the wicked."* The LXX here reads, *"And he shall smite the earth with the **word of his mouth**, and with the breath of his lips shall he destroy the ungodly one."* Paul, in 2 Thessalonians 2:8, refers to Isaiah 11:4 when he writes, *"And then shall that Wicked be revealed, whom the Lord shall consume with the spirit of his mouth, and shall destroy with the brightness of his coming."*

Some have thought that the phrase *"And out of his mouth goeth a sharp sword…"* indicated that Jesus would convert these who opposed him. This is not the case. The words in the above scriptures— *"smite," "slay," "destroy,"* and *"consume"*—do not indicate conversion. The picture of Jesus treading *"the winepress of the fierceness and wrath of*

---

113. In both Hebrew and Greek, *"the edge of the sword"* is literally *"the mouth of the sword"* and a *"two-edged sword"* is literally a *"two-mouthed sword"*

   "…with the edge (Hebrew, *pey,* mouth) *of the sword…"* Genesis 34:26; Exodus 17:13; Numbers 21:24; Deuteronomy 13:15; 20:13; Joshua 6:21; 8:24; 10:28, 32, 39; 11:11, 12, 14; 19:47; Judges 1:8,25; 4:15-16; 18:27; 20:37,48; 21:10; 1 Samuel 15:8; 22:19; 2 Samuel 15:14; 2 Kings 10:25; Job 1:15,17; Jeremiah 21:7.

   "…the edge (Greek, *stoma,* mouth) *of the sword…"* Luke 21:24; Hebrews 11:34.

   "…a two-edged (Hebrew, *pey,* mouth) *sword…"* Proverbs 5:4; Psalm 149:6.

   "…two-edged (Greek, *distomos,* two-mouthed) *sword…"* Hebrews 4:12; Revelation 1:16; see also Revelation 2:12.

Almighty God" is a picture not of conversions but of widespread death and destruction.

But how could the word of God bring physical death to such an extent that the *"fowls that fly in the midst of heaven"* are *"filled with the flesh"* of *"the kings of the earth, and their armies"* (Revelation 19:17-21)?

Solomon wrote, *"Death and life are in the power of the tongue"* (Proverbs 18:21). Elijah and Elisha both found that words from their mouths could bring physical death (2 Kings 1:9-17; 2:23-25). We usually think of the power of the Word of God in terms of giving life rather than death, and healing rather than infirmity. It is generally good to think in such terms, no doubt. Still, by words, the apostle Paul struck the sorcerer Elymas blind for a season (Acts 13:6-12), and by the words of Peter, Ananias and Sapphira fell dead (Acts 5:11). By the words of Moses (Numbers 16:28-33), *"the earth opened her mouth"* and swallowed Korah, Dathan, and Abiram, and their wives and children (Numbers 16:1-35; 26:9-11). By the words of Elijah, King Ahab's entire family—including himself, his wife, Jezebel, and his seventy sons—were destroyed (1 Kings 21:19-24, words; 22:34-38, Ahab died; 2 Kings 9:30-37, Jezebel, Ahab's wife killed; 10:1-10, Ahab's seventy sons killed). By the words of Moses, ten plagues were pronounced and came upon Egypt (Exodus 7-12).

If Jesus spoke the word, who would not die on the spot?

"...and he shall rule them with a rod of iron" (Revelation 19:15c).[114] In Revelation 2:27, it is the overcoming saints who *"rule them with a rod of iron,"* but this is because we will reign with Jesus.

---

114. The phrase, *"He shall rule them with a rod of iron"* is from Psalm 2:9, in the Septuagint version (LXX)

King James Version	The Septuagint Version
"Thou shalt break them with a rod of iron; thou shalt dash them in pieces like a potter's vessel" (Psalm 2:9).	*"Thou shalt rule them with a rod of iron; thou shalt dash them in pieces as a potter's vessel"* (Psalm 2:9).

"And he treadeth the winepress of the fierceness and wrath of Almighty God" (Revelation 19:15d), or literally, "the winepress of the wine of the wrath of the anger of God the Almighty." God's searing, unbounded rage was against the beast and his allies. The treading of the winepress is always indicative of a horrid loss of life.

Jesus Defeats the Beast and His Allies at Armageddon

This section, together with the previous one (Revelation 19:11-21), takes place immediately after the beast and the kings of the earth are gathered for "the battle of that great day of God Almighty" at Armageddon (Revelation 16:12-16). In this section we see the results of that battle.

"And I saw an angel standing in the sun..." (Revelation 19:17). His brightness indicates that this angel has just emerged from the presence of God. He has, therefore, God's latest message.

"And he cried with a loud voice, saying to all the fowls that fly in the midst of heaven, Come and gather yourselves together unto the supper of the great God; That ye may eat the flesh of kings, and the flesh of captains, and the flesh of mighty men, and the flesh of horses, and of them that sit on

And I saw an angel standing in the sun; and he cried with a loud voice, saying to all the fowls that fly in the midst of heaven, Come and gather yourselves together unto the supper of the great God;

18 That ye may eat the flesh of kings, and the flesh of captains, and the flesh of mighty men, and the flesh of horses, and of them that sit on them, and the flesh of all men, both free and

---

115. "Him that dieth of Jeroboam in the city shall the dogs eat; and him that dieth in the field shall the fowls of the air eat: for the Lord hath spoken it" (1 Kings 14:11).

"Him that dieth of Baasha in the city shall the dogs eat; and him that dieth of his in the fields shall the fowls of the air eat" (1 Kings 16:4).

"Thou shalt fall upon the mountains of Israel, thou, and all thy bands, and the people that is with thee; I will give thee unto the ravenous birds of every sort, and to the beasts of the field to be devoured.
Thou shalt fall upon the open field: for I have spoken it, saith the Lord God...
And, thou son of man, thus saith the Lord God, Speak unto every feathered fowl, and to every beast of the field,
Assemble yourselves, and come; gather yourselves on every side to my sacrifice that I do sacrifice for you, even a great sacrifice upon the mountains of Israel, that ye may eat flesh and drink blood...
Ye shall eat the flesh of the mighty, and drink the blood of the princes of the earth, of rams, of lambs, and of goats, of bullocks, all of them fatlings of Bashan.
And ye shall eat fat till ye be full, and drink blood till ye be drunken, of my sacrifice which I have sacrificed for you.
Thus ye shall be filled at my table with horses and chariots, with mighty men, and with all men of war, saith the Lord God" Ezekiel 39:4-5,17-20).

bond, both small and great.

them, *and the flesh of all men, both free and bond, both small and great"* (Revelation 19:17b-18).

19 And I saw the beast, and the kings of the earth, and their armies, gathered together to make war against him that sat on the horse, and against his army.

"Fowls" here are an indication that this great slaughter was to take place in the open field, not in a city.[115] (See 1 Kings 14:11; 16:4; 21:24.) *"Him that dieth of Ahab in the city the dogs shall eat; and him that dieth in the field shall the fowls of the air eat"* (1 Kings 21:24). This is in keeping with Armageddon, the great plain where this battle is to take place. A similar description of another battle in an open field is to be found in Ezekiel 39:4,17-20.

20 And the beast was taken, and with him the false prophet that wrought miracles before him, with which he deceived them that had received the mark of the beast, and them that worshipped his image. These both were cast alive into a lake of fire burning with brimstone.

*"And I saw the beast, and the **kings of the earth**, and their armies, gathered together to make war against him that sat on the horse, and against his army"* (Revelation 19:19).

"The kings of the earth" would include the ten kings who were to be allied with the beast (see Revelation 17:12-14), and also *"the kings from the sun-rising"* (Revelation 16:12c), who were the kings of the remnants of the old Babylonian, Medo-Persian, and Greek empires.

"And the beast was taken" (Revelation 19:20).

HALLELUJAH! *"THE BEAST WAS TAKEN, AND WITH HIM THE FALSE PROPHET!"* Just as Korah, Dathan, and Abiram, with their wives and children, *"**went down alive** into the pit, and the earth closed upon them"* (Numbers 16:33), so also the beast and the false prophet were both *"**cast alive** into a lake of fire burning with brimstone."* It was as though they had fallen into a volcanic crater just being born in the area of Armageddon.

21 And the remnant were slain with the sword of him that sat upon the horse, which sword proceeded out of his mouth; and all the fowls were filled with their flesh (Revelation 19:17-21).

"And the remnant were slain with the sword of him that sat upon the horse, which sword proceeded out of his mouth: and all the fowls were filled with their flesh" (Revelation 19:21).

Jesus' victory at Armageddon is complete.

Psalm 2 is fulfilled at this time. It reads as follows in the LXX version:

"Wherefore did the heathen rage, and the nations imagine vain things?

2 The kings of the earth stood up, and the rulers gathered themselves together, against the Lord, and against his Christ;
3 saying, Let us break through their bonds, and cast away their yoke from us.
4 He that dwells in the heavens shall laugh them to scorn, and the Lord shall mock them.
5 Then shall he speak to them in his anger, and trouble them in his fury.
6 But I have been made king by him on Sion his holy mountain,
7 declaring the ordinance of the Lord: the Lord said to me, Thou art my Son, today have I begotten thee.
8 Ask of me, and I will give thee the heathen for thine inheritance, and the ends of the earth for thy possession.
9 Thou shalt rule them with a rod of iron; thou shalt dash them in pieces as a potter's vessel" (Psalm 2:1-9, LXX).

The Meaning of Psalm 2:7

In the New Testament, the words from Psalm 2:7, *"Thou art my Son; this day have I begotten thee"* are quoted in reference to Jesus' resurrection from the tomb. Thus, His emergence from the tomb is compared to one's birth from a mother.

*"And we declare unto you glad tidings, **how that the promise which was made unto the fathers,***
*God hath fulfilled the same unto us their children, **in that he hath raised up Jesus again; as it is also written in the second psalm, Thou art my Son, this day have I begotten thee"*** (Acts 13:32-33).

"Concerning his Son Jesus Christ our Lord, which was made of the seed of David according to the flesh;
And declared to be the Son of God with power, *according to the spirit of holiness, **by the resurrection from the dead"*** (Romans 1:3-4)

*"And from Jesus Christ, who is the faithful witness, and **the first begotten of the dead**, and the prince of the kings of the earth. Unto him that loved us, and washed us from our sins in his own blood"* (Revelation 1:5).

Revelation 20
The Millennial Reign of Jesus

And I saw an angel come down from heaven, having the key of the bottomless pit and a great chain in his hand.

2 And he laid hold on the dragon, that old serpent, which is the Devil, and Satan, and bound him a thousand years,

3 And cast him into the bottomless pit, and shut him up, and set a seal upon him, that he should deceive the nations no more, till the thousand years should be fulfilled: and after that he must be loosed a little season (Revelation 20:1-3).

Satan Bound in Bottomless Pit; His Deception Ended

"And I saw an angel come down from heaven, having the key of the bottomless pit and a great chain in his hand." (Revelation 20:1) This angel was identified in Revelation 9:1,11. His name in Hebrew is *Abaddon*, in Greek, *Apollyon*.

"And he laid hold on the dragon, that old serpent, which is the Devil, and Satan, and bound him a thousand years" (Revelation 20:2).

Abaddon, or Apollyon, is clearly an angel of God. *"Dragon"* meant simply a large snake, *"that old serpent"*—that is, the serpent that seduced Eve in the Garden of Eden (Genesis 3:1-13).

In Revelation 13:2, the dragon's *"seat"* was Rome. *"The bottomless pit"* was thought of as beneath the city of Rome. With Rome now destroyed and bereft of inhabitants, Satan is seen as imprisoned beneath the ruined and desolate city.

"The thousand years." This time period is given in each verse from Revelation 20:2-7, but does not occur in any other scriptural passage. This raises the question: Is *"the thousand years"* a literal time period? There can be no question that the numeral "1000" would carry a significant symbolic meaning. Ten is the signature of governmental authority. A number multiplied by itself carries the same significance, but intensified. Here we have, not only 10 x 10, but 10 x 10 x 10, that is, greatly intensified, or intensified three times.

Three is the number of heaven. *"The thousand years"* would apparently indicate divine governmental authority intensified over a very wide area, and in which that authority is thoroughly enforced. The kingdom of heaven ruling upon the earth is thus signified.

But we can look at *"the thousand years"* from a different angle. Revelation was communicated to John in the Aramaic language, and in the Aramaic the word for *"thousand"* is *"alep."*

"Alep" is also the pronunciation of the first letter of the Aramaic alphabet, and as such, it is a symbol for God. So from a completely different approach the kingdom of God is symbolized, that is, *"the 'Alep' (or 'God') years."*

But may not *"the thousand years"* of the reign of Jesus be both symbolic and literal? Of course that's a possibility. But since the *"two hundred thousand thousand"* horsemen (Revelation 9:16) and the *"thousand six hundred furlongs"* (Revelation 14:20) were symbolic, but not literal, we could not assert with certainty that *"the thousand years"* must be taken literally.

However, in view of the current population explosion, and in view of the hundreds of language and dialect groups who still do not have the scriptures in their own language, and in view of the vast amount of time it takes to translate the Bible into even one language, perhaps a thousand years to bring the world under the lordship of Jesus is not unreasonable.

*And I saw **thrones**, and they sat upon them, and judgment was given unto them: and I saw the souls of them that were beheaded (Greek, pepelekismenon,*

The Reign of Jesus, with Those Raised in the First Resurrection

"And I saw thrones..." These are to be thrones of rulership and judgment. In the Old Testament the kings were also judges (as with Solomon, 1 Kings 3:16-28), and previously the judges were also rulers (as in the book of Judges). But are these

having been cut with an axe) *for the witness of Jesus, and for the word of God, and which had not worshipped the beast, neither his image, neither had received his mark upon their foreheads, or in their hands; and they lived and reigned with Christ a thousand years* (Revelation 20:4).

thrones in heaven or upon the earth? In Revelation 5:10b this question is settled in the *"new song"* of *"the four beasts and four and twenty elders."* They sang, *"and we* (or *they*) *shall reign on the earth."*

"…and they sat upon them…" Who sits upon these thrones? In 1 Corinthians 6:3a, Paul wrote, *"Do ye not know that the saints will judge the world?"* So these are not angels, but saints, as Paul also wrote, *"Know ye not that we shall judge angels?"* (1 Corinthians 6:3a). On these thrones are the twelve apostles (Matthew 19:28; Luke 22:30), and those of us who are martyred and who suffer (Greek, *hupomenomen*, endure) with Jesus (2 Timothy 2:12).[116] These (or *we*) would be judging not the souls of the departed dead, but judging and ruling for Jesus, and with Jesus, those living on earth in the millennium.

…and I saw the souls of them that were beheaded…

These *"souls"* were not to be thought of as disembodied souls, or spirits. *"Souls"* in Scripture are often used in reference to living persons. Thus, on Pentecost, there were added to the 120, *"about three thousand souls"* (Acts 2:41); *"…and fear came upon every soul"* (Acts 2:43); *"And we were in all in the ship two hundred threescore and sixteen souls"* (Acts 27:37). These were not disembodied souls, or spirits, at that time, but living persons. The *"souls"* John saw in Revelation 20:4 *"lived and reigned with Christ a thousand years."* They had *"part in the first resurrection"* (Revelation 20:6). As such they would be alive again!

---

116. On these *"thrones"* are the twelve apostles, and those who *"endure"* shall *"also reign with Him"*

"And Jesus said unto them, Verily I say unto you, That ye which have followed me, in the regeneration when the Son of man shall sit in the throne of his glory, ye also shall sit upon twelve thrones, judging the twelve tribes of Israel" (Matthew 19:28).

"And I appoint unto you a kingdom, as my Father hath appointed unto me;
That ye may eat and drink at my table in my kingdom, and sit on thrones judging the twelve tribes of Israel" (Luke 22:29-30).

"It is a faithful saying: For if we be dead with him, we shall also live with him:
If we suffer (Greek, *hupomenomen*, endure), *we shall also reign with him: if we deny him, he will also deny us:*
If we believe not, yet he abideth faithful: he cannot deny himself" (2 Timothy 2:11-13).

*But the rest of the dead lived not again until the thousand years were finished. This is **the first resurrection** (Revelation 20:5).*

"*...the rest of the dead...*" Does this phrase include all not slain with an axe, Christians and non-Christians alike? Then, if John were not slain with an axe, he would miss the first resurrection! Peter, according to tradition (see Eusebius' *Ecclesiastical History*, pg. 80), was crucified, but he was not slain with an axe! Would he be in the first resurrection? Or is John pointing to extreme cases—that even those beheaded would yet live again!

But some have interpreted Revelation 20:4-6 to mean that only those killed (not necessarily beheaded) would take part in this first resurrection.

In Revelation 16:15, John wrote, "*Behold, I [Jesus] come as a thief. **Blessed is he that watcheth, and keepeth his garments, lest he walk naked, and they see his shame.**" This passage is clearly written for the benefit of followers of Jesus who are physically alive just before the battle of Armageddon, which is introduced in the following verse (Revelation 16:16). But what kind of blessing is it if they are denied their part in the first resurrection?

While it was the clear intention of the beast to "*cause that as many as would not worship the image of the beast should be killed*" (Revelation 13:15b), still there would be scant prospect that he could get to them all in just three and a half years (Daniel 7:25; Revelation 11:3; 13:5). This time period, as we have pointed out previously (see comments on Revelation 13:7), would be a part of the second woe. *But after that we still see Christians alive in Rome.* The beast would not have killed them all.

God's angel would say to living Christians within Rome, "*Come out of her, **my people**, that ye be not partakers of her sins, and that ye receive not of her plagues*"[117] (Revelation 18: 4b). The phrase "*my*

---

117. God does not here issue a call to His children within Rome to escape *the wrath of man*—but He calls them out of Rome *to escape His wrath!*

The three woes (Revelation 8:13–11:19) included one and a half woes against Jerusalem, and one and a half woes against Rome. That part of the second woe which is against Rome (Revelation 11:3-13) is to last three and a half years, and it includes not only the plagues of the two witnesses against Rome, but also the war of the Roman Beast against the two witnesses, and against the Christians in Rome. *The second woe reveals the wrath of man.*

continued on next page

people" would refer to living Christians within Rome, after the three-and-a-half-year *"war with the saints"* in *"the second woe,"* and just before the destruction of Rome by the beast during *"the third woe."* Would God call them out of Rome to save their lives from His wrath only to withhold from them their part in the first resurrection?

Again, would Jesus give John a revelation that would contradict the revelation He gave Paul? No, of course not! But Paul wrote, *"For this we say unto you by the word of the Lord, that we which are alive and remain unto the coming of the Lord shall not prevent* (or, *precede,* or *'shall not obtain any advantage over')* *them which are asleep. For the Lord himself shall descend from heaven with a shout, with the voice of the archangel, and with the trump of God: and the **dead in Christ shall rise first: Then we which are alive and remain shall be caught up together with them** in the clouds, **to meet the Lord in the air:** and so shall we ever be with the Lord"* (1 Thessalonians 4:15-17; see also 1 Corinthians 15:51[118]).

So *"the first resurrection"* includes more than the martyrs!

Blessed and holy is he that hath part in the first resurrection: on such the   Still, John saw that a special blessing would belong to those who were killed by the Roman beast. He wrote, *"Blessed are the dead which die in the Lord **from henceforth:** Yea, saith the Spirit, that they may*

The third woe reveals the wrath of God. We see this third woe not only in Revelation 11:15-19, but also in Revelation 16:1-21 (and in other passages as well). The third woe includes the destruction of Rome by fire, the destruction of the beast, the false prophet, the beast's armies, and the armies of the kings of the sun-rising. It also includes a very great earthquake within Rome, and a horrible hailstorm which falls upon that city.

118. *"The first resurrection"* as seen in 1 Corinthians 15

"So also is the resurrection of the dead. it is sown in corruption; it is raised in incorruption:
It is sown in dishonour; it is raised in glory; it is sown in weakness; it is raised in power:
It is sown a natural body; it is raised a spiritual body. There is a natural body, and there is a spiritual body.
And as we have borne the image of the earthy, we shall also bear the image of the heavenly.
Now this I say, brethren, that flesh and blood cannot inherit the kingdom of God; neither doth corruption inherit incorruption.
Behold, I shew you a mystery; We shall not all sleep, but we shall all be changed,
In a moment, in the twinkling of an eye, at the last trump: for the trumpet shall sound, and the dead shall be raised incorruptible, and we shall be changed.
For this corruptible must put on incorruption, and this mortal must put on immortality"
(1 Corinthians 15:42-44, 49-53).

*second death hath no
power, but they shall
be priests of God and
of Christ, and shall
reign with him a
thousand years
(Revelation 20:6).*

*rest from their labours; and their works do follow
them"* (Revelation 14:13). The following three
verses (Revelation 14:14-16) reveal Jesus' reaping
(taking to heaven) those slain by the beast of
Rome. Revelation (5:8-10; 7:9-17; 14:2-3a; 15:2-4)
had prophetically pictured them already as being
in heaven. But what *special blessing* is to be theirs?

Jesus had spoken of *"the resurrection of the just"*
(Luke 14:14), as though it were to take place at a
time period distinct from the resurrection of the
unjust. He also spoke of those *"which shall be
accounted worthy to obtain that world, and the resurrection from the dead"* (Luke 20:35).

Paul had also seen the importance of striving by
every means he could to be a part of this first resurrection.[119] (Philippians 3:7-14). He had come to
see that this was not automatically his or ours, but
as Jesus had said, *"Strive to enter in at the strait
gate: for many, I say unto you, will seek to enter in,
and shall not be able"* (Luke 13:24).

Clearly, there are two aspects of our striving. One
aspect is simply to become a part of *"the first resurrection,"* and the second aspect is to reign with

---

119. *"And thou shalt be blessed; for they cannot recompense thee: for thou shalt be recompensed at the resurrection of the just"* (Luke 14:14).

*"And Jesus answering said unto them, The children of this world marry, and are given in marriage:
But they which shall be accounted worthy to obtain that world, and the resurrection from the dead
(Greek, ek nekron, out of dead ones), neither marry, nor are given in marriage:
Neither can they die any more: for they are equal unto the angels; and are the children of God, being
the children of the resurrection"* (Luke 20:34-36).

*"That I may know him, and the power of his resurrection, and the fellowship of his sufferings, being
made conformable unto his death;
If by any means I might attain unto the resurrection of the dead (Greek, exanastasis ton nekron,
out-resurrection from among the dead.).
Not as though I had already attained, either were already perfect: but I follow after, if that I may
apprehend that for which also I am apprehended of Christ Jesus.
Brethren, I count not myself to have apprehended: but this one thing I do, forgetting those things
which are behind, and reaching forth unto those things which are before,
I press toward the mark for the prize of the high (Greek, ano, above, high, up) calling of God in
Christ Jesus.
For our conversation (Greek, politeuma, citizenship) is in heaven; from whence also we look for the
Saviour, the Lord Jesus Christ:
Who shall change our vile body, that it may be fashioned like unto his glorious body, according to the
working whereby he is able even to subdue all things unto himself"* (Philippians 3:10-14,20-21).

*"Women received their dead raised to life again: and others were tortured, not accepting deliverance;
that they might obtain a better resurrection"* (Hebrews 11:35).

Christ on thrones of rulership and judgment immediately after that first resurrection. The special blessing that John had seen would include both aspects. These would be raised to life again in the first resurrection, and they would also be *"blessed"* by sitting on *"thrones"* on which they would judge and reign with Christ.

The reign of Jesus is clearly intended to bring all nations into subjection to Him. In this messianic kingdom Jesus will be able to enforce righteous standards, which the peoples of the world will not want. The question may fairly be asked, how will King Jesus enforce righteous standards in such matters as: fetal murder (abortion), child kidnapping, the physical and sexual abuse of children, the savage harassment of adults by unruly children, the sacrifice of children and infants to Satan, the use of children and adults in pornography, drug and alcohol abuse, nursing home abuse of the elderly, financial abuse of the bereaved by funeral homes, outrageous lawyer fees, outrageous Realtor commissions, outrageous hospital and surgical fees, and the teaching of secular humanism in public schools, which includes the teaching of evolution, moral relativity, and sexual permissiveness? Not only these, but how will King Jesus deal with the roots of immorality, such as unloving and insensitive spouses, self-centered living, being quick to judge and condemn, unfair and callous decisions?

The list of national ills screaming for solutions seems endless, and international relations have not even been touched. *But Jesus has a plan for dealing with all these ills in His coming kingdom!*

The Plan. In Philippians 3:20-21, we read, *"For our conversation (or citizenship) is in heaven; from whence also we look for the Saviour, the Lord Jesus Christ: Who shall change our vile body, that it may be fashioned like unto his glorious body, according to the working whereby he is able even to subdue all things unto himself."*

But how could subduing all things unto Himself accord with fashioning *"our vile body…like unto his glorious body"*?

Perhaps other passages of Scripture will help us here. We read:

"After that he [Jesus] *appeared **in another form** unto two of them, as they walked, and went into the country"* (Mark 16:12).

Jesus, in *"his glorious body,"* that is, His resurrection body, was able to appear *"**in another form**."* Then we, too, will have this ability when *"our vile body"* is *"fashioned like unto his glorious body."*

*"And their eyes were opened, and they knew him; and **he** [Jesus] **vanished out of their sight**"* (Luke 24:31).

Jesus was able to be unrecognized in His resurrection body, then He was able to make himself recognizable, and then He was also able to vanish. We, too, will have these abilities in our new bodies.

*"Then the same day at evening, being the first day of the week, **when the doors were shut** where the disciples were assembled for fear of the Jews, **came Jesus and stood in the midst**, and said unto them, Peace be unto you"* (John 20:19. See also John 20:26; Mark 16:14a.)

Jesus was able to pass through walls or shut doors, and then to appear suddenly. We, too, will have these abilities when we have our new bodies.

*"The other disciples therefore said unto him (Thomas, one of the twelve, called Didymus), We have seen the Lord. But he said unto them, **Except I shall see in his hands the print of the nails, and put my finger into the print of the nails, and thrust my hand into his side, I will not believe**…Then he saith he to Thomas, **Reach hither thy finger, and behold my hands; and reach hither thy hand, and thrust it into my side; and be not faithless, but believing**"* (John 20:25,27).

Jesus, in His resurrection body, was able to silently, invisibly, listen to conversations, and then later to confront an individual with his own words. We, too, will be able to do this in our new bodies.[120]

The apostle Paul also described our new bodies.

"So also is the resurrection of the dead. It is sown in corruption; it is raised in incorruption: (then it cannot be destroyed) *It is sown in dishonour; it is raised in glory: it is sown in weakness; it is raised in power: It is sown a natural body; it is raised a spiritual body"* (1 Corinthians 15:42-44).

With these new bodies, and with the special abilities that these new bodies will possess, the resurrected saints of all ages will be able to quickly detect the appearance of any evil. Our invisible, and powerful, bodies can enter any guarded room, overhear any rebellious plot, and quickly thwart attempts to carry out any rebellious or evil plans.

Revelation 2:26-27 describes our qualifications and work in these words: *"And he that overcometh, and keepeth my works unto the end, to him will I give power over the nations:...And he shall rule them with a rod of iron; as the vessels of a potter shall they be broken to shivers: even as I received of My Father."*

---

120. Faith in a coming resurrection from the dead as seen in the Old Testament

"So man lieth down, and riseth not: till the heavens be no more, they shall not awake, nor be raised out of their sleep.
O that thou wouldest hide me in the grave, that thou wouldest keep me secret, until thy wrath be past, that thou wouldest appoint me a set time, and remember me!
If a man die, shall he live again? all the days of my appointed time will I wait, till my change come. Thou shalt call, and I will answer thee: thou wilt have a desire to the work of thine hands" (Job 14:12-15).

"For I know that my redeemer liveth, and that he shall stand at the latter day upon the earth.
And though after my skin worms destroy this body, yet in my flesh shall I see God.
Whom I shall see for myself, and mine eyes shall behold, and not another; though my reins be consumed within me" (Job 19:25-27).

"Therefore my heart is glad, and my glory rejoiceth: my flesh also shall rest in hope.
For thou wilt not leave my soul in hell (Hebrew, Sheol); *neither wilt thou suffer thine Holy One to see corruption"* (Psalm 16:9-10).

"As for me, I will behold thy face in righteousness: I shall be satisfied, when I awake, with thy likeness" (Psalm 17:15).

"But go thou thy way till the end be: for thou shalt rest, and stand in thy lot at the end of the days" (Daniel 12:13).

"Thy dead men shall live, together with my dead body shall they arise. Awake and sing, ye that dwell in dust: for thy dew is as the dew of herbs, and the earth shall cast out the dead" (Isaiah 26:19).

We must not imagine that the nations will be pleased by this truly righteous rule, for there will yet be unsaved upon the earth, and they will resent any and all curbs upon their selfish and sinful activities. It will not be our ambition to be popular, but to be right in the eyes of Jesus our King and Master! *The plan* will be made effective in many ways. There may be enforced counseling of husbands and wives to remove the selfish and callous causes of sin in their lives. There would be immediate action against unrestrained wickedness, with correction where possible, and effective retribution where it is necessary. The greed of man will be challenged, and all people will be compelled to accept reasonable fees and commissions for their services.

In international relations, King Jesus will *"rebuke strong nations afar off"* (Micah 4:3), and we will enforce His orders. Disarmament will be worldwide, and war colleges will pass out of existence (Isaiah 2:4; Micah 4:3).[121]

In our day, and before the kingdom of God appears, the satanic New Age Movement will seek demonic and human solutions to the pressing problems of this world. But their solutions and efforts are in reality an attempt to picture Satan as a benevolent despot who alone is god and who is worthy of our devotion and worship, and to seek

---

121. Disarmament will be worldwide, and war colleges will pass out of existence

"But in the last days it shall come to pass, that the mountain of the house of the Lord shall be established in the top of the mountains, and it shall be exalted above the hills; and people shall flow unto it.

And many nations shall come, and say, Come, and let us go up to the mountain of the Lord, and to the house of the God of Jacob; and he will teach us his ways, and we will walk in his paths: for the law shall go forth of Zion, and the word of the Lord from Jerusalem.

And he shall judge among many people, and rebuke strong nations afar off; and they shall beat their swords into plowshares, and their spears into pruninghooks, nation shall not lift up a sword against nation, neither shall they learn war any more.

But they shall sit every man under his vine and under his fig tree; and none shall make them afraid: for the mouth of the Lord of hosts hath spoken it.

For all people will walk every one in the name of his god, and we will walk in the name of the Lord our God for ever and ever.

In that day, saith the Lord, will I assemble her that halteth, and I will gather her that is driven out, and her that I have afflicted;

And I will make her that halted a remnant. and her that was cast far off a strong nation: and the Lord shall reign over them in mount Zion from henceforth, even for ever" (Micah 4:1-7).

to make unnecessary the need for the kingdom of God. But Satan's true nature will be exposed, and his fraudulent plans will fail, at the victorious appearance of Jesus and His kingdom.

Satan Loosed *"When The Thousand Years Are Expired"*

And when the thousand years are expired, Satan shall be loosed out of his prison (Revelation 20:7).

Why, after God's greatest adversary is imprisoned, would he ever be loosed? The answer is that God, by His nature of holiness, must deal fairly with Satan.

As Abraham asked, *"Shall not the Judge of all the earth do right?"* (Genesis 18:25c). Thus God, even in war, cannot do other than deal with His greatest adversary fairly.

We see this in Daniel 7:21-22,26.

*"I beheld, and the same horn made war with the saints, and prevailed against them; Until the Ancient of days came, and **judgment was given to the saints of the most High**, and the time came that the saints possessed the kingdom…" "But the **judgment shall sit, and they shall take away his** (the little horn's, or beast's) **dominion**, to consume and to destroy it unto the end."*

So it is to be a judicial decision that takes away the kingdom of the beast, and gives it unto the resurrected saints, and the final end of Satan's rule will come in the same way.

The Nations Deceived; *"Gog and Magog"*

"And shall go out to deceive the nations which are in the four quarters of the earth, Gog and Magog, to gather them together to battle: the number of whom is as the sand of the sea" (Revelation 20:8).

At the close of *"the thousand years"* and of Jesus' work to *"put all enemies under his feet"* (1 Corinthians 15:25), Satan is *"loosed out of his prison, and shall go out to deceive the nations."*

It must be remembered that people want freedom to do as they please, even when they use their freedom to disobey God. In the kingdom of God there will be heavy constraints upon the freedom of people to do evil. These constraints would be strictly enforced by those of us who have received our glorified, or resurrection, bodies. *But the number of those who have resurrection bodies would be a static number* as there would be no new resurrections within this thousand-year period. Consequently, there would be *no increase* in the number of those with resurrection bodies, but the number of those living upon the earth *with natural bodies would increase greatly.* This would be particularly true because of the excellent health conditions, which we would enforce under the commands of our King Jesus! Thus, toward the end of "*the thousand years*" it would become more and more difficult to restrain evil, as we would not have enough resurrected saints to investigate, and to deal with, all the suspected problem areas.

Then, with the release of Satan, our problems with curtailing evil would quickly multiply. He would easily deceive those who have been restive under the constraints of the kingdom of God, and would gather them for war—"*...to deceive the nations which are in the four quarters of the earth, (as with) Gog and Magog...*"

John was given, by revelation, key insights into the nations listed as allied with Gog, of the land of Magog, in Ezekiel 38:5-6.[122] He was shown that

---

122. *"Gog and Magog"*

The phrase *"Gog and Magog"* comes, of course, from Ezekiel 38 and 39, and is used here in Revelation 20:8 to represent symbolically all the nations which are to be gathered against the Messiah at the close of the millennium.

The *"Gog and Magog"* of Revelation 20:8 would not be the original fulfillment of Ezekiel 38 and 39, but would be a secondary fulfillment. This is because in Ezekiel, *"Gog"* was a person, *"the chief prince of Meshech and Tubal"* (Ezekiel 38:2, 3; 39:1) and is referred to as *"him"* (Ezekiel 38:2). In Revelation 20:8, both *"Gog and Magog"* are nations. Also, in Ezekiel, Gog and Magog are gathered against Israel by God, while in Revelation both Gog and Magog are gathered into battle by Satan.

In its original fulfillment, Ezekiel 38 and 39 would have referred to an ancient battle, rather than to a battle in the present time, or in the future. This is because the names of some of the nations given have long ago ceased their existence as nations. This would be true of *"Meshech," "Tubal," "Gomer," "the house of Togarmah," "Sheba," "Dedan,"* and *"Tarshish."* Also, the weapons given in Ezekiel 38:4 and 39:9 indicate an ancient battle, not a modern-day or a future one. These ancient weapons include *"shields," "bucklers," "bows and arrows," "handstaves,"* and *"spears."* Finally, as we have emphasized in early chapters, all prophecies up to and including the second coming of Jesus were to have been fulfilled in the first century, A.D., and there are strong evidences within Ezekiel that the fulfillment of Ezekiel 38 and 39 would come after the return of the Jews from Babylonian captivity, and also after the rule of the Persian empire.

continued on next page

the five nations listed in these verses in Ezekiel came from widely separated areas, and came from different directions from Israel. These thoughts are condensed within the phrase, *"…the nations which are in the four quarters of the earth…"*

The battle described in Revelation 20:8-9 is not the same battle that Ezekiel described, but, as in that battle, the nations involved also came from widely separated areas, and from different directions. Because of their hostility to the kingdom of God, their numbers are immense, so immense that they are described as *"the sand of the sea."*

*And they went up on the breadth of the earth, and compassed the camp of the saints about, and **the beloved city**: and fire came down from God out of heaven, and devoured them* (Revelation 20:9).

"The Beloved City" of Jerusalem Protected

The picture, at the close of *"the thousand years,"* reveals an immense number of people surging toward *"the camp of the saints"* and *"the beloved city."* They are, doubtless, filled with wrath against the kingdom of God because they have loved the freedom to do evil far more than they have loved the practice of truth.

The phrase, *"the beloved city,"* identifies Jerusalem. (See Ecclesiasticus, or The Wisdom of Jesus the Son of Sirach 24:11, where *"the beloved city"* designates Jerusalem.[123])

Let's look at some of these evidences. Ezekiel 37, which prophesied the valley of dry bones, was a prophecy of the restoration of Israel to her land after the Babylonian captivity. Then, in Ezekiel 38 and 39, we see repeated references to the fact that the Jews had returned from captivity (Ezekiel 38:9,12; 39:23,25,27-28), obviously from Babylonian captivity as the return of the Jews in 1948 and thereafter could not have been prophesied because it would not have happened if the prophecies in Revelation had not been thrown into the future.

Also, in Ezekiel 38:5, *"Persia"* is named as one of the nations coming against the restored Israel. But because Persia was friendly to Israel throughout the entire period of Persian rule (539-333 B.C.), the fulfillment of Ezekiel's prophecy in Ezekiel 38 and 39 must have been intended to come after that.

Some have suggested the Scythians as the Magog of Ezekiel 38 and 39, and others have suggested Alexander the Great as the "Gog" intended, but neither of them fulfilled the role which Gog and Magog were prophesied to have.

Alexander the Great, in fact, was received peacefully by the Jews in Jerusalem, and he had a very congenial relationship with them. He *"offered sacrifice to God, according to the high priest's direction, and magnificently treated both the high priest and the priests"* (*Ant.* XI. VIII. 5).

The most likely candidate for the fulfillment of Ezekiel 38 and 39 would seem to be Antiochus IV Epiphanes, who was also prophesied against in Daniel 8:9-11, 23-25, and in Daniel 11:21-35, and who stormed Jerusalem in 169, 168, and in 167 B.C. Antiochus also tried to completely destroy

continued on next page

This momentous battle brings the first phase of the kingdom of God to completion. *"For he must reign, till he hath put all enemies under his feet"* (1 Corinthians 15:25). Soon the second phase of the kingdom of God must begin. *"Then cometh the end, when he shall have delivered up the kingdom to God"* (1 Corinthians 15:24a).

Satan *"Tormented" "for Ever and Ever"*

And the devil that deceived them was cast into the lake of fire and brimstone, where the beast and the false prophet are, and shall be tormented day and night for ever and ever (Revelation 20:10).

Satan, the adversary, the accuser, the great deceiver of mankind, must finally receive the punishment he deserves for his disobedience to God, for his opposition to God, for his deceiving of multitudes into hell.

The Judgment of All Mankind; the Resurrection; *"the Earth and the Heaven Fled Away"*

And I saw a great white throne, and him that sat on it, from whose face the earth and the heaven fled away; and there was found no place for them (Revelation 20:11).

The earth and the heavens are not permanent. They were created, and thus had a beginning. They will also have an end. Jesus said, *"Heaven and earth shall pass away, but my words shall not pass away"* (Matthew 24:35; see also Psalm 102:25-27, Isaiah 51:6; Matthew 5:18; Mark 13:31; Luke 16:17; 21:33; 2 Peter 3:10; Revelation 21:1,4).

In the events that follow in this section, John is inspired to follow a logical rather than a

---

the religion of the Jews and to turn them to the worship of other gods. It was no wonder, then, that God would say, *"Behold, I am against thee, O Gog"* (Ezekiel 38:3; 39:1). Because of repeated and miraculous victories by the Jews, Antiochus was defeated and in 164 B.C., he died insane.

The Roman encyclopedist, Pliny the Elder, wrote concerning Coela-Syria, *"Coela habet Apamiam Marsyia amne divisam a Nazarinorum Tetrarchia, Bambycem quam alio nomine Hierapolis vocatur, Syris vero Magog."* (*Naturalis Historia*, Pliny, lib. v., c.23). This is translated, *"Coela-Syria has Apamia separated from the tetrarchy of the Nazarenes by the river Marsyia; and Bambyce, otherwise called Hierapolis; but by the Syrians, Magog."*

So *"Magog"* still existed as a name of a place among the Syrians in the first century, A.D., when Pliny the Elder wrote. It was, no doubt, a remnant of some previous glory as only a city remained. Antiochus IV Epiphanes was over the Syrian part of the Greek empire. He must have been the *"Gog"* of Ezekiel 38 and 39.

123. *"Likewise in the beloved city he gave me rest, and in Jerusalem was my power"* (Ecclesiasticus, or The Wisdom of Jesus the Son of Sirach 24:11).

chronological order as the phrase, *"And I saw the dead, small and great, stand before God."* (Revelation 20:12a) must come after the phrase, *"And the sea gave up the dead which were in it; and death and hell* (Hades) *delivered up the dead which were in them."* (Revelation 20:13a). Also, since Paul has told us, by revelation, that *"the last enemy that shall be destroyed is death"* (1 Corinthians 15:26), then the verse *"And death and hell* (Hades) *were cast into the lake of fire. This is the second death"* (Revelation 20:14) may need to be placed chronologically after Revelation 20:15, which reads, *"And whosoever was not found written in the book of life was cast into the lake of fire."* The *"lake of fire"* is *"the second death"* (Revelation 20:14), but when the angel, Death, is destroyed, then death will be no more.

It might be well to list these final events in their probable chronological order.

1. *"Fire came down from heaven, and devoured them"* who had been deceived by Satan (Revelation 20:9b).

2. *"The devil that deceived them was cast into the lake of fire and brimstone"* (Revelation 20:10, see also Matthew 25:41).

3. *"And I saw a great white throne, and him that sat upon it…"* (Revelation 20:11a). We make a break here with the following phrase *("from whose face the earth and heaven fled away")*, as the phrase, *"And the sea gave up the dead which were in it,"* must occur before the sea vanishes.

4. *"And the sea gave up the dead which were in it; and death and hell* (Hades) *delivered up the dead which were in them…"* (Revelation 20:13a). This occurs before item 6 below, but it could be either simultaneous with, or before, item 5.

5. *"…from whose face the earth and heaven* (or sky) *fled away"* (Revelation 20:11b).

6. *"And I saw the dead, small and great, stand before God"* (Revelation 20:12a). They were resurrected before they stood before God, thus Revelation 20:12 follows after Revelation 20:13.

7. *"And whosoever was not found written in the book of life was cast into the lake of fire"* (Revelation 20:15).

8. *"And death and hell* (Hades) *were cast into the lake of fire. This is the second death"* (Revelation 20:14).

The chronological order of these last two verses is reversed on the strength of Paul's statement, *"The last enemy that shall be destroyed is death"* (1 Corinthians 15:26). Thus, after death is destroyed, then death (including *"the second death"*) will not be visited upon anyone ever again.

Also, it is clear that item 7 (Revelation 20:15) is not intended to be in chronological sequence, but rather is given here for emphasis. This is evident as John repeatedly emphasizes this point without regard for chronology. Thus we have:

"But the fearful, and unbelieving, and the abominable, and murderers, and whoremongers, and sorcerers, and idolaters, and all liars, shall have their part in the lake which burneth with fire and brimstone: which is the second death" (Revelation 21:8).

"And there shall in no wise enter into it any thing that defileth, neither whatsoever worketh abomination, or maketh a lie: but they which are written in the Lamb's book of life" (Revelation 21:27).

"For without are dogs, and sorcerers, and whoremongers, and murderers, and idolators, and whosoever loveth and maketh a lie" (Revelation 22:15).

The resurrection referred to above is of all who ever lived, the righteous and the unrighteous, except for those privileged to be in *"the first resurrection."*

The phrase "...*and the books were opened*" is found also in the judgment scene in Daniel 7:10. The phrase "...*and another book was opened, which was the book of life*" is similar in meaning to Daniel 12:1b, "...*and at that time thy people shall be delivered, every one that shall be found written in the book.*"

The books, or scrolls, would be the records kept in heaven of the deeds, good and bad, of every human being. In ancient times, a king's scribe did this (see Esther 6:1-3).[124] In heaven, our bad deeds are erased in these books if we ask forgiveness and receive cleansing through the blood of Jesus.

---

124. "*On that night could not the king sleep, and he commanded to bring the book of records of the chronicles; and they were read before the king. And it was found written, that Mordecai had told of Bigthana and Teresh, two of the king's chamberlains, the keepers of the door, who sought to lay hand on the king Ahasuerus. And the king said, What honour and dignity hath been done to Mordecai for this? Then said the king's servants that ministered unto him, There is nothing done for him*" (Esther 6:1-3).

Revelation 21

The New Heaven, the New Earth, and the New Jerusalem

And I saw a new heaven and a new earth: for the first heaven and the first earth were passed away; and there was no more sea (Revelation 21:1).

New Heaven and Earth

Compare this passage with two verses in Isaiah.

"For, behold, I create new heavens and a new earth: and the former shall not be remembered, nor come into mind" (Isaiah 65:17).

"For as the new heavens and the new earth, which I will make, shall remain before me, saith the Lord, so shall your seed and your name remain" (Isaiah 66:22).

The context of these Isaiah passages indicates that Isaiah had in mind a drastic change in an old order (either the new order that was under Zerubbabel, or that of the kingdom of the Messiah), but John, in a double reference of Isaiah's prophecies, sees that *"the earth and the heaven fled away"* at the presence of God (Revelation 20:11), and *"a new heaven and a new earth"* appeared. Thus, John saw a totally new creation. The *"sea"* which had been the cause of many shipwrecks, much suffering, and untold deaths *"was no more."*

"…and there was no more sea." The sea was not only a place of great danger, but also it was symbolic of the wicked. Isaiah 57:20 reads, *"But the wicked are like the troubled sea, when it cannot rest, whose waters cast up mire and dirt."* (See also Psalm 65:7; 93:3.) This is probably the basis of Revelation 17:15 in which the woman (Rome) sat upon the waters—the Roman Empire, the epitome of wickedness.

And I John saw the holy city, New Jerusalem, coming down from God out of heaven, prepared as a bride adorned for her husband.

3 And I heard a great voice out of heaven saying, Behold, the tabernacle of God is with men, and he will dwell with them, and they shall be his people, and God himself shall be with them, and be their God.

4 And God shall wipe away all tears from their eyes; and there shall be no more death, neither sorrow, nor crying, neither shall there be any more pain: for the former things are passed away.

See 2 Corinthians 11:2, *"...for I have espoused you to one husband, that I may present you as a chaste virgin to Christ"* (also Ephesians 5:23-32). Thus, the church is the bride of Christ.

God also saw Israel as His bride (Isaiah 54:5; 61:10).

The New Jerusalem Revealed

In this seventh prophetic unit we are given a closer look at the bride, the Lamb's wife, the New Jerusalem.

In this vision we will see the way in which the New Jerusalem is contrasted with Rome. We will also see the symbolic meaning of the angel's measurements of this wondrous city, the New Jerusalem. The 12 precious stones, which adorn the 12 foundations of the wall of the city, contain eight of the 12 stones that the Jewish high priest wore upon his breastplate. This reveals a Jewish flavor, but with a divine difference! The brightness of the glory of God and of the Lamb are the light of the city, in which we find the *"water of life"*[125] and the *"tree of life"* (Revelation 22:1-2). This should be an interesting outline!

---

125. The *"water of life"* refers to the Holy Spirit

"Jesus answered and said unto her, Whosoever drinketh of this water shall thirst again: But whosoever drinketh of the water that I shall give him shall never thirst; but the water that I shall give him shall be in him a well of water springing up into everlasting life" (John 4:13-14).

"In the last day, that great day of the feast, Jesus stood and cried, saying, If any man thirst, let him come unto me, and drink.
He that believeth on me, as the scripture hath said, out of his belly shall flow rivers of living water. (But this spake he of the Spirit, which they that believe on him should receive: for the Holy Ghost was not yet given; because that Jesus was not yet glorified.) (John 7:37-39).

"Therefore with joy shall ye draw water out of the wells of salvation" (Isaiah 12:3).

The above passage from Isaiah 12:3 was chanted by the priests on this very occasion, *"the last day, that great day of the feast."* On this day, water was carried in a golden pitcher from the pool of Siloam and poured upon the altar of sacrifice. This service was to commemorate the miracle of receiving water from a rock (Exodus 17:1-7; Numbers 20:1-13), but Jesus, on this occasion, invited them to receive *"rivers of living water,"* that is, the Holy Spirit.

5 And he that sat
upon the throne said,
Behold, I make all
things new. And he
said unto me, Write:
for these words are
true and faithful.

6 And he said unto
me, It is done. I am
Alpha and omega, the
beginning and the
end. I will give unto
him that is athirst of
the fountain of **the
water of life** freely.

7 He that overcometh
shall inherit all things;
and I will be his God,
and he shall be my
son.

8 But the fearful, and
unbelieving, and the
abominable, and mur-
derers, and whore-
mongers, and
sorcerers, and idol-
aters, and all liars,
shall have their part
in the lake which bur-
neth with fire and
brimstone: which is
the second death
(Revelation 21:2-8).

The City, The New Jerusalem, is Contrasted with Rome

The prophecies in Revelation have concerned Jerusalem and Rome. In this prophetic unit we see that the New Jerusalem, which descends from heaven, is contrasted with Rome!

Consider the following passages:

The New Jerusalem	Rome
*"And there came unto me **one of the seven angels which had the seven** vials (bowls) **full of the seven last** plagues, **and talked** with me, saying, **Come hither** and I will shew thee the bride, the Lamb's wife"* (Revelation 21:9).	*"And there came one **of the seven angels which had the seven** vials (bowls), **and talked with me, saying** unto me, **Come hither;** I will shew unto thee the judgment of the great whore that sitteth upon many waters"* (Revelation 17:1).

In the above two passages, two women, or cities, are contrasted. One is old, and great, and unfaithful, and worldly. The other is new, and holy, and faithful, and heavenly. The contrast continues:

*"And **he carried me away in the spirit to a great and high mountain,** and shewed me that great city, the holy Jerusalem, descending out of heaven from God"* (Revelation 21:10).	*"So he carried me away in the spirit into the wilderness: and I saw a woman sit upon a scarlet coloured beast, full of names of blasphemy, having seven heads and ten horns"* (Revelation 17:3).

The wilderness (a desert) represents the spiritual condition of the whore (Rome); while the great and high mountain represents the spiritual condition of the heavenly Jerusalem. The one is dry and empty; the other is exalted. The one is richly attired in purple and scarlet color—the glory of man; the other has *"the glory of God"* (Revelation 21:11).

11 Having the glory of God: and her light was like unto a stone most precious, even like a jasper stone, clear as crystal;	In Ezekiel 40–48, Ezekiel, for the most part, described a picture of idealized Judaism, but he also referred to the land (Ezekiel 47:13–48:29), and to *"the city"* (Ezekiel 40:2; 48:30-35).
	"The city" (in Ezekiel 48:30-35) has 12 gates named after the 12 tribes of Israel,[126] and this is the same as

---

126. *"And these are the goings out of the city on the north side, four thousand and five hundred measures. And the gates of the city shall be after the names of the tribes of Israel: three gates northward; one gate of Reuben, one gate of Judah, one gate of Levi.*
And at the east side four thousand and five hundred: and three gates; and one gate of Joseph, one gate of Benjamin, one gate of Dan.
And at the south side four thousand and five hundred measures: and three gates; one gate of Simeon, one gate of Issachar, one gate of Zebulun.
And at the west side four thousand and five hundred, with their three gates; one gate of Gad, one gate of Asher, one gate of Naphtali.
It was round about eighteen thousand measures: and the name of the city from that day shall be, The Lord is there" (Ezekiel 48:30-35).

*12 And had a wall great and high, and had **twelve gates,** and at the gates twelve angels, **and names written thereon, which are the names of the twelve tribes of the children** of Israel:*

13 on the east three gates; on the north three gates; on the south three gates; and on the west three gates.

14 And the wall of the city had twelve foundations, and in them the names of the twelve apostles of the Lamb (Revelation 21:11-14).

And he that talked with me had a golden reed to measure the city, and the gates thereof, and the wall thereof.

John saw also in Revelation 21:12-13. This seems to indicate that Ezekiel and John saw in visions the same city. But John seems to have been shown more about this city than Ezekiel had seen. John writes, *"And the wall of the city had twelve foundations, and in (or on) them the names of the twelve apostles of the Lamb"* (Revelation 21:14).

"The names of the twelve tribes of the children of Israel" (Revelation 21:12), and *"the names of the twelve apostles of the Lamb"* (Revelation 21:14) are both given to identify this *"New Jerusalem"* as the city of the *true Jews.*[127] They are *true Jews* because they have all received *"the Lamb"* as their Messiah.

The Meaning of the Measurements of the New Jerusalem

The angel's measurements of the New Jerusalem were to be of (1) *"the city"* and (2) *"the gates thereof, and the wall thereof."*

---

127. The early believers in Jesus saw themselves as the *true Jews.*

"They answered and said unto him, Abraham is our father. Jesus said unto them, If ye were Abraham's children, ye would do the works of Abraham" (John 8:39).

"For he is not a Jew, which is one outwardly; neither is that circumcision, which outward in the flesh: But he is a Jew, which is one inwardly; and circumcision is that of the heart, in the spirit, and not in the letter; whose praise is not of men, but of God" (Romans 2:28-29).

"Know ye therefore that they which are of faith, the, same are the children of Abraham. So then they which be of faith are blessed with faithful Abraham" (Galatians 3:7,9).

"That the blessing of Abraham might come on the Gentiles through Jesus Christ; that we might receive the promise of the Spirit through faith" (Galatians 3:14).

"There is neither Jew nor Greek, there is neither bond nor free, there is neither male nor female: for ye are all one in Christ Jesus. And if ye be Christ's, then are ye Abraham's seed, and heirs according to the promise" (Galatians 3:28-29)

"For we are the circumcision, which worship God in the spirit, and rejoice in Christ Jesus, and have no confidence in the flesh" (Philippians 3:3).

16 And the city lieth foursquare, and the length is as large as the breadth: and he measured the city with the reed, twelve thousand furlongs. The length and the breadth and the height of it are equal (Revelation 21:15-16).

Some commentators have felt that the height of the wall of this city, *"an hundred and forty and four cubits"* (Revelation 21:17), or 216 feet,[128] is small compared to the enormous height and size of this city (nearly 1500 miles in width, length, and height). But this misses the point. The real significance is in the symbolic meaning of the measurements. Thus, we gain nothing of value by figuring the precise height of the wall of the New Jerusalem, nor by comparing the height of the wall with the height of the city. The real importance here is in the numeral "144"—12 x 12. Twelve is the signature of Israel. A numeral multiplied by itself carries the same meaning, but intensified. So here the "144" signifies that this city is only for the true Jews. The angel was also to have measured *"the gates thereof,"* but that measurement is not given, unless the gates are the same height as the walls. The significance of these gates lies in the fact that there are *"twelve gates, and at the gates twelve angels, and names written thereon, which are the names of the twelve tribes of the children of Israel"* (Revelation 21:12). There are many twelves in this city. There are *"twelve foundations"* of the wall on which are *"the names of the twelve apostles of the Lamb"* (21:14). The city measured *"twelve thousand furlongs. The length and the breadth and the height of it are equal"* (Revelation 21:16). This seems to indicate that much of the city is arranged on a pattern of twelves, and very likely, a pattern of 144s. For instance, *"the tree of life"* was seen to *"bare twelve manner of fruits, and yielded her fruit every month"* (Revelation 22:2). Because there are 12 months, this would indicate 12 x 12, or a yearly production of 144 of the various kinds of fruits. The *"twelve gates"* remind one of the 12 gates in Jerusalem as Zerubbabel rebuilt it. In that city the 12 gates were named as follows:

---

128. 216 feet. But this would be 48' more, or 264' if John's angel used the same measurement as Ezekiel's angel which was a *"cubit and an hand breadth"* (Ezekiel 40:5; 43:13). This would have added about 4" for the *"hand breadth."*

1. *"The Gate of the Valley"* (Nehemiah 2:13,15), or *"The Valley Gate"* (Nehemiah 3:13).

2. *"The Gate of the Fountain"* (Nehemiah 2:14; 3:15), or *"The Fountain Gate"* (Nehemiah 12:37).

3. *"The Sheep Gate"* (Nehemiah 3:1; 12:39).

4. *"The Fish Gate"* (Nehemiah 3:3; 12:39).

5. *"The Old Gate"* (Nehemiah 3:6; 12:39).

6. *"The Dung Gate"* (Nehemiah 2:13; 3:13, 14; 12:31).

7. *"The Water Gate"* (Nehemiah 3:26; 12:37).

8. *"The Horse Gate"* (Nehemiah 3:28).

9. *"The East Gate"* (Nehemiah 3:29).

10. *"The Gate Miphkad"* (Nehemiah 3:31).

11. *"The Gate of Ephraim"* (Nehemiah 8:16; 12:39).

12. *"The Prison Gate"* (Nehemiah 12:39).

Thus, in the old Jerusalem, only one gate, *"The Gate of Ephraim,"* was given the name of one of the 12 tribes. But in the New Jerusalem, each of the tribes will be so honored. Both Ezekiel (48:30-35) and John (Revelation 21:12-13) had seen this. But Ezekiel, in giving the names of the 12 gates, leaves out gates named for Ephraim and Manasseh, and has one named for Joseph instead.

Ezekiel's vision (Ezekiel 40–48), and this one of John in Revelation (21:9–22:5), have so many points of both similarity and contrast that need to be carefully studied. This will enable us to understand John's vision more clearly.

Let's look at Revelation 21:16 again.

> *And the city lieth foursquare, and the length is as large as the breadth: and he measured the city with the reed, twelve thousand furlongs. The length and the breadth and the height of it are equal.*

In other words, the New Jerusalem may have been cube-shaped, just as the Holy of Holies in the temple was. (Some have suggested that Revelation 21:16 could also have been somewhat pyramid-shaped, but with four sides instead of three.[129] This is possible, but the important point is that the New Jerusalem is like the Holy of Holies in the temple, but greatly enlarged.)

In Ezekiel we read much of the temple, and of priests, and of sacrifices. Clearly, in Ezekiel the temple was the most important part of the city. But in Revelation, John writes, *"And I saw no temple (naon, sanctuary) therein: for the Lord God Almighty and the Lamb are the temple (naos, sanctuary) of it"* (Revelation 21:22). The Greek word for *"temple,"* with its precincts and courts, is *hieron* which is used 71 times in the New Testament, but not once in Revelation. In Revelation the Greek word translated *"temple"* is *naos*, meaning the inner sanctuary, or Holy of Holies, within the temple. This word is used 46 times in the New Testament, and 15 of those times are in Revelation. In Revelation 21:22, compared with Revelation 21:16, we see that the entire New Jerusalem is the Holy of Holies. Why? Because of the city's equal dimensions,[130] but even more because

---

129. Some visions of the new Jerusalem have seen it as pyramid-shaped, but John, in Revelation, does not describe the shape of the city.

"Caught Up to The Third Heaven

The Adullam children said they went to the third heaven. As they passed through the first heaven they could feel the air on their faces. Then, having passed the second heaven, they could look back upon the stars in their wonderful beauty, much as from a mountain height a person might gaze down upon a beautiful light-studded city below. From this starry heaven they passed on into the third heaven until they Came to The Heavenly Jerusalem. As they approached this heavenly city they could see its light in the distance. Coming nearer they could see the beautiful wall radiating its wonderful jasper light. The foundations were of indescribable beauty sparkling with red, yellow, orange, purple, blue, green, violet and all the colors of' the twelve most beautiful jewels. This city in the sky they saw as three cities in one. One city was suspended above another, the larger city below and the smaller cities on top making the total a sort of pyramid. Since this city John saw is surrounded by a wall two hundred feet high, and since the city is one thousand five hundred miles high, Bible students have supposed the heavenly city is not a cube but a pyramid.

"One of our small boys spoke in prophecy when in vision he was at the feet of the Lord and the Lord was talking to him. In this prophecy the Lord said that he made heaven big enough for everybody, that he has made it in three cities one above another, and that his throne is in the upper city" (From, Baker, H. A., *The Three Worlds*, Baker Book Publications, P. O. Box 3386, San Diego, California 92103, pg. 224, (See also *Visions Beyond the Veil*, pgs. 52-53 for such visions.)

130. The dimensions of the Holy of Holies were also equal in length, width, and height.

"the Lord God Almighty and the Lamb are the naos (the inner sanctuary, or Holy of Holies) *of it."*

So, to John, *"the New Jerusalem"* far excels the temple, the city, and the land that Ezekiel saw. It excelled the totality of Ezekiel's vision, both in size and in holiness. Ezekiel's vision had need of a temple, priests, and sacrifices. But all those things were not needed within the New Jerusalem, the new Holy of Holies.

Thus, the sacrifices (and the temple and the priests) Ezekiel saw were no longer necessary, as Jesus entered *"into heaven itself...to appear in the presence of God for us"* (Hebrews 9:24) for *"by his own blood he entered in once into the holy place, having obtained eternal redemption for us"* (Hebrews 9:12).

Thus, the city that Ezekiel saw—with its temple, priests, and sacrifices—represented an idealized Judaism. That is, Ezekiel's vision represented the highest that Judaism could ever become.

But the Jews, instead of attaining their highest, rejected their Messiah—Jesus—and killed those who did accept Him! Therefore, the vision of Ezekiel was replaced with a new vision, a more wonderful vision by far than Ezekiel's. Ezekiel's vision was of an idealized Judaism, based on a careful observance of the law. It would have been a tribute to man's righteousness. But Ezekiel's vision was not attainable. As Paul wrote, *"for if there had been a law given which could have given life, verily righteousness should have been by the law"* (Galatians 3:21). But no law could give life or righteousness.[131] John wrote, *"For the law was*

---

131. *"For what the law could not do, in that it was weak through the flesh, God sending his own Son in the likeness of sinful flesh, and for sin, condemned sin in the flesh:*
That the righteousness of the law might be fulfilled in us, who walk not after the flesh, but after the Spirit" (Romans 8:4-5).

"Who also hath made us able ministers of the new testament; not of the letter, but of the spirit; for the letter killeth, but the spirit giveth life" (2 Corinthians 3:6).

"I do not frustrate the grace of God: for if righteousness come by the law, then Christ is dead in vain" (Galatians 2:21).

"But that no man is justified by the law in the sight of God, it is evident: for, The just shall live by faith.

continued on next page

given by Moses, but grace and truth came by Jesus Christ" (John 1:17). Thus, those who received Jesus would have far more than Ezekiel's temple and city and land could offer. They would enter the new Holy of Holies, the "New Jerusalem" and live there with God eternally. And this "New Jerusalem" would not be the result of their own achievement; but it would be the result of God's wonderful grace!

And he measured the wall thereof, an hundred and forty and four cubits, according to the measure of a man, that is, of the angel (Revelation 21:17).

The significance of this passage lies in the number 144, which is the signature of true Israel. In the previous passage, 12,000 furlongs times the twelve edges of a cube, also yields 144,000 furlongs.

The phrases *"according to the measure of a man, that is, of the angel"* is generally misunderstood due to three factors:

(1) In modern times we never refer to an angel as a man, though in Scripture this was done quite often. Consider the following:

"...the man Gabriel...being caused to fly swiftly..." (Daniel 9:21). But Luke 1:26 refers to *"the angel Gabriel."*

In Genesis 19:1 we read of *"two angels"* who came to Sodom. But in Genesis 19:10, 12, and 16, these same *"two angels"* are referred to as *"the men."*[132]

And the law is not of faith: but, The man that doeth them shall live in them" (Galatians 3:11-12).

"For in Christ Jesus neither circumcision availeth any thing, nor uncircumcision, but a new creature" (Galatians 6:15).

"And be found in him, not having mine own righteousness, which is of the law, but that which is through the faith of Christ, the righteousness which is of God by faith" (Philippians 3:9).

132. *"And while they looked steadfastly toward heaven as he went up, behold, two men stood by them in white apparel;*
Which also said, Ye men of Galilee, why stand ye gazing up into heaven? this same Jesus, which is taken up from you into heaven, shall so come in like manner as ye have seen him go into heaven" (Acts 1:10-11).

Compare also Acts 10:3, 7, 22 with Acts 10:30 in regard to the same incident in the life of Cornelius.

"He saw in a vision evidently about the ninth hour of the day an angel of God coming in to him, and saying unto him, Cornelius" (Acts 10:3).

"And when the angel which spake unto Cornelius was departed, he called two of his household servants, and a devout soldier of them that waited on him continually" (Acts 10:7).

"And they said, Cornelius the centurion, a just man, and one that feareth God, and of good report among all the nation of the Jews, was warned from God by an holy angel to send for thee into his house, and to hear words of thee" (Acts 10:22).

"And Cornelius said, Four days ago I was fasting until this hour; and at the ninth hour I prayed in my house, and, behold, a man stood before me in bright clothing" (Acts 10:30).

In Genesis 32:24-32 we read the account of Jacob wrestling with the angel. But Genesis 32:24 reads, *"And Jacob was left alone; and there wrestled a man with him until the breaking of the day."*

So, in the phrase, *"according to the measure of a man,"* the *"man"* was *"the angel."*

(2) A cubit was more a method of measuring than it was a precise length. It was the length from a man's elbow to the tip of his middle finger. Hezekiah's tunnel, connecting the Pool of Siloam and the Spring of Gihon, was 1748 ft. The Siloam Inscription gave its length as 1200 cubits. This would have made the cubit used in this measurement equivalent to 17.5 inches. Egyptian cubit measuring sticks recovered have varied by as much as an inch, but they average 20.5 inches. Modern Bible interpreters generally place the cubit at 18 inches, but this is somewhat arbitrary on our part, to meet our psychological need for exactness. Thus, to assume that the phrase *"according to the measure of a man"* means that the angel used a human standard of measurement could hardly be true as there was no *human* standard of measurement for a cubit. In measuring, the angel used *"a golden reed"* (Revelation 21:15) based upon his own measurements (from his elbow to the tip of his middle finger). This is the same as the angel in Ezekiel's vision had done.

(3) Insufficient weight has been given to the similarity between this passage and Ezekiel 40–43, where an angel measured the courts and gates, the corridors and rooms, and the altar of the temple. This measuring was done with *"a measuring reed of six cubits long by the cubit and an hand breadth"* (Ezekiel 40:5). The angel's cubit was about a *"hand breadth"* longer than Ezekiel's cubit. Very likely, the angel in Revelation measured with a similar reed, that is, *"of six cubits long by the cubit and an hand breadth."* Such a reed would have gone evenly into 144 cubits, 24 times.

In Ezekiel 43:10, the angel in Ezekiel's vision said to him, *"Thou son of man, shew the house to the house of Israel, that they may be ashamed of their iniquities: and **let them measure the pattern**."* But if they did *"measure the pattern,"* their measurements would be quite different from the angel's, and so Ezekiel is reminded, *"The cubit is a cubit and an hand breadth"* (Ezekiel 43:13).

Thus, in Revelation 21:17, the angel's cubit is about four inches longer than John's cubit, if we allow about four inches for a *"hand breadth."*

We have been seeing the correspondences between the temple of Ezekiel's vision and the *"New Jerusalem"* of John's vision.

Let's look further at these correspondences.

The Visions of Ezekiel	The Revelation of John

An angel who has the appearance of a man guides both Ezekiel and John.

*"And he brought me thither, and, behold, there **was a man, whose appearance was like the appearance of brass...**"* (Ezekiel 40:3a).	*"...according to the measure of a man, that is, of the angel"* (Revelation 21:17b).

The angel in Ezekiel, and the one in Revelation, take *measurements*. In Ezekiel, of the temple; in Revelation, of the city, *"the New Jerusalem."*

"...so he measured the breath of the building, one reed; and the height, one reed" (Ezekiel 40:5b).	*"...and he measured the city with the reed, twelve thousand furlongs. The length and the breadth and the height of it are equal"* (Revelation 21:16b).

A special cubit was used both in Ezekiel and in Revelation.

"...and in the man's hand a measuring reed of six cubits long by the cubit and an hand breadth..." (Ezekiel 40:5, see also Ezekiel 43:13).	*"And he measured the wall thereof, an hundred and forty and four cubits, according to the measure of a man, that is, of the angel"* (Revelation 21:17).

Both *"the court"* about Ezekiel's temple and *"the New Jerusalem"* were *"foursquare."*

"So he measured the court, an hundred cubits long, and an hundred cubits broad, foursquare..." (Ezekiel 40:47a).

"And the city lieth foursquare, and the length is as large as the breadth..." (Revelation 21:16a).

In both Ezekiel and in Revelation *waters emerge suddenly*[133] and flow either *"from under the threshold"* (Ezekiel 47:1) or from *"the throne"* (Revelation 22:1b).

"...and, behold, waters issued out from under the threshold of the house eastward..." (Ezekiel 47:1).

"And he shewed me a pure river of water of life, clear as crystal, proceeding out of the throne of God and of the Lamb" (Revelation 22:1).

Both in Ezekiel, and in Revelation, *trees are on both sides of the river producing fruit for "meat," or food, and their leaves have healing qualities.*

"And by the river upon the bank thereof, on this side and on that side, shall grow all trees for meat, whose leaf shall not fade, neither shall the fruit thereof be consumed: it shall bring forth new fruit according to his months, because their waters they issued out of the sanctuary: and the fruit thereof shall be for meat, and the leaf thereof for medicine" (Ezekiel 47:12).

"In the midst of the street of it, and on either side of the river, was there the tree of life, which bare twelve manner of fruits, and yielded her fruit every month: and the leaves of the tree were for the healing of the nations" (Revelation 22:5).

---

133. The waters in Ezekiel 47:1-12 and in Revelation 22:1-2 are being contrasted, however, since natural waters are needed for natural man, and spiritual waters are needed for spiritual man.

    In Ezekiel, the waters were natural, but miraculous in their flow from under the threshold of the temple, and they became deeper the farther they flowed (Ezekiel 47:3-5). They were to have sweetened (or *"healed,"* verses 8-9) the waters of the Dead Sea, which is 26 percent mineral salts, so that *"a very great multitude of fish"* would live in it, and *"fishers shall stand upon it from Engedi even unto Eneglaim; they shall be a place to spread forth nets"* (Ezekiel 47:9-10).

    But, some *"miry places"* and marshes would not be *"healed,"* no doubt, because salt was important for the sacrifices (Leviticus 2:13; Ezekiel 43:24).

    But we who have followed Jesus have a *"better hope"* (Hebrews 7:19), a *"better testament"* (Hebrews 7:22), *"a better covenant, which was established upon better promises"* (Hebrews 8:6), *"God having provided some better thing for us, that they without us should not be made perfect"* (Hebrews 11:40).

continued on next page

Both Ezekiel and Revelation tell of a city with 12 gates named after the 12 tribes of Israel.

"And the gates of the City shall be after the names of the tribes of Israel" (Ezekiel 48:31a).

"And had a wall great and high, and had twelve gates, and at the gates twelve angels, and names written thereon, which are the names of the twelve tribes of the children of Israel" (Revelation 21:12).

And he measured the wall thereof, an hundred and forty and four cubits, according to the measure of a man, that is, of the angel (Revelation 21:17).

The Holy of Holies in Solomon's temple was 20 cubits in length, breadth, and height (1 Kings 6:20), and this seems to have been true in Ezekiel's temple also (Ezekiel 41:4), though Ezekiel does not give the height of the Holy of Holies.

The length, breadth, and height of the New Jerusalem were also equal, suggesting that the New Jerusalem was the new Holy of Holies (Revelation 21:16). This view is supported further by the passage, *"And I saw no temple therein: for the Lord God Almighty and the Lamb are the temple of it"* (Revelation 21:22).

So the correspondences between Ezekiel and Revelation point to the New Jerusalem as being the Holy of Holies—the place of the dwelling of God. (See Ezekiel 48:35, *"…and the name of the city from that day shall be, The Lord is there."*)

But the New Jerusalem of Revelation, while containing striking similarities to the temple of Ezekiel, also supercedes it in size and grandeur. The New Jerusalem also supercedes *"the city"* of Ezekiel.[134]

So the waters we read of in Revelation 22:1-2, like everything else in the New Jerusalem, will have a spiritual quality as *"corruption"* does not inherit *"incorruption"* (1 Corinthians 15:50).

(NOTE: See also scriptures and notes for Revelation 21:6.)

134. The New Jerusalem greatly supercedes the temple, the city, and the land of Ezekiel's vision, in size, grandeur, and in holiness

Notice also the fear, trembling, and death under the Old Covenant compared to the beauty, joy, and life provided under the New Covenant.

<u>Under the Old Covenant</u>

"For ye are not come unto the mount that might be touched, and that burned with fire, nor unto blackness, and darkness, and tempest,
And the sound of a trumpet, and the voice of words; which voice they that heard intreated that the word should not be spoken to them any more:

continued on next page

Ezekiel's city was *"four thousand and five hundred measures"* (Ezekiel 48:30,32-34) north, east, south, and west. Since a *"measure"* was that of a reed about ten feet long, this city would have been about 45,000 feet, or almost 8 3/4 miles, in any direction.

But the New Jerusalem far exceeds the old Jerusalem and that city seen by Ezekiel. It also far exceeds the borders that Ezekiel described for the land of Israel (Ezekiel 47:13-21). The New Jerusalem is 12,000 furlongs (Greek, *stadia*, 606 feet, Revelation 21:16). This would be a city roughly as large as from San Francisco, California, to Ketchikan, Alaska, to the Hudson Bay, to Kansas City, Missouri, and back to San Francisco!

Note: The New Jerusalem measures exactly 1378.97 miles; in round numbers, 1500 miles—in all directions.

The Glory of God Revealed in the Foundation Gemstones

And the building of the wall of it was of jasper:[135] *and the city was pure gold, like unto clear glass (Revelation 21:18).*

The *"jasper"* (Greek, *iaspis*) in this passage, and elsewhere in Revelation, has not been identified. It is not the jasper gemstone which we know by that name as Revelation 21:11 describes *"a jasper stone...clear as crystal,"* which would require a gemstone that was transparent or, at least, translucent, whereas the jasper gemstone known to us is opaque.

(For they could not endure that which was commanded, And if so much as a beast touch the mountain, it shall be stoned, or thrust through with a dart;
And so terrible was the sight, that Moses said, I exceedingly fear and quake:)"

<u>Under the New Covenant</u>

"But ye are come unto mount Sion, and unto the city of the living God, the heavenly Jerusalem, and to an innumerable company of angels,
To the general assembly and church of the firstborn, which are written in heaven, and to God the Judge of all, and to the spirits of just men made perfect,
And to Jesus the mediator of the new covenant, and to the blood of sprinkling, that speaketh better things than that of Abel.
Wherefore we receiving a kingdom which cannot be moved, let us have grace, whereby we may serve God acceptably with reverence and godly fear" (Hebrews 12:18-24,28).

135. IASPIS, a Phoenician word (cp. Heb. *Yash'pheh*, e.g., Exodus 28:30; 39:16), seems to have denoted a translucent stone of various colors, especially that of fire, Rev.4:3; 21:11, 18, 19. The sardius and the jasper, of similar colour, were the first and last stones on the breastplate of the High Priest, Ex.28:17, 20." -*Vine's Expository Dictionary of New Testament Words*, pg. 613

However, since *"the street of the city was pure gold, as it were transparent glass"* (Revelation 21:21c), and because the gold we know upon earth is opaque, not *"transparent,"* it may be that the heavenly gemstones sometimes have transparent qualities unlike those on earth.

The *"jasper"* of Revelation 4:3 is similar in appearance to *"a sardine stone,"* which is thought to be a ruby, a gem purplish-red in color.[136]

19 And the foundations of the wall of the city were garnished with all manner of precious stones. The first foundation was jasper; the second, sapphire; the third, a chalcedony; the fourth, an emerald;

20 The fifth, sardonyx; the sixth, sardius;[137] the seventh, chrysolyte; the eighth, beryl; the ninth, a topaz; the tenth, a chrysoprasus; the eleventh, a jacinth; the twelfth, an amethyst (Revelation 21:19-20).

The 12 precious stones that adorn the 12 foundations of the wall of the New Jerusalem remind one of the 12 gemstones upon the Jewish high priest's *"breastplate of judgment"* (Exodus 28:17-20; 39:10-13). But the colors of the gemstones upon the *"breastplate of judgment"* were in opposite sequence to the colors of a rainbow, whereas the colors of the gemstones of the 12 foundations of the New Jerusalem are in proper and correct sequence of the colors of the rainbow. The rainbow color order of the 12 foundation gemstones of the New Jerusalem seems to have been derived from the suggestion of a color order in opposite sequence to the rainbow in the Jewish high priest's *"breastplate of judgment."* Thus, as we shall herein document, the colors of the *"breastplate of judgment"* are reversed in the foundation gemstones of the New Jerusalem to become symbols of reconciliation, forgiveness, and of peace with God.

A quote from *The World Book Encyclopedia*[138] is helpful here.

---

136. *"And immediately I was in the spirit: and, behold, a throne was set in heaven, and one sat on the throne. And he that sat was to look upon like a jasper and a sardine stone: and there was a rainbow round about the throne, in sight like unto an emerald"* (Revelation 4:2-3).

137. *"sardius, n. [LL. sardius; Gr. sardios, sardion, a sard.]*
1. a precious stone, one of twelve set in the breastplate of the Jewish high priest; a ruddy stone, perhaps a ruby. Ex.xxviii.19.
2. a sard." -*Webster's New Twentieth Century Dictionary of the English Language*, pg. 1608

"sar-di-us (sar'di as), n. l. sard. 2. the precious stone in the breastplate of the Jewish high priest, thought to have been a ruby. [ME, t.L (Vulgate), t.Gk.: *m. sardios* (stone) of Sardis]" -*The American College Dictionary*, pg. 1077

NOTE: Thus, the sardius is thought to have been a ruby; a jasper, being of similar color as a sardius, would also be like a ruby in color.

138. *The World Book Encyclopedia*, Q-R, Vol. 16, pg. 126, 1983, by World Book, Inc.

The seven colors that appear in each rainbow are violet, indigo, blue, green, yellow, orange, and red. But these colors blend into each other so that the observer rarely sees more than four or five clearly. The amount of space each color takes up varies, and depends chiefly on the size of the raindrops in which a rainbow forms.

A complete bow shows two bands of colors. The inner and brighter one is called the primary bow. The outer and less distinct one is known as the secondary bow. The primary bow has the red coloring on the outside and the violet on the inside of the arch, while in the secondary bow, the colors appear as just the opposite.

The Identification of the Names and Colors of the Gemstones in the 12 Foundations of the New Jerusalem

There is some difficulty in identifying the names and colors of the gemstones in the 12 foundations of the New Jerusalem. For instance, the same gemstone in Greek is sometimes translated to indicate different gemstones in English.

Still, there does seem to be a basis for a rainbow order of colors on the foundation stones of the New Jerusalem because even when other gemstones are suggested, the color of the gemstone generally remains consistent with the rainbow color order.

The lists below give the foundation gemstones as given in the King James Version (KJV), the New English Bible (NEB), the Revised Standard Version (RSV), and Phillips. Variations from the King James Version are italicized.

	KJV	NEB	RSV	PHILLIPS
1	Jasper	Jasper	Jasper	Jasper
2	Sapphire	*Lapis lazuli*	Sapphire	Sapphire
3	Chalcedony	Chalcedony	*Agate*	*Agate*
4	Emerald	Emerald	Emerald	Emerald
5	Sardonyx	Sardonyx	*Onyx*	*Onyx*
6	Sardius	*Cornelian*	*Carnelian*	*Cornelian*

7 Chrysolite	Chrysolite	Chrysolite	*Goldstone*
8 Beryl	Beryl	Beryl	Beryl
9 Topaz	Topaz	Topaz	Topaz
10 Chrysoprasus	Chrysoprase	Chrysoprase	*Green Goldstone*
11 Jacinth	*Turquoise*	Jacinth	*Zircon*
12 Amethyst	Amethyst	Amethyst	Amethyst

In the above list, with eight changes from the King James Version, only two—agate (which is known in England as a ruby), and zircon, (which comes in yellow, brown, or red)—would change the color order. Other lists are given below from the Jerusalem Bible (JB), Today's English Version (TEV), the Concordant Literal New Testament (CLNT), and the New International Version (NIV).

	JB	TEV	CLNT	NIV
1	*Diamond*	Jasper	Jasper	Jasper
2	*Lapis lazuli*	Sapphire	*Lapis lazuli*	Sapphire
3	*Turquoise*	*Agate*	Chalcedony	Chalcedony
4	*Crystal*	Emerald	Emerald	Emerald
5	*Agate*	*Onyx*	Sardonyx	Sardonyx
6	*Ruby*	*Carnelian*	*Carnelian*	*Carnelian*
7	*Gold quartz*	*Yellow Quartz*	*Topaz*	Chrysolite
8	*Malachite*	Beryl	Beryl	Beryl
9	Topaz	Topaz	*Peridot*	Topaz
10	*Emerald*	*Chalcedony*	Chrysoprase	Chrysoprase
11	*Sapphire*	*Turquoise*	Amethyst	Jacinth
12	Amethyst	Amethyst	Garnet	Amethyst

In the above four lists, there are a total of 23 changes from the King James Version, of which ten are from the Jerusalem Bible. But of these 23 changes, only three of them would affect the color order of the rainbow. These three are the diamond and the crystal from the Jerusalem Bible and the agate in Today's English Version. Thus, in these lists the sapphire and the lapis lazuli are both blue; the chalcedony is green, and the turquoise is sky blue or greenish-blue—either one of which would sustain the rainbow order. The sardonyx combines the reddish sard with layers of onyx. The onyx is a quartz of various colors consisting of straight layers or bands, which could be red. The agate in the *Jerusalem Bible* for the fifth foundation gemstone is also of various colors arranged in stripes or bands. In England the agate is known as a ruby.

The sardius is not known by this name today. The prefix sard suggests a reddish color. It may have been a carnelian (or cornelian) or a ruby. In either case, the color red is indicated. A beryl may be green, blue, rose, white, or golden. Malachite is green, so the beryl and the malachite are both green and thus interchangeable. However, the topaz, which may also be yellow or green, would have to be the green topaz to maintain the rainbow order if the malachite were correct. A peridot is suggested in the *Concordant Literal New Testament* in place of the topaz. The peridot is a green variety of chrysolite, and thus is a possible alternative to the topaz in maintaining the rainbow color order.

The chrysoprase is an apple green or golden-green. The *Phillips* translation has here a green goldstone. The chalcedony suggested by *Today's English Version* was described by Pliny as possibly a green silicate of copper from near Chalcedon (Pliny, H. N. XXXIII. 21). The "emerald" in the *Jerusalem Bible* is green, and thus either chrysoprase, green goldstone, chalcedony, or emerald could be used here to maintain the color green for the tenth foundation gemstone.

The jacinth, from the Greek *huakinthos* is believed to represent a smoke blue, or blue gemstone. Because the sapphire (JB), and the turquoise (NEB and TEV) are blue and blue green, either would maintain the rainbow color order. The amethyst is purple, or violet, but it would not violate the color order as not every color must be represented, but only the correct order of colors must be maintained. The zircon (Phillips) may be in different colors, but if the Persian gold-colored "*zargun*" were meant, then the color order of the rainbow would be violated.

The amethyst is purple, or violet. The garnet (CLNT) that is used as a gemstone is a deep red transparent variety, and would be close enough to violet to be a possibility here. Thus, while the identification of the gemstones it sometimes difficult, the agreement on the colors intended by the gemstones is amazingly close.

NOTE: In these lists, there are simply too many disagreements among the translators as to the names and colors of the gemstones to constitute any sort of proof of either the rainbow color order, or later of a reverse rainbow color order, but still the correlations presented seemed to point in that direction.

Because *"the observer rarely sees more than four or five* (colors) *clearly,"* we must not expect all 14 colors of a complete bow to be shown on the 12 foundation gemstones of the New Jerusalem, but only that representative colors will be given in their proper sequence. Sometimes more than one gemstone will represent a single color.

In the chart below, the colors of the secondary bow, and then of the primary bow, are given in correct sequence, together with the names and colors of the foundation gemstones of the New Jerusalem, and helpful comments on some of them.

Rainbow Colors in Correct Sequence (14 Colors)	The Names and Colors of the Foundation Gemstones of the New Jerusalem		Comments on the Names and Colors of the Foundation Gemstones
Secondary Bow	Names	Colors	Comments
Violet	Jasper	Purplish-red	Henry W. Morris describes this stone from biblical and extra-biblical references as "a fine translucent stone, capable of different colors, primarily radiant white, but also with flashing fiery red and purple tints."[139]
Indigo (a deep violet-blue)	Sapphire	A deep blue	
Blue (a bluish-green)			

139. Morris, Henry M., *The Revelation Record*, Tyndale House, 1985, pg. 452.

Green	Chalcedony	Green	"a green silicate of copper"[140]
	Emerald	Shining green	
Yellow			
Red	Sardonyx	Red and white layers	A variety of onyx with deep red layers interspersed with white.

Thus, five foundation gemstones represent the secondary bow, which is fainter, while seven foundation gemstones remain to compose the primary bow, which is more distinct.

Rainbow Colors in Correct Sequence (continued)	The Names and Colors of the Foundation Gemstones of the New Jerusalem (continued)		Comments on the Names and Colors of the Foundation Gemstones (continued)
Primary Bow	Names	Colors	Comments
Red	Sardius	Red	A brilliant red stone of chalcedony quartz.
Orange	Chrysolyte	Golden yellow	"gold stone"
Yellow	Beryl	Yellow	The beryl gemstone comes in a variety of colors. The "golden beryl," however, is yellow.

140. *Vine's Expository Dictionary of New Testament Words*, pg. 181.

	Topaz	Yellow	The topaz also comes in a variety of colors, including pale green, but is most often yellow
Green	Chrysoprasus	Apple green	The chrysoprasus is probably a gold-tinted green gemstone.
Blue	Jacinth	Smoke blue (like blue smoke)	(Greek, *huakinthos*) The jacinth (hyacinth-colored) is believed to represent a blue gemstone.
Indigo			
Violet	Amethyst	Purple, or violet	The amethyst is undoubtedly the same as the beautiful purple stone known by that name today.

In Ezekiel 1:28, we read, "*As the appearance of the bow that is in the cloud in the day of rain, so was the appearance of the brightness round about. **This was the appearance of the likeness of the glory of the Lord.** And when I saw it, I fell upon my face, and I heard the voice of one that spake.*"

Ezekiel seems to have seen the glory of God often in the form of a rainbow. "*And, behold, the glory of the God of Israel was there, according to the vision that I saw in the plain*" (Ezekiel 8:4). That is, Ezekiel saw the glory of the Lord as a rainbow, just as he had seen it in Ezekiel 1:28. (See also Ezekiel 10:19-20; 43:3-5)

Thus, in Revelation 21:11, the New Jerusalem is described as "*having the glory of God,*" and this "*glory of God*" includes the rainbow colors of the gemstones composing the 12 foundations of the New Jerusalem.

The Identification of the Names and Colors of the 12 Gemstones on the Breastplate of the High Priest

As before, in the following lists, the colors of the gemstones correlate much more closely than does agreement on the gemstones themselves.

The eight lists below give the 12 gemstones on the breastplate of the Jewish high priest—*"the breastplate of judgment"*—as given in the King James Version (KJV), the Greek Septuagint (LXX), the New English Bible (NEB), the Jerusalem Bible (JB), the Revised Standard Version (RSV), The Living Bible (TLB), the Holy Bible by George Lamsa (Lamsa), and The Emphasized Bible by Rotherham (Rotherham). As before, variations from the King James Version are italicized.

	KJV	LXX	NEB	JB
1	Sardius	Sardius	*Sardin*	*Sard*
2	Topaz	Topaz	*Chrysolite*	Topaz
3	Carbuncle	*Emerald*	*Green felspar*	Carbuncle
4	Emerald	*Carbuncle*	*Purple garnet*	Emerald
5	Sapphire	Sapphire	*Lapis lazuli*	Sapphire
6	Diamond	*Jasper*	*Jade*	Diamond
7	A ligure	A ligure	*Turquoise*	*Hyacinth*
8	Agate	Agate	Agate	*Ruby*
9	Amethyst	Amethyst	*Jasper*	Amethyst
10	Beryl	*Chrysolite*	*Topaz*	Beryl
11	Onyx	*Beryl*	*Cornelian*	Onyx
12	Jasper	*Onyx*	*Green jasper*	Jasper

	RSV	TLB	LAMSA	ROTHERHAM
1	Sardius	*Jasper*	Sardius	Sardius
2	Topaz	Topaz	Topaz	Topaz
3	Carbuncle	*Emerald*	*Emerald*	*Emerald*
4	Emerald	*Carbuncle*	*Carbuncle*	*Carbuncle*
5	Sapphire	Sapphire	Sapphire	Sapphire
6	Diamond	Diamond	*Jasper*	Diamond
7	*Jacinth*	*Amber*	*Jacinth (zircon)*	*Opal*

8 Agate	Agate	*Cornelian*	Agate
9 Amethyst	Amethyst	Amethyst	Amethyst
10 Beryl	*Onyx*	Beryl	*Tarshish*
11 Onyx	*Beryl*	Onyx	*Sardonyx*
12 Jasper	Jasper	Jasper	Jasper

1. The first gemstone of the Jewish high priest's *"breastplate of judg-ment"* seems to have been of a reddish color. As previously noted, it may have been a ruby. The Jerusalem Bible here gives "sard," which is a brownish-red chalcedony.

2. In the second gemstone lists (see above), the topaz and the chryso-lite, or goldstone, are both yellow, though a topaz may also be olive-green.

3. The third gemstone is given as carbuncle, emerald, or green feldspar, which are all green.

4. In the fourth gemstone in the above lists, only the "purple garnet" (NEB) would be out of color sequence.

5. In the fifth gemstone both the sapphire and the lapis lazuli (NEB) are blue.

6. The sixth gemstone, which the King James Version, the Jerusalem Bible, the Revised Standard Version, The Living Bible, and Rotherham's give as "diamond," is given as "jasper" by the Septuagint, and by George Lamsa's translation from the Aramaic. While diamonds come in every color of the rainbow, and black, still we usually think of diamonds as clear. The Amplified Bible has here in Exodus 28:18 *"diamond [so called at that time]."* Clearly, the cor-rect stone intended here has not been identified.

7. The seventh gemstone, "a ligure" (KJV, LXX), has not been identified with any gemstone known today. The "turquoise" (bluegreen) (NEB), "hyacinth" (smoke blue) (JB), "jacinth" (smoke blue) (RSV, Lamsa), "amber" (yellow, or brownish yellow) (TLB), "opal" (found in many colors, often a milky white) (Rotherham), reveals an uncertainty here. Still, all of these stones, except the amber, could represent a blue or cloudy sky between the secondary and the primary bow.

8. The eighth gemstone, the "agate" (variegated) (KJV, LXX, NEB, RSV, TLB, Rotherham) is also given as "ruby" (purplish-red) (JB), and "car-nelian" (red) (Lamsa).

9. The ninth gemstone, the "amethyst," is agreed to in all of our lists, except the NEB, which gives "jasper," a purplish-red.

10. The tenth gemstone, "beryl" (yellow, or green) (KJV, JB, RSV, TLB, Lamsa) , would, if yellow, be the same color as the "chrysolite" (LXX), or "topaz" (NEB). I cannot identify the "Tarshish stone" (Rotherham).

11. The eleventh gemstone, "onyx" (KJV, JB, RSV, Lamsa), "beryl" (LXX, TLB), "cornelian" (NEB), and "sardonyx" (Rotherham) seems too uncertain to be identified.

12. The twelfth gemstone is generally given as jasper, which fits our color scheme in opposite sequence to the rainbow, although the LXX gives this as onyx, and the NEB as "green jasper," which would not fit.

However, "there is more here than meets the eye." The colors of the foundation gemstones bear a reverse resemblance to the colors of the 12 gemstones that are upon the *"breastplate of judgment"* (Exodus 28:15-20; 39:10-13) which was worn by the Jewish high priest.

To illustrate this, we will place the colors of the rainbow *in reverse order*, and then list the names and colors of the gemstones in the high priest's *"breastplate of judgment"* in their correct order. Explanatory comments will help to enlighten, as before.

Rainbow Colors in Reverse Sequence (14 Colors)	The Names and Colors of the 12 Gemstones of the "Breastplate of Judgment"		Comments on the Names and Colors of the Gemstones on the "Breastplate of Judgment"
Secondary Bow	Names	Colors	Comments
Red	Sardius	Red	
Orange			
Yellow	Topaz	Yellow	
Green	Carbuncle	Green	
	Emerald	Green	
Blue	Sapphire	Blue	

Indigo			
Violet	(jasper), or		This identification is uncertain, however.
	Diamond (KJV)	Clear	This could represent the clear space between the secondary bow and the primary bow.
	(Jacinth), or	Smoke blue	Possibly representing a cloudy blue sky
	a Ligure (KJV)		between the secondary bow and the primary bow
	Agate	Variegated	The identification here is uncertain.

Primary Bow	Names	Colors	Comments
Violet	Amethyst	Purple, or violet	
Indigo			
Blue			
Green			
Yellow	Beryl	Yellow	The beryl comes in different colors. The Yellow Green beryl is yellowish-green.

			The Golden beryl is yellow. In this case, either one would be possible.
Orange	Onyx		This identification is doubtful.
Red	Jasper	Red	This translates the Hebrew word, *yashpheh.* Jasper is a quartz of various colors, including red.

This indicates that the 12 gemstones in the *"breastplate of judgment"* carried an opposite meaning to the colors of the rainbow. The rainbow symbolized an end to God's wrath, or in other words, peace and reconciliation, and this is the meaning of the rainbow colors of the foundation gemstones of the New Jerusalem.

And the twelve gates were twelve pearls; every several gate was of one pearl: and the street of the city was pure gold, as it were transparent glass.

The Glory of God Revealed in the Gates and Within the City

In Isaiah 54:11-12 we read, *"O thou afflicted, tossed with tempest, and not comforted, behold, I will lay thy stones with fair columns, and lay thy foundations with sapphires. And I will make thy windows of agates, and thy gates of carbuncles, and all thy borders of pleasant stones."*

In the same way, God desires to give to His own afflicted people the glories of the New Jerusalem. In this city the gold is transparent, the pearls are enormous, and the trees produce a variety of fruit—not just once a year, but every month.

22 And I saw no temple therein: for the Lord God Almighty and the Lamb are the temple of it.

Wherever God is, there is His true temple, whether in our hearts, or in the midst of the New Jerusalem. The sun and the moon, which vanished when *"the earth and heaven fled away"* from before the face of God (Revelation 20:11), are no

23 And the city had no need of the sun, neither of the moon, to shine in it: for the glory of God did lighten it, and the Lamb is the light thereof.

24 And the nations of them which are saved shall walk in the light of it: and the kings of the earth do bring their glory and honour into it.

25 And the gates of it shall not be shut at all by day: for there shall be no night there.

longer needed as *"the glory of God did lighten"* the city, and *"the Lamb is the light thereof."*

This agrees with what we know of God and of Jesus from other passages of scripture, as

"God is light, and in him is no darkness at all" (1 John 1:5b).

"Who only hath immortality, dwelling in the light which no man can approach unto; whom no man hath seen, nor can see: to whom be honour and power everlasting. Amen" (1 Timothy 6:16).

"In him (Jesus) was life; and the life was the light of men... That was the true Light, which lighteth every man that cometh into the world" (John 1:4,9, see also John 8:12).

Revelation 21:23-27 is based upon Isaiah 60 (entire chapter). It would be good for one to study Isaiah 60.[141] It must be remembered, however, that Isaiah 60, like Ezekiel 40–48, reveals the promises given to an idealized Judaism, a worthy Judaism. But, as

---

141. *"Arise, shine; for thy light is come, and the glory of the Lord is risen upon thee.*
   For, behold, the darkness shall cover the earth, and gross darkness the people: but the Lord shall arise upon thee, and his glory shall be seen upon thee.
   And the Gentiles shall come to thy light, and kings to the brightness of thy rising. Lift up thine eyes round about, and see: all they gather themselves together, they come to thee: thy sons shall come from far, and thy daughters shall be nursed at thy side.
   Then thou shalt see, and flow together, and thine heart shall fear, and be enlarged; because the abundance of the sea shall be converted unto thee, the forces of the Gentiles shall come unto thee.
   The multitude of camels shall cover thee, the dromedaries of Midian and Ephah; all they from Sheba shall come: they shall bring gold and incense; and they shall shew forth the praises of the Lord.
   All the flocks of Kedar shall be gathered together unto thee, the rams of Nebaioth shall minister unto thee: they shall come up with acceptance on mine altar, and I will glorify the house of my glory.
   Who are these that fly as a cloud, and as the doves to their windows?
   Surely the isles shall wait for me, and the ships of Tarshish first, to bring thy sons from far, their silver and their gold with them, unto the name of the Lord thy God, and to the Holy One of Israel, because he hath glorified thee.
   And the sons of strangers shall build up thy walls, and their kings shall minister unto thee: for in my wrath I smote thee, but in my favour have I had mercy on thee.
   Therefore thy gates shall be open continually: they shall not be shut day nor night; that men may bring unto thee the forces of the Gentiles, and that their kings may be brought.
   For the nation and kingdom that will not serve thee shall perish; yea, those nations shall be utterly wasted.
   The glory of Lebanon shall come unto thee, the fir tree, the pine tree, and the box together, to beautify the place of my sanctuary; and I will make the place of my feet glorious.
   The sons also of them that afflicted thee shall come bending unto thee; and all they that despised thee shall bow themselves down at the soles of thy feet; and they shall call thee, The city of the Lord, The Zion of the Holy One of Israel.
   Whereas thou hast been forsaken and hated, so that no man went through thee, I will make thee an eternal excellency, a joy of many generations.

continued on next page

26 And they shall bring the glory and honour of the nations into it.

27 And there shall in no wise enter into it any thing that defileth, neither whatsoever worketh abomination, or maketh a lie: but they which are written in the Lamb's book of life (Revelation 21:21-27).

Hebrews 8:6 (see also Hebrews 7:19 *"better hope"*; 7:22 *"better testament"*[142]) tells us, Jesus *"is the mediator of a better covenant, **which was established upon better promises.**"* So the promises of Isaiah 60 were for a natural, repentant, but purified Israel. But *"God having provided some better thing for us…"* (Hebrews 11:40a), indicates that we shall have an inheritance much more blessed than even that which Isaiah saw. Nevertheless, here are some correspondences between Revelation 21:23-27 and Isaiah 60.

Revelation 21

23 "And the city had no need of the sun, neither of the moon, to shine in it: for the glory of God did lighten it, and the Lamb is the light thereof."

24 "And the nations of them which are saved shall walk in the light of it: and the kings of the earth do bring their glory and honour into it."

Isaiah 60

19 "The sun shall be no more thy light by day; neither for brightness shall the moon give light unto thee: but the Lord shall be unto thee an everlasting light, and thy God thy glory."

3 "And the Gentiles shall come to thy light, and kings to the brightness of thy rising."

Thou shalt also suck the milk of the Gentiles, and shalt suck the breast of kings: and thou shalt know that I the Lord am thy Saviour and thy Redeemer, the mighty One of Jacob.

For brass I will bring gold, and for iron I will bring silver, and for wood brass, and for stones iron: I will also make thy officers peace, and thine exactors righteousness.

Violence shall no more be heard in thy land, wasting nor destruction within thy borders; but thou shalt call thy walls Salvation, and thy gates Praise.

The sun shall be no more thy light by day, neither for brightness shall the moon give light unto thee; but the Lord shall be unto thee an everlasting light, and thy God thy glory.

Thy sun shall no more go down; neither shall thy moon withdraw itself: for the Lord shall be thine everlasting light, and the days of thy mourning shall be ended.

Thy people also shall be all righteous: they shall inherit the land for ever, the branch of my planting, the work of my hands, that I may be glorified.

A little one shall become a thousand, and a small one a strong nation: I the Lord will hasten it in his time.

142. The *"Better"* Passages of Hebrews

"For the law made nothing perfect, but the bringing in of a better hope did; by the which we draw nigh unto God" (Hebrews 7:19).

"By so much was Jesus made a surety of a better testament" (Hebrews 7:22).

"But now hath he obtained a more excellent ministry, by how much also he is the mediator of a better covenant, which was established upon better promises" (Hebrews 8:6).

continued on next page

25 "And the gates of it shall not be shut at all by day: for there shall be no night there."	*11 "Therefore thy gates shall be open continually; they shall not be shut day nor night; that men may bring unto thee the forces of the Gentiles, and that their kings may be brought.*
26 "And they shall bring the glory and honour of the nations into it."	*13 "The glory of Lebanon shall come unto thee, the fir tree, the pine tree, and the box together, to beautify the place of my sanctuary; and I will make the place of my feet glorious."* (See also Isaiah 60:5-10,12-17.)
27 "And there shall in no wise enter into it any thing that defileth, neither worketh abomination, or maketh a lie: but they which are written in the Lamb's book of life."	*21 "Thy people also shall be all righteous: they shall inherit the land for ever, the branch of my planting, the work of my hands, that I may be glorified."* (See also vss. 17-18.)

In Isaiah 60, however, the Gentiles would provide *"the multitude of camels," "the dromedaries of Midian and Ephah,"* and *"they shall bring gold and incense"* (Isaiah 60:6).

Besides these, we also read, *"All the flocks of Kedar shall be gathered together unto thee, the rams of Nebaioth shall minister unto thee: they shall come up with acceptance on mine altar, and I will glorify the house of my glory"* (Isaiah 60:7).

In Revelation 21:22, however, there is *"no temple therein,"* and therefore no altar for burnt offerings. So what would be *"the glory and honour of the nations"* which would be brought into the New Jerusalem?

Because *"corruption"* cannot *"inherit incorruption"* (1 Corinthians 15:50b), and because we are now to *"offer the sacrifice of praise to God continually, that is, the fruit of our lips giving thanks to his name"* (Hebrews 13:15), it would appear that *"the nations of them which are saved"*[143] and

---

"And these all, having obtained a good report through faith, received not the promise; God having provided some better thing for us, that they without us should not be made perfect" (Hebrews 11:39-40).

143. The phrase *"the nations of them which are saved"* (Revelation 21:24a) is probably derived from Isaiah 60:3-16,22, in which *"the Gentiles shall come to thy light, and kings to the brightness of thy rising"* (Isaiah 60:3), and in which *"a little one shall become a thousand, and a small one a strong nation"* (Isaiah 60:22).

But we have *"a better covenant, which was established upon better promises"* (Hebrews 8:6; see notes), and in these *"better promises"* Jesus tells us, *"For in the resurrection they neither marry, nor are given in marriage, but are as the angels of God in heaven"* (Matthew 22:30). The need for sex will someday vanish altogether.

"the kings of the earth" would be bringing the fruit of their lips, that is, new melodies and lyrics with which to praise God, new compositions and poems with which to adore and to worship Him, and His wonderful Son, Jesus Christ.

In Isaiah 60:9-10, *"the ships of Tarshish"* would *"bring thy sons from far"* and *"the sons of strangers shall build up thy walls."* But we have *"a better covenant, which was established upon better promises"* (Hebrews 8:6), and in the *"new earth"* that John saw, *"there was no more sea"* (Revelation 21:1) upon which *"the ships of Tarshish"* might sail, and the *"holy Jerusalem...had a wall great and high"* (Revelation 21:12) already when it was seen *"descending out of heaven from God."*

Thus, the holy Jerusalem that John saw is both enormously larger, and far more holy than even Isaiah had seen. In Isaiah's vision Jerusalem was prophesied to become the best that men could give God. In John's vision it would be the best that God could give us.

But who are *"the nations of them which are saved"* (Revelation 21:24a), who live upon the *"new earth"* (Revelation 21:1) but obviously outside the walls of the New Jerusalem?

In Scripture we read that *"there is neither Jew nor Greek, there is neither bond nor free, there is neither male nor female: for ye are all one in Christ Jesus"* (Galatians 3:28).

So these are not Gentile nations in the present-day sense.

There are three matters that must be understood in order to answer this question:

(1) These all have resurrection bodies. (See 1 Corinthians 15:50, *"Now this I say, brethren, that flesh and blood cannot inherit the kingdom of God; neither doth corruption inherit incorruption."*)

(2) In the New Jerusalem, and in the new Earth—as it is now in heaven—we will all have different degrees of glory depending upon the degree of our surrender to the ways of Jesus. Thus, some of us will be closer to God and to Jesus in the New Jerusalem, and some will dwell outside the New Jerusalem, but upon the new Earth. These are all saved and have their resurrection bodies, but in their previous earthly lives were lacking in the works that are needed in a Christian's life. These are described in 1 Corinthians 3:10-15. They are saved, but their works are burned up. They are *"saved; yet so as by fire."*

(3) Since purity of heart is necessary to see God (Matthew 5:8; Hebrews 12:14), many who are saved are not prepared, at first, to enter into His

glorious presence. They are *"just spirits,"* but not yet made perfect (Hebrews 12:23).

These, then, dwell outside the city, but they are learning unselfish service so that they may eventually dwell within the city. They *"do his commandments";* they have the *"right to the tree of life"; "and may enter in through the gates into the city"* (Revelation 22:14).

These will have *"kings"* over them, and will learn more perfectly to follow Jesus. Apparently, these will have national boundaries, or administrative districts, closer to or farther from the New Jerusalem.

Revelation 22
Setting Things Right

One of the richest contrasts we find in the book of Revelation is with the book of Genesis, the first book of the Bible. Just as Genesis started and established the world as we know it, we see many of the same things being removed or closed in the closing words of Revelation.

The first words of Genesis are:	The Near-closing words in Revelation are:
"In the beginning God created the heavens and the earth" (1:1)	*"I saw a new heaven and a new earth"* (21:1)
"The gathering together of the waters called He Seas" (1:10)	*"And there was no more sea"* (21:1)
"The darkness He called Night" (1:5)	*"There shall be no night there"* (21:25; 22:5)
"And God made two great lights" (sun and moon) (1:16)	*"And the city had no need of the sun, neither of the moon"* (21:23)
"In the day that thou eatest thereof thou shalt surely die" (2:17)	*"And there shall be no more death"* (21:4)
"I will greatly multiply thy sorrow" (3:16)	*"Neither shall there be any more pain"* (21:4)
"Cursed is the ground for thy sake" (3:17)	*"And there shall be no more curse"* (22:3)

(Adapted from *Halley's Bible Handbook*)

Let us see how God sets right all the corruption and damage of sin in the earth.

And he shewed me a pure river of water of life, clear as crystal, proceeding out of the throne of God and of the Lamb (Revelation 22:1).

The Blessedness of Those Who Live Within the New Jerusalem

Ezekiel (47:1-12) and Zechariah (14:8) had seen this river also, as had David (Psalm 36:8; 46:4).[144]

But this river, like all else upon the new Earth, has a spiritual quality quite unlike that which is known in the present world. We read, *"Because the creature (Greek, ktisis, creation) itself also shall be delivered from the bondage of corruption into the glorious liberty of the children of God"* (Romans 8:21). Thus, we see that the *"new heaven"* and the *"new earth"* have been radically changed and have taken on an incorruptible dimension.

---

144. The river seen by Ezekiel, Zechariah and David was miraculous, but natural. The river in Revelation 22:1 is spiritual.

"Afterward he brought me again unto the door of the house; and, behold, waters issued out from under the threshold of the house eastward: for the forefront of the house stood toward the east, and the waters cane down from under from the right side of the house, at the south side of the altar.
Then brought he me out of the way of the gate northward, and led me about the way without unto the utter gate by the way that looketh eastward; and, behold, there ran out waters on the right side.
And when the man that had the line in his hand went forward eastward, he measured a thousand cubits, and he brought me through the waters; the waters were to the ancles.
Again he measured a thousand, and brought me through the waters; the waters were to the knees.
Again he measured a thousand, and brought me through; the waters were to the loins.
Afterward he measured a thousand; and it was a river that I could not pass over: for the waters were risen, waters to swim in, a river that could not be passed over.
And he said unto me, Son of man, hast thou seen this? Then he brought me, and caused me to return to the brink of the river.
Now when I had returned, behold, at the bank of the river were very many trees on the one side and on the other.
Then said he unto me, These waters issue out toward the east country, and go down into the desert, and go into the sea: which being brought forth into the sea, the waters shall be healed.
And it shall come to pass, that every thing that liveth, which moveth, whithersoever the rivers shall come, shall live: and there shall be a very great multitude of fish, because these waters shall come thither: for they shall be healed; and every thing shall live whither the river cometh.
And it shall come to pass, that the fishers shall stand upon it from Engedi even unto Eneglaim; they shall be a place to spread forth nets; their fish shall be according to their kinds, as the fish of the great sea, exceeding many.
But the miry places thereof and the marishes thereof shall not be healed; they shall be given to salt.
And by the river upon the back thereof, on this side and on that side, shall grow all trees for meat, whose leaf shall not fade, neither shall the fruit thereof be consumed: it shall bring forth new fruit according to his months, because their waters they issued out of the sanctuary: and the fruit thereof shall be for meat, and the leaf thereof for medicine" (Ezekiel 47:1-12).

"And it shall be in that day, that living waters shall go out from Jerusalem; half of them toward the former sea, and half of them toward the hinder sea: in summer and in winter shall it be.
And the Lord shall be king over all the earth: in that day shall there be one Lord, and his name one" (Zechariah 14:8-9).

"They shall be abundantly satisfied with the fatness of thy house; and thou shalt make them drink of the river of thy pleasures" (Psalm 36:8).

"There is a river, the streams whereof shall make glad the city of God, the holy place of the tabernacles of the most High" (Psalm 46:4).

In John 4:10-11,14 and in John 7:38-39, Jesus spoke of *"living water"* in reference to the Holy Spirit. Jeremiah (2:13; 17:13) had also referred to God as *"the fountain of living waters."*[145] These scriptures seem to point to the spiritual quality of this *"water of life."* For instance, in our world the rivers run into the sea (Ecclesiastes 1:7), but in the new Earth this will not be so as *"there was no more sea"* (Revelation 21:1b).

In the midst of the street of it, and on either side of the river, was there the (or, a) tree of life, which bare twelve manner of fruits, and yielded her fruit every month: and the leaves of the tree were for the healing of the nations (Revelation 22:2).

The Greek reads not *"the tree of life,"* but *"a tree of life."* There must have been three trees—one in the street, and one on each side of the river. The final phrase of this verse, *"...and the leaves of the tree were for the healing of the nations"* is based on Ezekiel 47:12, *"And by the river upon the bank thereof, on this side and on that side, shall grow all trees for meat* (food), *whose leaf shall not fade, neither shall the fruit thereof be consumed: it shall bring forth new fruit according to his months, because their waters issued out of the sanctuary: and the fruit thereof shall be for meat* (food), *and the leaf thereof for medicine."*

However, because we will have incorruptible bodies (1 Corinthians 15:42,53-54), we must understand this *"healing"* in the sense of Psalm 147:3, *"He healeth the broken in heart, and bindeth up their wounds."*

And there shall be no more curse: but the throne of God and of the Lamb shall be in it; and his servants shall serve him:

"...no more curse." In Leviticus 26, and in Deuteronomy 27 and 28 we have written *the curse* of the law. But *"Christ hath redeemed us from the curse of the law"* (Galatians 3:13), that is, from curse that is in the law.[146] These curses will all be gone in the New Jerusalem.

---

145. *"For my people have committed two evils; they have forsaken me the fountain of living waters, and hewed them out cisterns, broken cisterns, that can hold no water"* (Jeremiah 2:13).

   "O Lord, the hope of Israel, all that forsake thee shall be ashamed, and they that depart from me shall be written in the earth, because they have forsaken the Lord, the fountain of living waters" (Jeremiah 17:13).

146. Many of the curses of the law are given in Deuteronomy 27:15-26, and 28:15-68, and elsewhere. In Galatians 3:6-14 (see below), Paul explains that *"Christ hath redeemed us from the curse of the law,"* and Revelation 22:3 confirms this.

   "Even as Abraham believed God, and it was accounted to him for righteousness. Know ye therefore that they which are of faith, the same are the children of Abraham.

continued on next page

4 And they shall see his face; and his name shall be in their foreheads (Revelation 22:3-4).

"And they shall see his face..." because they are now pure in heart. (Matthew 5:8; 1 Corinthians 13:12; Hebrews 12:14; 1 John 3:2-3) To see God's face was the hope of Job (Job 19:26-27), and Jesus desired that we might behold His glory (John 17:24).

"...and his name shall be in their foreheads," as in Revelation 3:12; 14:1. Slaves sometimes bore the name of their master on their foreheads. We who are love-slaves to God will be able to manifest that we belong to Him.

And there shall be no night there; and they need no candle, neither light of the sun; for the Lord God giveth them light: and they shall reign for ever and ever (Revelation 22:5).

John reiterates that *"there shall be no night there"* (see Revelation 21:25b), and that *"they shall reign for ever and ever. "*

Our reigning with God, and with Jesus, is a theme given repeatedly in prophetic scriptures. Thus,

"But the saints of the most High shall take the kingdom, and possess the kingdom for ever, even for ever and ever" (Daniel 7:18).

"...and the time came that the saints possessed the kingdom" (Daniel 7:22b).

"And the kingdom and dominion, and the greatness of the kingdom under the whole heaven, shall be given to the people of the saints of the most High, whose kingdom is an everlasting kingdom, and all dominions shall serve and obey him" (Daniel 7:27).

"For if by one man's offense death reigned by one; much more they which receive abundance of grace and of the gift of righteousness shall reign in life by one, Jesus Christ" (Romans 5:17).

"If we suffer, we shall also reign with him: if we deny him, he also will deny us" (2 Timothy 2:12).

And the scripture, foreseeing that God would justify the heathen through faith, preached before the gospel unto Abraham, saying, In thee shall all nations be blessed.
So then they which be of faith are blessed with faithful Abraham.
For as many as are of the works of the law are under the curse: for it is written, Cursed is every one that continueth not in all things which are written in the book of the law to do them.
But that no man is justified by the law in the sight of God, it is evident: for, The just shall live by faith.
And the law is not of faith: but, The man that doeth them shall live in them.
Christ hath redeemed us from the curse of the law, being made a curse for us; for it is written, Cursed is every one that hangeth on a tree: That the blessing of Abraham might come on the Gentiles through Jesus Christ; that we might receive the promise of the Spirit through faith" (Galatians 3:6-14).

"To him that overcometh will I grant to sit with me in my throne, even as I also overcame, and am set down with my Father in his throne" (Revelation 3:21).

"And they sung a new song, saying, Thou art worthy to take the book, and to open the seals thereof: for thou wast slain, and hast redeemed us to God by thy blood out of every kindred, and tongue, and people, and nation. 10 And hast made us unto our God kings and priests: and we shall reign on the earth" (Revelation 5:9-10).

And he said unto me, These sayings are faithful and true: and the Lord God of the holy prophets sent his angel to shew unto his servants the things which must shortly be done.

7 Behold, I come quickly: blessed is he that keepeth the sayings of the prophecy of this book (Revelation 22:6-7)

John's Epilogue

This concluding section of Revelation reiterates and reemphasizes the themes of the nearness of the return of Jesus, and the necessity of a holy life to have the *"right to the tree of life"* and to *"enter in through the gates into the city."* (Revelation 22:14).

Thus, it is interesting to note that the phrase in Revelation 22:6, *"to shew unto his servants the things which must shortly be done,"* is no different at all in the Greek from the phrase in Revelation 1:1, *"to shew unto his servants things which must shortly come to pass."*

In both places the Greek, with the literal translation, reads:

deixai	*tois*	*doulois*	*autou*	*Ha*
to point out	to the	bond-servants	of himself	the things

dei	*genesthai*	*en*	*tachei*
it behooves	to have done	in, or with	speed.

In this concluding section it may sometimes seem difficult to know just when the angel is speaking as a mouthpiece for Jesus, and when he is speaking on his own. By applying here the principle given in Revelation 1:1, we understand that God gave this revelation to Jesus, who gave it to His angel to give to John for us.

In verses 7,12-13,16, and 18-20 of this chapter (22) the angel most likely is speaking as a mouthpiece for Jesus, while in verses 6,9-11,14-15, and 17 he is speaking on his own.

The angel is *"one of the seven angels which had the seven vials* (or, bowls) *full of the seven last plagues"* (Revelation 21:9), who had been speaking with John throughout the previous section (that is, from Revelation 21:9–22:5), and here (Revelation 22:6) continues to speak to him.[147]

The angel is sometimes referred to as *"the Spirit"* (Revelation 22:17; see also Acts 8:26,29,39; also Revelation 1:1 compared with Revelation 2:7,11,17,29; 3:6,13,22; also Revelation 1:4 compared with 4:5 and 8:2; also Revelation 5:6 compared with 15:6 and 16:1).[148]

---

147. *"The seven spirits which are before His* (God's) *throne"* are also *"the seven angels which stood before God"*

"John to the seven churches which are in Asia: Grace be unto you, and peace, from him which is, and which was, and which is to come; and from the seven Spirits which are before his throne..." (Revelation 1:4).

"I charge thee before God, and the Lord Jesus Christ, and the elect angels, that thou observe these things without preferring one before another, doing nothing by partiality" (1 Timothy 5:21).

"And the angel answering said unto him, I am Gabriel, that stand in the presence of God; and am sent to speak unto thee, and to shew thee these glad tidings" (Luke 1:19).

"And I saw the seven angels which stood before God; and to them were given seven trumpets" (Revelation 8:2).

"And I beheld, and, lo, in the midst of the throne and of the four beasts, and in the midst of the elders, stood a Lamb as it had been slain, having seven horns and seven eyes, which are the seven Spirits of God sent forth into all the earth" (Revelation 5:6).

"The seven spirits of God sent forth into all the earth" are the *"seven angels having the seven last plagues"*

"For as for the stone which I have set before the face of Jesus, on the one stone are seven eyes: behold, I am digging a trench, saith the Lord Almighty, and I will search out all the iniquity of that land in one day" (Zacharias III.10 LXX).

"And there shall come forth a rod out of the root of Jesse, and a blossom shall come up from his root: and the Spirit of God shall rest upon him, the spirit of wisdom and understanding, the spirit of counsel and strength, the spirit of knowledge and godliness shall fill him;
the spirit of the fear of God. He shall not judge according to appearance, nor reprove according to report: but he shall judge the cause of the lowly, and shall reprove the lowly of the earth: and he shall smite the earth with the word of his mouth, and with the breath of his lips shall he destroy the ungodly one. And he shall have his loins girt with righteousness, and his sides clothed with truth" (Esaias XI.1-5 (LXX).

"And I saw another sign in heaven, great and marvelous, seven angels having the seven last plagues; for in them is filled up the wrath of God" (Revelation 15:1, see also Revelation 15:6-8; 16:1; 17:1; 21:9 for references to this second group of seven spirits, or angels. See also the footnote at Revelation 15:1).

148. The angel of Jesus who gave the Revelation is sometimes referred to as *"The Spirit"*

"The Revelation of Jesus Christ, which God gave unto him, to shew unto his servants things which must shortly come to pass; and he sent and signified it by his angel unto his servant John:" (Revelation 1:1).

continued on next page

Except for the brief introduction of two matters relating to John's near sin of attempting to worship an angel (Revelation 22:8-9),[149] and the warnings against tampering with the contents of this book (Revelation 22:18-19), the principle emphasis of this concluding section is the soon-coming of Jesus (as in Revelation 22:6-7,10-12,20) and our being ready for that event (as in Revelation 22:7,11-12,14-15,17).

Revelation 22:7 reads, *"Behold, I come quickly: blessed is he that keepeth the sayings of the prophecy of this book."* Jesus had previously warned the churches to repent or He would come to them quickly. Thus, we read in Revelation 2:5, to the church at Ephesus, *"Remember therefore from whence thou art fallen, and repent, and do the first works; or else I will come unto thee quickly, and will remove thy candlestick out of his place, except thou repent."* Without repentance, the first century church at Ephesus would be judged along with the world at the coming of Jesus.

To the church in Pergamos, Jesus had said, *"Repent; or else I will come unto thee quickly, and will fight against them with the sword of my mouth"* (Revelation 2:16). *"The sharp sword with two edges"* (Revelation 2:12b), with which he would fight against the beast and the kings of the earth and their armies (Revelation 19:15,19-20), would be used against those in the church at Pergamos who *failed* to repent.

To Thyatira, Jesus had said, *"But that which ye have already hold fast till I come"* (Revelation 2:25). Jesus clearly intended to come in the lifetimes of those He was here admonishing.

To the church at Sardis, Jesus had said, *"Remember therefore how thou hast received and heard, and hold fast and repent. If therefore thou shalt not watch, I will come on thee as a thief, and thou shalt not know what hour I will come upon thee"* (Revelation 3:3).

To the church at Philadelphia, Jesus said, *"Behold, I come quickly: hold that fast which thou hast, that no man take thy crown"* (Revelation 3:11).

And so, in Revelation 22:7,12 and 20, Jesus reiterates this theme, *"Behold, I come quickly."*

"He that hath an ear, let him hear what the Spirit saith unto the churches..." (Revelation 2:7,11,17,29; 3:6,13,22).

"I Jesus have sent mine angel to testify unto You these things in the churches. I am the root and the offspring of David, and the bright and morning star" (Revelation 22:16).

"And the Spirit and the bride say, Come. And let him that heareth say, Come. And let him that is athirst come. And whosoever will, let him take the water of life freely" (Revelation 22:17).

149. Note: See notes at Revelation 19:10 on "Angels are such awesome beings, that they must often admonish people not to fear them"

Revelation 22:7 reads, again, *"Behold, I come quickly: blessed is he that keepeth the sayings of the prophecy of this book."* The last part of this verse is from Revelation 1:3, *"Blessed is he that readeth, and they that hear the words of this prophecy, **and keep those things which are written therein:** for the time is at hand."*

The theme throughout Revelation had been on the soon coming of Jesus, and the need to repent in preparation for His coming. Those themes are reiterated in this final section of Revelation.

And I John saw these things, and heard them. And when I had heard and seen, I fell down to worship before the feet of the angel which shewed me these things.

9 Then saith he unto me, See thou do it not: for I am thy fellowservant, and of thy brethren the prophets, and of them which keep the sayings of this book: worship God (Revelation 22:8-9).

The Angel Restrains John from Committing a Forbidden Act

John had nearly committed a forbidden act a second time (see Revelation 19:10), but the angel restrained him. Why would John do this? Because the appearance of an angel is so very awesome! Daniel had lost all of his strength in the presence of an angel (Daniel 10:8-11). Manoah's wife had unknowingly been visited by an angel, and described his appearance to her husband (Judges 13:6) saying, *"A man of God came unto me, and his countenance was like the countenance of an angel of God, very terrible..."*

10 And he saith unto me, Seal not the sayings of the prophecy of this book: for the time is at hand (Revelation 22:10).

"Seal Not the Sayings...The Time Is at Hand"

Daniel was told, *"But thou, O Daniel, shut up the words, and seal the book, even to the time of the end"* (Daniel 12:4), and *"Go thy way, Daniel: for the words are closed up and sealed till the time of the end"* (Daniel 12:9).

That which Daniel had *"sealed"* because the time of its fulfillment was so distant, John had unsealed because *"the time is at hand"* (Revelation 1:3b; 22:10b).

11 He that is unjust, let him be unjust still: and he which is filthy, let him be filthy still: and he that is righteous, let him be righteous still: and he that is holy, let him be holy still.

12 And, behold, I come quickly; and my reward is with me, to give every man according as his work shall be (Revelation 22:11-12).

*I am Alpha and Omega, the beginning and the end, **the first and the last*** (Revelation 22:13).

There's Hardly Time Left to Repent

The thought here is that Jesus' coming was so close at hand that a person would hardly have time left to repent. The emphasis, repeatedly, in this section is upon the soon coming of Jesus. The following verse, Revelation 22:12, reinforces this point, *"And, behold, I come quickly; and my reward is with me, to give every man according as his work shall be."*

The Authority for This Prophecy Is Jesus

In Revelation 1:8, God the Father had said, *"I am Alpha and Omega,"* and in Isaiah 48:12, He refers to Himself as, *"I am he; I am the first, I am also the last."*

But here, Jesus is rightfully able to use these names, or titles, of God, the Father. Jesus said, *"I am come in my Father's name…"* (John 5:43). He was sent by His Father, to do the will of His Father, and carrying all the authority and all the titles and names of His Father.[150] Jesus, also, as the Word of God, was in the beginning with His Father (John 1:2).

---

150. Compare the following passages.

"Thus said Jehovah, king of Israel, and his Redeemer, Jehovah of Hosts: 'I am the first, and I the last, and besides Me there is no God" (Isaiah XLIV.6 Young's).

"Lift up, O gates, your heads, And be lifted up, O doors age during, and come in doth the king of glory!
Who is this—'the king of glory?' Jehovah - strong and mighty, Jehovah, the mighty in battle.
Who is He—this 'king of glory?' Jehovah of hosts–He is the king of glory" (Psalm XXIV.7-8,10 Young's).

"I am Alpha and Omega, the beginning and the end, the first and the last" (Revelation 22:13).

"Which none of the princes of this world knew: for had they known it, they would not have crucified the Lord of glory" (1 Corinthians 2:8).

continued on next page

14 Blessed are they that do his commandments, that they may have right to the tree of life, and may enter in through the gates into the city.

The Righteous Are Blessed; the Wicked Are Punished

The nations, or peoples, would come through *"the gates into the city,"* as in Revelation 21:24-26. *"The tree (Greek, xulon, wood) of life,"* which was kept from man after he sinned in the garden of Eden (Genesis 3:22-24), is now given to redeemed man. According to Genesis 3:22, by eating from this tree of life one would *"live for ever."*

15 For without are dogs, and sorcerers, and whoremongers, and murderers, and idolaters, and whosoever loveth and maketh a lie (Revelation 22:14-15).

"For without are dogs…" *"Without"* here emphasizes that the unrighteous could not enter the city at all. Elsewhere we have learned that they were *"in the lake which burneth with fire and brimstone: which is the second death"* (Revelation 21:8b). The punishment of the wicked had been given often in the final chapters of Revelation (see Revelation 20:15; 21:8,27).

"Dogs." George Lamsa, who was raised with the Aramaic language, writes that *"dogs"* refers to *"vicious men."* *"In the East,"* he says, *"heretics, vicious men and gossipers are called dogs."* Paul, in his epistle, also warns the faithful to *"beware of dogs,"* that is, *"heretics and troublemakers."*[151]

16 I Jesus have sent mine angel to testify unto you these things in the

"I Jesus." "and the Spirit and the Bride"

In spite of the nearness of the time of the coming of Jesus that was indicated by the words, *"He that is*

"Behold, the Lord God will come with strong hand, and his arm shall rule for him: behold, his reward is with him, and his work before him. He shall feed his flock like a shepherd: he shall gather the lambs with his arm, and carry them in his bosom, and shall gently lead those that are with young" (Isaiah 40:10-11).

"A voice is crying—in a wilderness—prepare ye the way of Jehovah, make straight in a desert a highway to our God" (Isaiah XL. 3 Young's).

"Now the God of peace, that brought again from the dead our Lord Jesus, that great shepherd of the sheep, through the blood of the everlasting covenant" (Hebrews 13:20).

Compare also Isaiah 53:1 with John 12:38-41 where *"the arm of the Lord"* refers to Jesus.

"In those days came John the Baptist, preaching in the wilderness of Judea. For this is he that was spoken of by the prophet Esaias, saying, The voice of one crying in the wilderness, Prepare ye the way of the Lord, make his paths straight" (Matthew 3:1,3).

151. Lamsa, George M., *New Testament Commentary*, A. J. Holman Company, pgs. 362, 614-615.

churches. I am the root and the offspring of David, and the bright and morning star.

17 And the Spirit and the bride say, Come. And let him that heareth say, Come. And let him that is athirst come. And whosoever will, let him take the water of life freely (Revelation 22:16-17).

For I testify unto every man that heareth the words of the prophecy of this book, If any man shall add unto these things, God shall add unto him the plagues that are written in this book:

19 And if any man shall take away from the words of the book of this prophecy, God shall take away his part out of the book of life, and out of the holy city, and from the things which are written in this book (Revelation 22:18-19).

20 He which testifieth these things saith, Surely I come quickly. Amen. Even so, come,

unjust, let him be unjust still…" the angel, or Spirit, of Jesus now urges *"whosoever"* to come. The time of His coming was very close, but if one came immediately, he might still gain the right to enter in through the gates into the city, and have a right to the tree of life.

Solemn Warnings against Tampering with the Contents of This Book

The *"plagues"* here may be a reference to *"the seven last plagues"* (Revelation 15:1), which we saw in Revelation 16, but we especially have here a reference to Revelation 19:11-21, in which Jesus returns to destroy his enemies by the sword of His mouth, and also a reference to Revelation 20:15, in which *"whosoever was not found written in the book of life was cast into the lake of fire."*

Deuteronomy 4:2 and 12:32 also included solemn warnings against tampering with the contents of the book.

"Ye shall not add unto the word which I command you, neither shall ye diminish aught from it, that ye may keep the commandments of the Lord your God which I command you" (Deuteronomy 4:2).

"What thing soever I command you, observe to do it: thou shalt not add thereto, nor diminish from it" (Deuteronomy 12:32).

"Even so, Come, Lord Jesus"

Jesus certainly intended to come quickly. He was very willing to do so. But His coming was thrown

Lord Jesus
(Revelation 22:20).

into the future by the massive repentance and turning to Him within the Roman Empire, and also by the failure of the Jews to repent and to receive their Messiah and His wonderful kingdom.

But all this is changing. And as it changes, we are able to stand in the place John stood, and to be as close to Jesus' return as John would have been had the event not been thrown into the future! John was about 26 years away if we take the last year of the reign of Domitian, *"the eighth"* (Revelation 17:11) Roman emperor, or *"king,"* and then subtract from that date the date this book was written (A.D. 70).

Are we 26 years away from Jesus' second coming? Very likely we are! And if so, then we can be as excited as John was when he said, *"Even so, come, Lord Jesus."*

21 The grace of our Lord Jesus Christ be with you all. Amen (Revelation 22:21).

Concluding Benedictions

A benediction was a regular part of the temple service in which the name of Yahweh (Jehovah) was put upon the Hebrew people. Benedictions were used both at the beginning and at the end of epistles. At the beginning, Paul commonly wrote, *"Grace be to you and peace from God our Father, and from the Lord Jesus Christ."* (See Romans 1:7; 1 Corinthians 1:3; 2 Corinthians 1:2; Galatians 1:3; Ephesians 1:2; Philippians 1:2; Colossians 1:2; 1 Thessalonians 1:1; 2 Thessalonians 1:2; 1 Timothy 1:2; 2 Timothy 1:2; Philemon 3.)

At the end of his epistles, Paul always gave a benediction in which *"grace"* was invoked and imparted to those who were a part of the covenant family. In Philippians 4:23 and in 2 Thessalonians 3:18 the benediction is the same as Revelation 22:21. Both Galatians 6:18 and Philemon 25 are almost identical, *"The grace of our Lord Jesus Christ be with your spirit. Amen."*

A shortened form is given, with slight variations, in five epistles, *"Grace be with you all. Amen."* (See

Colossians 4:18; 1 Timothy 6:21; 2 Timothy 4:22; Titus 3:15; Hebrews 13:25.)

A beautiful and well-known benediction comes from 2 Corinthians 13:14, *"The grace of the Lord Jesus Christ, and the love of God, and the communion of the Holy Ghost, be with you all. Amen."*

Paul wrote very similar benediction in 1 Corinthians 16:23: *"The grace of our Lord Jesus Christ be with you."*

Thus, John, like Paul, concludes with blessing his readers and his hearers with the *grace* of Jesus, which we are to receive by faith.

Lord Jesus, extend to us Your grace, and come more fully into our lives. Make us like You, Lord Jesus! Prepare us for Your holy and heavenly kingdom in Your city, the New Jerusalem. Amen

Appendix A

The Use of Symbolic Numbers in Daniel

Revelation provides an interesting study of the use of symbolic numbers. We have seen repeatedly

(1) that numbers have meanings, and

(2) that a number multiplied by itself carries the same meaning, but intensified (as in 40 x 40 which equals 1600 (Revelation 14:20), for example).

In Daniel 8:13-14 and 12:8,11-12, we see a completely different use of symbolic numbers. In these passages of Daniel, symbolic numbers reveal the Hebrew concepts of

(1) the lengthening of days, and

(2) the shortening of days.

By understanding these concepts, we will also be able to appreciate the prophecies regarding the 2,300 evenings mornings, and also in regard to the 1,290 days and the 1,335 days.

In Daniel 8:13-14, and in Daniel 12:8,11-12, we read as follows in the King James Version.

Daniel 8:13-14

Daniel 12:8,11-12

Then I heard one saint speaking, and another saint said unto that certain saint which spake, How long shall be the vision concerning the daily sacrifice and the transgression of desolation, to give both the sanctuary and the host to be trodden under foot?

*14 And he said unto me, Unto **two thousand and three hundred days*** (Hebrew, *ereb boqer, evenings mornings*); *then shall the sanctuary be cleansed.*

*And I heard, but I understood not: then said I, O my Lord, what shall be **the end of*** (Hebrew, *acharith,* after) *these things?*

11 And from the time that the daily sacrifice shall be taken away, and the abomination that maketh desolate set up (Hebrew, *nathan,* "to the giving out of the desolating abomination" from *Young's Literal Translation of the Bible*), *there shall be **a thousand two hundred and ninety days.***

*12 Blessed is he that waiteth, and cometh to **the thousand three hundred and five and thirty days.***

The Hebrew concepts of the lengthening and shortening of days are basic for our understanding of the above passages. These concepts seem to have developed both from scriptural passages that tie God's blessings to lengthened days, His wrath and displeasure to shortened days, and also to the constant lengthening and shortening of the number of days in the Hebrew year.

Thus, we read in Proverbs 10:27, "*The fear of the Lord prolongeth days: but the years of the wicked shall be shortened.*" In the passages that follow we will see that in every case the lengthening of days indicated God's blessing and approval, and in every case a shortening of days indicated God's displeasure and disapproval.

Lengthened Days

Shortened Days

*But thou shalt have a perfect and just weight, a perfect and just measure shalt thou have: that **thy days may be lengthened** in the land which the Lord thy God giveth thee* (Deuteronomy 25:15).

*He weakened my strength in the way; **he shortened my days*** (Psalm 102:23).

*The **days** of his youth hast thou **shortened**: thou hast covered him with shame* (Psalm 89:45).

*And if thou wilt walk in my ways, to keep my statutes and my commandments, as thy father David did walk, then I will **lengthen thy days** (1 Kings 3:14; See also Deuteronomy 30:20; Job 12:12; Psalm 21:4; Proverbs 3:2,16).*

*And except that the Lord had shortened those days, no flesh should be saved: but for the elect's sake, whom he hath chosen, he hath **shortened the days** (Mark 13:20; See also Matthew 24:22).*

The passages in Mark 13:20 and Matthew 24:22 carry our above concepts a step farther. Days were "*shortened*" so that God's wrath would not fall upon His "*elect*," as in Habakkuk 3:2, "*...in wrath remember mercy.*" The opposite must also be true, then, that days were lengthened so that the fullness of God's blessings could come.

Daniel 8:13-14 gives us an example of the lengthening of days; while Daniel 12:11 gives us an example of the shortening of days.

Daniel 8:13-14 refers to the three years (which are pictured here as very full years, that is, three years of leap years), in which Mattathias, and his son, Judas Maccabaeus, confronted the much superior Syrian forces under Antiochus Epiphanes in battle after battle. The Jewish forces, under the leadership of Judas Maccabaeus, *did not suffer a single defeat in this time period of exactly three year's duration,* and this was the meaning of the symbolic number "*two thousand and three hundred evenings mornings.*" These battles are described in 1 Maccabees 1:59–4:55.

Daniel 12:11 refers to the time period from the destruction of the temple and of the removal of the altar of burnt offering in A.D. 70, to the fall of Masada on 15 Nisan, A.D. 74. In this time period the Jewish forces *did not gain a single victory against the Romans,* and this was the meaning of the symbolic number of "*a thousand two hundred and ninety days.*" Thus, in Daniel 8:13-14 the prophetic meaning of the symbolic numbers was that the Jewish forces would go from victory to victory until the sanctuary would be cleansed, while in Daniel 12:11, the meaning is that the Jewish forces would go from defeat to defeat until God's punishment upon the Jews for the pile of human fecal matter within a wing of the temple ("*the abomination that maketh desolate*") had finally given out.

In giving support to the above positions, some knowledge of the Hebrew calendar is necessary. The Hebrews did not use a solar calendar of 365 1/4 days. They used a lunar calendar which usually had 354 days, but it often varied between 353 days and 355 days. Samuel, a Jewish authority on their calendar, said, "*The lunar year consists of no fewer than 352, nor of more than 356 days.*" (Richard Siegel and Carl Rheins, *The Jewish Almanic,* A

Bantam Book, October 1980, pg. 306.) *The shortest possible Hebrew year was 352 days.* However, Samuel's above quote applied only to common, or regular years, of 12 months' duration.

Thus, every two or three years a thirteenth month was intercalated, or added, to their 12-month calendar to prevent the Jewish feasts from drifting backward through the seasons. In a leap year the final month of Adar became two months—Adar Rishon (Adar I) and Adar Sheni (Adar II). In regular years Adar is always 29 days. In leap years Adar I is 30 days and Adar II is 29 days.

A lunar month is actually 29 days, 12 hours, 44 minutes, and 3 1/3 seconds. Thus, a leap year of thirteen months would be 383 days, 21 hours, 32 minutes, and 43 1/3 seconds. But, in Daniel's time such calculations, while close, were not that precise. It will become obvious that Daniel was using a leap year of 383 1/3 days.

The above facts will help us in understanding Daniel 8:14. We need to recall that, in the King James Version, the phrase "*Unto two thousand and three hundred days*" is more accurately translated, "*Unto two thousand and three hundred evenings mornings.*" The "*evenings mornings*" would be a reference to the evening and morning sacrifices, which would usually have taken 1,150 days to accomplish. Thus, "*two thousand and three hundred evenings* (and) *mornings*" would actually be 1,150 days!

It is known from 1 Maccabees 1:54, 59 and 4:52-54 that the time lapse referred to in Daniel 8:13-14 was exactly three years to the very day. These passages read, "*On the fifteenth day of the month Kislev in the year 145* (that is, 167 B.C. by our calendar) '*the abomination of desolation' was set up on the altar*" (1 Maccabees 1:59). "*On the twenty-fifth day of the month they offered sacrifice on the pagan altar which was on top of the altar of the Lord*" (1 Maccabees 1:59). "*Then, early on the twenty-fifth day of the ninth month, the month Kislev, in the year 148* (that is 164 B.C., or three years *later to the very day) sacrifice was offered as the law commands on the newly made altar of burnt-offering. On the anniversary of the day when the Gentiles had profaned it, on that very day, it was rededicated...*" (1 Maccabees 4:52-54).

But, how can 1,150 days be made to equal three years to the very day? The answer lies in our new understanding of the use of symbolic numbers, in which the 1,150 days are symbolic of lengthened days revealing God's wonderful blessings upon the Maccabees and those who fought with them. These blessings are symbolized by three years (to the day) of leap years.

Thus,

383 1/3 days in a normal Jewish leap year

X 3

1,150 days (1/2 of 2,300 "*evenings* (and) *mornings*")

It took three years to the day for the wrath of God to have ended when the Gentiles sacrificed upon a pagan altar that was placed upon the altar of God. That action was the abomination that had caused desolation then.

But, as we shall now see, the abomination that caused the desolation of the Second Temple and of the city of Jerusalem in A.D. 70 was not placed by the Gentiles, but by the Jews themselves!

In *Wars*, II. XIX. 4, Josephus writes of the Roman general, Cestius, who on the 30th of Hyperbereteus [Tishri] of A.D. 66, brought his troops into Jerusalem. On this occasion the Jews "*retreated into the inner part of the city, and into the temple.*"

In *Wars*, II. XIX. 5, we read,

> *Thus did the Romans make their attack against the wall for five days, but to no purpose. But on the next day, Cestius took a great many of his choicest men, and with them the archers, and attempted to break into the temple at the northern quarter of it; but the Jews beat them off from the cloisters, and repulsed them several times when they were gotten near to the wall, till at length the multitude of the darts cut them off, and made them retire...*

In the above passage, then, we see that the Jews were a total of six days within the temple. They had no sewage facilities there, of course, so what did they do when they needed to eliminate their bodily fecal material? In Daniel 9:27, we read in the King James Version, "...*and for the overspreading of abominations he shall make it desolate.*" But the Hebrew word translated, "*overspreading*" is "*kahnahph,*" which literally means "*wing.*" The LXX, which was translated about 280 B.C., took it to refer to the temple and translated this phrase, "...*and on the temple shall be the abomination of desolations.*"

The *Concordant Literal Old Testament* here reads, "...*on a wing of the sanctuary shall be desolating abominations...*" This seems to express the correct meaning of the phrase.

George Lamsa, who was raised in an Aramaic culture and who spoke the Aramaic language, in his commentary, *Gospel Light* (A.J. Holman Co., Philadelphia, pg. 132), writes thus in his comments on Matthew 24:15:

> *When a city is besieged by an invading army its inhabitants take
> refuge in the citadel, churches and other holy places because they offer
> the best protection from the enemy... During the siege, conditions
> grow worse and hardships increase. The most serious situation is
> caused by the filth and refuse which accumulate in the streets and in
> the holy places where people have taken refuge...During war time, this
> refuse stands piled high on street corners, courtyards and around holy
> places, resulting in disease and plague...Jesus had this in mind in his
> reference to "the sign of the abomination of desolation accumulating
> in the holy place." ...Jesus predicted the fall of Jerusalem was
> near...Even the sacred shrines which the Jews so highly revered were to
> be defiled by themselves and later disgraced by an invading army.
> These predictions actually happened when the city fell before Titus in
> A.D. 70.*

So in the Hebrew months of Tishri and Marchesvan, about October or
November of A.D. 66, the Jews themselves defiled the temple, fulfilling the
words of Jesus, "*When ye therefore shall see the abomination of desolation,
spoken of by Daniel the prophet, stand in the holy place...*" God's wrath for
the Jews' defilement would not be ending when Jerusalem was destroyed,
and when the temple was burned and thrown down. His wrath would last
1,290 days longer. This 1,290 days signified the shortened days of a 44-
month period. The shortest possible Jewish year was 352 days, and so that
is the figure that must be used here when God's displeasure with the Jews
is at its greatest. This 1,290-day period is figured then as follows:

352 days in the shortest possible Hebrew year

x 3 years

1,056 days in three shortened Hebrew years, and with no leap years
at all, a total of 36 months.

+176 days; 1/2 of 352 days; no leap year; six months added, for a
total now of 42 months.

1,232 days of 3 1/2 shortened years.

29 days. A 352-day year would have 8 29-day months,

29 Days, and 4 30-day months, so two shortened months in a
row, of 29 days, was possible.

1,290 days. Forty-four shortened months. This was the time period
between the destruction of the temple, and of the altar of
burnt offering, to the fall of Masada on the 15th of Nisan,
A.D. 74.

The final verse of this study is Daniel 12:12, which reads, "*Blessed is he that waiteth, and cometh to the thousand three hundred and five and thirty days.*"

The 1,335 days is 45 days longer than the 1,290 days. This would indicate a 30-day month, and a half of a 30-day month. God's blessing has come to those who have survived. Those who are here called "*blessed*" were those referred to in Daniel 12:1, "*...and at that time thy people shall be delivered, every one that shall be found written in the book.*"

These "*blessed*" ones of Daniel 12:12 are also "*the 144,000*" of Revelation 7:4 and of Revelation 14:1,3. They are also the "*woman clothed with the sun*" of Revelation 12:1.

They are "*blessed*" because they have trusted in Jesus in that they fled Jerusalem when He told them to do so (Matthew 24:16; Mark 13:14; Luke 21:20,-21). They are "*blessed*" because after the fall of Masada, they returned to Jerusalem, to "*the mount Sion*" (Revelation 14:1), and "*the Lamb*" stood there with them. They are "*blessed*" because the 1,290 shortened days for those unbelieving Jews who stayed in Jerusalem and died there are over, and now the lengthened days for them have returned.

NOTE: The temple in Jerusalem was destroyed on the ninth of Ab, A.D. 70, according to the rabbis, and on the tenth of Ab, A.D. 70, according to Josephus (*Wars*, VI. IV. 5). The brazen altar, or altar of burnt offering, was still standing when the temple was burning (*Wars*, VI. IV. 6). It is not known whether the altar of burnt offering was destroyed on that day or not, but because of the intense heat which burnt the temple, the altar may have melted or partially melted, on that same day, and removed a few days later

We present, then, these figures:

From 10 Ab, A.D. 70 to 10 Ab, A.D. 71 is...	352	days
From 10 Ab, A.D. 71 to 10 Ab, A.D. 72 is...	352	days
From 10 Ab, A.D. 72 to 10 Ab, A.D. 73 is...	352	days
From 10 Ab, A.D. 73 to 10 Shevat, A.D. 74 is...	176	days
From 10 Shevat, A.D. 74 to 10 Nisan, A.D. 74 is...	58	days
	1,290	days

But 10 Nisan, A.D. 74 is not 15 Nisan, A.D. 74 the day of the fall of Masada—and our figures would be 1,295 days if we went to 15 Nisan, A.D. 74; that is five days too many.

In this matter we have no history to help us. We do not know the date on which the altar of burnt offering was "*taken away*," or removed! We must here *"walk by faith, not by sight"* (2 Corinthians 5:7). We assert on the basis of Daniel 12:11 that the altar of burnt offering, on which the *"daily sacrifice"* was offered, was *"taken away"* on 15 Ab, A.D. 70, and thus the 1,290 days met the prophetic requirements. An offering could be made without a temple, but it could not be made without an altar as the altar was commanded for this purpose (Exodus 27:1-8; 38:1-7). Therefore, the *"daily sacrifice"* was *"taken away"* only when the altar of burnt offering was—on 15 Ab, A.D. 70.

For many years history books and encyclopedias have given the date for the fall of Masada as 73 AD. However, Emil Schurer in his work, *The History of the Jewish People in the Age of Jesus Christ,* pg. 515, relates the following:

> *Two new inscriptions show clearly that he* (L. Flavius Silva) *cannot have become legatus of Judea before* A.D. *73, and consequently that the fall of Masada must belong in spring* A.D. *74, at the earliest.*

Another quotation from Emil Schurer's above mentioned work states,

> *Meanwhile Lucilius Bassus died, and it fell to his successor, Flavius Silva, to capture Masada.*

> *When Eleazar saw that there was no longer any hope of resisting the assault, he addressed the garrison, asking them first to kill their own families, and then one another. This was done. When the Romans entered, they discovered with horror that no work remained for them to do. Thus the last bulwark of the revolt was conquered, in April of probably* A.D. *74. (pgs. 512-513)*

Footnote 139 adds,

> *According to Wars, VII. 9. 1 (401), the mass suicide of the garrison of Masada took place on 15 Xanthicus* (Nisan, March/April), *i.e. on the feast of Passover. The year is not mentioned. But since just prior to this, VII. 7. 1 (219), there is a reference to the fourth year of Vespasian, it has always been thought that the conquest of Masada must have occurred in the spring of* A.D. *73. But two new inscriptions giving the career of Flavius Silva show that he can not have gone as legatus to Judea before* A.D. *73. (pg. 513)*

The phrases in Daniel 12:7, referring to *"a time, times, and an half"* and *"when he shall have accomplished to scatter the power of the holy people,"* were a reference to the length of time (3 1/2 years), and the results of the Roman-Jewish War of A.D. 66-70. Daniel's question in Daniel 12:8, *"O my Lord, what shall be after these things?"* shows clearly that he had in mind the events after the defeat of the Jews in that war. The angel's answer fit

Daniel's question, and gave the ending of God's wrath at Masada and His blessing after that on the people who had been delivered.

In the phrase in Daniel 12:11, "...*and the abomination that maketh desolate set up*," the words "*set up*" are from the Hebrew word, *nathan*. *Nathan* is translated by 69 different words or phrases in the King James Version.

The most numerous of these translations are:

deliver	156 times	make	108 times
give	1023	set (forth)	101

Young's Literal Translation of the Bible renders *nathan* here as "*giving out*." This gives a completely different view of this matter. When something is "*set up*," it is beginning; whereas "*giving out*" would indicate its end.

The meaning here seems to be that from the time the daily sacrifice is taken away, until the total end of the desolation brought about by a horrible abomination, will be 1,290 days.

The calculation of a lunar leap year at 383 1/3 days in Daniel's time would be even more accurate than it appears, since the earth's rotation is slowing now at the rate of 1.7 seconds per year. *At the present rate* of the slowing of the earth, it would have rotated at an hour and ten minutes faster in Daniel's time. However, in the past the rate of slowing is believed to have been faster.

The phrase "*redeeming the time*" (Ephesians 5:16; Colossians 4:5) is related to the concept of the shortening of days. Repentance would buy back the time.

The campaigns of Judas Maccabaeus against the Syrian armies of Antiochus Epiphanes are given in 1 Maccabees. Judas Maccabaeus and his forces went from victory to victory until the temple in Jerusalem was cleansed. The following data from 1 Maccabees is also in the *Antiquities of the Jews*, by Josephus, XII. VII. 1-6.

1 Maccabees	Against Syrian general
3:10-12	Apollonius
3:13-24	Seron
4:1-15	Gorgias
4:26-35	Lysias

Josephus, in telling about the desolation of the temple for three years, states (*Ant.* XII. VII. 6), "*And this desolation came to pass according to the prophecy of Daniel, which was given four hundred and eight years before,*" so Josephus saw Daniel 8:13-14, and other passages as referring to this time period.

Because the Jews, at the time of the destruction of Jerusalem, had no fixed calendar, each new month began when the new moon became visible. The new moon's appearance was confirmed by witnesses before the Sanhedrin in Jerusalem. The new month was then "*sanctified*" by the Sanhedrin, and messengers were sent out to announce the beginning of the new month.

And because the Sanhedrin was destroyed with the fall of Jerusalem, no means were left to the Jewish people to declare new months, nor to intercalate a thirteenth month. Thus, in the time period to which the 1,290 days of Daniel 12:11 applies, no leap year would have been possible and, at least in that sense, a shortened year was literally, as well as figuratively, true.

Josephus records that on "*the seventeenth day of Panemus [Tamuz], the sacrifice called 'the Daily Sacrifice' had failed, and had not been offered to God for want of men to offer it....*" (*Wars*, VI. II. 1) But the phrase in Daniel 12:11, "*...the daily sacrifice* **shall be taken away**," seems to imply more than this. The Hebrew word *sur*, which is translated here "*taken away*," means "*to be turned aside*," and is also translated by such words and phrases as the following in the King James Version:

depart   73

be removed   5

The thought here is to take, or remove, to another place. This did not happen when the daily sacrifice failed on 17 Tamuz, A.D. 70. At that point neither the sacrifices, nor the temple, nor the altar of burnt offering had been taken, or removed, anywhere. At that point in time the necessary priests for officiating at the daily sacrifice had been killed, but the physical means for continuing the daily sacrifices were still intact.

The rabbis taught that a sacrifice could take place without the temple, but not without the altar. Thus, when the altar of burnt offering was removed, "*the daily sacrifice*" was fully "*taken away.*"

The Abomination
of Desolation

In a previous chapter on "Understanding Applicable Old Testament Passages," we stated that "Matthew 24:1-29, Mark 13:1-25, Luke 21:5-26, and Revelation 6–9 all refer to the events preceding the destruction of Jerusalem, and to the destruction of Jerusalem itself." Jesus describes in these passages from the Gospels a turbulent time in Jewish history. He tells of false Messiahs, wars and rumors of wars, famines and pestilences and earthquakes—and for those who believe in Him, they must suffer persecution and betrayal.

At this particular time in Jewish history, Messianic expectations were in the air. Much of this was from the prophet Daniel. He (9:24-27) had prophesied the coming of the Messiah 483 years from the decree of Cyrus (2 Chronicles 36:22-23; Ezra 1:1-4; Isaiah 44:28; 45:13). Jesus, in referring to this time period—*the only time period in Scripture to which His words could refer*—announced, "*The time is fulfilled, and the kingdom of God is at hand: repent ye, and believe the gospel.*" (Mark 1:15).

Others had capitalized on this expectation of the Messiah. The Herodians claimed that Herod, because he was the ruler, must be the Messiah. An

"*Egyptian*" who "*made an uproar*" (Acts 21:38; Josephus, *Antiquities*, XX. VIII. 6.) claimed to be God's prophet, and Josephus writes that when the Romans had surrounded Jerusalem, there were "*a great number of false prophets*" (*Wars*, VI. V. 2).

Judea was struck with famine in the reign of Claudius (Acts 11:28-29; Josephus, *Antiquities*, XX. II. 5), and wars and tumults were constant throughout this entire period.

Daniel had often referred to the time of the conclusion of his prophecy as "*the time of the end.*" This was the time of the coming of the Messiah and of the destruction of Jerusalem, and also the times that were nearing those events. It was also the time for the appearance of the kingdom of God (Daniel 2:34-35,44-45; 7:13-14,18,22,27). The early church definitely believed that they were living in the last times. Below are passages from Daniel and from the epistles indicating these things.

Daniel	Epistles
"*…even to the time of the end*" (11:35).	"*I say, brethren, the time is short*" (1 Corinthians 7:29).
"*…at the time of the end*" (11:40).	"*…upon whom the ends of the world are come*" (1 Corinthians 10:11).
"*…even to the time of the end*" (12:4).	"*Hath in these last days…*" (Hebrews 1:2).
"*How long shall it be to the end of these wonders?*" (12:6).	"*…but now once in the end of the world*" (Hebrews 9:26).
"*O my Lord, what shall be the end of these things?*" (12:8).	"*But the end of all things is at hand…*" (1 Peter 4:7).
"*Go thy way, Daniel: for the words are closed up and sealed till the time of the end*" (12:9).	"*Little children, it is the last time*" (1 John 2:18).

These events would have come as prophesied, except that repentance threw them far into the future. Domitian, the prophesied beast (Revelation 17:11), began his reign in A.D. 81 over the Roman Empire. His reign ended with his violent death on September 18, A.D. 96. Because his reign was to have ended with the return of Jesus (Revelation 19:11-20), this seems to indicate that the second coming of Jesus would have been about A.D. 96.

But how are we to understand the following parallel passages from Matthew (24:15-21), Mark (13:14-19), and Luke (21:20-24), which tell of the *sign* by which Jewish followers of Jesus would know that they were to leave Jerusalem and Judea.

Matthew 24:15-21	Mark 13:14-19	Luke 21:20-24
15 When ye therefore shall see the **abomination of desolation**, spoken of by Daniel the prophet, stand in the holy place (whoso readeth, let him understand;) Then let them which be in Judea flee into the mountains; Let him which is on the housetop not come down to take anything out of the house: Neither let him which is in the field return back to take his clothes.	14 But when ye shall see the **abomination of desolation** spoken of by Daniel the prophet, where it ought not, (let him that readeth understand,) then let them that be in Judea flee to the standing mountains: And let him that is on the housetop not go down into the house, neither enter therein, to take anything out of his house: And let him that is in the field not turn back again for to take up his garment.	20 And when ye shall see **Jerusalem compassed with armies**, then know that the desolation thereof is nigh. Then let them which are in Judea flee to the mountains; and let them which are in the midst of it depart out; and let not them that are in the countries enter thereinto.
19 And woe unto them that are with child, and to them that give suck in those days!	17 But woe to them that are with child, and to them that give suck in those days!	22 For these be the days of vengeance, that all things which are written may be fulfilled.
20 But pray ye that your flight be not in the winter, neither on the sabbath day:	18 And pray ye that your flight be not in the winter.	23 But woe unto them that are with child, and to them that give suck, in those days! for there shall be great distress in the land, and wrath upon this people.
21 For then shall be great tribulation, such as was not since the beginning of the world to this time, no, nor ever shall be.	19 For in those days shall be affliction, such as was not from the beginning of the creation which God created unto this time, neither shall be.	24 And they shall fall by the edge of the sword, and shall be led away captive into all nations; and Jerusalem shall be trodden down of the Gentiles, until the times of the Gentiles be fulfilled.

As we can see from the above passages, that which Luke (21:20) refers to as "*Jerusalem compassed with armies*" is in Matthew 24:15 and Mark 13:14 referred to as "*the abomination of desolation spoken of by Daniel the prophet.*" From this we see a very close connection between "*Jerusalem compassed with armies*" and the "*abomination of desolation.*" Clearly, then, "*the abomination of desolation*[152]" occurred when Jerusalem was surrounded with armies.

Jerusalem was compassed, or surrounded, with armies by the Roman general Cestius in A.D. 66. Cestius then withdrew his armies from Jerusalem "*without any reason in the world*" (*Wars*. II. XIX. 7). At this time the Jewish followers of Jesus departed en masse from Jerusalem, and went to Pella, beyond the Jordan River. It was at the time when the Roman general Cestius surrounded Jerusalem that the "*abomination of desolation*" occurred. It was so understood by the early Jerusalem Jews who believed in Jesus, and because they correctly understood this, their lives were spared in the Jewish-Roman War of A.D. 66 to 70.

Some have thought that the "*abomination of desolation*" was the idolatrous insignia on the Roman standards being brought into the temple. But this is impossible, since the "*abomination of desolation*" was to "*stand in the holy place*"—a part of the temple where the priests ministered (Matthew 24:15). This bringing of Roman standards, or ensigns, into the holy place did not occur until "*the burning of the holy house*" (the temple) (Josephus, *Wars*. VI. VI. 1), at the end of the Jewish-Roman War, and much too late for any surviving Jewish followers of Jesus to have fled anywhere. "*The holy place*" was a part of the temple proper, and it was enclosed and hidden from public view. Perhaps this will give us a hint of things occurring there.

In *Gospel Light*, by George Lamsa, we read the following in a section discussing the "Abomination of Desolation."

> When a city is besieged by an invading army its inhabitants take refuge in the citadel, churches and other holy places because they offer the best protection from the enemy. From these strategic points, the warriors defend the city against the invading army for months or even for years. During the siege the inhabitants cannot go out nor can any enter. The water supply is cut off and wells are dug to furnish water for a

---

152. In scripture, many things are referred to as "*abominations*." An abomination would be anything so horrid and detestable that one would be astounded by it. Whenever the early followers of Jesus were astounded by a most horrid evil standing in the holy place of the temple, they were to leave Jerusalem. Some of the things said to be abominations were: the worshiping of idols (2 Chronicles 15:8; Jeremiah 44:3,4); the casting of filth upon a person (Nahum 3:6); the eating of unclean animals (Leviticus 11: 11-20); a false balance (Proverbs 11:1); lying lips (Proverbs 12:22); homosexuality (Leviticus 18:22) and others. Solomon lists seven abominations (Proverbs 6:16-19).

famine-stricken population. During the siege, conditions grow worse and hardships increase. The most serious situation is caused by the filth and refuse which accumulate in the streets and in the holy places where people have taken refuge. Eastern cities do not now have sewers. The refuse is taken out weekly and thrown into the fields for fertilizing. During wartime, this refuse stands piled high on street corners, court-yards and around holy places, resulting in disease and plague.

Jesus had this in mind in his reference to "the sign of the abomination of desolation accumulating in the holy place." Jesus predicted the fall of Jerusalem was near. The historic city and its holy places were doomed. It was to be besieged and captured by Roman forces and the temple destroyed. Even the sacred shrines, which the Jews so highly revered, were to be defiled by themselves and later disgraced by an invading army. These predictions actually happened when the city fell before Titus in A.D. 70.

Lamsa's view of human excrement accumulating in the temple is supported by his translation of Matthew 24:15 and Mark 13:14, which uses the word "*accumulating*" rather than "*standing*." Thus his rendering of Matthew 24:15 from the Aramaic is:

When you see the sign of uncleanness and desolation, as spoken by the prophet Daniel, accumulating in the holy place (whoever reads will understand)...

This view of human waste accumulating in the holy place of the temple is in accord with what we read in Josephus (*Wars*. II. XIX. 4-5), in regard to the Jewish-Roman War that began in A.D. 66. After we read that the Roman general Cestius "*put the Jews to flight and pursued them to Jerusalem*," we have the following testimony that the "*seditious*," or militant Jews, retreated into the temple. This is important, because this is the place and also the time when we would have to expect the "*abomination of desolation*" to occur.

*Now as for the people, they were kept under by the seditious; but the seditious themselves were greatly affrighted at the good order of the Romans, and retired from the suburbs, and retreated into the inner part of the city, and **into the temple**.*

But how long were they in the temple? Would it have been long enough for this horrible abomination to occur?

*Thus did the Romans make their attack against the wall for **five days**, but to no purpose. But on the **next day** (six days now), Cestius took a great many of his choicest men, and with them the archers, and **attempted to break into the temple** at the northern quarter of it; but the Jews beat them off from the cloisters (of the temple), and repulsed them several times when they were gotten near to the wall.*

Here then, are the "*seditious*," the militant Jews, at least six days in the temple—without sewage facilities to care for their bodily waste. No wonder Matthew and Mark add the words "*whoso readeth let him understand*," as though they were saying, "*we trust we will not need to be more explicit than this.*"

An additional thought on this matter comes to us from Deuteronomy 23:12-14.

> *Thou shalt have a place also without the camp, whither thou shalt go forth abroad: And thou shalt have a paddle upon thy weapon; and it shall be, when thou wilt ease thyself abroad, thou shalt dig therewith, and shalt turn back and cover that which cometh from thee: For the Lord thy God walketh in the midst of thy camp, to deliver thee, and to give up thine enemies before thee; therefore shall thy camp be holy: that he see no unclean thing in thee, and turn away from thee.*

The above verses indicate that God would "*turn away*" from His covenant people if He should see human waste lying about the camp. How much more of an abomination this would be defiling the very holy place in the temple.

But how are we to understand the phrase "*spoken of by Daniel the prophet*" (Matthew 24:15; Mark 13:14)?

Three passages in Daniel 9:27; 11:31; 12:11 refer to this. Daniel 11:31, however, was a prophecy of the defiling of the temple by Antiochus Epiphanes of Syria, in 167 B.C. In his defilement, Antiochus Epiphanes had built an altar upon God's altar and "*slew swine upon it.*" (*Ant.* XII. V. 4). This action was termed in 1 Maccabees 1:54, "*the abomination of desolation*," but because there were many abominations and because this was long before Jesus spoke of that which was future in His time, this passage does not concern us here.

Daniel 9:27 and Daniel 12:11 are placed below for our comparison.

Daniel 9:27

"*And he* (the Messiah) *shall confirm the covenant with many for one week* (one seven-year period): *and in the midst of the week he shall cause the sacrifice and the oblation to cease,* **and for the overspreading of abominations he shall make it desolate,** *even until the consummation, and that determined shall be poured upon the desolate.*"

Daniel 12:11

"*And from the time that the daily sacrifice shall be taken away,* **and the abomination that maketh desolate** *set up, there shall be a thousand two hundred and ninety days.*"

The temple is not directly mentioned in either of the above passages, but it is assumed in the references to sacrifices in both passages, and Jesus so understood it in His reference to "*the holy place*" (Matthew 24:15). The phrase "*the overspreading of abominations*" (Daniel 9:27) aptly pictures the spreading of human waste in the holy place of the temple.

Also, neither passage (9:27 nor 12:11) in the King James Version uses the specific phrase "*the abomination of desolation*," though this phrase does appear in the Greek Septuagint in Daniel 12:11. Some English translations, such as the *Concordant Literal Old Testament* and *The New English Bible*, also use the phrase "*the abomination of desolation*" in Daniel 12:11.

We conclude this study with two quotes from Josephus. Josephus, incidentally, was born in A.D. 37 or 38 into a priestly family. He became a priest, himself, and also a Pharisee, and thus would have known the way in which the Jews interpreted the very passages that we have been discussing.

> *...yet did these prophets foretell many things...for there was a certain ancient oracle* (or prophecy, Daniel's no doubt) *of those men, that the city should be taken, and the sanctuary burnt, by right of war, when a sedition should invade the Jews, and **their own hand should pollute the temple of God**. Now while these zealots did not disbelieve these predictions, they made themselves the instruments of their accomplishment* (*Wars*. IV. VI. 3)

> *In the very same manner Daniel also wrote concerning the Roman government, and that our country should be made desolate by them* (*Ant*. X. XI. 7).

Finally, if Jesus viewed Daniel 9:27 and 12:11 as referring to the time of the Jewish-Roman War of A.D. 66–70, then many modern books dealing with the prophecies of Daniel have been quite mistaken. Modern commentators have generally broken off the last week (seven-year period) of Daniel and thrown it far into the future. They also have claimed that Daniel 11:36 through Daniel 12:13 were future because, as they have claimed, there was nothing in history to which these prophecies could refer. But are these claims valid? Our next appendix will deal with these matters and will show that there was no break in Daniel's prophecies, but that they are prewritten history covering the time of Daniel until the destruction of Jerusalem in A.D. 70.

Appendix C

Fulfillments of Daniel's Prophecies

The prophecies of Revelation are based upon the prophecies of Daniel. The two books are so closely related that they could be called Revelation I and Revelation II. This is because Revelation picks up the prophetic themes of Daniel and expands upon them. (See section in Introduction on "Themes Common to Daniel and Revelation.")

Revelation especially expands on the themes of Daniel, such as the destruction of Jerusalem (Daniel 9:26; 12:1, 6, 7; Revelation 6:1-8; 8:7–9:19), which occurred in A.D. 70, and the destruction of Rome (Daniel 2:40-45; 7:7-8,11,19-27; Revelation 6:12-17; 11:3-13; 14:8; 14:17-20; 16:1-11,19; 17:1–18:23), which is yet future because of a great repentance as explained in the chapter "Why God Spared Rome."

The purpose of the following study is to show that the historical fulfillment of Daniel 11 and 12 covers major events affecting the Jews from the time of Cyrus the Great through the reign of Herod the Great, and the Roman-Jewish War, of A.D. 66-70 to the destruction of the last Jewish holdouts at Masada (see Appendix A on "The Use of Symbolic Numbers in Daniel"), and finally, to the blessing on those who waited until 45 days after the destruction at Masada, that is, the blessing of returning to Jerusalem by the Jerusalem Jews who believed in Jesus (Daniel 12:1c,12; Revelation 14:1).

Daniel 11:1 Also I in the first year of Darius the Mede, even I, stood to confirm and to strengthen him.

The four kings referred to in Daniel 11:2 are Cyrus the Great; Cambyses, the son of Cyrus; Darius I Hystaspes; and Xerxes.

Darius the Mede, or Astyges, had taken Babylon in 538 B.C. by usual chronology, and had reigned two years. Then Cyrus reigned for nine years. The usual chronology is about 80 years too long in the Persian period, and I am reluctant to give it.

2 And now will I shew thee the truth. Behold, there shall stand up three kings in Persia;

Cambyses (the Ahasuerus of Ezra 4:6) reigned seven years. Darius I Hystaspes (Ezra 4:5-24; 5:5, 6; 6:1,12,14-15; 7:1-26; the Artaxerxes in Nehemiah 2:1; 5:14; 13:6; and the Ahasuerus of the Book of Esther) reigned 35 years. He was the first king to invade Greece, but was defeated at the battle of Marathon.

Xerxes reigned 21 years. He also was defeated by the Greeks.

and the fourth shall be far richer than they all: and by his strength through his riches he shall stir up all against the realm of Grecia.

This *"mighty king"* was Alexander the Great, who began his invasion of the Persian empire in 336 B.C. The chronology of the Greek empire period and on may be considered reliable.

3 And a mighty king shall stand up, that shall rule with great dominion, and do according to his will.

4 And when he shall stand up, his kingdom shall be broken, and shall be divided toward the four winds of heaven; and not to his posterity, nor

After the death of Alexander the Great, his kingdom was divided into four parts. His son, Alexander Aegus, was never able to take the throne, as he and his mother Roxana were slain by Cassander. Alexander's empire, after being divided into four parts, was ruled by Alexander's four generals, who each ruled one of the four parts. These

according to his dominion which he ruled: for his kingdom shall be plucked up, even for others beside those.

four generals were Seleucus, Cassander, Lysimachus, and Ptolemy.

Others ruled minor parts of the original empire.

5 And the king of the south shall be strong, and one of his princes; and he shall be strong above him, and have dominion; his dominion shall be a great dominion.

"*The king of the south*" referred to Ptolemy I. He was the founder of the Egyptian part of the Greek empire, which continued from 323 to 30 B.C., when Rome took over Egypt.

6 And in the end of years they shall join themselves together; for the king's daughter of the south shall come to the king of the north to make an agreement: but she shall not retain the power of the arm; neither shall he stand, nor his arm: but she shall be given up, and they that brought her, and he that begat her, and he that strengthened her in these times.

"*...in the end of years.*" Literally, "*after some years*," that is, about 65 years.

The king of the south (Egypt), and the king of the north (Syria), having been in war, agreed to terminate it in 250 B.C. Berenice, the daughter of Ptolemy II Philadelphus, married Antiochus II Theos, king of Syria, on condition that Antiochus would put away his wife, Laodice, and her children, which he did. Later, Antiochus recalled Laodice and her children, but she caused him to be poisoned, and Berenice to be murdered, and then placed her own son, Callinicus (Seleucus II) upon the throne.

7 But out of a branch of her roots shall one stand up in his estate, which shall come with an army, and shall enter into the

The "*branch of her roots*" was Berenice's brother, Ptolemy III, who had just succeeded to the Egyptian throne. He came with an army against Seleucus II, son of Laodice, and defeated him.

fortress of the king of the north, and shall deal against them, and shall prevail:

8 And shall also carry captives into Egypt their gods, with their princes, and with their precious vessels of silver and of gold; and he shall continue more years than the king of the north.

Berenice's brother, Ptolemy III, plundered Seleucia, Susa, and Babylonia to the borders of India. He took many captives back to Egypt, and also took back the Egyptian gods that Cambyses, King of Persia, took from Egypt 300 years before. For these reasons, the Egyptians called him Ptolemy Euergetes; Euergetes meaning benefactor.

Seleucus II died due to falling from a horse. Ptolemy III lived four or five years longer.

9 So the king of the south shall come into his kingdom, and shall return into his own land.

10 But his sons shall be stirred up, and shall assemble a multitude of great forces: and one shall certainly come, and overflow, and pass through: then shall he return, and be stirred up, even to his fortress.

Ptolemy III invaded the kingdom of Seleucus II a second time, but having heard of a rebellion in Egypt, he returned to Egypt to suppress it. Otherwise, he would have completely destroyed Syria. The sons of Seleucus II were Seleucus III and Antiochus III, called the Great. Seleucus III assembled a great multitude of forces to recover his father's dominions, but was poisoned by two of his own generals after a reign of two years. His brother, Antiochus III, was then proclaimed king. He retook Seleucia, and regained Syria, even to the borders of Egypt.

11 And the king of the south shall be moved with choler (or, fury), and shall come forth and fight with him, even with the king of the north: and he shall set forth a great multitude; but the multitude shall be given into his hand.

Ptolemy Philopater, "Lover of Father," "*the king of the south*," reigned over Egypt, 221–204 B.C. Antiochus III the Great declared war on him about 219 B.C. Ptolemy Philopater defeated Antiochus in the battle of Raphia near Gaza, 217 B.C.

12 And when he hath taken away the multitude, his heart shall be lifted up; and he shall cast down many ten thousands: but he shall not be strengthened by it.	Ptolemy Philopater became greatly exalted by destroying many in his own land, especially the Jews. He was not strengthened by his victories, as his kingdom was in constant decline due to misrule by subordinates who were favorites of his.
13 For the king of the north shall return, and shall set forth a multitude greater than the former, and shall certainly come after certain years with a great army and with much riches.	Antiochus the Great, who reigned over Syria 233–187 B.C., returned to fight the Egyptians 14 years after his defeat at Raphia, with a greater army than before, and with many riches from his campaign to restore the eastern parts of his empire.
14 And in those times there shall many stand up against the king of the south: also the robbers of thy people shall exalt themselves to establish the vision; but they shall fall.	The "*robbers of thy people*," or "*the sons of breaching of your people*," refer to the Jews who rejected their religion, and sided first with Egypt, and then with Syria, in seeking to help fulfill the prophecy of liberating Judea. They fell under the wrath of the Egyptians, who, under their general, Scopas, subdued Palestine.
15 So the king of the north shall come, and cast up a mount, and take the most fenced cities: and the arms of the south shall not withstand, neither his chosen people, neither shall there be any strength to withstand.	Antiochus the Great and Philip of Macedonia united in conquering Egypt in 198 B.C. The "*king of the south*" here is Ptolemy V, called Epiphanes, the Illustrious. Egypt was defeated, and Palestine was again under the Seleucids. (Rome, for the first time, interfered to make Antiochus surrender his conquests. Not daring to disobey Rome, Antiochus made peace with Ptolemy, and betrothed to him his daughter, Cleopatra, 193 B.C.) Antiochus the Great came to recover Judea. He defeated Scopas, taking several fenced cities, and none of the Egyptian generals were able to oppose him.

16 But he that cometh against him shall do according to his own will, and none shall stand before him: and he shall stand in the glorious land, which by his hand shall be consumed.

Antiochus the Great came against Ptolemy V and did as he pleased in his conquests. At first, Antiochus the Great showed great favor to the Jews who helped supply him with provisions and helped him in reducing the garrison of Scopas. He brought back the dispersed and freed the priests from all tribute. But in time Judea was reduced to poverty by his long wars.

17 He shall also set his face to enter with the strength of his whole kingdom, and upright ones with him; thus shall he do: and he shall give him the daughter of women, corrupting her: but she shall not stand on his side, neither be for him.

Antiochus the Great intended to march into Egypt, but chose instead to make a covenant of peace with Ptolemy, giving him his own daughter, Cleopatra.

Antiochus acted as if he were influenced by nothing but upright views in his covenant with Ptolemy. The phrase *"daughter of women"* refers to the beauty of Cleopatra. Antiochus planned to corrupt Cleopatra, causing her to be a snare to Ptolemy, but instead she helped her husband and put him on guard against her father.

18 After this shall he turn his face unto the isles, and shall take many: but a prince for his own behalf shall cause the reproach offered by him to cease; without his own reproach he shall cause it to turn upon him.

After making peace with Egypt, Antiochus the Great fitted out a great fleet of ships. He subdued most of the maritime places on the Mediterranean Sea and took many islands, including Rhodes, Samos, Colophon, and others. The Romans defeated Antiochus in Asia Minor, causing him to abandon much of the land he had taken. Thus *"the reproach"* Antiochus planned to cause Rome to suffer was turned on himself.

19 Then he shall turn his face toward the fort of his own land: but he shall stumble and fall, and not be found.

Antiochus the Great turned back to his own fort in Antioch. Obliged to raise 15,000 talents for Rome to pay for the war, he marched into his eastern provinces to exact the unpaid taxes and perished in a war in Luristan, 187 B.C.

20 Then shall stand up in his estate a

The *"raiser of taxes"* who succeeded Antiochus the Great was his son, Seleucus IV, called Philopater,

raiser of taxes in the glory of the kingdom: but within few days he shall be destroyed, neither in anger, nor in battle.	who reigned 187–176 B.C. He was compelled to pay the yearly war indemnity exacted by Rome. To do this, he sent Heliodorus to Jerusalem to rob the temple but as it turned out, he was assassinated by Heliodorus, who wanted to be king.
21 And in his estate shall stand up a vile person, to whom they shall not give the honour of the kingdom: but he shall come in peaceably, and obtain the kingdom by flatteries.	This *"vile person"* refers to Antiochus IV Epiphanes, who reigned from 175–163 B.C. All of verses 21 to 35 refer to this man. The true heir of Seleucus IV was another son, Demetrius, who was being held as a hostage in Rome. This gave Antiochus Epiphanes the opportunity to gain the throne by *"flatteries."* The books of 1 and 2 Maccabees, though not inspired, give historically correct data about Antiochus.
22 And with the arms of a flood shall they be overthrown from before him, and shall be broken; yea, also the prince of the covenant.	With the help of the arms of his supporters, his competitors for the throne were overthrown and broken. The *"prince of the covenant,"* Onias, the high priest, was deposed, and Jason, who had given Antiochus a great sum of money, was installed in Onias' place (2 Maccabees 4:4-10).
23 And after the league made with him he shall work deceitfully: for he shall come up, and shall become strong with a small people.	The *"league,"* or agreement between Antiochus and Jason was broken because Menelaus offered Antiochus more money than Jason had, and Menelaus became the high priest. Thus, Antiochus acted *"deceitfully"* with Jason (2 Maccabees 4:23-29). *"A small* (or, few) *people."*
24 He shall enter peaceably even upon the fattest places of the province; and he shall do that which his fathers have not done, nor his fathers' fathers; he shall scatter among them the prey, and spoil, and	After becoming king, Antiochus Epiphanes laid claim to Coelesyria, Palestine, and Phoenicia, so war broke out between Syria and Egypt. The phrase, *"he shall enter peaceably,"* is better translated in the RSV, *"without warning he shall come into the richest parts of the province."* Antiochus divided the spoils of war, as well as his own revenues, among his friends and subjects. He would even go out into the street and throw handfuls of money to any that would get it.

riches: yea, and he shall forecast his devices against the strong holds, even for a time.

25 And he shall stir up his power and his courage against the king of the south with a great army; and the king of the south shall be stirred up to battle with a very great and mighty army; but he shall not stand: for they shall forecast devices against him.

He strengthened his strongholds on the border of Egypt, and made preparations for war with Egypt. Antiochus Epiphanes made war on Egypt. He was victorious and took Ptolemy Philometer, the ruler of Egypt, as a prisoner. Antiochus then had himself crowned king of Egypt (171–167 B.C.). *"About this time Antiochus undertook his second invasion of Egypt"* (2 Maccabees 5:1).

"They shall forecast devices against him," or *"for plots shall be devised against him."* This refers to Antiochus' plots to turn key men away from Ptolemy. These plots were successful and helped defeat Ptolemy.

26 Yea, they that feed of the portion of his meat shall destroy him, and his army shall overflow: and many shall fall down slain.

They that were fed by Ptolemy were corrupted in their loyalty to him. This was done by Antiochus Epiphanes, and caused the fall of Egypt.

27 And both these kings' hearts shall be to do mischief, and they shall speak lies at one table; but it shall not prosper: for yet the end shall be at the time appointed.

Both Antiochus Epiphanes and Ptolemy Philometer sat at the same table professing love for each other, yet both were planning how to ruin the other. The Romans demanded that Antiochus surrender Egypt, and so his plans did not prosper.

28 Then shall he return into his land with great riches; and his heart shall be against the holy covenant; and he shall do exploits, and return to his own land.

Antiochus, after conquering Egypt, returned to Antioch with the spoils of Egypt. Hearing that there had been great rejoicing in Jerusalem because they heard a report of his death, he *"took Jerusalem by storm, and ordered his troops to cut down without mercy everyone they met and to slaughter those who took refuge in houses"* (2 Maccabees 5:11-12). He also entered the temple, guided by Menelaus, the high priest.

29 At the time appointed he shall return, and come toward the south; but it shall not be as the former, or as the latter.	Antiochus IV Epiphanes again invaded Egypt. The *"former"* refers to his victory over the Egyptian army at Pelusiam, and the *"latter"* to his subjugation of all Egypt, except Alexandria. Josephus records this invasion by Antiochus (*Ant.* XII. V. 2, 3).
30 For the ships of Chittim shall come against him: therefore he shall be grieved, and return, and have indignation against the holy covenant: so shall he do; he shall even return, and have intelligence with them that forsake the holy covenant.	At this point the book of 1 Maccabees begins to describe the wickedness of Antiochus Epiphanes. The *"ships of Chittim"* refers to Roman warships. The Roman legate ordered Antiochus to stop this war, and drew a circle around Antiochus demanding that Antiochus give his answer before stepping out of the circle. Antiochus yielded to the Roman demand when he was only seven miles from Alexandria, Egypt. This is what *"grieved"* him. Turning his fury upon the Jews, he took Jerusalem by storm; slew 40,000 Jews, sold many as slaves; boiled swine's flesh and sprinkled the broth in the temple and on the altar; and broke into the Holy of Holies, taking away the golden vessels and any other treasures, leaving the temple empty. Many Jews forsook Jewish worship and he honored them.
31 And arms shall stand on his part, and they shall pollute the sanctuary of strength, and shall take away the daily sacrifice, and they shall place the abomination that maketh desolate.	*"Burnt-offerings, sacrifices, and libations in the temple were forbidden; sabbath days and feast days were to be profaned; the temple and its ministers were to be defiled. Altars, idols, and sacred precincts were to be established; swine and other unclean beasts to be offered in sacrifice. They must leave their sons uncircumcised; they must make themselves in every way abominable, unclean, and profane, and so forget the law and change all their statutes. The penalty for disobedience was death"* (1 Maccabees 1:45-50).
32 And such as do wickedly against the covenant shall he corrupt by flatteries: but the people that do know their God shall be strong, and do exploits.	Antiochus corrupted Menelaus, the high priest, to act against the Jews who remained loyal to God. *"The people that do know their God shall be strong, and do exploits"*—this refers to the Maccabees, a name given to a Jewish priest, Mattathias, who had five sons: John, Simon, Judas, Eleazar, and Jonathan. These, in succession, led the Jewish

revolt against Antiochus Epiphanes—and eventually won!

33 And they that understand among the people shall instruct many, yet they shall fall by the sword, and by flame, by captivity, and by spoil, many days.

Daniel 11:33-35 refers to the war between the Maccabees and Antiochus Epiphanes. The Maccabees retook Jerusalem, then cleansed and rededicated the temple, three years to the day after Antiochus Epiphanes had polluted it.

Because of the constant warfare many fell, or died, and constant warfare was necessary to gain and preserve their freedom.

34 Now when they shall fall, they shall be holpen (helped) *with a little help: but many shall cleave to them with flatteries.*

Appendix A has material that deals with the Maccabean revolt, and the meaning of the symbolic numbers in Daniel 8:13-14.

35 And some of them of understanding shall fall, to try them, and to purge, and to make them white, even to the time of the end: because it is yet for a time appointed.

36 And the king shall do according to his will; and he shall exalt himself, and magnify himself above every god, and shall speak marvelous things against the God of gods, and shall prosper till the indignation be accomplished: for that that is determined shall be done.

"*The king*" refers to Herod the Great, who reigned as king of the Jews from 37–4 B.C. While Herod built temples to several gods, including Yahweh, he served none of them. He is the one who slaughtered the babes of Bethlehem in order to kill the Messiah (Matthew 2:16). Herod's kingly line would "*prosper*," or continue, until God's "*indignation…accomplished*" against Jerusalem in A.D. 70. The last king of Herod the Great's lineage was Herod Agrippa II, who died without having children, thus ending the kingly line.

37 Neither shall he regard the God of his fathers, nor the desire

Herod the Great was half Jewish and half Edomite. The Edomites were descendents of Esau, Jacob's brother. "*The God of his fathers*" refers to

of women, nor regard any god: for he shall magnify himself above all.

Yahweh. Herod did not regard Him in the way he appointed the high priest, or in the slaughter of the babes of Bethlehem, or in placing a Roman eagle on the gate of the temple in Jerusalem.

38 But in his estate shall he honour the God (god) of forces: and a god whom his fathers knew not shall he honour with gold, and silver, and with precious stones, and pleasant things.

The phrases *"god of forces (fortresses)"* and *"a god whom his fathers knew not"* are both references to Augustus Caesar. Herod continually honored Augustus with such gifts as are described here. He also built a magnificent seaport and named it Caesarea. He rebuilt Samaria, and renamed it Sebaste (a name for Augustus). *"He built many cities which he called Caesareas"* (*Wars*, I. 21. 2).

39 Thus shall he do in the most strong holds with a strange god, whom he shall acknowledge and increase with glory: and he shall cause them to rule over many, and shall divide the land for gain.

"In the most strong holds"—a reference to the Tower of Antonia, which was built next to the temple. It was a fortress, and named after Mark Antony, *"a strange god,"* who, with his wife Cleopatra, ruled over Egypt. *"He shall cause them to rule over many"*—"them" being a reference to Augustus and to Mark Antony. *"Shall divide (or, parcel) the land for gain."* Herod parceled out the land about the strongholds to his friends as an additional security measure. Josephus refers to this (*Ant.* XV, 8, 5).

40 And at the time of the end shall the king of the south push at (or, with) him: and the king of the north shall come against him like a whirlwind, with chariots, and with horsemen, and with many ships; and he shall enter into the countries, and shall overflow and pass over.

"At the time of the end," the final end of the Greek empire, and the beginning of Roman rule in Egypt. The Battle of Actium is here described. *"The king of the south,"* Mark Antony, aided by Cleopatra, made a *"push with"* Herod the Great against Syria, which had become a Roman province. *"The king of the north,"* Augustus Caesar, overwhelmed Antony. *"Ships"* were decisive in this battle. Herod had sent supplies, but no troops. With Mark Antony's defeat, Herod submitted himself to Augustus and changed sides. Augustus accepted Herod's submission.

Augustus entered Judea (*"the glorious land"*). *"Many countries shall be overthrown,"* that is, Augustus took regions of Africa, Upper Cilicia,

41 He shall enter also into the glorious land, and many countries shall be overthrown: but these shall escape out of his hand, even Edom, and Moab, and the chief of the children of Ammon.

Paphlogonia, Thrace, Pontus, Galatia, and other provinces from Illyrica to Armenia.

"*But these shall escape…*" Augustus sent an expedition under Aelius Gallus, in which he was joined by 500 of Herod's guards (*Ant.* XV. 9. 3.), and went into the countries named. As we read in *Ancient Universal History*, Vol XIII, pg. 498, quoted from Philip Mauro, *The Seventy Weeks and the Great Tribulation*, pgs. 154-155, "*The bad success that attended Aelius in this expedition deterred both him and others from any further attempts on that country.*"

42 He shall stretch forth his hand also upon the countries: and the land of Egypt shall not escape.

43 But he shall have power over the treasures of gold and of silver, and over all the precious things of Egypt; and the Libyans and the Ethiopians shall be at his steps.

As Augustus ("*the king of the north*" of verse 40) advanced toward Egypt, he wanted to obtain Cleopatra's treasures of gold, silver, precious stones, ivory, and cinnamon. Cleopatra had removed these treasures to some large monuments she had erected near the temple of Isis, to keep them from Augustus Caesar. However, by a strategy, as related in Plutarch's *Life of Mark Antony*, Augustus was able to obtain all of these.

James Farquharson wrote (quoted from *The Seventy Weeks and the Great Tribulation*, pg. 156) in regard to the phrase, "*and the Libyans and the Ethiopians shall be at his steps,*" "*The conquest of Egypt and maritime Libya laid inner Libya and Ethiopia open to the steps, that is, as we may interpret the term, to the inroads of Augustus Caesar, and his officers, of which advantage was soon taken by them.*" Thus, when Augustus returned from Africa to Rome, Cornelius Balbus completed the conquest of Libya and Ethiopia.

44 But tidings out of the east and out of the north shall trouble him: therefore he shall go forth with great fury to destroy, and utterly to make away many.

The "*him*" and "*he*" of verses 44 and 45 do not refer to Augustus Caesar, but back to Herod the Great. See the comments of Bishop Horsely on Isaiah 18, "*To those to whom the prophetic style in the original is not familiar, but to those only, I think, it will appear strange that a pronoun should refer to an antecedent at so great a distance.*" Thus, this was not unusual in the Hebrew. "*Tidings out of the east"* would refer to *"wise men from the east"* (Matthew 2:1) and *"out of the north"* refers to letters that Antipater, Herod's oldest son, arranged to have written to Herod, informing Herod that two other sons of Herod had spoken strongly to Augustus Caesar against their father (*Ant.* XVII. IV. 3).

45 And he shall plant the tabernacles of his palace between the seas in the glorious holy mountain; yet he shall come to his end, and none shall help him.	*"Between the seas,"* that is, between the Mediterranean and the Dead Sea. *"Yet he shall come to his end, and none shall help him."* Josephus describes Herod's end in detail, giving his diseased condition and the remedies prescribed by his physicians. But nothing helped. (See *Ant.* XVII. VI. 5.)
Daniel 12:1 And at that time shall Michael stand up, the great prince which standeth for the children of thy people: and there shall be a time of trouble, such as never was since there was a nation even to that same time: and at that time thy people shall be delivered, every one that shall be found written in the book.	*"Shall Michael stand up."* This refers to the *"war in heaven"* (Revelation 12:7-12), which took place in May, A.D. 66. (See Chapter 12, "The Woman Clothed With the Sun.") *"A time of trouble, such as never was since there was a nation even to that same time…"* Jesus, in Matthew 24:21 and Mark 13:19 (see also Luke 21:22) referred this to the destruction of Jerusalem in A.D. 70. *"Thy people shall be delivered."* These were those referred to in Revelation as the *"hundred and forty and four thousand of all the tribes of the children of Israel,"* and the *"woman clothed with the sun"* (Revelation 7:4; 12:1). These were the Jerusalem Jews who believed in Jesus, and departed Jerusalem for Pella in A.D. 66.
2 And many of them that sleep in the dust of the earth shall awake, some to everlasting life, and some to shame and everlasting contempt.	Verse 12:2 is often used of the resurrection of the dead, and it may have a secondary reference to that. But the primary reference here is to those *"dead in trespasses and sins"* (Ephesians 2:1,5; see also Colossians 2:13) who were *"quickened,"* or given life through the gospel. See Ephesians 5:14, *"Wherefore he saith, Awake thou that sleepest, and arise from the dead, and Christ shall give thee light."* Also, *"Shake*

thyself from the dust; arise, and sit down, O Jerusalem..." (Isaiah 52:2). *"Some to everlasting life,"* that is, those who received Jesus as their Messiah and were faithful to Him. *"And some to...everlasting contempt,"* that is, those of whom the Epistle of the Hebrews was written, who believed for a while, and then went back to Judaism.

3 And they that be wise shall shine as the brightness of the firmament; and they that turn many to righteousness as the stars for ever and ever.

"They that be wise," as in Proverbs 11:30, *"he that winneth souls is wise."* This verse is on the same subject as the previous one, but is for the one who is used of Jesus in soul-winning.

4 But thou, O Daniel, shut up the words, and seal the book, even to the time of the end: many shall run to and fro, and knowledge (or, evil) shall be increased.

See Concordant Version[153], *"...when many will swerve as evil will increase."* Josephus (*Wars*, V. X. 5.) wrote, *"It is impossible to go distinctly over every instance of these men's iniquity. I shall, therefore, speak my mind here at once briefly: That neither did any other city suffer such miseries, nor did any age ever breed a generation more fruitful in wickedness than this was, from the beginning of the world."* Josephus, in the above quote, was referring to the Jews at the time of the destruction of Jerusalem in A.D. 70.

Dr. Ginsburg, who published an edition of the Hebrew text, suggested that we read "evil" instead of "knowledge" here in Daniel 12:4. A late edition of the Septuagint reads "adikia" or "injustice." The reason for this suggestion is that "do," the stem of the word "knowledge" in Hebrew, is nearly identical to "ro," the stem of the word "evil."

5 Then I Daniel looked, and, behold, there stood other two, the one on this side of

"How long shall it be to the end of these wonders?," that is, to the end of the events given in Daniel 12:1. In that verse, *"shall Michael stand up,"* *"there shall be a time of trouble,"* and *"thy people shall be*

---

153. See Knoch, A.E., *Concordant Studies in the Book of Daniel,*, Concordant Publishing Concern, 15570 West Knochaven Drive, Saugus, California 91350, pgs. 429-430.

the bank of the river, and the other on that side of the bank of the river.

delivered." These events occurred, or commenced, in A.D. 66.

6 And one said to the man clothed in linen, which was upon the waters of the river, How long shall it be to the end of these wonders?

7 And I heard the man clothed in linen, which was upon the waters of the river, when he held up his right hand and his left hand unto heaven, and sware by him that liveth for ever that it shall be for a time, times, and an half; and when he shall have accomplished to scatter the power of the holy people, all these things shall be finished.

"A time, times, and an half..." or three and a hald years. This was the length of time of the Roman-Jewish War of A.D. 66-70.

8 And I heard, but I understood not: then said I, O my Lord, what shall be the end of (Hebrew, *achariyth,* after) *these things?*

"What shall be after these things?" or, what shall be after the three and a half years in which the *"power of the holy people"* shall be *"scattered"* (or, *"shattered"*).

9 And he said, Go thy way, Daniel: for the words are closed

"Many shall be purified," a reference to *"thy people shall be delivered, every one that shall be found written in the book"* (Daniel 12:1). The angel is recapping that

up and sealed till the time of the end.

10 Many shall be purified, and made white, and tried; but the wicked shall do wickedly: and none of the wicked shall understand; but the wise shall understand.

which he has given. "*But the wicked…*," a reference to "*…when many will swerve as evil will increase.*" "*But the wise…*," a reference to Daniel 12:3, "*And they that be wise shall shine…*"

11 And from the time that the daily sacrifice shall be taken away, and the abomination that maketh desolate set up (Hebrew, nathan, "*to the **giving out** of the desolating abomination*" from Young's Literal Translation of the Bible), *there shall be a thousand two hundred and ninety days.*

(See Appendix A, "The Use of Symbolic Numbers in Daniel.") The 1290 days referred to the 44 months from 15 Ab, A.D. 70 to 15 Nisan, A.D. 74, or from the removal of the altar of burnt offering ("*the daily sacrifice shall be taken away*") to the fall of Masada, with the suicide death of 960 Jews, including women and children ("*the giving out of the desolating abomination*").

12 Blessed is he that waiteth, and cometh to the thousand three hundred and five and thirty days.

"*Blessed is he that waiteth…*" This refers to the 144,000, that is, to the Jerusalem Jews who believed in Jesus and fled to Pella in A.D. 66. They are blessed because they survived the Roman-Jewish War of A.D. 66-70, and returned to Jerusalem after that war.

13 But go thou thy way till the end be: for thou shalt rest, and stand in thy lot at the end of the days.

This prophecy of Daniel 11 and 12 ended then at the fall of Masada on 15 Nisan, A.D. 74.

Daniel had also, in chapters 2 and 7, prophesied the coming of four great world empires, the last one being the Roman Empire. John, in Revelation, saw more clearly just how Daniel's prophecies were to happen. Soon the prophecies regarding the Roman Empire will begin again to be fulfilled. The "*beast*," the head of the European Community, will persecute the Christians for three and a half years. "*Two witnesses*" will oppose him with miracle power. Ten kings and the "*beast*" will break away from the European Community (the revived Roman Empire) and burn Rome with fire. The "*kings from the sun-rising*" and their armies, together with the armies of the "*beast*," and the armies of the ten kings who are allied with the "*beast*," will attempt to fight the returning Jesus. Jesus will be victorious, and will return to reign on earth, and we will reign with Him! HALLELUJAH! Lift up your heads! The time of His coming is drawing nigh!

Chronological
Chart of Revelation

"Write the things which thou hast seen, and the things which are, and the things which shall be hereafter" (Revelation 1:19).

From Revelation 6:1 to 22:5

4 B.C.	A.D. 62	A.D. 64	A.D. 66	A.D. 66	A.D. 68
Herod Attempts to kill Jesus ------------- The dragon (Satan) stood ready to devour the Man Child (Jesus) as soon as he was born. Rev 12:3-5; Mt 2:1-18	The gospel *"preached to every creature under heaven."* Col 1:23 Written in 62 AD or before. ------------- The angel *"having the everlasting gospel to preach unto them that dwell on the earth, and to every nation, and kindred, and tongue, and people."* Rev 14:6-7	Nero kills the Christians in Rome ------------- Their Blood continues unceasingly to cry out for God to act to *"avenge"* them. Rev 6:9-11	Jerusalem *"compassed about with armies."* Luke 21:20 ------------- *"The abomination of desolation"* (Mt 24:15) occurs as human fecal matter piles up on a wing of the temple. Dan 9:27 ------------- The Jerusalem church (the 144,000) removes to Pella, where they are *"sealed,"* or protected. Rev 7:1-8 ------------- The *"woman"* (true Israel) is also the Jerusalem church. Her flight into the *"wilderness"* is the flight to Pella. Rev 12:1-6,14	War in heaven! Seen from earth! Rev 12:7-12; Dan 12:1	Nero is killed, following an attempted suicide. ------------- He is *"the beast,"* which had *"the wound by a sword"* or *"dagger."* Rev 13:14 ------------- He is *"the beast that was"* (had lived) *"and is not"* (no longer lived). Rev 17:8 ------------- His persecuting spirit would return in the person of the *"eighth king.* Rev 17:11

A.D. 70	A.D. 70	A.D. 70	A.D. 70	A.D. 70	A.D. 74
John receives the Revelation on the isle of Patmos. Rev 1:9	**The First Seal** The rider on the white horse "the Conquering Spirit" comes as Titus begins his conquest of Jerusalem. ------------ **The Second Seal** Three Jewish armies within Jerusalem fight each other as Roman soldiers approach Jerusalem. Rev 6:3-4 ------------ **The First Trumpet** Great boulders, or "*hail*," from Roman catapults assault Jerusalem. Rev 8:7	**The Third Seal** Famine increases in Jerusalem. Rev 6:5, 6 ------------ **The Fourth Seal** Death increases in Jerusalem. Rev 6:7-8 ------------ **The Second Trumpet** Jerusalem falls to the Romans. Rev 8:8 ------------ **The Third Trumpet** Simon bar Giora, the main Jewish general, is taken captive by the Romans. Rev 8:10-11	**The Fourth Trumpet** "*Woe*" is upon Jerusalem as the city comes under Roman military rule. Rev 8:12-13 Note: The 1290 days of Dan 12:11 begin with the destruction of the temple and the altar of burnt offerings and extends to the fall of Masada on Nisan 15, A.D. 74.	**The Fifth Trumpet** Roman soldiers force Jewish survivors into slavery. Rev 9:1-11 ------------ **The Sixth Trumpet** Jews captured in the fall of Rome are forced to entertain their captors by their violent deaths. Rev 9:13-19	The Jerusalem church returns from Pella to Jerusalem. Rev 14:1 ------------ Note: This event was prophesied in Dan 12:12, "*Blessed is he that waiteth, and cometh to the thousand three hundred and five and thirty days.*"

The following events were originally planned for about A.D. 81-96 (the reign of Domitian) but were thrown into the future by a great repentance in Rome, and by the failure of the Jews to repent and receive their Messiah and His kingdom.

Domitian, the "*eighth*" Roman emperor, or king, is the prophesied "*beast*" who was to "*make war*" against the Christians, as "*the two witnesses*" send plagues upon Rome. Rev 13:7; Rev 11:3-13; Dan 7:21	The First Bowl of God's Wrath "*Sores*" or *wounds* upon those who take the mark of the beast, and who worship his image, as civil war begins among the nations of the Roman Empire. Rev 16:1-2	The Second Bowl of God's Wrath "*The sea*" (Roman Empire) becomes stale "*blood*" as the civil war destroys multitudes throughout the Roman Empire. Rev 16:3	The Third Bowl of God's Wrath "*The rivers and the fountains of waters*" (the city of Rome) becomes "*blood*" as the slaughter moves from the Roman provinces to Rome. Rev 16:4-7	The Fourth Bowl of God's Wrath "*The sun*," the representative of fire, symbolizes the burning of Rome by "*the beast*" and his allies. Rev 16:8-9; 17:16

The Fifth Bowl of God's Wrath	The Sixth Bowl of God's Wrath	The Seventh Bowl of God's Wrath	The Millennial Reign of Christ Rev 20:4-6
The *"darkness"* of smoke, from Rome's burning rises and darkens the Roman provinces. Rev 16:10-11; 18:9,18; 19:3	The Roman *"beast"* meets *"the kings from the sun-rising"* at Armageddon. Rev 16:12-16	The Return of Jesus Christ. Rome is hit by an earthquake, dividing the city into three parts. The cities of the nations fall. Jesus, the Messiah, captures the Roman *"beast"* and *"the false prophet." "These both were cast alive into a lake of fire burning with brimstone."* Rev 19:20 (see also Rev 16:17-21; 19:11-21) As Jesus returns, *"they that are Christ's"* (1 Cor 15:23) are raised to meet Him (1 Thess 4:14-18) and to reign with Him throughout the millennium (Rev 20:4-6). Satan is *"bound"* for *"a thousand years."* Rev 20:2	At the close of the millennium, Satan is *"loosed"* for a final battle. He and his followers lose and are cast into the lake of fire. Rev 20:3,7-10 **The Final Judgment** Rev 20:11-15 **The Holy City, New Jerusalem Rev 21:2-22:5**

Bibliography

Author	Document
	The Septuagint (Hebrew to Greek) Translation of the Old Testament (LXX)
	World Book Encyclopedia
Baker, H.A.	Plains of Glory and Gloom
Baker, H.A.	The Three Worlds
Baker, H.A.	Visions Beyond the Veil
Barclay, Henry	Commentary on Revelation
Biederwolf, William E.	The Second Coming Bible
Bridger, David; Eban, Abba; Eban, Abra	The Jewish Encyclopedia
Bromiley, Geoffery W. (Editor)	International Standard Bible Encyclopedia
Dake, Finis Jennings	Dake's Annotated Bible
Dio Cassius	Roman History
Epiphanius	De Mensuris et Ponderibus (Treatise on Weights and Measures)
Eusebius	Ecclesiastical History
Haley, John W.	Alleged Discrepancies of the Bible
Hastings, James (Editor)	The Encyclopedia of Religion and Ethics (1929 edition)
Hislop, Alexander	The Two Babylons
Horsely, Bishop	Comments on Isaiah 18
Jesus, Son of Sirach	Ecclesiasticus (Apocrapha)
Josephus, Flavius	Antiquities of the Jews
Josephus, Flavius	The Life of Flavius Josephus
Josephus, Flavius	Wars of the Jews (Bella Judaica)
Knoch, A. E. (Editor)	Concordant Literal New Testament

Knoch, A. E.	Concordant Studies in the Book of Daniel
Lamsa, George	Gospel Light
Lamsa, George	Holy Bible (notes at Isaiah 14:31)
Lamsa, George	New Testament Commentary
LaTourette, Kenneth Scott	History of Christianity
Ludwig, Charles	Rulers of New Testament Times
Mauro, Phillip	The Seventy Weeks and The Great Tribulation
Moeller, Henry R.	The Legacy of Zion
Morris, Henry M.	The Revelation Record
Pliny	Naturalis Historia
Robertson, A. T.	Redating the New Testament
Robertson, A. T.	Word Pictures in the New Testament
Schonfield, Hugh I.	The Passover Plot
Schurer, Emil	The History of the Jewish People in the Age of Jesus Christ
Siegel, Richard; Rheins, Carl	The Jewish Almanac, Oct. 1980
Swete, Henry	Commentary on Revelation
Taylor, Kenneth	The Living Bible
Vine, William E.	Vine's Expository Dictionary of New Testament Words
Wansbrough, Henry (Editor)	The Jerusalem Bible
Whitaker, H.A.	Revelation: A Biblical Approach
Young, James	Young's Analytical Concordance
Young, James	Young's Literal Translation of the Bible

The Revelation...God Gave
Order Form

Postal orders: 4556 Appian Way #37
El Sobrante, CA 94803

Telephone orders: 510-932-7084

E-mail orders: tgcase@mindspring.com

Please send *The Revelation...God Gave* to:

Name: _____

Address: _____

City: _____ State: _____

Zip: _____

Telephone: (_____) _____

Book Price: $29.95

Shipping: $3.00 for the first book and $1.00 for each additional book to
cover shipping and handling within US, Canada, and Mexico.
International orders add $6.00 for the first book and $2.00 for
each additional book.

Or order from:
ACW Press
5501 N. 7th. Ave. #502
Phoenix, AZ 85013

(800) 931-BOOK

or contact your local bookstore